THE GREAT TREASURES

THE GOLDSMITH'S ART FROM ANCIENT EGYPT TO THE 20TH CENTURY

CHARTWELL
BOOKS, INC.

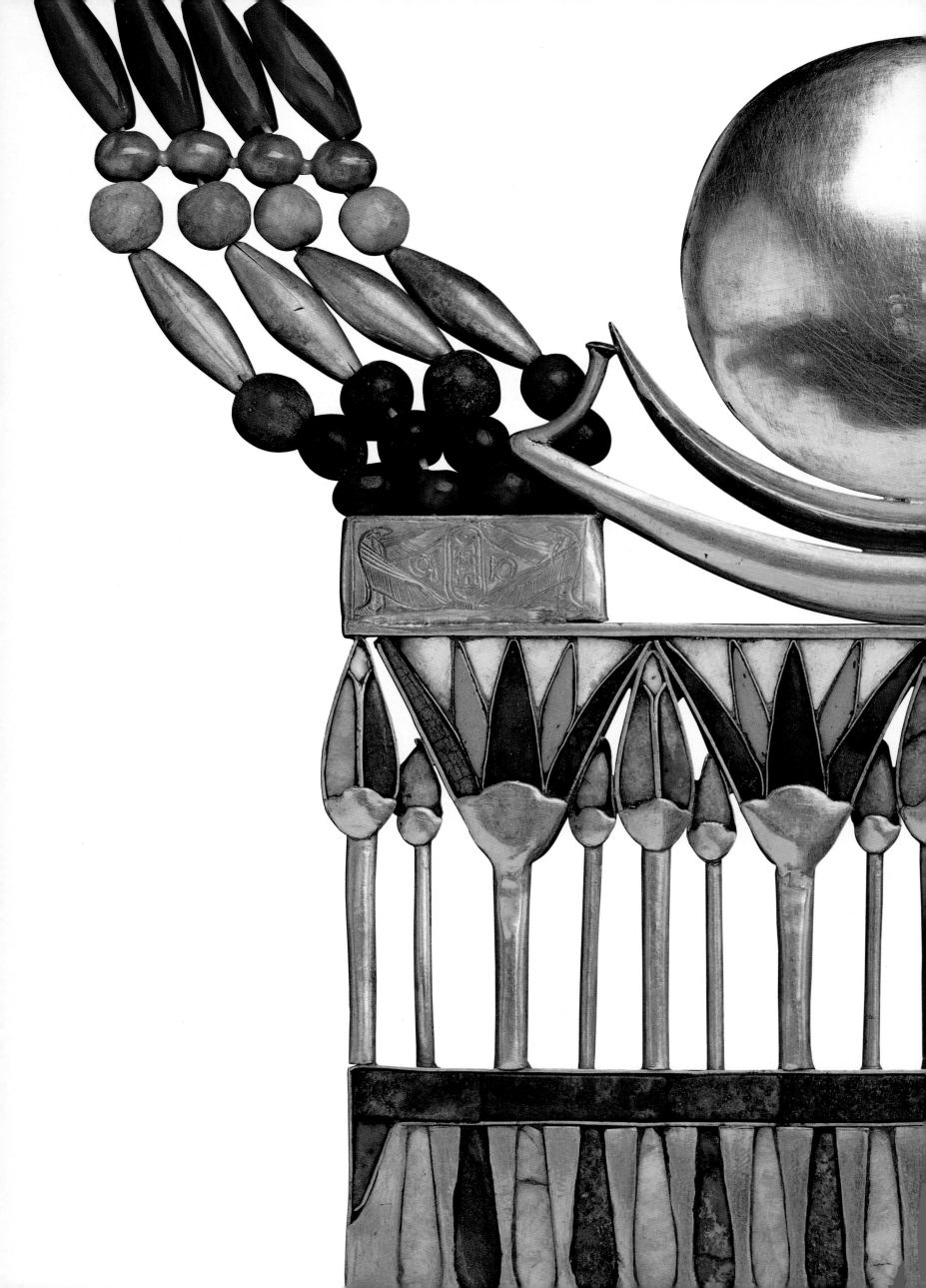

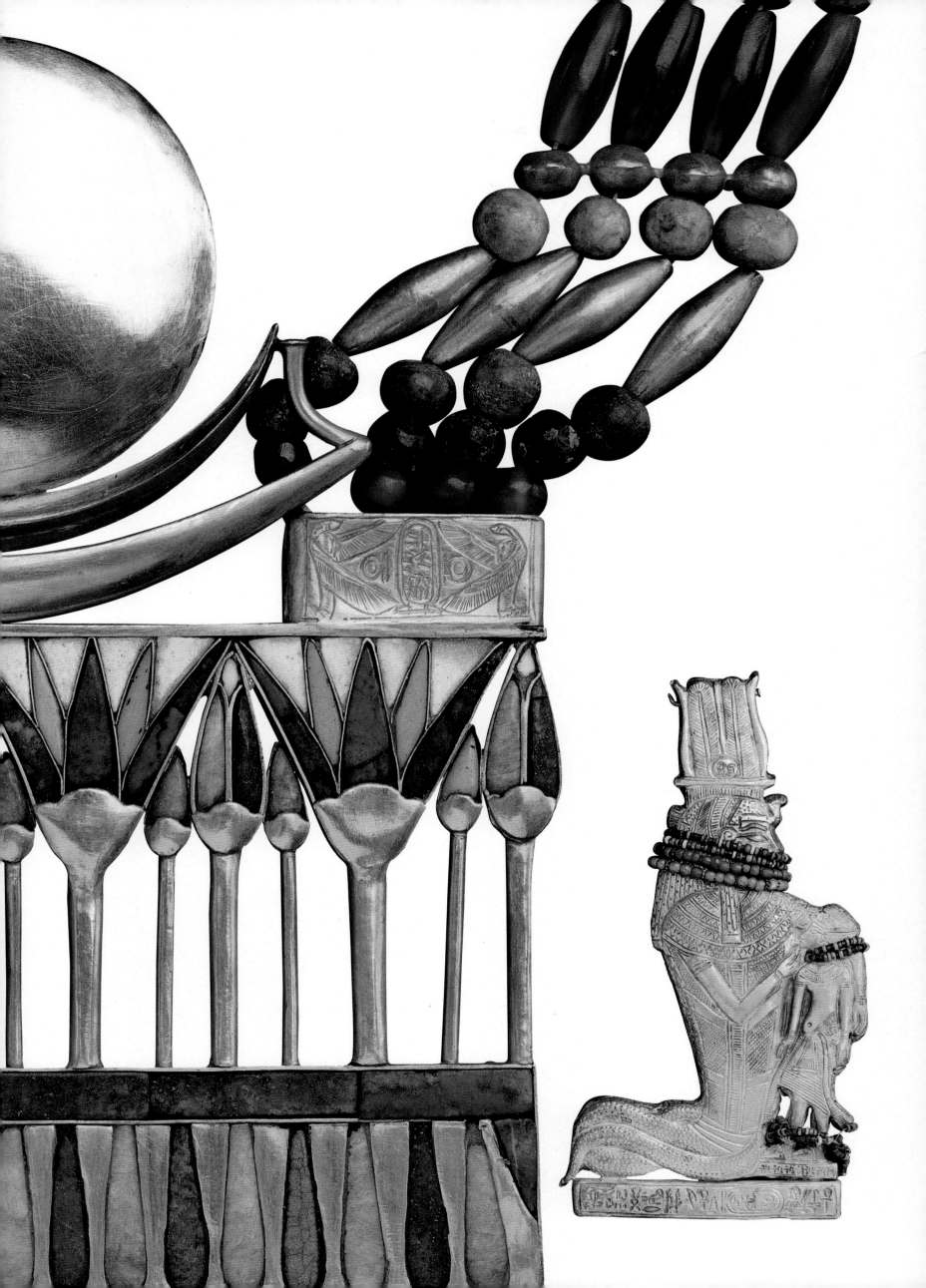

Editor
Gianni Guadalupi

Editorial Direction
Valeria Manferto De Fabianis

Editorial Coordination
Livio Bourbon
Bianca Filippone
Giulia Gaida

Translation
Neil Frazer Davenport
Ann Ghiringhelli
A.B.A., Milan
C.T.M., Milan

Graphic Design
Clara Zanotti

Jacket Design
Lisa Vaughn

The editor would like to thank the following people and institutions for their kind cooperation in the realization of this book: Dr. Walter Alva from the Muséo Arqueológico Nacional Bruning de Lambayeque, Lima; Ente Fiera di Vicenza; Mr. Jan-Peder Lamm and Ms. Siv Falk from the Statens Historiska Museet, Stockholm; Prof. Maurizio Scarpari of Università di Venezia; Dr. Marilena Mosco from the Museo degli Argenti, Firenze.
A special thanks to Michela Cassa and Mariella Sampietro for their valuable assistance.

CONTENTS

PREFACE — page 8

INTRODUCTION — page 12
by Gianni Guadalupi

THE PHARAOH'S GOLD — page 34
by Adela Oppenheim

MYCENAE AND THE GOLDEN MASK — page 56
by Furio Durando

JEWELS FOR THE BEAUTEOUS HELEN — page 66
by Salvatore Ciro Nappo

MAGIC IN PHOENICIAN GOLD — page 78
by Maria Rosaria Visone

GOLDEN JEWELS FROM HELLAS — page 92
by Furio Durando

THE TREASURE OF PHILIP II OF MACEDON — page 106
by Furio Durando

SCYTHIAN GOLD FROM THE STEPPES — page 112
by Paola D'Amore

JEWELS FOR THE ETRUSCAN ARISTOCRACY — page 122
by Antonella Magagnini

ROMAN JEWELRY — page 142
by Salvatore Ciro Nappo

BARBARIC SPLENDORS — page 152
by Bente Magnus

THE MIRAGE OF EL DORADO — page 162
by Giuseppe Mazzocchi

THE TREASURE OF SIPÁN — page 182
by Giuseppe Mazzocchi

THE TREASURE DESIRED BY THEODELINDA — page 198
by Roberto Conti

VENICE AND BYZANTIUM IN ST. MARK'S TREASURE — page 206
by Renato Polacco

A SACRED CROWN FOR THE HUNGARIAN ROYAL FAMILY — page 216
by Renato Polacco

1 *This magnificent brooch is characterized by a central square emerald weighing 136.25 carats. A piece from the Czars' jewelry, it was mounted in the early nineteenth century and measures 3.6 by 3.25 centimeters.*

2–3 *The central section of a pectoral in gold and lapis lazuli, found in the tomb of Tutankhamen, features lotus and papyrus flowers supporting the lunar sphere transported on a gold boat.*

3 bottom right *This amulet is in gilded wood, decorated with carnelian and feldspar beads, glass paste, and gold. Standing 14 centimeters high, it was also found among the grave goods in Tutankhamen's tomb.*

4–5 *This plaque in embossed gold decorated the quiver containing the bow and arrows of a Scythian warrior. It dates from the fourth century B.C. and was discovered in Ukraine.*

6–7 *The plate in embossed and chased gold was discovered in Bulgaria. With a diameter of 25 centimeters, it shows three concentric orders of Negroid heads and a ring of acorns; it dates from the fourth century B.C.*

A GOLDEN EAGLE
FOR EMPRESS GISELA   page 220
by Giovanna Baldissin Molli

OVIEDO: MEDIEVAL SACRED GOLD   page 224
by Giuseppe Mazzocchi

GEMS AND HARDSTONE VASES
OF THE MEDICEAN TREASURY   page 228
by Mario Scalini

THE JEWELS OF THE GALLEON NUESTRA
SEÑORA DE LAS MARAVILLAS   page 236
by Giuseppe Mazzocchi

ST. PETER'S BASILICA: A TREASURE
OF FAITH AND ART   page 240
by Msgr. Michele Basso

CHARM AND LUXURY IN
THE GOLD OF FRANCE   page 246
by Piero Pazzi

THE BRITISH CROWN JEWELS   page 258
by Anna Keay

VIENNA'S IMPERIAL TREASURE   page 266
by Bruce Leimsidor

CROWNS AND JEWELS OF BAVARIA   page 274
by Sabine Heym

THE KREMLIN'S DIAMONDS   page 286
by Gianfranco Giraudo

THE GOLDEN TALE
OF THE TOPKAPI   page 298
by Giuseppe Mazzocchi

STATUES IN GOLD
FROM MYSTERIOUS THAILAND   page 312
by Fiorella Rispoli

THE JEWELS OF THE MAHARAJA   page 320
by Maria Ausilia Albanese

CARTIER, THE KING
OF THE GOLDSMITHS   page 330
by Alessandra Quattordio

BIOGRAPHIES, BIBLIOGRAPHIES,
AND PHOTOGRAPHIC CREDITS   page 334

PREFACE

Precious metal and stone work—common to all peoples on Earth, but in diverse forms depending on historical period and geographical location—has produced products of rare beauty through the technical skill of artisans gifted with creativity and style. While in little over 300 pages it is impossible to include all the jewelry and gold collections in the world, this volume will present some of the indisputably best ones in terms of size, elegance of execution, and historical importance.

The brilliant showcases in this book follow the chronological development of the goldsmith's art, in the places where these precious objects were created. We will see the celebrated, majestic, and intriguing gold mask of Tutankhamen, as well as gold from Greek and Roman workshops, skillfully molded into precious objects for personal adornment as well as ritual and votive use. Our voyage continues as we retrace the steps of other Mediterranean peoples, Etruscans and Phoenicians, whose jewelry is uncommonly majestic, with gold relief and granulation.

As master goldsmiths traveled with their repertoire of techniques and styles, Viking objects similar to Roman medallions appeared throughout Scandinavia, and Scythian pec-torals decorated with battle scenes reflected those made by Greek artisans for buyers in Hellas. At the same time, we will see statuettes and other votive objects found in the territories where pre-Columbian peoples flourished, with religions that honored the sun, a deity that only gold was worthy enough to represent.

Coming back to the Old Continent, from the dawn of the Middle Ages to the Renaissance in flower, we will see a wealth of precious stones, used along with semiprecious gems and colored glass to create magnificent jewels; many became the pride of the sacred treasures of churches and

cathedrals, and the even more sumptuous jewels of English, French, and German royalty. The concept of treasure interweaves with that of collecting, but the treasure is also the precious content of legendary sunken coffers. Our gaze will shift to the horizons of gold art, to the Orient, among the arabesques of Topkapi and the sarpech of Indian manufacture, to Thai statues. Our adventure closes at the threshold of the third millennium, with perhaps the most evocative name of this "minor" art: Cartier.

The Editor

9

INTRODUCTION

Perhaps in the very beginning one of our distant ancestors was dazzled, as any child might be today, by a glittering pebble on a stream bed, the sparks of which were those of a miniature sun, a fragment of blazing star that had somehow fallen onto Earth. Etymology seems to confirm this theory: in Sanskrit, the progenitor of all the Indo-European languages, the word *hari* means both gold and the sun. Herein lies the magic of the relation-ship between man and the metal that has always symbolized not only wealth, but also purity, incor-ruptibility, and power, and which found its fullest

expression in the fascinating but fallacious dreams of the alchemists.

When that distant ancestor completed his simple gesture of gathering and keeping what he found, he unwittingly set in train many more significant matters: the birth of aesthetics, the discovery of beauty, the dawn of collecting. Later, much later, somebody more astute or more fortunate than others discovered that this apparently hard substance became malleable when heated and could be shaped into many different forms, as could silver, another metal that, rather than the sun, resembled the moon.

Fire and hammers were the tools of the first gold-smiths, and soon scintillating objects began to adorn the robes of priests, the homes of the powerful, and the mysterious chambers of divinity. Small gold ornaments have been found in dolmens and menhirs, the pious tributes of the faithful of the late Stone Age. These were prototypes of the votive offerings still today placed alongside images of the Madonna or Buddha. In the history of goldsmithing can be read not only the millennial development of what is probably the oldest art, but also the sequence of religious beliefs, the rise and fall of terrestrial empires, the vicissitudes of the great dynas-ties, the births and deaths of entire civilizations, and the exploits of archaeologists, who have

brought to light once again
many of the treasures that
dazzle us from these pages.

It appears that in antiquity
gold was relatively abundant
compared with the present day.
Archaeological remains suggest that
when the first great civilizations arose in
the irrigated lands of Mesopotamia and Egypt, on
the Persian plateau and on the islands of the Aegean,
centered on the great Crete, the goldsmiths' art was
already widely diffused and extremely sophisticated.

In the fabulous Babylonia of the almost mythical
Semiramide, in the Persepolis of the Great King, in
the city-states that flourished and declined one after
the other in the Fertile Crescent—named for the
abundance of its crops and herds—sovereigns
and merchants, princes and favorites,
adventurers and priests literally dressed
in gold, wearing great plated pectorals,
belts, bracelets, necklaces, plaques, and
rings. Palaces and temples glowed; gold was
even used to decorate walls and ceilings, doors and
furniture, as well as statues of divinities.

*13 The reliquary of
St. Elizabeth is considered
to be the most precious piece
in the Stockholm Museum
of Antiquity. It was made
to contain the skull of
St. Elizabeth of Thuringia,
the daughter of King*

The warrior kings glittered like the sun god of whom
they were the progeny and terrestrial representatives.
When they left for, or returned from, some campaign
of conquest they carried golden swords at their belts
and wore ceremonial gold armor. An example of stunningly sophisticated elegance is the gold helmet in the
form of a wig found in a tomb at Ur and dating back
four thousand years.

We have all heard of the so-called Treasure of Priam,
found by Heinrich Schliemann during his successful
excavation of the nine superimposed cities of Troy.
There is a famous photograph taken by the rather

swashbuckling archaeologist to celebrate not only
the discovery of these jewels, but also his success in
smuggling them out from under the very noses of
the Ottoman authorities: in the photograph, they
are being worn by his attractive wife in the role of
a resuscitated Helen of Troy.

On the far side of that sea celebrated by Homer
and crossed by the long ships of the Greeks sailing
to lay siege to Ilium, in the lost city of Mycenae
with its Cyclopean walls, mortuary masks in sheet
gold have been brought to light, along with daggers
decorated with gold and silver inlays, spiral volutes,

*Andrea II of Hungary,
who was born in A.D. 1207
and canonized in 1235.
The jewel has a long and
complicated history: the
oldest section is an agate
cup from the late Roman or
possibly Byzantine period;
its gold mount dates to the
eleventh century.*

13

14 top left *The "Ankh" or the "Cross of Life" is a frequently recurring motif in Egyptian iconography; here it is used to decorate the frame of a wood mirror covered with gold and colored glass paste. The relic was found among the objects of the young pharaoh's personal funerary cache. It stands 27 centimeters high.*

14–15 top *The serpent with huge outspread wings that forms this large collar in chased gold is one of the ritual figures that occur most frequently in Egyptian iconography. The jewel was found by Howard Carter in November 1922, in the tomb of the young pharaoh.*

14–15 bottom *The posture and tension of the group of running lions are the most significant elements in the decoration of this dagger blade inlaid with gold. The piece comes from Mycenae and dates to 1550 B.C. It is one of the most characteristic objects of the Achean world, in which hunting and war were fundamental pursuits.*

and scenes of hunting and fleeing lions. In the Minoan Crete of Daedalus, architect of the labyrinth who, as well as being capable of making the wings with which he escaped, is also considered to be the father of all arts, including that of the goldsmiths, the tombs of Mochlos have given us pendants, necklaces, and rings with decoration. However, the cream of the Cretan production was elsewhere around the world, exported or pillaged by military expeditions, including the rings with collets and the gold chalices of the treasure of Mycenae which recall the cup of Nestor celebrated in the *Iliad*.

The true treasure chest of antique jewelry is Egypt, a treasure trove that infinite generations of grave robbers have never succeeded in exhausting, as demonstrated by the most surprising and fantastic archaeological discovery of our century, that of the tomb of Tutankhamen. Appropriately, this discovery was accompanied—like all treasures worthy of the name—by a curse, in this case invoked by the pharaohs, a tenacious legend that no rational explanation could ever deflate. As well as the gold objects that are the pride of Egyptian collections around the world, from Cairo to London by way of Munich and Turin, the ancient civilization of the

15 This beautiful gold box with inlays in colored glass paste had a ritual function as a container for unguents. The box is in the form of a double scroll with a hinged lid, and comes from the extremely rich funerary cache of Tutankhamen.

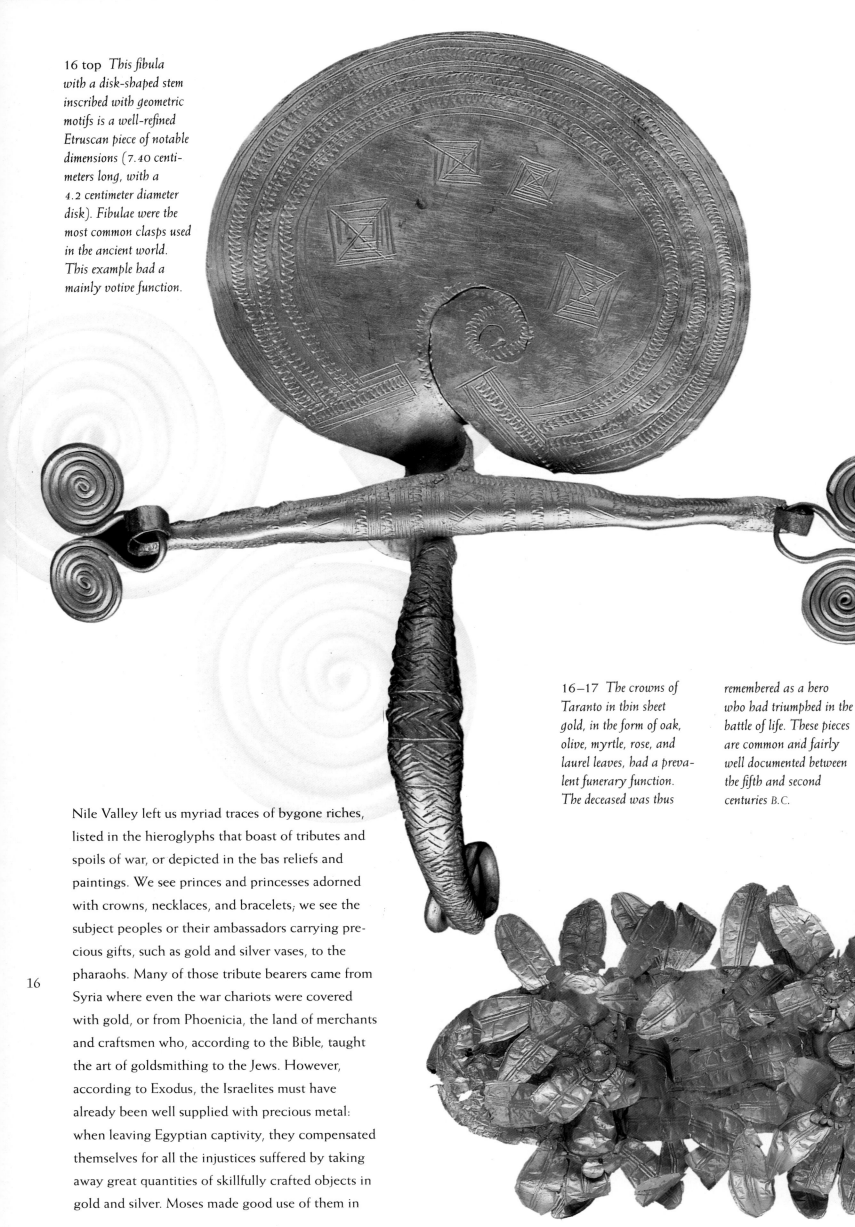

This fibula with a disk-shaped stem inscribed with geometric motifs is a well-refined Etruscan piece of notable dimensions (7.40 centimeters long, with a 4.2 centimeter diameter disk). Fibulae were the most common clasps used in the ancient world. This example had a mainly votive function.

16–17 The crowns of Taranto in thin sheet gold, in the form of oak, olive, myrtle, rose, and laurel leaves, had a prevalent funerary function. The deceased was thus remembered as a hero who had triumphed in the battle of life. These pieces are common and fairly well documented between the fifth and second centuries B.C.

16

Nile Valley left us myriad traces of bygone riches, listed in the hieroglyphs that boast of tributes and spoils of war, or depicted in the bas reliefs and paintings. We see princes and princesses adorned with crowns, necklaces, and bracelets; we see the subject peoples or their ambassadors carrying precious gifts, such as gold and silver vases, to the pharaohs. Many of those tribute bearers came from Syria where even the war chariots were covered with gold, or from Phoenicia, the land of merchants and craftsmen who, according to the Bible, taught the art of goldsmithing to the Jews. However, according to Exodus, the Israelites must have already been well supplied with precious metal: when leaving Egyptian captivity, they compensated themselves for all the injustices suffered by taking away great quantities of skillfully crafted objects in gold and silver. Moses made good use of them in

17 top *The celebrated Tazza Farnese is a cameo in sardonyx with a diameter of 20 centimeters. Its obverse portrays the head of Medusa. Lorenzo the Magnificent, who owned the piece, considered it to be the most important object in his collection of ancient semiprecious stones. Today it is conserved in the National Archaeological Museum at Naples.*

17 bottom *Like the majority of Roman jewels, these two engraved rings come from Pompeii and date from the Augustan Age. These rings demonstrate the Roman goldsmiths' talent in the art of glyptic sculpture.*

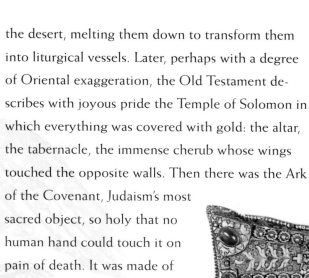

the desert, melting them down to transform them into liturgical vessels. Later, perhaps with a degree of Oriental exaggeration, the Old Testament describes with joyous pride the Temple of Solomon in which everything was covered with gold: the altar, the tabernacle, the immense cherub whose wings touched the opposite walls. Then there was the Ark of the Covenant, Judaism's most sacred object, so holy that no human hand could touch it on pain of death. It was made of cedar wood covered with plaques of gold and studded with onyx, while the seven-branched candelabrum, a venerated symbol of Israel, was of solid gold. These two masterpieces of Jewish craftsmanship are both lost; archaeologists of the Indiana Jones ilk are still searching for them around Jerusalem. One legend has it that the candelabrum was taken to Rome following the destruction of the Holy City by the legions of Titus in A.D. 70, and that it ended up at

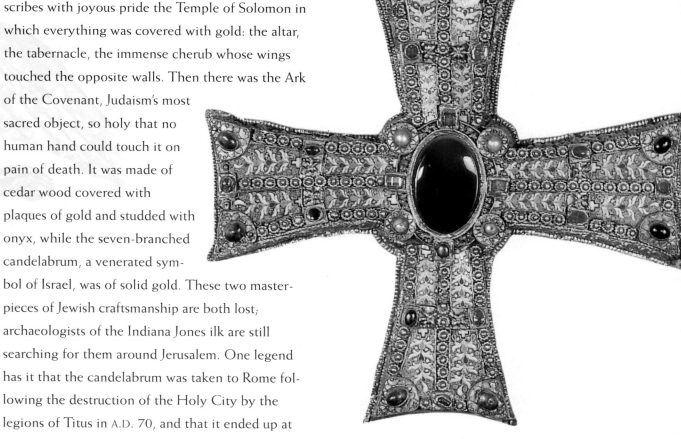

the bottom of the Tiber to save it from a barbarian invasion.

The throne of Midas, the king of Phrygia, must have been an equally sensational piece. Midas, of course, was so incalculably wealthy that the authors of the myths attributed to him the power of transforming everything he touched into gold (a poisoned gift from Dionysus to punish him for his greed: he risked dying of hunger because even the food he brought to his mouth turned to gold). The throne, which appears to belong to the world of history

18 and 19 Gold, gemstones, enamels, and extremely delicate embossing and filigree work in gold and silver distinguish the altar-reliquary by Vuolvinio, an artist who grew up in the Carolingian culture and was active in the first half of the ninth century A.D. The

frontal, signed by the artist "Vuolvinus Magister Phaber," is considered one of the triumphs of medieval goldworking and is conserved in the Basilica of Sant'Ambrogio in Milan. It measures 220 by 85 centimeters.

19

20 *This clasp was intended to be worn with a cope, the long cloaklike garment worn by bishops and the pope. The jewel is encrusted with precious stones and pearls. It depicts, with rare technical virtuosity given its reduced dimensions, a scene from the Annunciation within a cuspate architectural setting. This piece dates from the medieval Gothic period and is conserved in the Treasury of the Cathedral of Aachen.*

rather than legend, was made of solid gold and was donated to the temple at Delphi in order to earn the favor of Apollo, such magnificence being more appropriate to a god than a mere mortal.

The traditions of opulence established in what was then called Asia Minor were no less extravagant. When Alexander the Great moved to conquer the Orient, he found gold plate encrusted with precious stones, and cups and plates of silver in the baggage of the defeated King Darius. And Pompey, the con-

ber of jewels, brooches, necklaces, earrings, and other items featuring both geometric and anthropomorphic decoration. But the Greeks traveled throughout the world as the merchant heirs to the Phoenicians, and jewels of Hellenic fabrication have been found, for example, in the funerary mounds of the Scythians, a nomadic tribe of horsemen who wandered the infinite plains of the present-day Ukraine and who loved to adorn not only themselves but also their horses with pectorals and medallions in gold and silver.

In the West, Etruscan goldworking was particularly admired and flourished in the seventh century B.C. The cemeteries have left us with numerous fine pieces, the burial places of that era being known as the "tombs of gold," with Vulci, Cerveteri, Vetulonia, and Palestrina among the richest. The Etruscan craftsmen obtained particularly fine results with the techniques of granulation and filigree. Subsequently, however, the Etruscan political decline also affected artistic production: the earlier fine sophistication was replaced by rougher work, the objects lost originality and became increasingly similar to those of the Hellenic Orient.

Having, through a series of irresistible conquests, become the capital of an empire that it proudly boasted covered almost the entire ecumene—that is to say, the entire inhabited world—Rome concentrated the riches of the annexed nations in its temples and palaces. First, the consuls and then the emperors accumulated in the city the treasures that derived from their military triumphs—the plundering, the tributes and the sackings—and that unheard-of abundance of precious metals bred in the austere and sober conquerors a taste for jewels that was immediately condemned by the moralists of the era. Luxury was boundless and rampant. Plutarch tells that in certain Roman houses the furniture was of solid gold and silver. The Domus Aurea, the first true imperial palace, built by Nero, was so-called because it had walls covered with sheets of gold. Caligula, following the example set by the Oriental monarchs, gave a banquet for a thousand guests with chased gold and silver plate. Of all this opulence, relatively little remains: the excavation of the buried Pompeii has brought to light a few jewels from the Augustan Age, and other scattered relics have been discovered else-

20

21 *The* Pala d'Oro *in St. Mark's Basilica in Venice is the absolute masterpiece of Venetian-Byzantine goldworking. It was created with an incredible quantity of precious and semiprecious stones—over 2,500 total— and colored enamels. The detail shows one of the three saints depicted with extreme solemnity below the central medallion with Christ Almighty. The* Pala d'Oro *measures 3 by 1 meters.*

queror of Mithridates IV of Pontus, counted two thousand gold chalices studded with gems in his spoils. At Alexandria in Egypt, the Ptolemaic dynasty gave banquets at which the guests ate and drank from gold and the plate was changed for every course.

Little has survived of Greek goldsmithing: the great city of Ephesus in Lydia and the small town of Camirus on the island of Rhodes are the two main centers where chance has led to the finding of a num-

22 right *This automaton in the form of a ship with carillon trumpets forms part of the Imperial Treasure of Vienna. It was perhaps one of the pieces in the extrovert collection of Rudolph II of Prague. This work in gold was the fruit of the imagination of the German goldsmith Hans Schlottheim, active between the sixteenth and seventeenth centuries.*

22 left *This triton, encrusted with precious stones and with a torso of pearl, is a pendant made by the goldsmiths of the Florentine grand-ducal workshops early in* A.D. *1600. It is a particularly felicitous example of the taste for bizarre jewels of exquisite craftsmanship favored by Mannerism and, subsequently, the baroque culture. The jewel can be seen in the Museo degli Argenti in Florence.*

where in the vast imperial territories, such as the so-called Treasure of Hildesheim. The incalculable patrimony of the patrician families and the emperors may still lie underground in the capital and the imposing villas built in the pleasant countryside of Lazio and Campania. Or perhaps, when the Nemesis arrived and the predator city was in turn preyed upon, all was carried away in the barbarians' saddle-packs.

These barbarians were not, however, merely thieves and destroyers; goldsmithing was in fact their craft of choice, and the talented artists who served the nobles and kings of those fearsome peoples were as skilled as their colleagues in the civilizations they overran. We know, for example, what the Gothic goldsmiths were capable of from the treasury attributed to their king Athanaric, found in 1837 at Petroasa in Romania.

The cache contained twenty-two extraordinary pieces in solid gold, but human greed led to its partial dispersal.

Another treasure, this time belonging to two of the last Gothic kings of Spain, Recesvinto and Svintila, was brought to light in 1858 at Guarrazzar, a village near Toledo (the former capital of the Gothic kingdom, overrun during the Arab invasion). There were gold crowns set with sapphires, pearls, and red glass. Many other precious barbarian manufactures have been found in French and Italian cemeteries: ornaments for clothing and the harnesses of horses, in particular small gold crosses that were eye-catching testimony to the conversion of their owners to Christianity, swords with gold hilts, plated armor.

The Duomo of Monza zealously conserves the treasure of the Lombard Queen Theodelinda, including the famous Iron Crown worn by numerous kings of Italy up to Napoleon. The crown is decorated with enamels and gemstones, and has an internal iron circlet that is said to have been cast from one of the nails used to crucify Jesus.

While in the West the Roman Empire crumbled under the blows inflicted by invaders, it survived for many centuries in the East, with Constantinople, its beautiful capital, becoming the center of the world. The Byzantine imperial court cloaked itself in new splendors: the basileus, who was no mere monarch

23 top *The celebrated Saltcellar of Francis I by Benvenuto Cellini in gold and enamel depicts Neptune and Ceres. It was commissioned from the Florentine sculptor and goldsmith by Francis I of France. It was eventually presented to the archduke Ferdinand of Tyrol. Created in A.D. 1543, it is today one of the prized exhibits in the Imperial Treasury of Vienna.*

23 bottom *This vase with gold lid and base has a body made from a large coconut and is another of those late-sixteenth-century jewels designed to arouse the wonder of the spectator by combining art and nature in a novel and audacious manner. The piece is conserved in the Narodni Museum in Prague.*

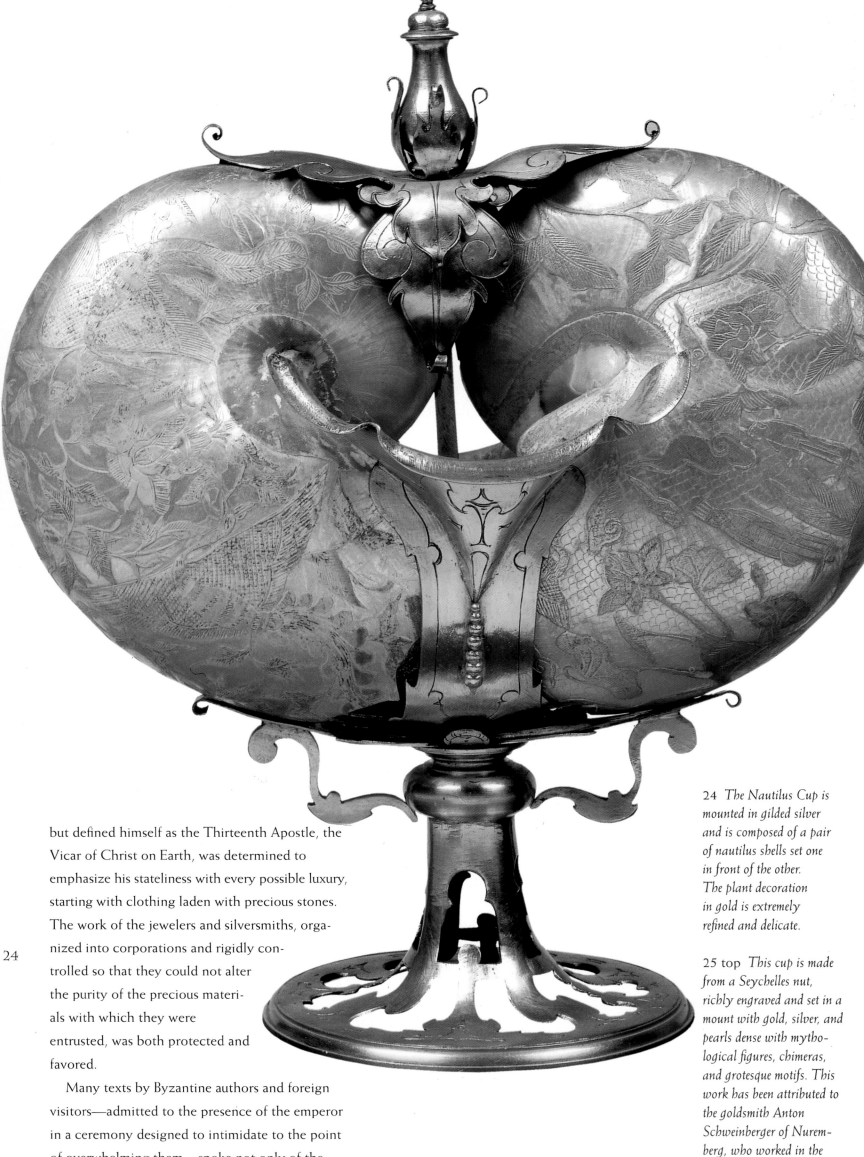

but defined himself as the Thirteenth Apostle, the Vicar of Christ on Earth, was determined to emphasize his stateliness with every possible luxury, starting with clothing laden with precious stones. The work of the jewelers and silversmiths, organized into corporations and rigidly controlled so that they could not alter the purity of the precious materials with which they were entrusted, was both protected and favored.

Many texts by Byzantine authors and foreign visitors—admitted to the presence of the emperor in a ceremony designed to intimidate to the point of overwhelming them—spoke not only of the regal pomp, but also of the marvels amassed in the

24

24 *The Nautilus Cup is mounted in gilded silver and is composed of a pair of nautilus shells set one in front of the other. The plant decoration in gold is extremely refined and delicate.*

25 top *This cup is made from a Seychelles nut, richly engraved and set in a mount with gold, silver, and pearls dense with mythological figures, chimeras, and grotesque motifs. This work has been attributed to the goldsmith Anton Schweinberger of Nuremberg, who worked in the service of Rudolph II of Prague.*

churches of the so-called Incomparable City, above all the imperial basilica of Hagia Sophia. Constantinople was the main center of production of precious objects: its craftsmen were commissioned by churches and convents throughout the Christian world. From St. Mark's Basilica in Venice to the monastery of Monte Cassino, these artisans produced liturgical furnishings from crosses to altarpieces and the most diverse objects, ranging from enameled and gem-encrusted bookbindings for illuminated codices to panels for the doorways of ecclesiastical buildings.

For their part, the Byzantine emperors were accustomed to demonstrating their munificence by donating the masterpieces produced by their goldsmiths to western monarchs, abbots, popes, and bishops. It was also by copying and drawing inspiration from Byzantine art that the goldworking of Europe revived, especially during the Ottonian period around the year 1000. In the meantime, the cult of the saints and the veneration of their mortal remains had given rise to a new genre of objects: reliquaries, sacred cases that were fashioned in the shape of their content, be

25 bottom This rock crystal heron is a magnificent cup with an engraved lid, enriched with a gold and enamel rim. It is an example of the taste for exquisite ceremonial tableware that was so popular at the noble and princely courts of late-sixteenth-century Europe.

it a leg, an arm, or a head. They were made of gold or silver and were increasingly embellished with enamels and precious stones. Every church attempted to gather as many as possible (and many priests in whom the passion for collecting overwhelmed all scruples stooped to theft in order to procure them); not only did they guarantee supernatural protection, but they also attracted crowds of pilgrims thanks to whose offerings the sanctuaries prospered. Still today we can admire in the treasuries of cathedrals and monasteries fabulous reliquaries, their splendor banishing all thought of their macabre contents. It should also be remembered that

among the masterpieces of Romanesque goldsmithing is the great gold altar by Vuolvinio in the basilica of Sant'Ambrogio in Milan and the crown of the Holy Roman Emperor executed in gold, filigree, precious stones, pearls, and enamels for the coronation of Otto I in A.D. 936, now conserved in the Kunsthistorisches Museum of Vienna.

In 1204 Constantinople suffered the same fate as Rome: the Byzantine empire fell and was dismantled by the Crusaders, who had treacherously attacked it rather than attempting to liberate the Holy Sepulchre. The spoils were immense: entire ships laden with precious cargo poured jewels and reliquaries into the ports of western Europe, especially Venice, where doge Enrico Dandolo—aging, blind, but still fearsome—had orchestrated the enterprise and guided the conquerors. St. Mark's Basilica was filled with statues, gold, silver, agate vases, and gems which were used to embellish the already dazzling *Pala d'Oro*. Above the pronaos were set the four gilded horses that had previously adorned the hippodrome of Byzantium. That flood of riches was not to remain intact: many of the jewels were dismantled and melted down; the materials were used to create objects more in keeping with changing tastes.

Western patronage, with the exception of the royal courts, was primarily religious and determined by liturgical needs. At that time there were few who could afford to purchase jewels. And even those who could permit themselves luxuries—wealthy merchants, for example—were forbidden to do so by the sumptuary laws: in the late thirteenth century, Philip the Handsome, king of France, prohibited the bourgeois from wearing jewelry, rings, belts, bracelets, or otherwise. Opulence was to be the preserve of the nobility, but even it displayed fairly sober tastes, according to the images that have been handed down to us. Statues and paintings show figures whose clothing principally features two forms of jewelry: clasps and buckles. Buttons were not used, and garments were closed with laces, hooks, and clasps. The relatively large belt buckles frequently featured hunting or courtship scenes.

The verticality typical of the Gothic style which in architecture was expressed in the towering spires of the cathedrals, was also applied to jewelry: for exam-

ple, the Crown of Lancaster, donated by Henry IV of England to his daughter Blanche on the occasion of her marriage to the Elector Palatinate in 1402, now to be found in Munich; or the templelike monstrances with their walls of crystal or translucent enamel, a technique born in Switzerland around Basel and from there dispersed throughout the Christian world. Other centers of goldsmithing that were particularly active in the International Gothic period were Siena, Milan, and Venice, where the interminable *Pala d'Oro* was finally completed with almost two thousand pearls and gemstones set in a fashion that was to have a profound influence on contemporary European jewelry.

Favored by the patronage of princes and popes, goldsmithing in Renaissance Italy reached its greatest heights. In the competition held in 1401 for the second door of the Baptistery of Florence, a date that marks the inauguration of a new era, the prin-

27 *The shield that accompanied the armor of Charles IX is also richly decorated. A battle scene of notable violence depicts the victory of Marius over Jugurtha, the king of Numidia. Panoplies, masks, and the royal monogram "K," are repeated along the border of the shield, framing the central motif. Charles IX's armor was an eminently decorative object, but also offered the king adequate protection.*

26 *The helmet of Charles IX of France is attributed to the Parisian goldsmith Pierre Redon. Dating from 1572, it is in finely chased gold with reliefs in translucent enamel. The helmet is a clear example of the ostentatious luxury of the court of the last Valois sovereigns; the siege of a turreted city of a vaguely exotic form is depicted below a grotesque mask.*

27

28 *The jewelry box of Anna of Austria is made of gold, densely decorated with relief-work, chasing, and an extraordinary wealth of leaves and flowers. It dates to the middle of the seventeenth century and is conserved in the Louvre.*

29 left *The diamond brooch of the Order of the Holy Spirit is a jewel dating from the middle of the eighteenth century, created by the court goldsmith Jacquemin. It is an excellent example of fine French royal jewelry. The brooch is encrusted with 400 diamonds mounted on silver; the largest stone forms the body of a dove, a small ruby representing its beak.*

cipal entrants were goldsmiths; indeed, the eventual winner was Lorenzo Ghiberti.

Many of the multi-talented and greatest figures of the times were also active in this field; their versatility is unimaginable today in an era of increasing specialization. Among these artists were Pollaiuolo, Verrocchio, Brunelleschi, and Benvenuto Cellini, the creator of one of the most beautiful of the Renaissance works, the *Saltcellar of Francis I,* King of France. In the last years of his life, Cellini devoted himself to the writing of an essay, the *Trattato dell'Oreficeria e della Scultura,* published in 1568, in which he discussed the working of gold and silver, enamels, seals, and various precious stones. He was perhaps the most famous goldsmith in history due to the publication of an autobiography that combined fact and fiction and became a bestseller.

While the quantity of gold and silver available was vastly expanded by the discovery of America and the subsequent siphoning of its riches (leading to the loss of most of the gold manufactures of the Aztecs and the Incas, melted down by the Conquistadores), artists such as Raphael, Giulio Romano, Dürer, and Holbein the Younger supplied designs to the craftsman jewelers. This period also saw the rise of modern collecting: the *Wunderkammern,* or "Chambers of Marvels," in which the great nobles and patrons such as Ferdinand of Hapsburg and his nephew Rudolph, the

future emperor, accumulated works of art of all kinds, together with natural curiosities such as narwhal tusks and mandrake roots. Goldsmithing played an extremely important role in these collections, both because gems and jewels were themselves objects worthy of collection, and because the goldsmiths were commissioned to produce frames and mounts for other pieces.

Imbued with magical powers, precious stones became integral parts of aristocratic clothing: sewn onto both male and female garments, they were used to emphasize waistlines, to fasten pleats and ruffs, and they sparkled at the top of slits, harmonizing with the "mobile" jewelry, such as necklaces, pendants, and chains. Pearls, imported on a large scale from the eastern and western seas initially on the Portuguese and Spanish, then Dutch, French, and British ships, were commonly worn, together with gold chains which were frequently superimposed; we see them, for example, scattered over the sumptuous dresses of Queen Elizabeth I of England.

Another jewel typical of the Renaissance was the "insignia," an ornament originally worn on male cloaks, then hung round the neck as a pendant. They featured scenes, portraits, fantastic creatures, and regal animals, such as lions and birds, ships, and divinities; the most stunning example is the Canning Triton Pendant, today conserved in the

Victoria and Albert Museum in London.

The goldsmiths' techniques were also applied to precision instruments; from the middle of the sixteenth century, magnifying glasses, dividers, astrolabes, compasses, quadrants, and armillary spheres were designed and decorated with extreme sophistication. And out of the goldsmiths' workshops came not only the first pocket watches, enameled, engraved, and set with colored stones, but also complicated mechanisms designed to animate human and animal figurines known as *automata*, or automatons. The technique of champlevé enjoyed particular success in France, where it was also applied to ceremonial weapons. In 1572 the Parisian Pierre Redon created two exceptional pieces for his king, Charles IX: the helmet and shield in enameled and gold-plated iron that are today conserved in the Louvre.

It was France and the court of Versailles—in that seventeenth century declared by Voltaire to be the century of Louis XIV, the Sun King—that dictated the fashions of the whole of Europe, including the

field of jewelry. Unfortunately, financial pressures at the end of his reign obliged the king to melt down the gold plate and silver furniture that adorned his fabulous palace; however, a number of exceptional objects remain as testimony to the taste of the era: the jewelry box of Anna of Austria, now in the Louvre; the bowl made for the Dauphin in 1690 by Sébastien Leblond, which is also conserved in the Paris museum; and an assortment of writing and toilet sets, ornaments, and snuff boxes. In 1715, on the death of the Sun King, more than four hundred master goldsmiths were active in Paris. Among them was Claude II Ballin, who made the grandiose centerpieces for the tables of the imperial Russian

29 right *One of the most famous objects in the collection of the French crown is the mirror said to have belonged to Maria de' Medici. In reality it was acquired by Louis XIV. This magnificent Venetian work dates from circa 1600. It features an exceptional series of multicolored gems, including agates, onyx, gray jaspers, sardonyx, 18 cameos, 2 garnet busts, 3 large emeralds, diamonds, and rubies.*

court now exhibited in the Hermitage at St. Petersburg. The baroque period featured a number of important German craftsmen whose increasingly extravagant compositions included not only gold, silver, and precious stones but also shells, horns, and rock crystal.

The seventeenth century adopted the airy lightness of the rococo style exemplified in the jewels of the Elector Palatine conserved in the Museo degli Argenti of Florence, the Crown of Bavaria in the Residenzmuseum of Munich, the diamond brooch of the Order of the Holy Spirit in the Louvre, and the crown of Louis XV by Duflos. The excavations of Herculaneum and Pompeii, and the neoclassicism that began to take hold in the second half of the century brought Greek, Etruscan, and Roman models back into fashion. In Italy the leading figure in this respect was a goldsmith from Rome, Fortunato Pio Castellani, who collected antique pieces in order to study the techniques by which they were made and their iconography. We are indebted to him for the revival of filigree and granulation, as well as renewed interest in engraved and sculptured cameos, that endured throughout the last century.

The nineteenth century was character-

30–31 This unusual pendant designed by Lalique and sold in 1901 depicts the face of a woman. The piece terminates with a baroque pearl hung from the streaming hair that is crowned with four silver poppies; the female features glow in cold enameled crystal.

30 bottom right This pair of earrings features diamonds and rubies; it was designed by Cartier.

31 top An extremely delicate play of enamels and diamonds characterizes this dragonfly brooch, designed by Lacloche. The dragonfly was one of the most popular Art Nouveau themes.

30 top left This ribbon-shaped brooch of diamonds is a fine example of Art Deco jewelry, which preferred geometric forms and an absence of color in favor of the exclusive dazzling white of diamonds. The brooch by Boucheron is 15.5 centimeters long and dates from 1930.

30

30 bottom left and center Two floral brooches designed by the celebrated American company Tiffany, with diamonds, sapphires, and moonstones.

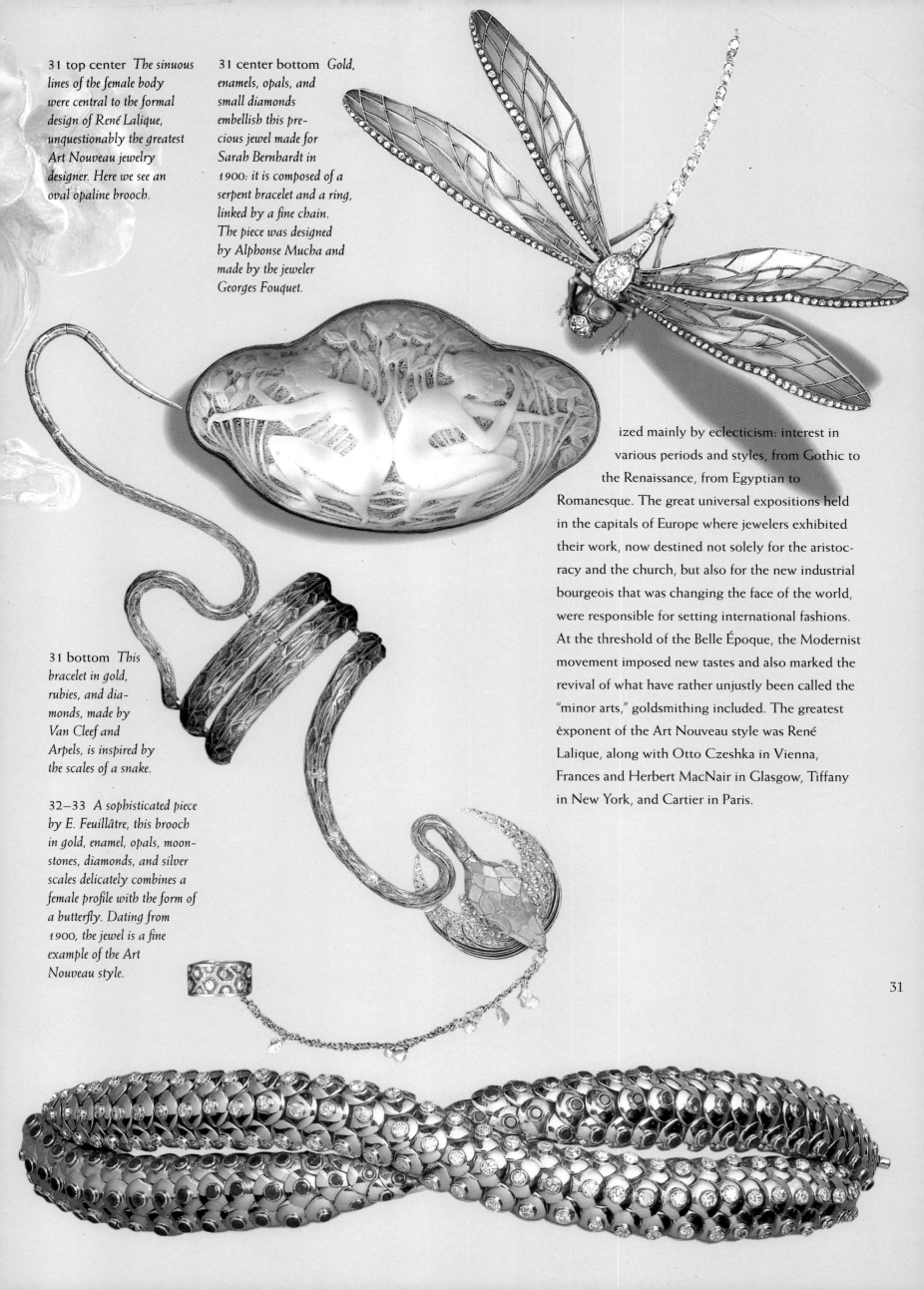

31 top center *The sinuous lines of the female body were central to the formal design of René Lalique, unquestionably the greatest Art Nouveau jewelry designer. Here we see an oval opaline brooch.*

31 center bottom *Gold, enamels, opals, and small diamonds embellish this precious jewel made for Sarah Bernhardt in 1900: it is composed of a serpent bracelet and a ring, linked by a fine chain. The piece was designed by Alphonse Mucha and made by the jeweler Georges Fouquet.*

31 bottom *This bracelet in gold, rubies, and diamonds, made by Van Cleef and Arpels, is inspired by the scales of a snake.*

32–33 *A sophisticated piece by E. Feuillâtre, this brooch in gold, enamel, opals, moonstones, diamonds, and silver scales delicately combines a female profile with the form of a butterfly. Dating from 1900, the jewel is a fine example of the Art Nouveau style.*

ized mainly by eclecticism: interest in various periods and styles, from Gothic to the Renaissance, from Egyptian to Romanesque. The great universal expositions held in the capitals of Europe where jewelers exhibited their work, now destined not solely for the aristocracy and the church, but also for the new industrial bourgeois that was changing the face of the world, were responsible for setting international fashions. At the threshold of the Belle Époque, the Modernist movement imposed new tastes and also marked the revival of what have rather unjustly been called the "minor arts," goldsmithing included. The greatest exponent of the Art Nouveau style was René Lalique, along with Otto Czeshka in Vienna, Frances and Herbert MacNair in Glasgow, Tiffany in New York, and Cartier in Paris.

THE PHARAOH'S GOLD

34 and 35
The funerary mask of Tutankhamen is made of solid gold with inlays of several materials, including turquoise, lapis lazuli, and glass. The mask is 54 centimeters tall and 40 wide at shoulder level. It is an idealized image of the king and was placed over the wrappings that covered the head of the pharaoh. Along with other precious objects deposited in Tutankhamen's tomb, it is displayed in the Egyptian Museum, Cairo.

The treasure of Pharaoh Tutankhamen is undoubtedly the most celebrated archaeological discovery ever made in ancient Egypt, and the king's adornments certainly rank among the world's great collections of royal jewelry. Ironically, this most famous royal tomb is actually one of the smallest and most obscure burial sites prepared for an Egyptian monarch. Tutankhamen himself, who reigned at the end of the New Kingdom's Eighteenth Dynasty, was not one of Egypt's great rulers. We know few facts about Tutankhamen's life; even such basic questions as the identity of his parents and the cause of his death have been the subjects of intense scholarly debate and speculation.

The period preceding Tutankhamen's reign was characterized by tremendous religious, political, and artistic upheaval. During the reign of Pharaoh Akhenaten (Amenophis IV, 1353–1335 B.C.)—known as the Amarna period, after Akhenaten's new capital city—the worship of Egypt's complex pantheon of deities was sharply curtailed. Veneration of Amun, Egypt's chief deity during the New Kingdom, was particularly suppressed. In place of this multitude of deities, religious observance centered upon Aten, a solar god depicted as a sun disk with rays ending in human hands. This religious transformation also had political consequences; the priests who presided over Egypt's cultic installations wielded considerable secular power, greatly diminished under the authority of the new Aten

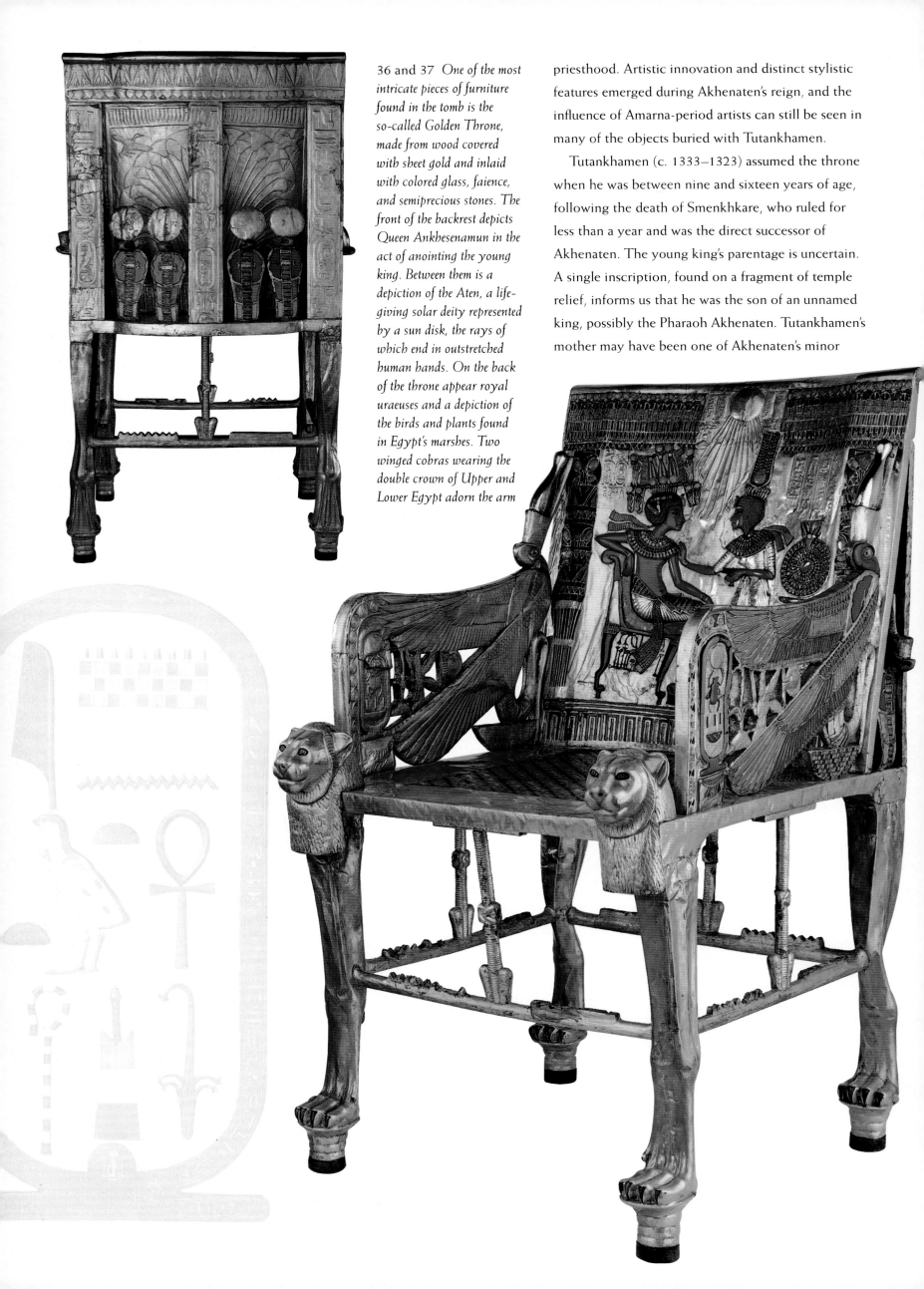

36 and 37 *One of the most intricate pieces of furniture found in the tomb is the so-called Golden Throne, made from wood covered with sheet gold and inlaid with colored glass, faience, and semiprecious stones. The front of the backrest depicts Queen Ankhesenamun in the act of anointing the young king. Between them is a depiction of the Aten, a life-giving solar deity represented by a sun disk, the rays of which end in outstretched human hands. On the back of the throne appear royal uraeuses and a depiction of the birds and plants found in Egypt's marshes. Two winged cobras wearing the double crown of Upper and Lower Egypt adorn the arm*

priesthood. Artistic innovation and distinct stylistic features emerged during Akhenaten's reign, and the influence of Amarna-period artists can still be seen in many of the objects buried with Tutankhamen.

Tutankhamen (c. 1333–1323) assumed the throne when he was between nine and sixteen years of age, following the death of Smenkhkare, who ruled for less than a year and was the direct successor of Akhenaten. The young king's parentage is uncertain. A single inscription, found on a fragment of temple relief, informs us that he was the son of an unnamed king, possibly the Pharaoh Akhenaten. Tutankhamen's mother may have been one of Akhenaten's minor

38 and 39 *This pectoral is filled by a representation of the sky goddess Nut in the form of a vulture with outstretched wings. The piece is made of gold, carnelian, and colored glass. To either side of the vulture's head appear the king's names and epithets associated with the pharaoh. The pectoral was found in the tomb's so-called treasury inside the base of a statue of Anubis, a jackal deity connected with the afterlife.*

39

wives, since his chief wife, Nefertiti, is believed to have borne only daughters. Ankhesenamun, the third daughter of Akhenaten and Nefertiti, became Tutankhamen's queen and she is frequently depicted on objects found in the tomb.

Historically, the period of Tutankhamen's reign is most notable for the demise of the Aten cult and the restoration of traditional religious practice; Amun was once again supreme. Because of the king's youth, it is questionable whether or not he played an active role in the events that shaped his reign. Rather, power seems to have resided with the high officials who surrounded the young king. Examination of Tutankhamen's mummy indicates that he died between the ages of nineteen and twenty-six, after a reign of less than ten years. The cause of the pharaoh's death remains controversial, and suggestions have been made that the king was murdered, presumably by power-hungry officials. However, the poor condition of Tutankhamen's bodily remains does not allow firm conclusions as to the cause of his death.

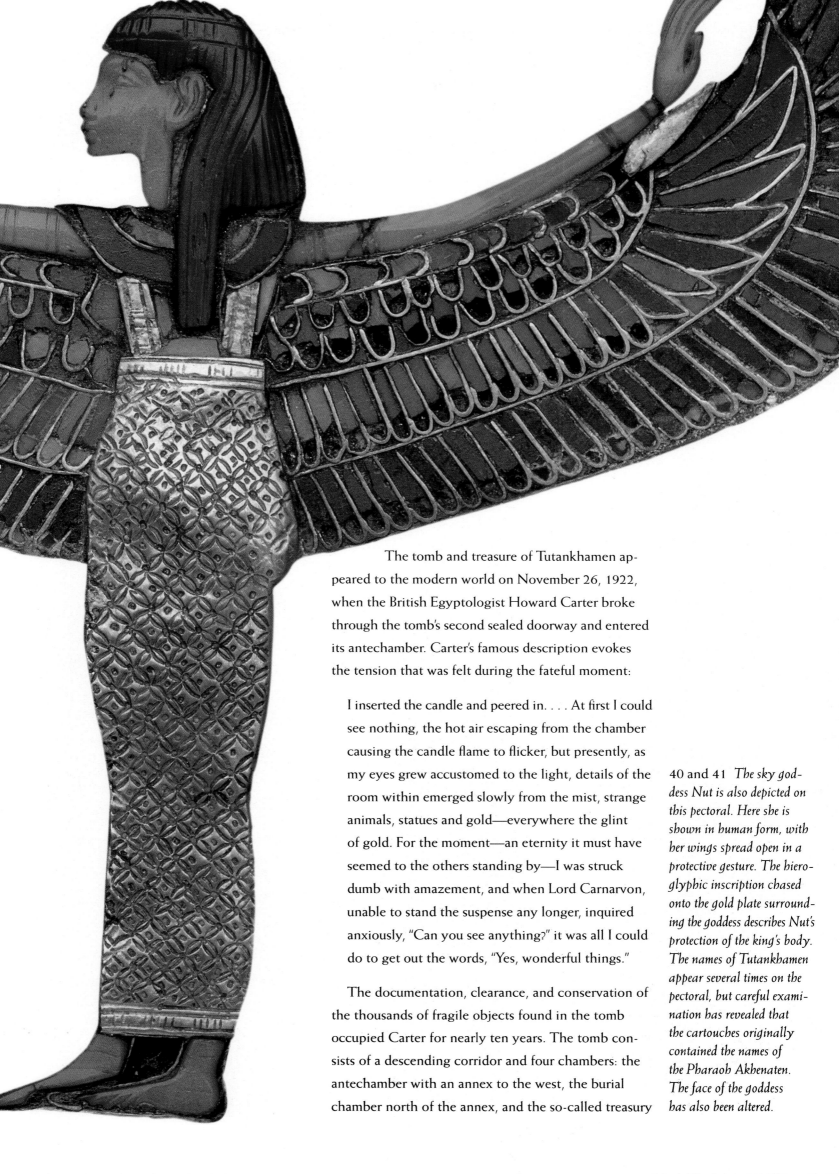

The tomb and treasure of Tutankhamen appeared to the modern world on November 26, 1922, when the British Egyptologist Howard Carter broke through the tomb's second sealed doorway and entered its antechamber. Carter's famous description evokes the tension that was felt during the fateful moment:

> I inserted the candle and peered in. . . . At first I could see nothing, the hot air escaping from the chamber causing the candle flame to flicker, but presently, as my eyes grew accustomed to the light, details of the room within emerged slowly from the mist, strange animals, statues and gold—everywhere the glint of gold. For the moment—an eternity it must have seemed to the others standing by—I was struck dumb with amazement, and when Lord Carnarvon, unable to stand the suspense any longer, inquired anxiously, "Can you see anything?" it was all I could do to get out the words, "Yes, wonderful things."

The documentation, clearance, and conservation of the thousands of fragile objects found in the tomb occupied Carter for nearly ten years. The tomb consists of a descending corridor and four chambers: the antechamber with an annex to the west, the burial chamber north of the annex, and the so-called treasury

40 and 41 The sky goddess Nut is also depicted on this pectoral. Here she is shown in human form, with her wings spread open in a protective gesture. The hieroglyphic inscription chased onto the gold plate surrounding the goddess describes Nut's protection of the king's body. The names of Tutankhamen appear several times on the pectoral, but careful examination has revealed that the cartouches originally contained the names of the Pharaoh Akhenaten. The face of the goddess has also been altered.

41

42 and 43 Scarab beetles
are included on many of
Tutankhamen's ornaments.
These beetles roll balls
of dung containing their
eggs along the ground;
the young beetles later
emerge from these balls.
The ancient Egyptians
identified the dung ball
with the rising sun and
saw the scarabs as
powerful symbols of
regeneration. All these
jewels include representations of scarabs and many
have the hieroglyphic
sign for the sun god Ra
above, and the basket
sign transliterated as
Neb below, thus form-
ing one of the pharaoh's
names—Nebkheprura,
which can be trans-
lated as "Lordly mani-
festation of Ra." Similar
motifs are found on
the bracelet clasp
and the pectoral.
The ornate necklace
is an example of the
baroque tendencies
displayed by some of
the objects found in
Tutankhamen's tomb.

east of the burial chamber. Each chamber was crammed with a variety of objects, some of which were made for Tutankhamen, while others appear to have originally belonged to different members of the royal family. Although popular belief holds that the tomb of Tutankhamen was left undisturbed after the king's burial, Carter found clear evidence that plunderers had twice entered the tomb, probably not long after the king was interred. The robbers seem to have removed a considerable amount of jewelry, as well as vessels made of precious metals, linen, and cosmetics.

The tomb contained a variety of seemingly utilitarian objects, such as chairs, beds, and boxes, some of which were presumably used by the king during his brief lifetime. Other objects belonged to the funerary realm and were created specifically for the tomb. It should be noted, however, that the ancient Egyptians did not make a sharp distinction between the secular and the religious: objects of everyday

life are often covered with scenes that have ritual significance. Along the same lines, the king himself was not only a political leader but also a semidivine figure. Both sacred and utilitarian objects were gilded and embellished with elaborate chased or repoussé depictions of deities or the king engaged in various rituals. Scenes were also constructed by means of intricate inlays formed from semiprecious stones and glass. Pieces placed in the tomb are not a collection of random artifacts or treasures. Instead, many objects clearly belong to a ritual program intended to aid and guide the king on his journey through the next world.

One of the most stunning objects recovered from Tutankhamen's tomb is the so-called Golden Throne, found in the antechamber beneath a hippopotamus-shaped bed. The throne is covered with complex iconographic symbols that refer to kingship, divine

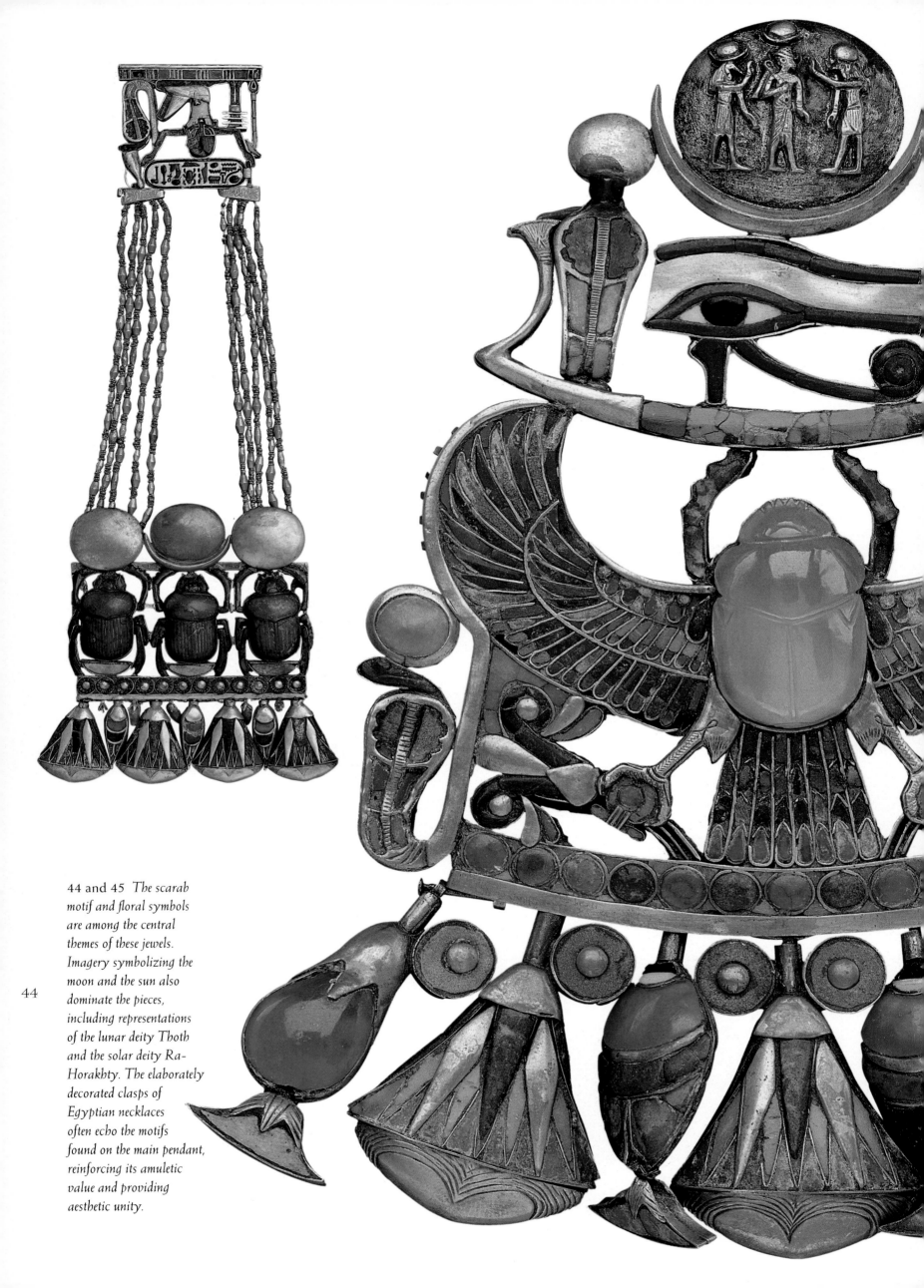

44 and 45 *The scarab motif and floral symbols are among the central themes of these jewels. Imagery symbolizing the moon and the sun also dominate the pieces, including representations of the lunar deity Thoth and the solar deity Ra-Horakhty. The elaborately decorated clasps of Egyptian necklaces often echo the motifs found on the main pendant, reinforcing its amuletic value and providing aesthetic unity.*

44

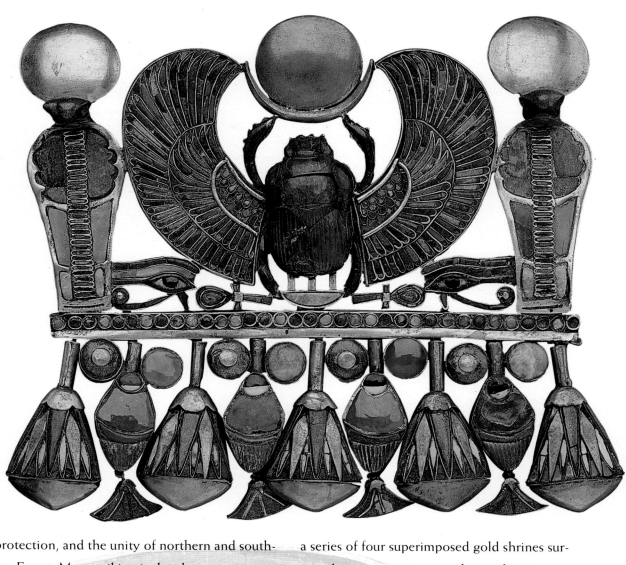

protection, and the unity of northern and southern Egypt. Most striking is the elegant scene on the front of the throne's backrest, which depicts Queen Ankhesenamun anointing her seated husband. Iconographic and stylistic elements indicate that the throne was designed and executed by artisans in Akhenaten's capital at Amarna. Most notable is the representation of the Aten, the sun disk with rays ending in human hands, which fills the upper center section of the scene. The tender interaction of king and queen is also typical for Amarna-period art, as are the king's sagging belly and the queen's generously proportioned thighs and buttocks.

Tutankhamen's mummy was placed inside a series of four superimposed gold shrines surrounding a quartzite sarcophagus that, in turn, held three coffins; the innermost coffin was made of solid gold. Most magnificent is the solid gold mask that covered the mummy's head and shoulders. Comparison between the mask and the mummy of the king show that the mask presents the general features of Tutankhamen. However, the mask is not a portrait in the modern sense but rather an image of the serenity and eternal youth that the young king would enjoy in the afterlife. Tutankhamen's role as king of Egypt is explicitly shown by the royal symbols that adorn the mask: the *nemes* headcloth, rendered with alternating stripes of gold and inlaid blue glass; the cobra and vulture rearing on the forehead; and the long, inlaid false beard.

The king's mummy was covered with more than 150 pieces of jewelry and other ornaments, all of which were believed to have amuletic powers that would protect his body throughout eternity. Items of jewelry were also found in each of the tomb's chambers, with the majority of pieces deposited in the so-called treasury. Tutankhamen's jewels seem to fall into three general categories: objects created for inclusion in the tomb, jewelry the pharaoh wore during his life, and altered pieces that belonged to

46 The goddess Nekhbet, shown in the form of a vulture with the Atef crown. Here, she embraces the pharaoh, who wears the enveloping garment characteristic of Osiris, lord of the dead.

46–47 The sisters Nephthys and Isis crouch on either side of a large scarab. The juxtaposition of scarab, sun disk, and uraeuses alludes to the daily rebirth that the king was believed to undergo after death.

47

the king's predecessors. Careful examination of the cartouches found on several of Tutankhamen's pectorals indicates that they once contained different royal names.

Much of our knowledge of New Kingdom Egyptian jewelry is a based on the spectacular objects found in Tutankhamen's tomb. The ornaments display a lavish use of materials, with complex combinations of religious symbols and hieroglyphic signs, including the names of the king placed inside an elongated oval known as a cartouche. The ancient Egyptians did not have the precious gems that form the centerpieces of Western jewelry; rather, they used semiprecious stones such as lapis lazuli, carnelian, turquoise, feldspar, jasper, and calcite. Gold was an important element in most pieces of royal jewelry, particularly since deities were believed to have golden bodies; silver appears less frequently. Manmade materials, such as glass and faience, were also employed.

Neck ornaments, in the form of pectorals and collars, are among the most impressive and dazzling

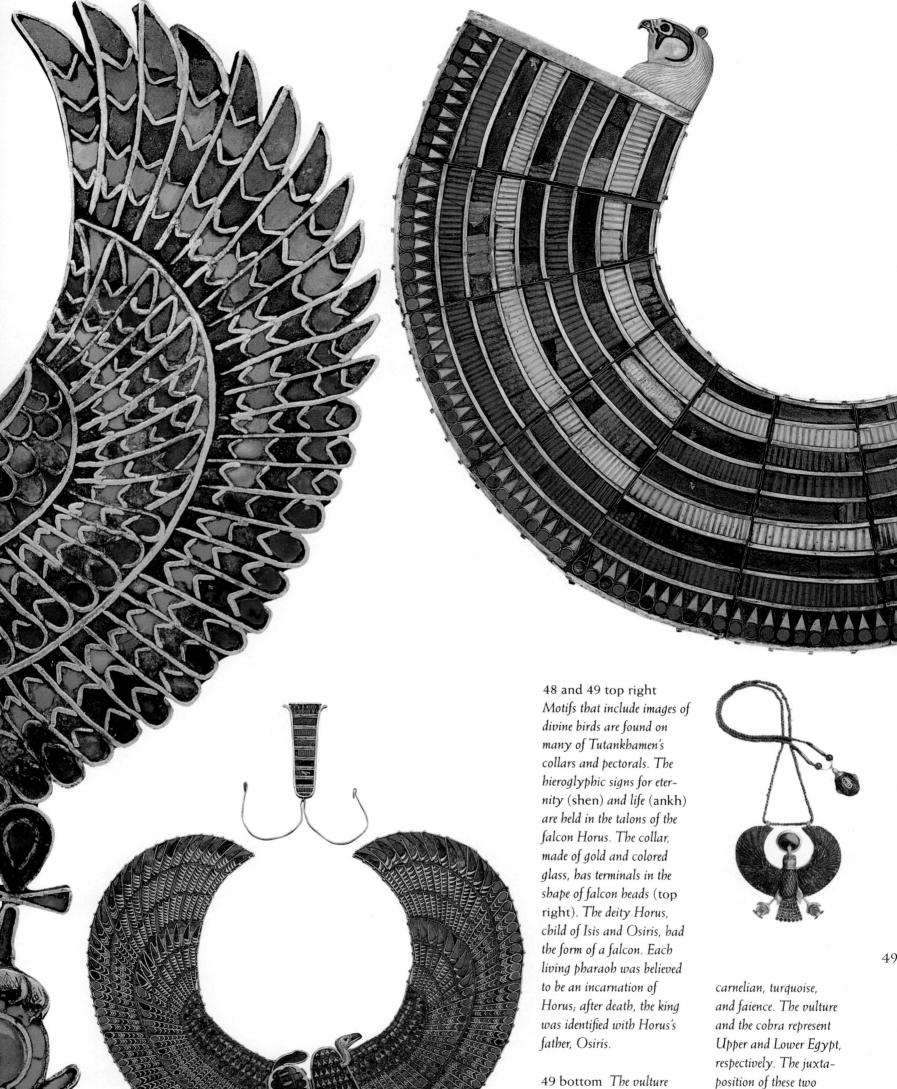

48 and 49 top right
Motifs that include images of divine birds are found on many of Tutankhamen's collars and pectorals. The hieroglyphic signs for eternity (shen) and life (ankh) are held in the talons of the falcon Horus. The collar, made of gold and colored glass, has terminals in the shape of falcon heads (top right). The deity Horus, child of Isis and Osiris, had the form of a falcon. Each living pharaoh was believed to be an incarnation of Horus; after death, the king was identified with Horus's father, Osiris.

49 bottom *The vulture goddess Nekhbet appears on this collar with the cobra goddess Wadjet to one side. Nekhbet's outspread wings are covered with inlays of*

carnelian, turquoise, and faience. The vulture and the cobra represent Upper and Lower Egypt, respectively. The juxtaposition of these two animals symbolizes the unity of southern and northern Egypt and the king's authority over the entire country.

49

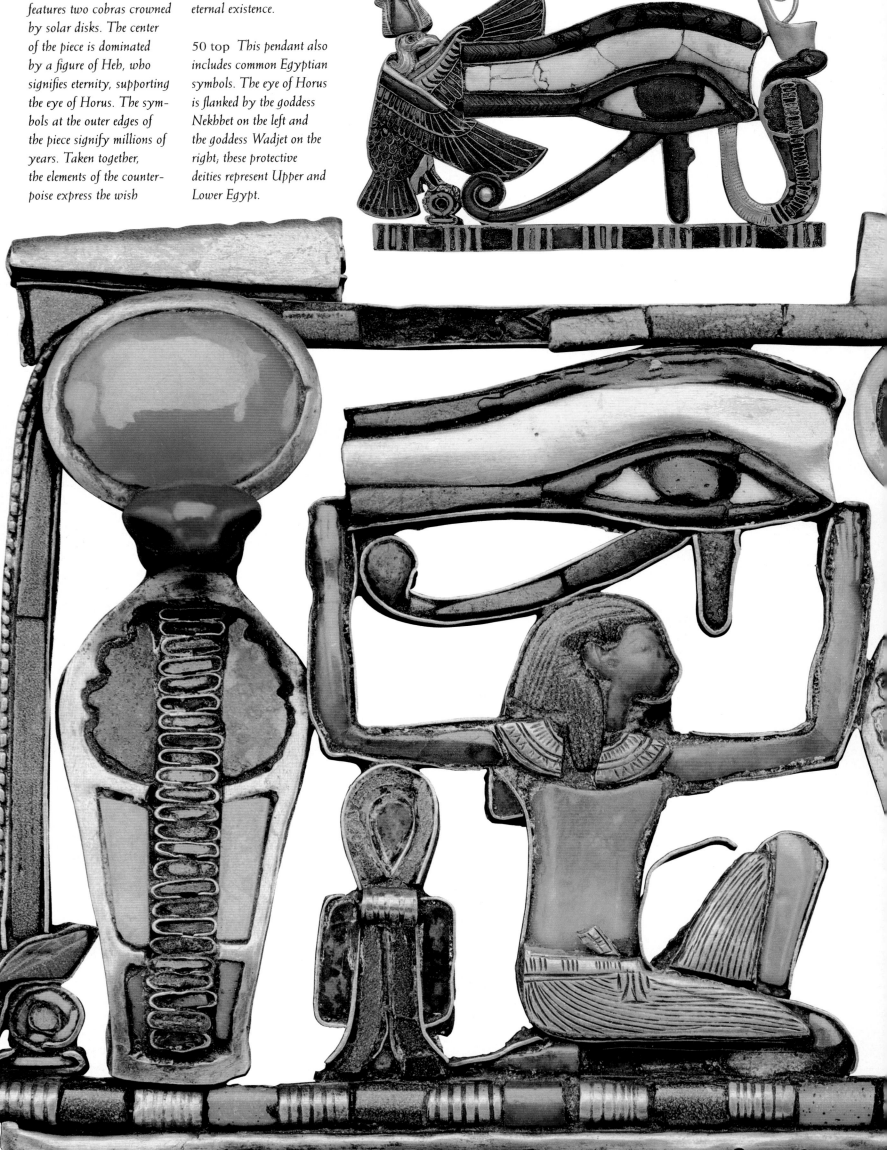

50–51 This counterpoise features two cobras crowned by solar disks. The center of the piece is dominated by a figure of Heb, who signifies eternity, supporting the eye of Horus. The symbols at the outer edges of the piece signify millions of years. Taken together, the elements of the counterpoise express the wish that the king be granted eternal existence.

50 top This pendant also includes common Egyptian symbols. The eye of Horus is flanked by the goddess Nekhbet on the left and the goddess Wadjet on the right; these protective deities represent Upper and Lower Egypt.

51 right *A faience Wadjet eye with a cobra in front of it is depicted on this amulet. This symbol is usually identified with the god Horus, but here the inscription connects it with the sun god Ra. The amu-let is suspended from a strand of cylindrical faience and gold beads, some of which are embellished with gold granulation. The piece was one of many ornaments placed around the neck of the deceased pharaoh.*

jewels found in Tutankhamen's tomb. Generally, pectorals are roughly rectangular in form, with a patterned, shrine-shaped outer frame that encloses either divine figures intended to protect the king or symbols relating directly to the ruler himself. Designs and figures were created by means of tiny, individually shaped pieces of semiprecious stones, inserted into cells formed by gold strips attached to a gold base plate. The artisans who created Tutankhamen's pectorals sometimes created pieces that displayed irregular edges and complex projections at the top, bottom, and sides. Pectorals were suspended from long strands of beads and were secured by elaborately inlaid clasps that often repeated design elements found on the main piece.

52–53 center *This bracelet displays alternating rows of scarabs and Wadjet eyes, separated by ball beads. The clasp is formed by an amethyst scarab in a gold setting. Patterned gold granulation surrounds the scarab, while uraeuses flank it on either long end.*

52 left and 53 right
*Earrings first appear in
Egypt during the Second
Intermediate Period. They
were worn by both men
and women, though during
the period in which Tutankhamen lived, men gener-
ally did not wear earrings
after puberty. The earrings
are made from gold, car-
nelian, calcite, quartz,
and glass. One pair
(right) includes tiny
images of the king
standing between
uraeuses, while above
the king is a Horus
falcon with outstretched
wings. The pharaoh is
not only Horus himself
but, in a paradox that is
common in Egyptian
religious belief, he is also
protected by Horus.*

Collars stretched from shoulder to shoulder across
the upper chest. Such ornaments could be made
from interconnected strands of individual beads, but
some of the collars found in Tutankhamen's tomb
were created using the same inlay technique as that
just described for pectorals. One of the most splendid of these collars combines representations of
the snake goddess Wadjet and the vulture goddess
Nekhbet. These protective deities, representing
Lower and Upper Egypt, also adorn the forehead
of the king's funerary mask. Nekhbet has enormous
wings that are covered with a dazzling array of
brilliantly colored inlays.

The extended wings of falcons, vultures, scarabs,
and female deities are often found on pieces of
Tutankhamen's jewelry, perhaps not only because

of the religious symbolism inherent in these representations but also because they allowed artisans to create virtuoso displays of magnificent color.

Several pairs of earrings were found in Tutankhamen's tomb, but during this period of Egyptian history males generally stopped wearing these ornaments once they reached adulthood. Earrings were first worn in Egypt during the Second Intermediate Period, a transitional era that preceded the New Kingdom, and their appearance probably is a result of foreign influence. Egyptian earrings were large objects, threaded through the ear by means of thick posts. Prominent holes are visible on the ears of Tutankhamen's mummy mask, but these were covered with gold foil disks rather than earrings, indicating that the king had reached adulthood before his death.

Like most of the jewelry found in Tutankhamen's tomb, his bracelets are elaborately worked and often crowded with a multitude of complex motifs. Large

scarabs, which project outward from the surface of the bracelet, are a common part of wrist ornaments. In addition to serving as a powerful symbol of regeneration and rebirth, the scarab beetle also figures prominently in one of Tutankhamen's five names.

The tomb of Tutankhamen is one of the only pharaoh's burial places to have escaped large-scale robbery. The treasures it contained provide both an invaluable impression of the richness of the pharaonic court and a tantalizing reminder of how much of Egyptian artistry and craftsmanship has been lost. Historically, Tutankhamen was a minor pharaoh who ruled during a difficult period of Egyptian history, and one can only speculate about the treasures that must have belonged to Egypt's more prominent rulers. Yet only the golden face of Tutankhamen remains, captivating us with its serene gaze and providing a rare glimpse into the opulent world of ancient Egypt.

54 and 55 At the center of the pectoral, a winged scarab is flanked by the goddesses Nephthys (left) and Isis (right). The back of the scarab is inscribed with a passage from the Book of the Dead, an ancient Egyptian guide to the afterlife. That the pectoral was probably made at Amarna is indicated by the inclusion of the name of Aten at the top of the column of text directly in front of Isis. The full lips and the down-turned corners of the goddesses' mouths are also characteristic of Amarna-period art.

MYCENAE AND THE GOLDEN MASK

56 top *Gold funerary mask from Tomb V of Circle A at Mycenae. It is the type with a rounded, highly convex face and globular, protruding eyes. Found in Tomb V, where Heinrich Schliemann also discovered the celebrated funerary mask wrongly attributed to Agamemnon.*

56 bottom *This gold mask is modeled in the broad, modestly convex facial type, with just a few simple details. These are, of course, conventionalized facial features, as there was no individualized portraiture in Mycenaean art.*

The Mycenaean civilization flourished in the Peloponnese and other areas of Greece between the seventeenth and twelfth centuries B.C. The name derives from Mycenae on the plain of Argolis, the well-known home of the house of Atreus, celebrated in the Homeric epics and the tragedies of Aeschylus. The ancient city was discovered and excavated from the 1870s onward by Heinrich Schliemann and numerous other archaeological missions.

The distinguishing characteristics of the Mycenaean civilization have long been identified: at the top of the social pyramid was the *wanax*; there followed a warrior elite; then proprietors of land and resources involved in the organization and coordination of an active artisan and mercantile class involved in enterprises of vast economic scope. A writing system known as Linear B was developed; considerable documentation survives. Clay tablets were fired in the conflagrations that almost everywhere marked the end of the Mycenaean centers; these conserve texts in an Indo-European language closely related to the successive Hellenistic dialects and are testimony to the careful economic management practiced by the Mycenaeans.

57 The most beautiful of the Mycenaean masks is the "Mask of Agamemnon." In reality, it belonged to a Mycenaean king who lived in the first half of the sixteenth century B.C. and was buried in Tomb V of Circle A. The carefully wrought detail in the facial features—the beard and mustache rendered with dense hatching, the facial convexities in the embossed modeling —indicates that a talented artist made the piece.

58 top *A lynx hunting wild ducks along a watercourse with papyrus plants: this image, with its exotic theme and Egyptian origins, adorns one side of the blade of a bronze dagger with inlays of niello, gold and silver, from Circle A, Tomb V.*

58–59 center *This bronze dagger blade with inlays of niello, gold and silver is datable to the first half of the fifteenth century B.C. The decoration derives from the Minoan "Marine Style." The piece is from the small tholos tomb at Routsi, near Pylos.*

58–59 bottom *Another celebrated bronze dagger was also discovered in Tomb IV of Circle A at Mycenae. It features niello-work inlays of gold and silver and depicts a lion-hunting scene, a theme dense with metaphorical meanings. According to the scholar M. Benzi, the theme is Mycenaean, but the style is Minoan and the piece can be attributed to a Cretan artist.*

The role played by this civilization as a great commercial power of the Bronze Age Mediterranean is confirmed by the numerous finds of Mycenaean manufactures made throughout the Mediterranean basin and in many areas of inland Europe and the Near East. The attractive ceramics, finely worked metal manufactures, and precious fabrics, however, were but the most prestigious of the goods exported throughout the Mediterranean of antiquity on Mycenaean ships. These vessels could, moreover, count on a network of decentralized trading stations, the so-called emporia, which probably had the function of distributing the exports and gathering raw materials from various regions.

The excavations conducted for more than a developing on two levels linked by staircases and centered on the primary nucleus of the *megaron*, the basic domestic and cultural structure of the Helladic world.

Notable funerary architecture also survives. The grandiose *tholos* (false dome) tombs, dating from the fifteenth to the thirteenth centuries B.C., perhaps derive from Cretan or Anatolian models, reserved for the *wanakes* and their families. These tombs represent the culmination of a tradition: in the seventeenth and sixteenth centuries B.C., the dead of the ruling class were buried in similarly imposing excavated tombs.

The best-known examples are the six underground chambers excavated by Schliemann in

century on the plain of Argolis, at Laconia, Phthiotis, Boeotia, and Attica have also revealed the basic characteristics of Mycenaean architecture: the most fascinating sites are those of Mycenae, Tiryns, and Pylos. In the first two the powerful megalithic walls that protected the "palace" of the *wanax* and a "proto-urban" space, destined for a number of figures close to the king in terms of rank or activity, are well conserved. At Pylos the regular and functionally efficient planning of the residence of the Homeric Nestor is well documented, the building

59 *This magnificent rhyton (a religious zoomorphic vessel used for libations) was made in sheet gold. It was shaped in the form of a lion's head by an artist whose style has, according to the experts, much in common with the products of the craftsman who produced the "Mask of Agamemnon." This rhyton was discovered in Tomb IV of Circle A. Its small dimensions and measured realism make the talent of the artist who executed the embossing and engraving all the more impressive.*

60 left *This long brooch in gold and silver was found on the body of a woman buried in Tomb III of Circle A at Mycenae. The handle features a female figure similar in many respects to the traditional Cretan "Lady of the Snakes"; the general style of the piece is also Cretan, with strong Egyptian iconographic overtones.*

60

funerary Circle A, incorporated within the city by the last extension of the walls.

The most famous and most widely admired gold treasures of the Mycenaean civilization were found in these tombs, along with the remains of nineteen persons (eight men, nine women, and two children). These masterpieces include the stunning funerary masks placed over the faces of the deceased, the services of gold plate, the personal jewelry, and the ceremonial and functional arms that can be admired on these pages.

This impressive testimony to the wealth of the "lords" of Mycenae and its ostentation in the funerary ceremony that preceded burial provoke questions that are, at least in part, still unanswered. Where did the Mycenaeans obtain their gold, given the scarcity of deposits in the Hellenic territories? The Mycenaean term *ku-ru-so*, which appears frequently on the clay tablets in Linear B and is clearly related to the more recent *chrysos* of classical Greek, means "gold" and is a Semitic linguistic borrowing. Egyptian and Middle Eastern origins have been

60 right *The "Nestor's Cup," wrongly identified because of the fertile imagination of Schliemann, was discovered in Tomb IV of Circle A at Mycenae. It is made from a single thick gold sheet; the handles, decorated with animal figures, are applied.*

60–61 *This diadem, deposited in Tomb III of Circle A, is made from a thin elongated oval sheet of gold. Its embossed decoration with stylized floral motifs is a characteristic feature of the most clearly Mycenaean decorative tradition.*

61 bottom *A small hexagonal wooden box lined with gold plaquettes, found in Tomb V of Circle A. The decoration of this piece with hunting scenes, clumsily rendered by a Mycenaean artist revealing a horror vacuii, is not of particular interest.*

hypothesized, partly due to the widespread evidence of economic and commercial contacts between the civilization of the "Fertile Crescent," Anatolia, and the Mycenaeans. Neither can we exclude the possibility that the precious metal arrived from the distant lands south of the Iberian peninsula, where the Tartessian-Mycenaean interactions were of interest.

What is certain, however, is that from a stylistic point of view the Mycenaean goldsmiths were heavily influenced by Crete. The local formal substrata, which leaned toward abstract and geometric decorative motifs, were enriched and stimulated by the Minoan tradition based on naturalism and figuration, both through the import of Minoan manufactures and through the probable, albeit not demonstrable, activities of Cretan artists in Mycenaean centers. And Crete was, it should not be forgotten, the great cultural bridge between the Oriental and the Aegean worlds, the crucible for the synthesis of the cultural and formal models of the East that were best received

62 top *This small gold cup decorated with embossed intertwining spirals distributed in two registers and separated by a marked bulge midway up the sides was also found in Tomb V of Circle A at Mycenae. The decorative motif was originally Minoan and has been developed here with great skill.*

and most easily adaptable in the West.

A number of the objects found in the tombs of Circle A at Mycenae are typically Mycenaean, especially the six gold masks in embossed and engraved sheet metal. Among these is the celebrated example attributed by Schliemann to Agamemnon, the king of Mycenae and the commander of the Achaean expedition in the Trojan War described in the *Iliad.* In reality the masks belonged to a *wanax* who died toward the middle of the sixteenth century B.C., three hundred years before the son of Atreus! The symbolic value of such splendor is increased by its

consignment to the obscurity of a tomb; the significance of these objects does not appear to be limited to the simple perpetuation in precious materials of the features of the deceased, because they were actually depicted according to conventions. The weapons inlaid with figurative motifs are also conceptually typical of this warrior civilization, but their decoration presents clearly Minoan formal influences. The technique used for these objects was that of inlays with niello, a shiny black-blue substance probably of Egyptian origin, used as an adhesive to attach gold and silver to bronze.

62 bottom *From the outstanding tholos tomb of Vapheio, most probably belonging to a Mycenaean "prince," came rich gold objects, including this beautiful gold cup decorated in repoussé. A masterpiece by a Cretan goldsmith, working in the exquisite naturalistic style typical of Minoan art in the fifteenth century B.C.*

62–63 *This exceptional image of a well-known cup in sheet gold is from a late fifteenth-century* B.C. *tholos tomb at Dendra, Argolis, containing a sumptuous royal funerary cache. The decoration with marine animals typical of contemporary Minoan ceramics suggests a date in the fifteenth century* B.C. *and a provenance from a Cretan workshop.*

64–65 A typically aristocratic theme is illustrated on the face of this small signet ring, found in Tomb IV of Circle A at Mycenae. A biga is being driven furiously by a charioteer chasing a large deer with many-branched antlers. The hunter is ready to loose the fatal arrow from his bow, but the action seems to be suspended.

64 center This second signet ring bears a processional scene: four demons carrying ritual vessels to a goddess seated on a throne. The ring was discovered at Tiryns outside the stratigraphic context. It dates from the fifteenth century B.C. and apparently originated in a Minoan workshop.

64 bottom A scene perhaps depicting a hierogamy (holy marriage) is on this signet ring from the fifteenth century B.C., found at Tiryns together with the preceding piece.

65 bottom This fourth signet ring, on the other hand, comes from Tomb IV of Circle A at Mycenae, and features an engraved dueling scene. Like the others, it belongs to a female burial cache.

JEWELS FOR THE BEAUTEOUS *Helen*

66–67 Undoubtedly the most popular among the splendid jewels of the "Treasure of Priam" is the Greater Diadem, composed of a thin gold chain half a meter long from which 90 individual smaller chains with cascades of leaflike pendants hang vertically, jingling and sparkling in the light. These chains terminate in double-arrowhead pendants. The piece is made of sheet gold and dates to circa 2400–2300 B.C.

67 top *The internal part of this pair of earrings highlights the goldsmith's technical mastery. The pendants are composed of a very fine chain in which tiny leaves are inserted.*

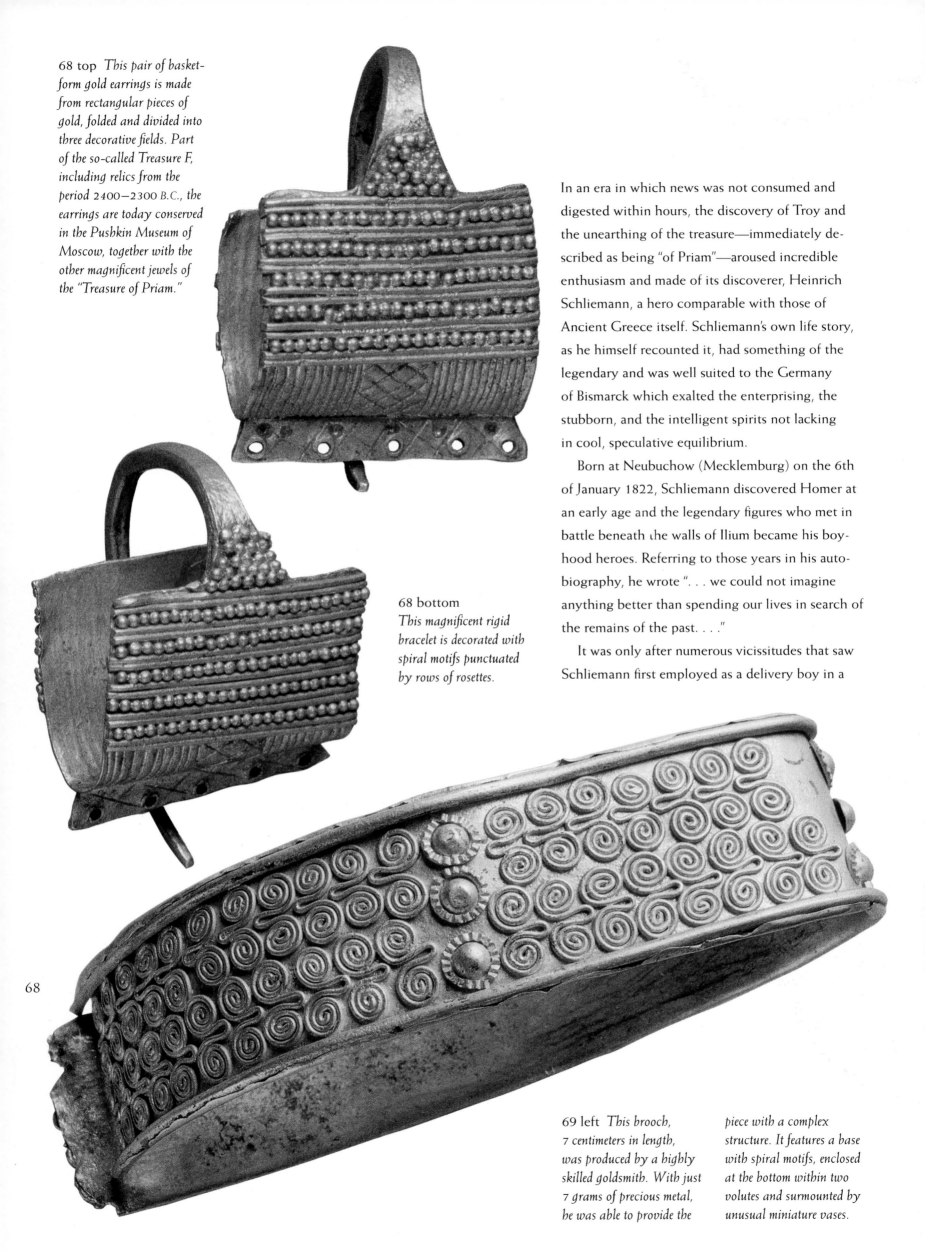

68 top *This pair of basket-form gold earrings is made from rectangular pieces of gold, folded and divided into three decorative fields. Part of the so-called Treasure F, including relics from the period 2400–2300 B.C., the earrings are today conserved in the Pushkin Museum of Moscow, together with the other magnificent jewels of the "Treasure of Priam."*

68 bottom
This magnificent rigid bracelet is decorated with spiral motifs punctuated by rows of rosettes.

In an era in which news was not consumed and digested within hours, the discovery of Troy and the unearthing of the treasure—immediately described as being "of Priam"—aroused incredible enthusiasm and made of its discoverer, Heinrich Schliemann, a hero comparable with those of Ancient Greece itself. Schliemann's own life story, as he himself recounted it, had something of the legendary and was well suited to the Germany of Bismarck which exalted the enterprising, the stubborn, and the intelligent spirits not lacking in cool, speculative equilibrium.

Born at Neubuchow (Mecklemburg) on the 6th of January 1822, Schliemann discovered Homer at an early age and the legendary figures who met in battle beneath the walls of Ilium became his boyhood heroes. Referring to those years in his autobiography, he wrote ". . . we could not imagine anything better than spending our lives in search of the remains of the past. . . ."

It was only after numerous vicissitudes that saw Schliemann first employed as a delivery boy in a

69 left *This brooch, 7 centimeters in length, was produced by a highly skilled goldsmith. With just 7 grams of precious metal, he was able to provide the piece with a complex structure. It features a base with spiral motifs, enclosed at the bottom within two volutes and surmounted by unusual miniature vases.*

grocery, then as a cabin boy on a transatlantic liner, and finally as a business agent in St. Petersburg in Russia, that he found his true vocation. Business seemed to appeal to his enterprising nature and he founded a successful trading company. It allowed him to accumulate sufficient wealth to retire in 1863, then devote himself to matters he had long dreamed of. For a number of years he traveled extensively, visiting Sweden, Italy, Egypt, and Syria, as well as Japan, China, and the United States, before settling in Paris in 1866 with the intention of making an intensive study of archaeology and preparing himself for the realization of his life's work.

In 1868 he made a pilgrimage to the sites celebrated by Homer and decided that the time had come to bring to light the cities described in the *Iliad* and the *Odyssey*. He wanted to demonstrate to the scientific community that the Homeric poems were based on historical fact and not mere fantasy.

In 1871, having purchased an excavation permit from the Turkish government, he began working on the mound of Hissarlik, which he believed to be the site of ancient Troy. The excavations immediately revealed an extremely complex and monumental

69 bottom Some of the jewels discovered by Schliemann were produced by the same craftsman; this brooch, in fact, presents decorative and technical features similar to those of the two preceding pieces.

70–71 top *The Lesser
Diadem is composed of a
slim band of sheet gold from
which are hung 64 fine
double-link vertical chains.
The 50 central ones are
shorter, with the seven to
either side being longer. The
chains terminate with pendants in the form of idols.*

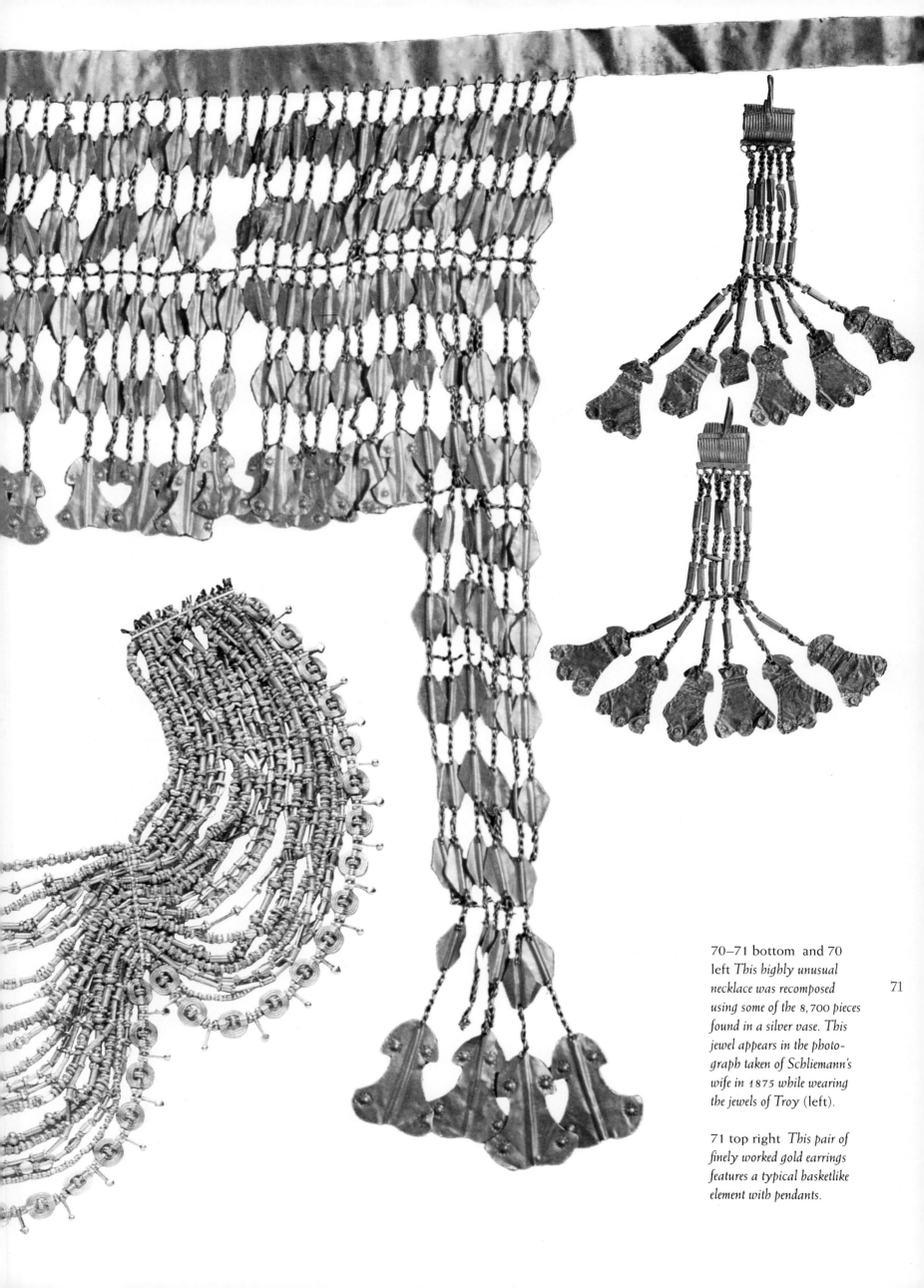

70–71 bottom and 70 left *This highly unusual necklace was recomposed using some of the 8,700 pieces found in a silver vase. This jewel appears in the photograph taken of Schliemann's wife in 1875 while wearing the jewels of Troy (left).*

71 top right *This pair of finely worked gold earrings features a typical basketlike element with pendants.*

72–73 top *These various necklace elements also date from the period 2400–2300 B.C. The beads assembled were of varied and original forms: rounded, smooth, dentate, barrel shaped, truncated cones, square, tubular, winged, or simple spheres.*

72 bottom *These crescent-moon-shaped earrings are finely decorated with granulation work.*

73 bottom *This flat necklace element, composed of four spirals soldered together, is again in pure gold. It was made from thin, narrow strips of gold rolled up at each end. The join between the two is perforated to allow for the thread.*

stratigraphic sequence. In fact, nine phases were identified in the city occupying the entire mound, dating from the start of the third millennium B.C. to the Roman period.

Schliemann, later assisted by W. Dörpfeld, identified Homeric Troy in the sixth strata, dated between 1500 and 1000 B.C. On the basis of subsequent archaeological investigations that confirmed the nine phases of the city, the American C. Blegen corrected Schliemann's interpretation. The city of the sixth strata was, in fact, destroyed by an earthquake that can be dated to around 1300 B.C., not by a fire which instead occurred in the subsequent phase; it was, therefore, in that seventh strata that the Troy of Homer was to be seen.

During Schliemann's third dig, lasting from February to June 1873, he made his great discovery. About 8–9 meters below the city wall and the architectural elements that he recognized as the Scaean Gate and the palace of Priam of the *Iliad*, he found a cache of 250 objects in gold that was immediately baptized the "Treasure of Priam."

He described the find in the following terms in *Trojan Antiquities:*

> I came across a large object in copper of an extremely unusual shape . . . behind it I thought I could see gold. . . . As I found these objects all together or inserted one in another in a square pile, it appears certain that they were once enclosed in a wooden chest like those of Priam's palace mentioned in the *Iliad*.
>
> This seems all the more probable given that close to the objects I found a long copper key. . . .

Schliemann recounts that, in order to save the treasure from the greed of his workers, he had to send them away, moving up their lunch break and, helped by his wife, ". . . who was ever ready to wrap

objects in her shawl and carry them away . . . ," he recovered the priceless relics himself, using a long knife and ignoring the risk that the high wall above might collapse.

Schliemann described the jewels he found in the following terms:

> In a large silver vase I found . . . two splendid gold diadems, a diadem of exceptional craftsmanship and four earrings fashioned with great skill. Over them were 56 gold earrings of a very unusual shape and 8,750 small gold rings, perforated prisms and cubes, gold buttons and so on, that evidently belonged to other jewels. There followed six gold bracelets and, at the very top, two small gold cups. I also found two pieces of gold 5 centimeters long and each having 21 small holes.

The discovery of the treasure aroused a great sensation and there were inevitably those who denigrated the find, some of whom went so far as to claim the jewels were fakes. The polemic was in part fed by Schliemann himself; in his own diary he claimed that the discovery had been made on the

17th of June 1873, rather than the 31st of May. The discrepancy in the dates was due to his wish to involve his wife in the discovery; unfortunately, she was in Athens on the 31st of May. Whatever Schliemann's intentions may have been, the fact that his wife was not present aroused some doubt as to the veracity of his account.

What is undeniable, however, is that the photograph of Schliemann's wife wearing the so-called Greater Diadem and earrings and a necklace belonging to the treasure was soon seen throughout the world.

Schliemann smuggled the treasure to Athens, arousing the ire of the Turkish authorities, whom he reimbursed with 50,000 gold francs, a vast sum in those days. Having become the sole owner of the "Treasure of Priam," Schliemann bequeathed it to the Ethnological Museum of Berlin.

The German archaeologist was responsible for further remarkable discoveries, such as the royal tombs at Tiryns and Mycenae that were also extremely rich in gold.

74 and 75 *A simple earring of exquisite elegance (top left) was crafted with a three-branched shape, departing from the solid central hook. The earring below features six branches decorated geo-* *metrically with rows of small beads. Two necklaces (center) were reconstructed using the elements found in the silver vase. A pair of boatlike earrings (bottom right) is decorated with rows of beads.*

Following an operation on his ears, Schliemann died on the 26th of December 1890, at Naples; he had traveled there to see the latest discoveries at Pompeii and Herculaneum, ignoring the risks of convalescence. The funeral ceremony was held in Athens and attracted a vast crowd. A bust of Homer was placed on the coffin.

The treasure, long conserved in the Museum of Berlin, was transferred to the so-called Zoo Bunker on the eve of the Second World War. Found by the Russians when they entered the city as conquerors on the 26th of May 1945, it was transferred to Moscow as spoils of war. To this day, it is conserved and exhibited in all its splendor at the Pushkin Museum.

While not wishing to detract from the romantic interpretation of Heinrich Schliemann, it should be pointed out that the treasure he believed to have belonged to Priam actually dates to a period at least 1,000 years before the Trojan War. It is, nonetheless, an extremely important expression of the culture of the Bronze Age; moreover, it is undeniable that Schliemann's excavations provided a fundamental resource for scholars of these remote periods in the history of the Mediterranean.

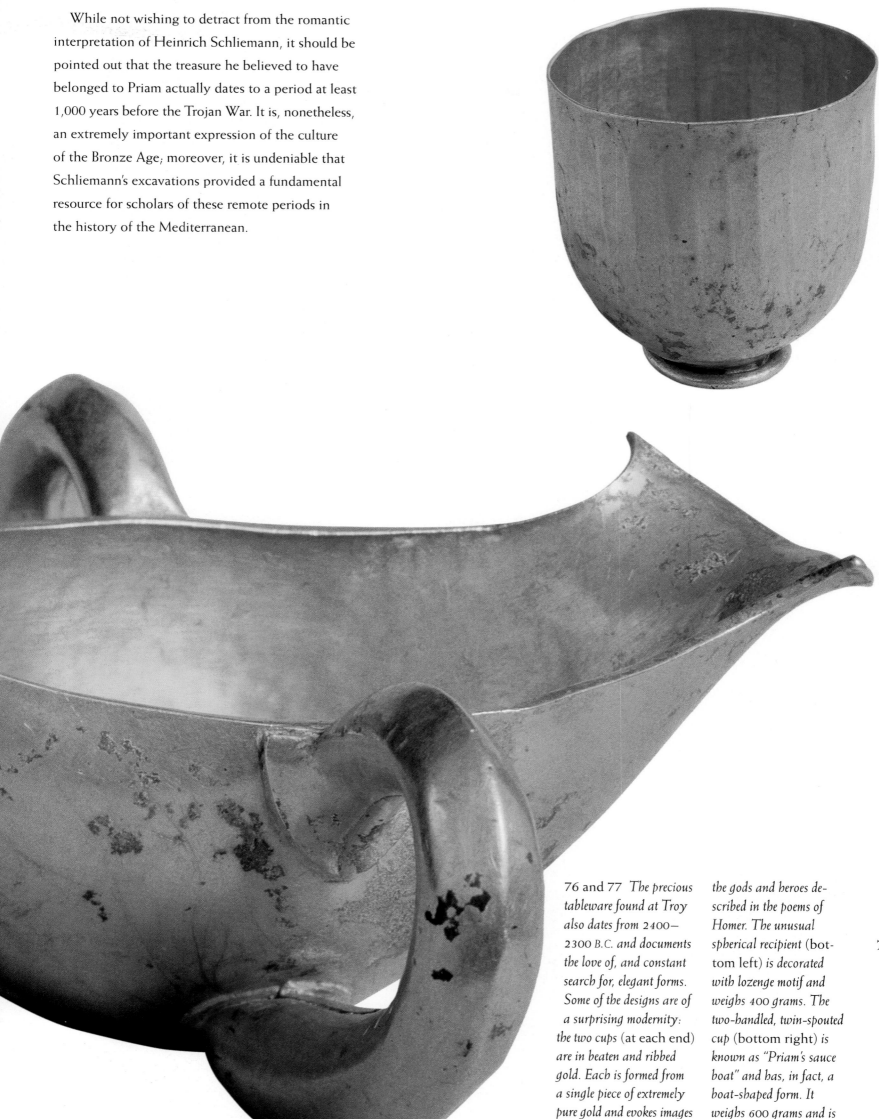

76 and 77 The precious tableware found at Troy also dates from 2400–2300 B.C. and documents the love of, and constant search for, elegant forms. Some of the designs are of a surprising modernity: the two cups (at each end) are in beaten and ribbed gold. Each is formed from a single piece of extremely pure gold and evokes images of the opulent banquets of the gods and heroes described in the poems of Homer. The unusual spherical recipient (bottom left) is decorated with lozenge motif and weighs 400 grams. The two-handled, twin-spouted cup (bottom right) is known as "Priam's sauce boat" and has, in fact, a boat-shaped form. It weighs 600 grams and is also made of pure gold.

MAGIC IN PHOENICIAN GOLD

78 top *This gold bowl is engraved with scenes of Egyptian, Syrian, and Mycenaean inspiration. Found at Ugarit, it is today conserved in the museum at Aleppo in Syria.*

"One day arrived the Phoenicians, famous navigators," runs a Homeric verse, consecrating the image of a people associated with the sea, masters of its routes and secrets. They were expert seamen and explorers, as well as skilled and astute traders.

The Phoenicians (or Sidonians, to use their older name, perhaps linked to the supremacy assumed by the city of Sidon in the ninth century B.C.) were ancient inhabitants of the Syrian-Palestinian coastal region roughly corresponding to present-day Lebanon. We attribute the invention of the letters of the alphabet to the Phoenicians, known in antiquity as master navigators, skilled craftsmen, and talented entrepreneurs. The first written testimony, that is to say, the Bible, the *Iliad*, and the *Odyssey*, together with other classical literary sources, express positive and flattering verdicts on the technical and craft skills of the Phoenicians.

79 *This exceptional example of a ceremonial ax with a gold handle is decorated with divine figures, using the extremely old granulation technique. Along with filigree-work, granulation was widely used by the Phoenicians. The piece was part of the treasure of Byblos and dates from the nineteenth to eighteenth centuries B.C. It is today conserved in the National Museum at Beirut.*

78 bottom *This elaborate gold cup with embossed hunting scenes is proof of the notable technical skills of the Phoenician goldsmiths, who were influenced by the Egyptian culture and those of the Middle and Far East. The cup, dating from the fifteenth to fourteenth centuries B.C., is 19 centimeters in diameter; it was found at Ugarit.*

They came to dominate the Mediterranean, trading small-scale, sophisticated manufactures such as Tyrian purple dye and spices, or jewels in gold, silver, and semiprecious stones produced in their specialty workshops, for other precious goods.

The prerequisites for commercial expansion of the Phoenician cities are to be found in a series of historical events that took place in the Mediterranean basin from the second half of the second millennium B.C. These momentous events included the invasion of the "Peoples of the Sea," the sudden weakening of Egyptian maritime dominance, and the collapse of Mycenaean power. The Phoenician trading activities during the last two centuries of the second millennium were principally concentrated in the eastern Mediterranean regions, such as Egypt, the south coast of Anatolia, and Cyprus. There was also intensive trade with the neighboring kingdom of Israel. The Old Testament reports that, at the time of his alliance with Hiram, the sovereign of

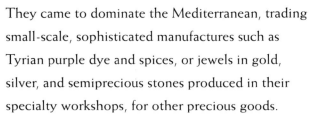

80 and 81 *Gold funerary masks were widely produced by the Phoenician craftsmen. Most of the masks have been found in tombs, which demonstrates that they had an apotropaic function and were laid on the deceased's face. The examples seen here date from the fifth and fourth centuries B.C. and can now be seen in the Musée du Louvre, Paris.*

Tyre, King Solomon was so impressed by the Phoenicians' sophisticated craftsmanship that he commissioned them to construct the great works he promoted, first and foremost the temple of Jerusalem. No expense was spared to secure their services; in fact, in the Bible it is written that Solomon promised to reward Hiram's workers and craftsmen "in the measure he requested."

It was the search for raw materials to craft in the workshops of their homeland that encouraged the Phoenicians to leave their ports and sail the routes opened by the Mycenaean navigators. They undertook voyages of exploration and founded

82 top left and bottom right *The two images show a versatile gold ring: on one side is a winged scarab, a recurrent magical symbol in the Phoenician culture. On the other side appears an engraved image of Egyptian origin, the eye of Horus. The ring dates from the period between the seventh and sixth centuries B.C. and is conserved in the Musée du Bardo in Tunis.*

82 center *This stirrup pendant features a carnelian scarab on an elaborate gold mount. On the reverse side of the stone, Isis is depicted in the company of the young Horus.*

colonies in lands at the confines of the known world and beyond. These colonies included Carthage and Utica in North Africa, Sulcis and Tharros on the west coast of Sardinia, the island of Mozia off Sicily, and extended even beyond the Pillars of Hercules (that is, beyond the Strait of Gibraltar, where Hercules erected the columns marking the edge of the world) with Cadiz, Huelva, and Sexi established along the south coast of the Iberian peninsula.

The Phoenicians' talent was seen at its best in the minor arts, such as the working of ivory to produce ciboria, amulets, and precious inlays for wooden furnishings such as chairs or beds; intaglio on precious

or semiprecious stones, such as lapis lazuli, used for pendants or seals. Alongside these activities, one of the most characteristic Phoenician crafts was that of goldsmithing, associated with art forms that predated the birth of a Phoenician cultural identity in the Syrian-Palestinian region. Of interest in this regard is the documentation from the third and second millennia B.C. provided by Byblos. A city with a favorable geographical position, Byblos was the natural port of call on the routes linking the Syrian-Palestinian coast with Egypt. It became the principal source of the Cedar of Lebanon wood that was highly prized by the pharaohs. The sumptuous jewels deposited as votive offerings in the sanctuary, the most important religious site in a Phoenician

82–83 This pectoral, one of the oldest yet discovered, came from the tomb of King Abi Shemu of the eighteenth century B.C. Several details recalling Egyptian iconography are clearly visible. The piece from Byblos is today conserved in the Musée du Louvre.

83 bottom The figures of Horus and Anubis seen in this amulet, standing 2.5 centimeters high, were found in a tomb on Malta and date to the seventh or sixth century B.C.

city, and the rich funerary caches of the sovereigns of Byblos, who loved to surround themselves with the attributes of pharaonic regality, are particularly enlightening: they document the extremely close relationship between Byblos and Egypt, the wealth of the city, and the technical virtuosity of the local goldsmiths, who combined semiprecious stones and vitreous paste in cloisonné work. The pectorals and gold medallions with embossed and cloisonné decorations found at Tell el-Ajjiul (the ancient Gaza) and Ras Shamra (the ancient Ugarit) are characterized by the presence of types and motifs that were to be widely used during the course of the first millennium, that is to say, during the Phoenician era.

Undoubtedly, the commissioning and use of jewelry in gold and silver (evidence of the latter being relatively rare, because of the perishability of the material) was primarily due to demand from high-ranking local patrons who had privileged con-

tacts with the Eastern world and for whom jewels were symbols of wealth and power. The figurative motifs used in jewelry attest to the fact that the plundering of the Egyptian repertory was by no means casual; nor was it a case of simple repetition. Rather, designs were chosen for their cultural significance and magical-religious values.

Strongly convinced of the survival of the spirit after death, the Phoenicians buried their dead in tombs excavated in rock and placed a series of inscriptions on their sarcophagi. These texts provide evidence of a constant preoccupation with the possible violation of the tomb and the concept of the state of death as a long rest that must never be disturbed. In the Phoenician world, the concept of an afterlife, a second existence, as understood in the Egyptian religion, was linked to a fear of the influence of evil demons, who were warded off with magical rites and objects such as spells, potions, and amulets of good fortune. From the Syrian region comes, for example, a pendant amulet dating from the sixth century B.C.: it features a long incantation in which the two Phoenician deities Sasm and Horun are invoked against two evil powers that operate in the dark of night. Thus, in order to guarantee a tranquil existence in the afterlife, the deceased's tomb was filled with various objects—particularly amulets and scarabs, to which symbolic meanings and apotropaic powers were attributed. The masks that are frequently found in Phoenician and Punic tombs of both cremated and interred males and females were intended to prevent evil spirits from disturbing the sleep of the dead. The demoniacal male heads in the form of pendants deposited in the tombs are to be interpreted as

84 top left This elegant gold earring with an elongated, acorn-shaped pendant is from Tharros. It is a typical product of the seventh century B.C. and is almost 7 centimeters long. It is conserved in the National Archaeological Museum at Cagliari.

84 center These unusual basket-form earrings were found at Carthage and have been dated to the sixth century B.C.

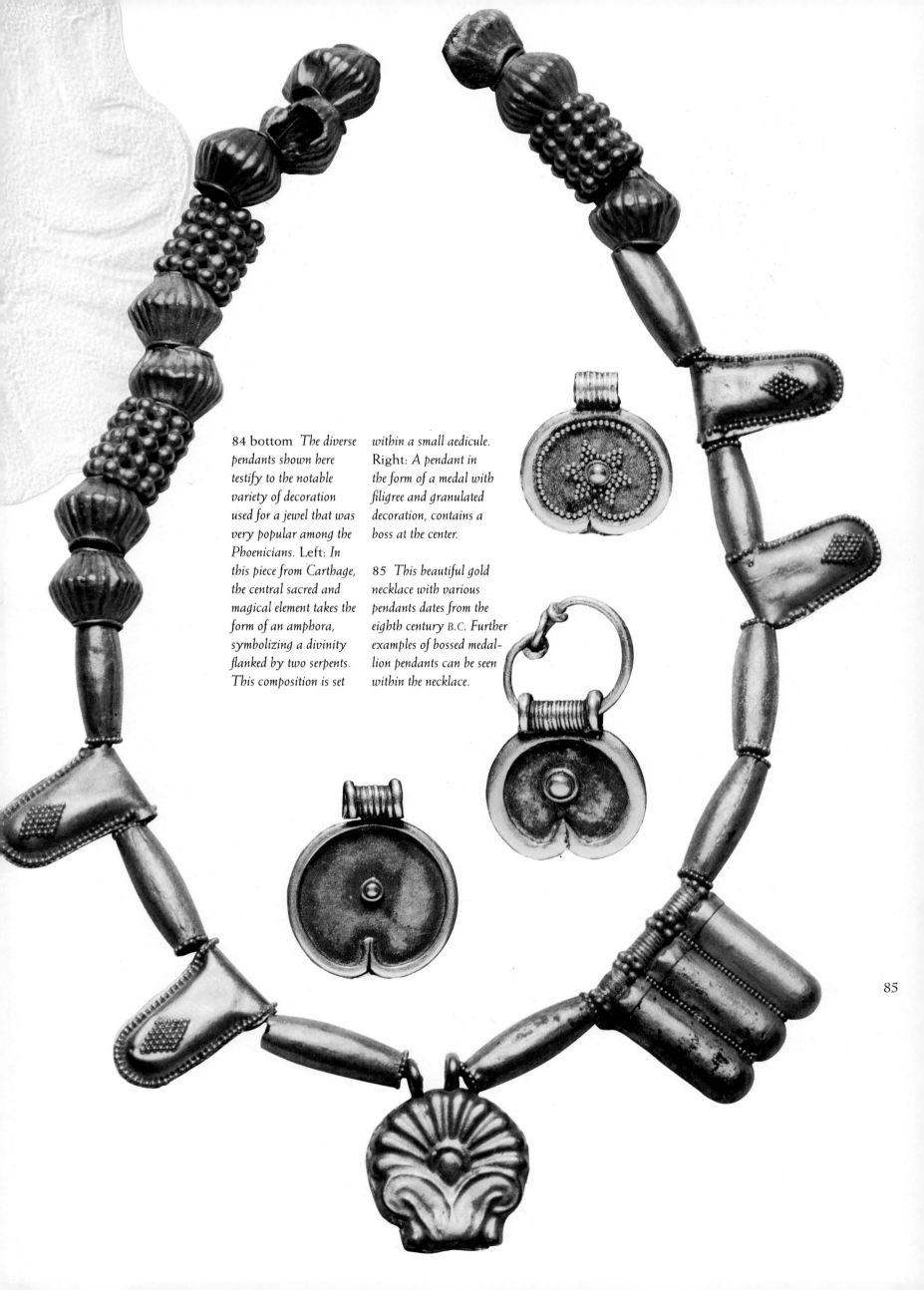

84 bottom *The diverse pendants shown here testify to the notable variety of decoration used for a jewel that was very popular among the Phoenicians. Left: In this piece from Carthage, the central sacred and magical element takes the form of an amphora, symbolizing a divinity flanked by two serpents. This composition is set within a small aedicule. Right: A pendant in the form of a medal with filigree and granulated decoration, contains a boss at the center.*

85 *This beautiful gold necklace with various pendants dates from the eighth century* B.C. *Further examples of bossed medallion pendants can be seen within the necklace.*

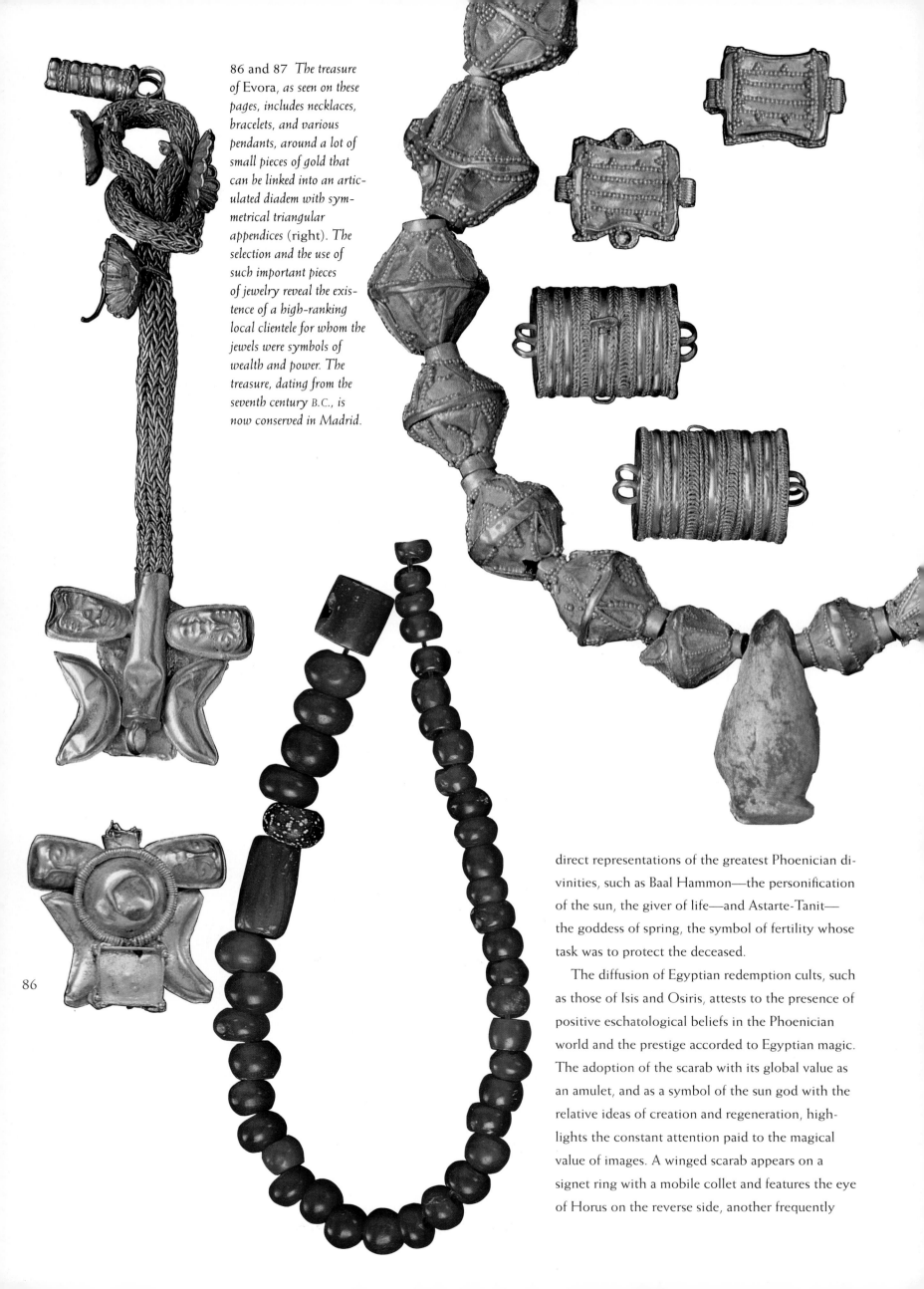

86 and 87 *The treasure of Evora, as seen on these pages, includes necklaces, bracelets, and various pendants, around a lot of small pieces of gold that can be linked into an articulated diadem with symmetrical triangular appendices (right). The selection and the use of such important pieces of jewelry reveal the existence of a high-ranking local clientele for whom the jewels were symbols of wealth and power. The treasure, dating from the seventh century* B.C., *is now conserved in Madrid.*

86

direct representations of the greatest Phoenician divinities, such as Baal Hammon—the personification of the sun, the giver of life—and Astarte-Tanit—the goddess of spring, the symbol of fertility whose task was to protect the deceased.

The diffusion of Egyptian redemption cults, such as those of Isis and Osiris, attests to the presence of positive eschatological beliefs in the Phoenician world and the prestige accorded to Egyptian magic. The adoption of the scarab with its global value as an amulet, and as a symbol of the sun god with the relative ideas of creation and regeneration, highlights the constant attention paid to the magical value of images. A winged scarab appears on a signet ring with a mobile collet and features the eye of Horus on the reverse side, another frequently

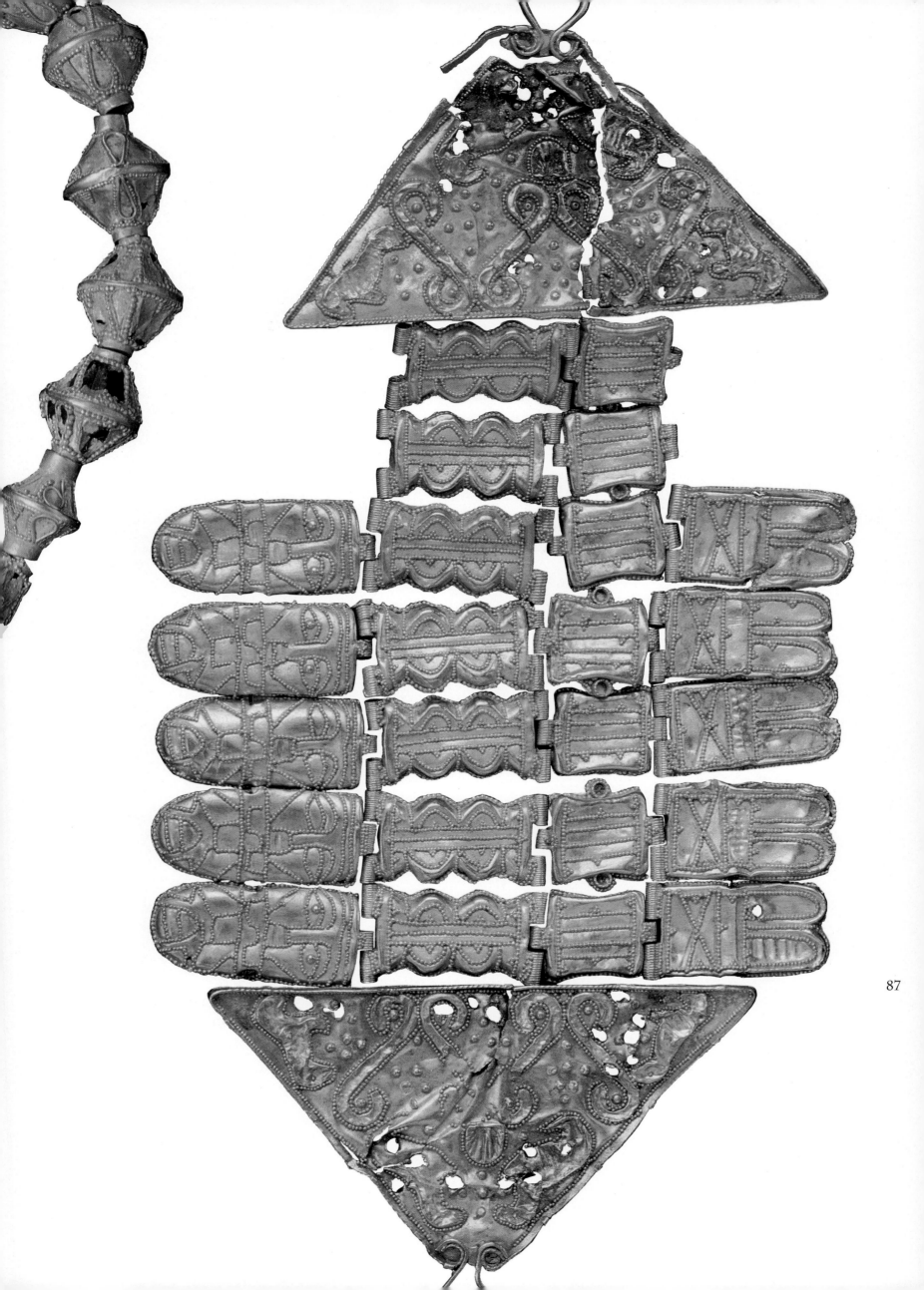

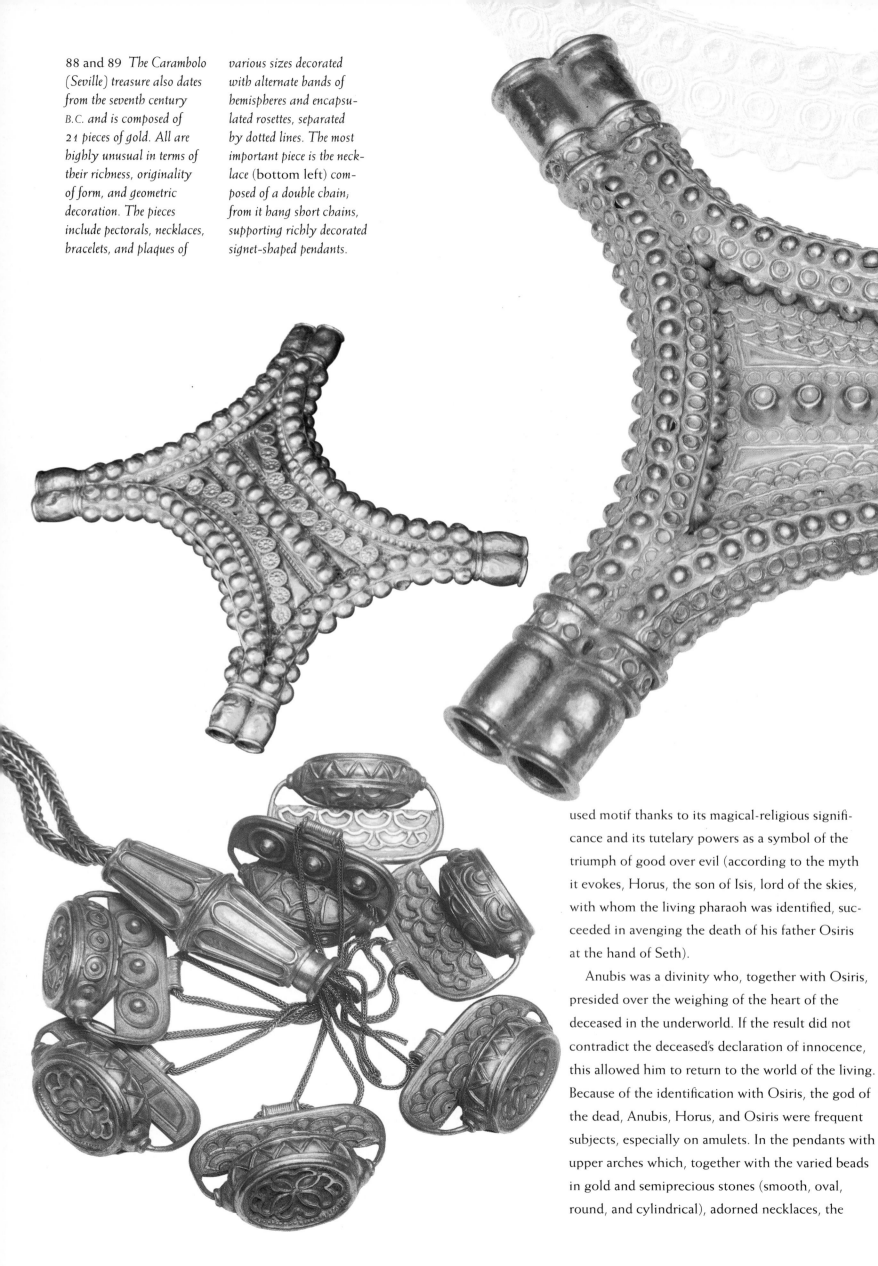

88 and 89 *The Carambolo (Seville) treasure also dates from the seventh century* B.C. *and is composed of 21 pieces of gold. All are highly unusual in terms of their richness, originality of form, and geometric decoration. The pieces include pectorals, necklaces, bracelets, and plaques of various sizes decorated with alternate bands of hemispheres and encapsulated rosettes, separated by dotted lines. The most important piece is the necklace (bottom left) composed of a double chain; from it hang short chains, supporting richly decorated signet-shaped pendants.*

used motif thanks to its magical-religious significance and its tutelary powers as a symbol of the triumph of good over evil (according to the myth it evokes, Horus, the son of Isis, lord of the skies, with whom the living pharaoh was identified, succeeded in avenging the death of his father Osiris at the hand of Seth).

Anubis was a divinity who, together with Osiris, presided over the weighing of the heart of the deceased in the underworld. If the result did not contradict the deceased's declaration of innocence, this allowed him to return to the world of the living. Because of the identification with Osiris, the god of the dead, Anubis, Horus, and Osiris were frequent subjects, especially on amulets. In the pendants with upper arches which, together with the varied beads in gold and semiprecious stones (smooth, oval, round, and cylindrical), adorned necklaces, the

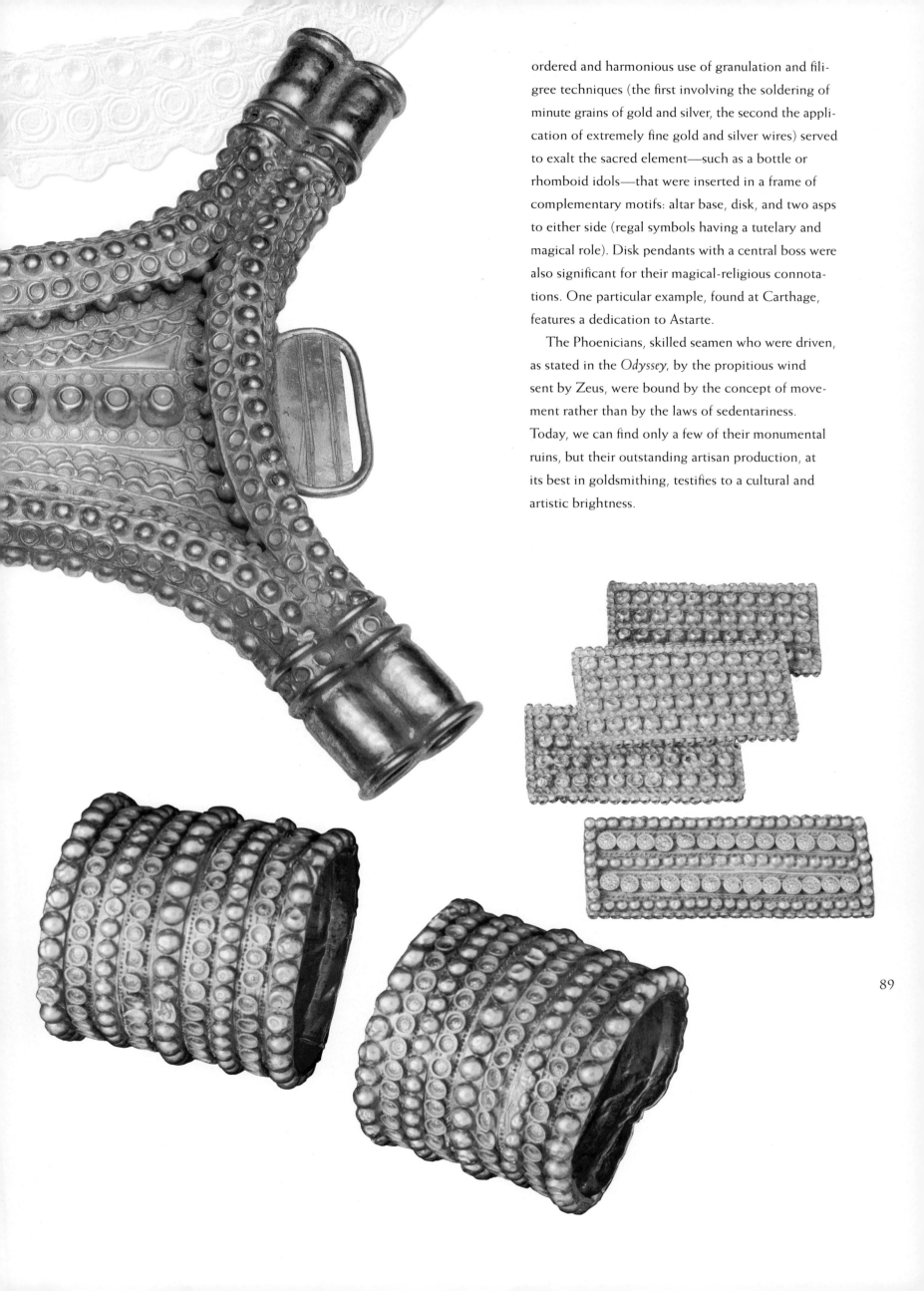

ordered and harmonious use of granulation and filigree techniques (the first involving the soldering of minute grains of gold and silver, the second the application of extremely fine gold and silver wires) served to exalt the sacred element—such as a bottle or rhomboid idols—that were inserted in a frame of complementary motifs: altar base, disk, and two asps to either side (regal symbols having a tutelary and magical role). Disk pendants with a central boss were also significant for their magical-religious connotations. One particular example, found at Carthage, features a dedication to Astarte.

The Phoenicians, skilled seamen who were driven, as stated in the *Odyssey*, by the propitious wind sent by Zeus, were bound by the concept of movement rather than by the laws of sedentariness. Today, we can find only a few of their monumental ruins, but their outstanding artisan production, at its best in goldsmithing, testifies to a cultural and artistic brightness.

89

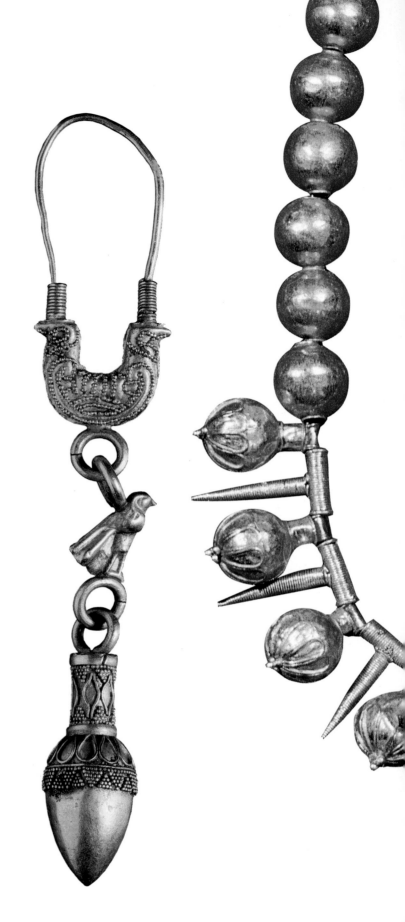

90 top left *This beautiful necklace with acorn pendant comes from the Sardinian Mountains of the Moon and dates from the fourth century* B.C. *It is 24.8 centimeters long.*

90 top right *The particularly sophisticated, 10-centimeter-long earring has a double falcon-and-acorn pendant and dates from the seventh or sixth* century B.C. *The fine decoration skillfully alternates granulation, embossing, and filigree, revealing its provenance from Tharros.*

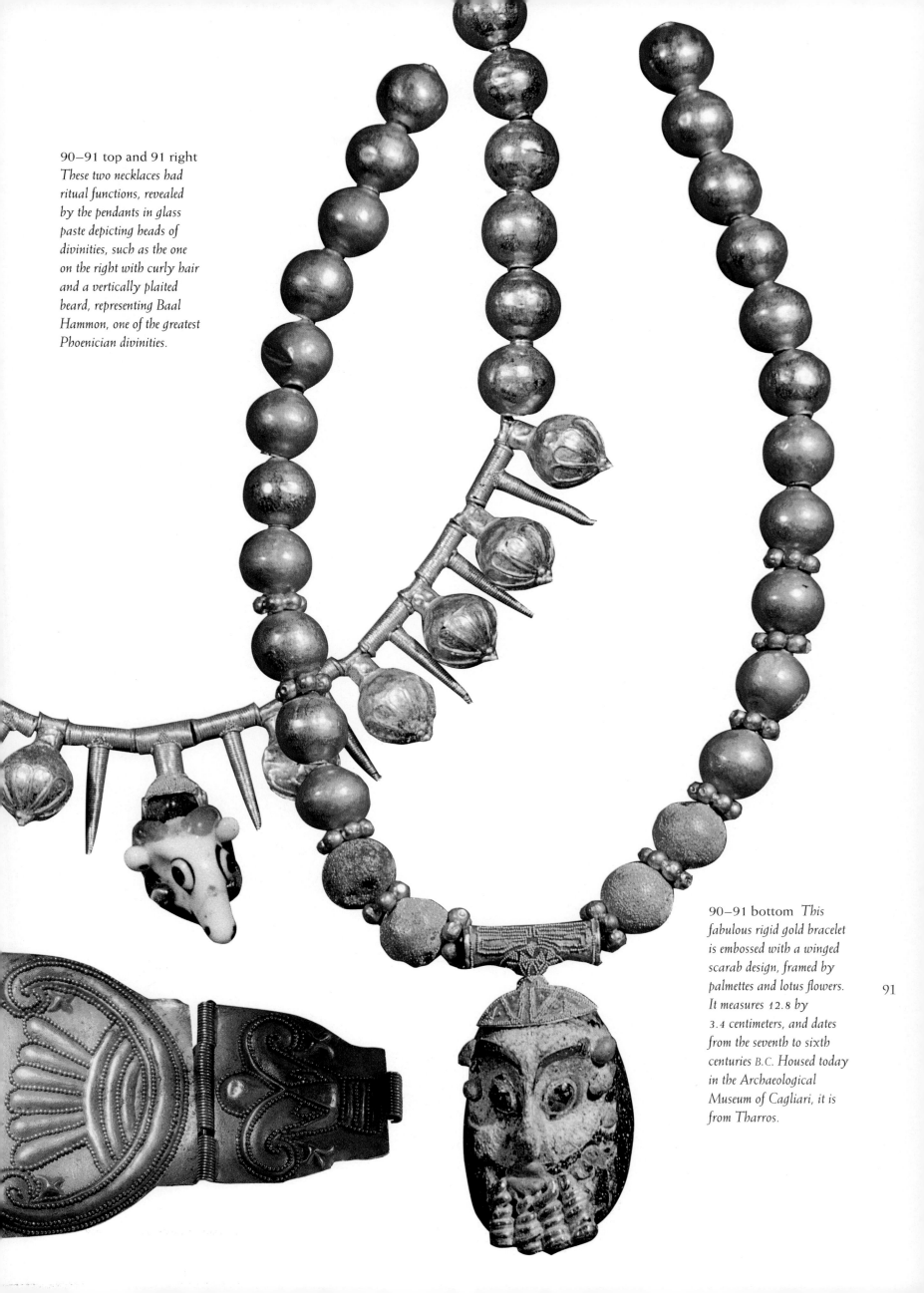

90–91 top and 91 right
These two necklaces had ritual functions, revealed by the pendants in glass paste depicting heads of divinities, such as the one on the right with curly hair and a vertically plaited beard, representing Baal Hammon, one of the greatest Phoenician divinities.

90–91 bottom This fabulous rigid gold bracelet is embossed with a winged scarab design, framed by palmettes and lotus flowers. It measures 12.8 by 3.4 centimeters, and dates from the seventh to sixth centuries B.C. Housed today in the Archaeological Museum of Cagliari, it is from Tharros.

91

GOLDEN JEWELS FROM *H*ELLAS

92 top *This large stud in embossed lamina, decorated with plant motifs, was found in the votive treasury on the Sacred Way in Delphi; it is datable to the sixth century B.C.*

92 bottom *This semicircular embossed appliqué is from the same treasury; decorating it is an apotropaic image of a fearsome-looking Gorgon in flight.*

93 below *These two lavishly embossed and incised plaques have richly decorated borders and five pendants in the form of pomegranates. They are made from electrum, a sometimes natural, sometimes man-made alloy of gold (80%) and silver (20%), used for the archaic coins of many Ionian cities. Depicted on their rectangular surface is the terrifying Potnia Theron, the "Mistress of Animals," dominating two rampant creatures at her sides.*

93 right *This piece of gold lamina with embossed and incised decorative motifs and appliqué rosettes was probably once used to face a piece of wooden furniture; it came from the votive treasury on the Sacred Way in Delphi and is dated around 550 B.C. Natural and fantasy worlds merge in the figures of winged horses, griffins, sphinxes, lions with slaughtered prey, bulls, deer, and panthers set in the panels.*

94 left *A masterpiece of Greek goldwork in post-Classical style (fourth century B.C.) is this rhyton, or jug, shaped like the head of an Amazon. It was found, with many other gold objects, in the so-called Panagurishte hoard, in Bulgaria, in a region of Thrace ruled in ancient times by wealthy sovereigns.*

94 right *From the same source came this amphora rhyton in embossed lamina, a gem of Thracian-Greek goldsmithing. It is decorated with scenes from the "Seven against Thebes." On opposite sides of the base are two holes with heads of Africans, allowing two people to drink simultaneously from the hanging vessel.*

The history of the goldsmith's art in Ancient Greece is closely linked with that of Greek art as a whole. Developments in the design of gold jewelry and artifacts reflected trends in painting and sculpture. It is not unusual to see archaeological finds that offer faithful examples of the creations of goldsmiths and the tastes of their clientele: figures of deities and humans—especially female forms—wearing jewelry or shown amid furnishings and objects that include precious metals; mirrors

decorated by Attic and Italiot pottery painters; rare surviving funerary frescoes; statuary and stone or bronze reliefs; and pottery.

It is apparent, particularly from data regarding the first few centuries of Greek civilization, that for the Greeks (as for other peoples) ownership of gold and precious metals was one of the factors that best expressed the power exercised by the apex of the social pyramid over the lower strata. And if ownership was backed by direct or indirect control of the sources of supply, so much the better.

The decline that followed the collapse of the Mycenaean civilization in Greece in the twelfth to eleventh centuries B.C. can be seen in the total absence of precious artifacts, both in the few modest settlements and in the scantily adorned necropolises. The extremely small populations of these communities are a clear indication of the effects of the interruption of maritime trade and the invasion of the Dorians, the last Indo-Europeans to arrive in Greece. In the space of a few generations, nothing remained except recollections passed down in epic poems, telling of the golden treasures of Nestor at Pylos, of Odysseus at Ithaca, of Menelaus at Sparta. Also gone, along with these riches, was every trace of the great artistic tradition that had created the masterpieces of Minoan and Mycenaean goldwork, courageous alternatives to the models prevailing in Egypt and the Near East.

In the tenth to eighth centuries B.C., with the country's rapid demographic, economic, and commercial recovery and the creation of the poleis, the cultural characteristics that eventually became the essence of Greek civilization began to take shape. This was the period of the Geometric style. One of its manifestations was a significant revival of the goldsmiths' art. Jewelry and artifacts were created in increasing abundance, naturally in response to commissions from the

95 top Also from Panagurishte is this rhyton with goat protome, in embossed and incised lamina. Decorating its edge are figures of Olympian deities Hera, Apollo, Artemis, and Nike.

95 bottom Another rhyton from Panagurishte is shaped like a deer's head. On the neck are two scenes: Heracles capturing the hind of Ceryneia and Theseus fighting the bull of Marathon. Both share stylistic elements typical of Greek artistry in the late fourth century B.C.

ruling elite, whose economic power came from control over land and livestock and ownership of arms. Indications from literary sources—from the Homeric poems onward—confirm the evidence presented by archaeological finds. An important role was evidently played by highly talented Phoenician, Phoenician-Cypriot, and Cretan goldsmiths who traveled in these regions: these master craftsmen taught their art to others, introducing traditions that soon became rooted in the intensely active Greek poleis and colonies of this era, particularly from the ninth century B.C. onward.

The goldwork of these centuries is not outstandingly ornate or elegant. In this field, too, we see the austere taste for abstract design and synthesis of form embodied by Geometric art. The jewels found in the richest tombs are mostly earrings made from twisted wire or simple filigree, pendants, gold bands and fibulae in finest gold leaf, studs and buttons used to decorate fabrics. The ornamental motifs are generally geometric, much the same as used for pottery and bronzes, with an occasional foray into stylized figurative designs. The influence of the Orient led to rapid acquisition of decorative techniques such as granulation, used to "embroider" rows of tiny gold beads in relief on laminae of

96 bottom *A fragment of a gold crown found in 1804 during excavations in the area of Piraeus, the great port of Athens, shows the virtuosity of Greek goldsmiths in the fourth century* B.C. *The stem is in gold leaf on a bronze core; the myrtle flowers and leaves are also in ultrafine lamina and gold wire; the stamens in each calyx are made from tiny gold balls. The piece is conserved in the British Museum in London.*

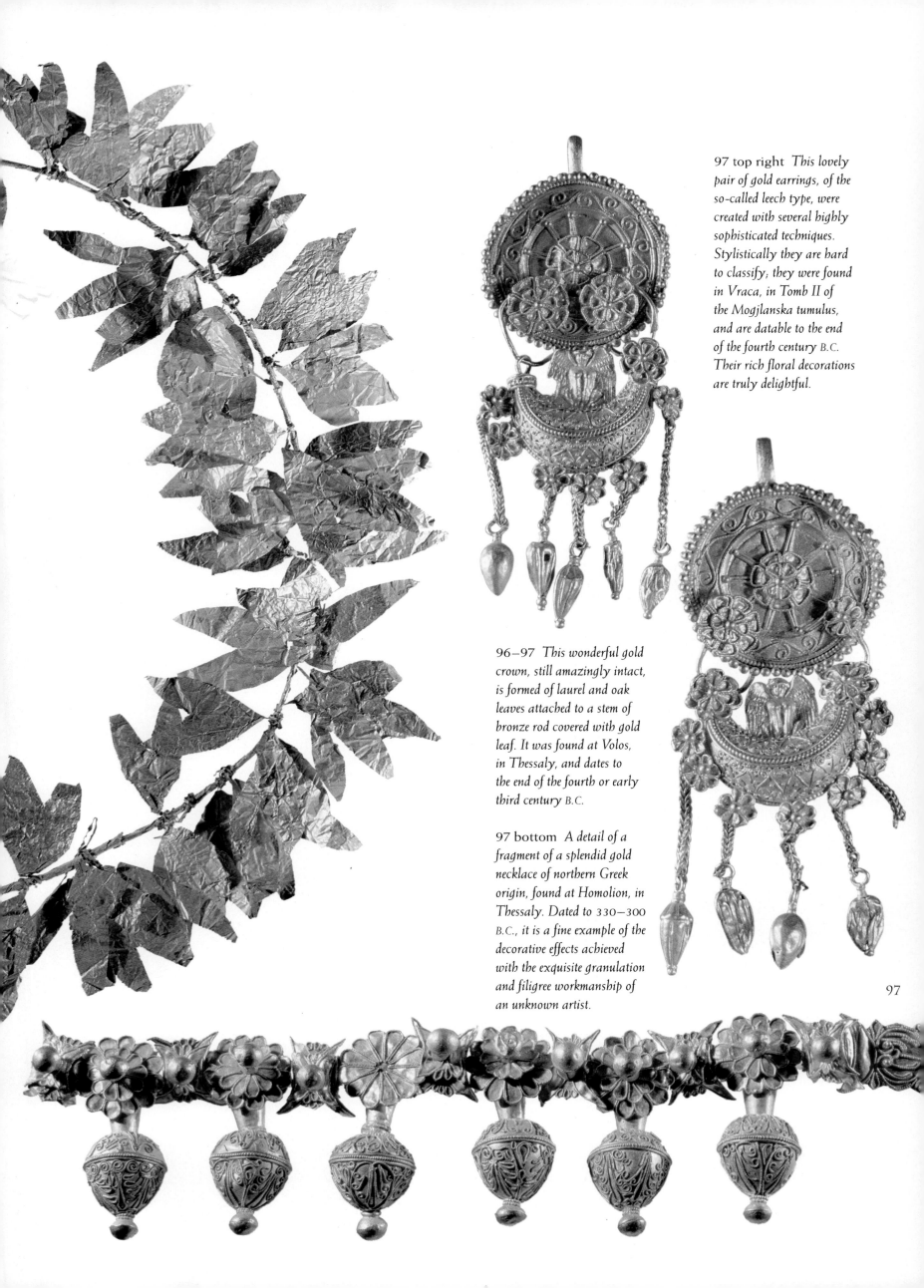

97 top right This lovely pair of gold earrings, of the so-called leech type, were created with several highly sophisticated techniques. Stylistically they are hard to classify; they were found in Vraca, in Tomb II of the Mogjlanska tumulus, and are datable to the end of the fourth century B.C. Their rich floral decorations are truly delightful.

96–97 This wonderful gold crown, still amazingly intact, is formed of laurel and oak leaves attached to a stem of bronze rod covered with gold leaf. It was found at Volos, in Thessaly, and dates to the end of the fourth or early third century B.C.

97 bottom A detail of a fragment of a splendid gold necklace of northern Greek origin, found at Homolion, in Thessaly. Dated to 330–300 B.C., it is a fine example of the decorative effects achieved with the exquisite granulation and filigree workmanship of an unknown artist.

97

varying thickness, to form geometric patterns or sinuous curvilinear frames. It also encouraged decorative use of figured subjects, animals in particular. Significant examples of this typical Geometric repertory are offered by the Athenian cemetery of Dipylon-Kerameikos and other Attic sites (above all, Eleusis), as well as Euboea (Lefkandi) and Crete (Khaniale Tekke and Ideon Cave).

Greek cultural and artistic life truly blossomed in the subsequent Orientalizing period (end of the eighth to the end of the seventh centuries B.C.), encouraged by numerous factors: colonial expansion in the West and its consolidation in Anatolian Ionia and on the Pontus Euxinus (Black Sea), with isolated settlements or trading posts also along the north African coast; evolution of the political model, in the forms of aristocracy-led oligarchy or tyranny; establishment of an impressive Mediterranean-wide trade network, with the involvement of Phoenicians, Greeks, Etruscans, and other peoples. With the more extensive influence of Oriental

art, the so-called Orientalizing style caught on throughout the West: in Greece it was the form of artistic expression favored by the aristocracies and, above all, by the tyrannies.

From Asia Minor to Ionia and Dodecanese, gold was abundant in both quality and quantity. In terms of luxury and variety, the objects it was used to make bear a resemblance to the fabulous riches of Asian kings of that era (Gyges, Croesus, Midas).

98 left This stud with embossed and filigree decoration portrays the head of Heracles, crowned by the lion skin; dated to 300–250 B.C., it comes from Tumulus III at Kralevo.

98 bottom Along with two similar ones, this medallion with the helmeted head of Athena, produced in 330–300 B.C., was found at Homolion (Thessaly).

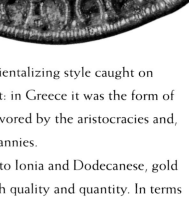

98–99 *Embellishing the splendid gold necklace from Tomb IX at Roccagloriosa (Salerno, Italy) are pendants with alternating lion and female heads. Produced in 400–350 B.C. with granulation and embossing techniques, it offers an excellent example of the virtuosity of Tarentine workshops, where it was made for the "Lady of Lucan" later buried in this tomb.*

99 top *The griffins decorating these earrings hark back to the fanciful bestiaries so popular in the Oriental iconography of antiquity, extensively borrowed by the Greeks. The earrings were created with embossing, engraving, and filigree techniques.*

99 top right *Engraved on a red carnelian of exceptional transparency set in a gold ring is a dove, probable symbol of pure and devoted love. Dating to the first half of the fourth century B.C., the ring is part of a rich collection of gems now kept in the British Museum in London.*

99 bottom right *This magnificent triple spiral bracelet, made entirely from embossed and incised gold, came from the already mentioned Tomb 9 at Roccagloriosa and is dated earlier than the mid-fourth century B.C. Its decorative elements are comprised of terminals with snake protomes, women's faces, and masks of a Satyr and a bearded Silenus. It may not be possible to trace its origin to a specific workshop, but it certainly came from a Hellenized area of the Black Sea, the only place where objects comparable with this jewel can be seen.*

Amazing examples have been unearthed on Rhodes (Ialisos, Kamiros, Lindos) and in other sites influenced by the splendid creations of the Aegean goldsmiths.

In Attica, on the other hand, austere customs limited accumulation and ostentation of gold artifacts. However, in most parts of the Greek world, people felt a keen sense of belonging— ethnically, religiously, culturally, and politically— to the urban communities established in previous centuries. This spirit underlay the practice of offering riches in the form of gifts made of gold, primarily within a religious context: often splendid offerings were donated to the foremost sanctuaries of the Greek world (as is evident at the Artemision in Ephesus and, to a lesser degree, in Olympia and Delphi).

A distinctive feature of jewelry of the Orientalizing period was the imaginative way in which goldsmiths reelaborated and personalized the vast Levantine iconography, with its "bestiaries," its

100 top Discovered in a tomb at Capua, in Italy's Campania region, this lovely necklace was created in a workshop in Tarentum between the fourth and third centuries B.C. Beautifully executed in gold mesh with embossed and engraved lion heads, finished with enameling, it offers further evidence of the inexhaustible inventiveness and creativity of the city's goldsmiths.

demons, and its opulence, clearly evident in the virtuoso application of several techniques simultaneously: repoussé, filigree, granulation, knurling, incising, punching, stamping. And the results are to be seen in magnificent earrings, exceptionally rich necklaces and pectorals, bands made of gold and yellow electrum.

Abandonment of the exotic leanings of Orientalizing art coincided with the establishment of Greek cultural supremacy in the Mediterranean (sixth century B.C.). Greek art had now moved further and further away from Oriental models and

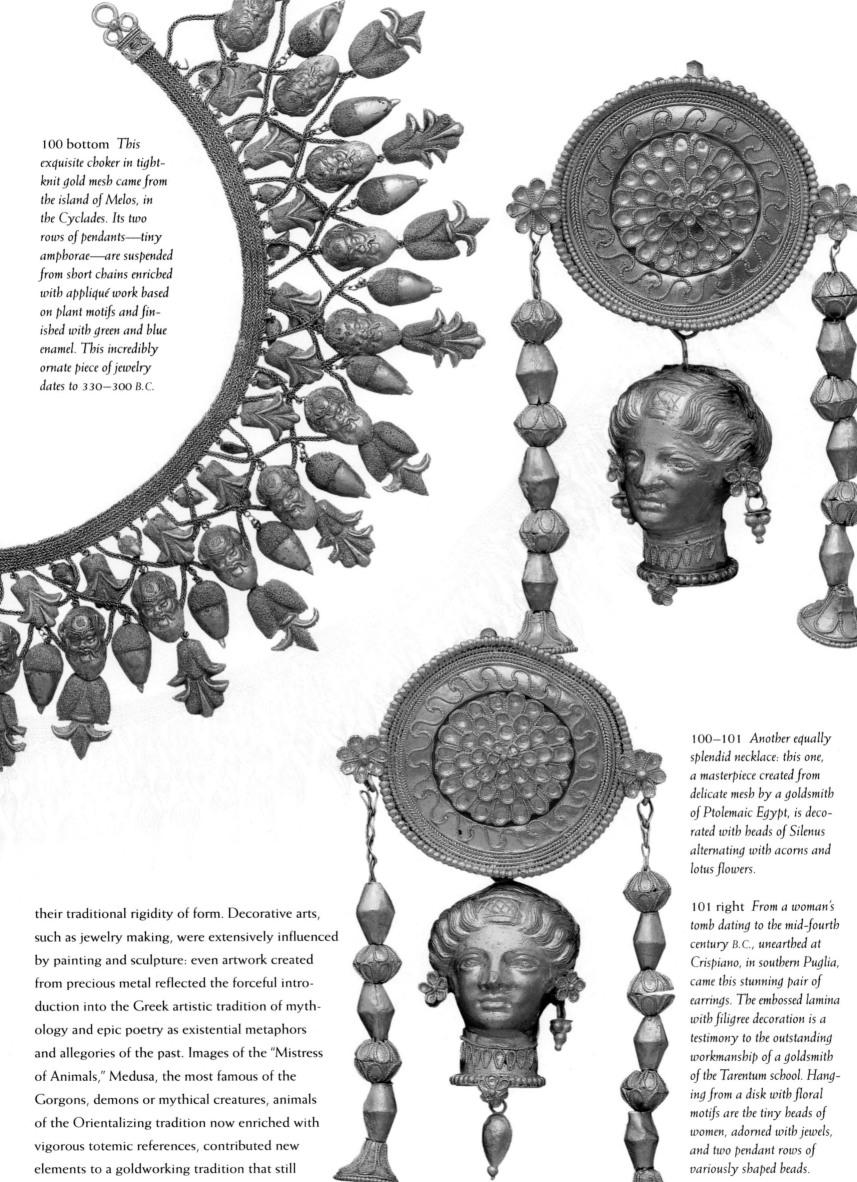

100 bottom *This exquisite choker in tight-knit gold mesh came from the island of Melos, in the Cyclades. Its two rows of pendants—tiny amphorae—are suspended from short chains enriched with appliqué work based on plant motifs and finished with green and blue enamel. This incredibly ornate piece of jewelry dates to 330—300 B.C.*

their traditional rigidity of form. Decorative arts, such as jewelry making, were extensively influenced by painting and sculpture: even artwork created from precious metal reflected the forceful introduction into the Greek artistic tradition of mythology and epic poetry as existential metaphors and allegories of the past. Images of the "Mistress of Animals," Medusa, the most famous of the Gorgons, demons or mythical creatures, animals of the Orientalizing tradition now enriched with vigorous totemic references, contributed new elements to a goldworking tradition that still

100—101 *Another equally splendid necklace: this one, a masterpiece created from delicate mesh by a goldsmith of Ptolemaic Egypt, is decorated with heads of Silenus alternating with acorns and lotus flowers.*

101 right *From a woman's tomb dating to the mid-fourth century B.C., unearthed at Crispiano, in southern Puglia, came this stunning pair of earrings. The embossed lamina with filigree decoration is a testimony to the outstanding workmanship of a goldsmith of the Tarentum school. Hanging from a disk with floral motifs are the tiny heads of women, adorned with jewels, and two pendant rows of variously shaped beads.*

102 top *Engraved on this simple signet ring is an image normally interpreted as Odysseus with the dog Argus, perhaps intended as an allegory of faithfulness or lasting friendship. The work of a goldsmith of Tarentum, it dates to 300 B.C.*

102 center *Inspired by Macedonian models but actually made in Tarentum, this necklace was found among grave goods in a tomb at Ginosa, dated to the early third century B.C. Its most prominent feature—a complicated Heracles knot—is decorated with plant motifs obtained with granulation and knurling.*

102–103 bottom *The superb diadem found at Santa Eufemia—now part of the British Museum's collections of gold jewelry and artifacts—is one of the most fascinating examples of the artistry of the goldsmiths of Tarentum in the Hellenistic period, when their virtuosity reached its greatest heights. Eyecatchingly placed on the upper edge, where it emerges from thickly bunched foliage and floral elements, is a head attributed by some to the Gorgon, by others to Helios.*

placed greatest emphasis on purely decorative and abstract designs.

It was still common practice to make splendid votive offerings (*anathemata*) to the deities worshipped in sanctuaries scattered about the Greek world. An outstanding example of an object made from precious gold lamina, hammered around a silver core, is the bull discovered at Delphi, in the famous votive treasury buried at the end of the fifth century B.C. along the Sacred Way in the sanctuary of Pythian Apollo.

Between the sixth and fifth centuries B.C., increasingly widespread use was made of precious metals in the production of ornamental weapons; furnishings were also trimmed with gold, a sign of the prosperity now commonplace, particularly in parts of the Greek world where oligarchies still had the upper hand or tyrannies were long established, as in Magna Graecia. Perfect mastery of goldsmithing techniques meant that craftsmen had an amazing range of solutions to draw on. Even the traditional method of setting gems and hardstones—or brightly colored *pâte de verre*—in gold continued to be followed, due to highly refined engraving techniques: glyptic art of the Classical and Hellenistic periods has left examples of an exceptional level.

103 left *This diadem, with its highly original assortment of decorative elements, is possibly the most beautiful piece of gold jewelry ever produced in Tarentum. An unknown artist of the third century B.C. has attached to a piece of bent lamina an amazingly ornate composition of berries, leaves, and flowers, held together by a ribbon. The diadem is made all the more sumptuous by the addition of details in garnet, carnelian, and polychrome enamel, today still perfectly preserved.*

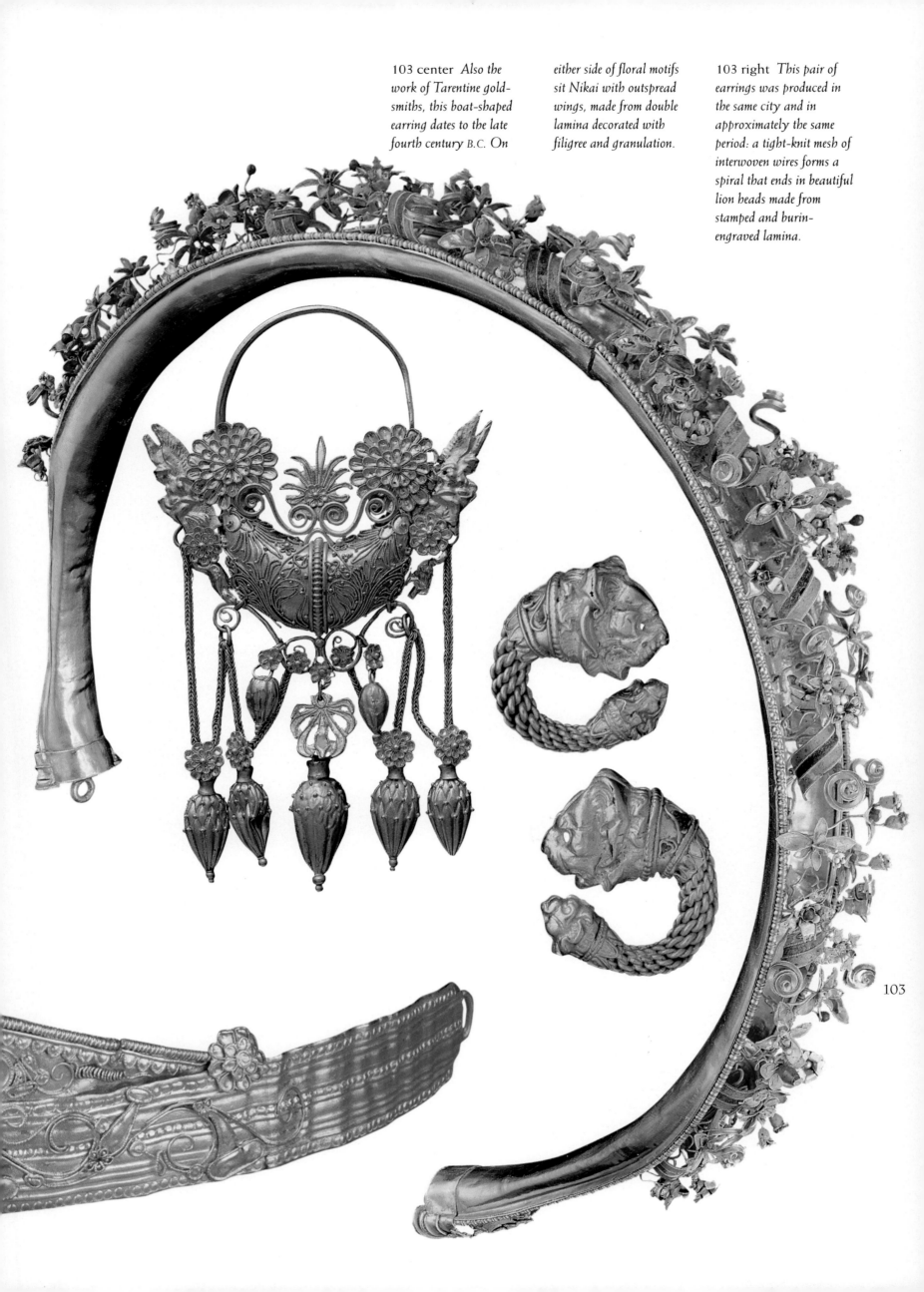

103 center *Also the work of Tarentine goldsmiths, this boat-shaped earring dates to the late fourth century B.C. On either side of floral motifs sit Nikai with outspread wings, made from double lamina decorated with filigree and granulation.*

103 right *This pair of earrings was produced in the same city and in approximately the same period: a tight-knit mesh of interwoven wires forms a spiral that ends in beautiful lion heads made from stamped and burin-engraved lamina.*

103

104 left *Standing more than half a meter high, the scepter of Tarentum is displayed among the collections of the British Museum in London. It is one of the rarest and most precious pieces of Tarentine goldwork. Reportedly owned by a priestess between the third and second centuries B.C., its shaft is covered with thin gold mesh and surmounted by a Corinthian capital and oak leaves.*

From the fifth century B.C. onward the creations of Greek goldsmiths were exported beyond the boundaries of the city-states of Magna Graecia, from the Black Sea to southern Italy. A discerning and extremely wealthy clientele existed in the prosperous kingdoms of Macedonia and Thrace—regions already blessed with substantial reserves of precious metals obtained from vast deposits throughout the Balkans. The courts of the satraps and small dynasties of Asia Minor were also avid customers.

In the Western world, the capital of jewelry making from the fourth century onward was undoubtedly Tarentum. Founded by settlers from Sparta in 706 B.C., this city eventually became the last outpost of Greek culture in southern Italy, defiant in the face of the colonial ambitions of first the Italiots, then the Romans, who moved from the interior toward the coast and from the center south. The influence of Hellenistic art—and its jewelry production, too—can be seen in the magnificent pieces unearthed in the tombs of prominent figures, mostly women, who were members of the land-owning and entrepreneurial aristocracy in the vast territory of Puglia and other more distant regions (Campania, Lucania, Calabria). Master craftsmen skilled in all the most refined techniques, the goldsmiths of Tarentum created jewels of stunning decorative richness. For objects of this kind, ornamentation took precedence over every other function: floral motifs were abundant (and were preferred to figured designs) and beauty for beauty's sake was the

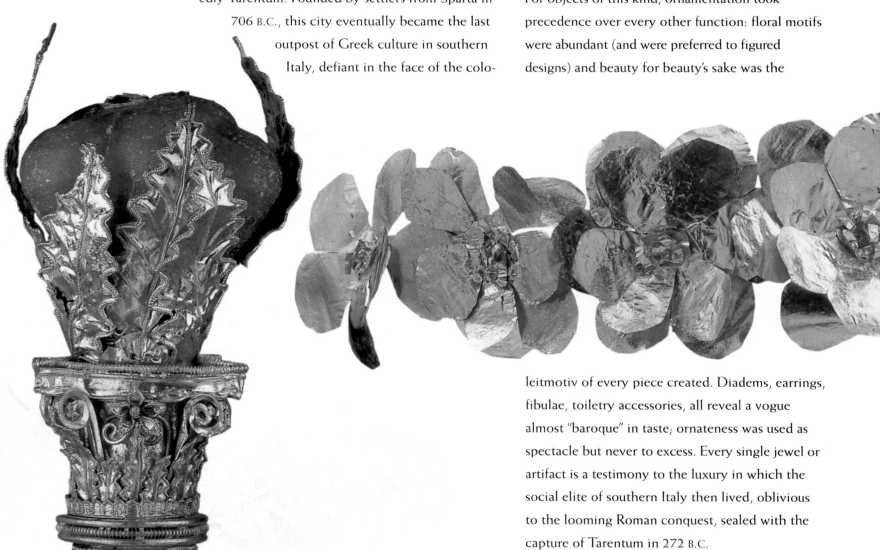

leitmotiv of every piece created. Diadems, earrings, fibulae, toiletry accessories, all reveal a vogue almost "baroque" in taste; ornateness was used as spectacle but never to excess. Every single jewel or artifact is a testimony to the luxury in which the social elite of southern Italy then lived, oblivious to the looming Roman conquest, sealed with the capture of Tarentum in 272 B.C.

104–105 A great many crowns and diadems were found in the rich Tarentine necropolises of the Hellenistic period. The ones shown here have been chosen to illustrate the enormous variety of decorations in gold leaf and glass pastes. All these pieces, dating from the fourth through second centuries B.C., can now be seen in the beautiful National Museum of present-day Tarento.

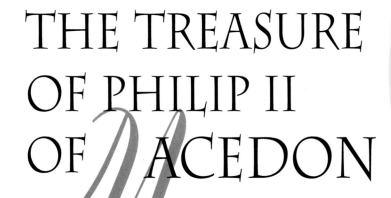

THE TREASURE
OF PHILIP II
OF *M*ACEDON

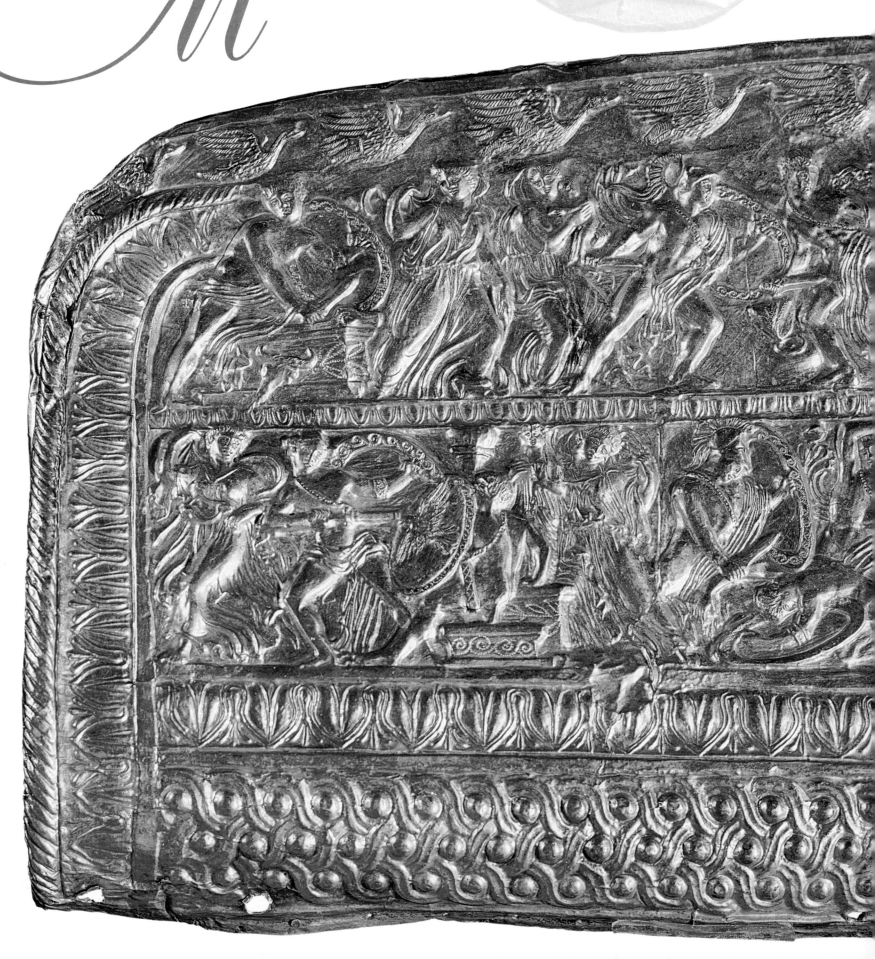

106–107 *Inside the splendid gilded silver quiver found in the tomb of Philip II at Vergina was a leather holder for the bow and arrows, which were also found in the burial chamber. The figured frieze, set between geometric and zoomorphic motifs, relates events connected with the capture and sack of Troy; it exemplifies the pictorial language typical of art in the fourth century B.C. and it is, in certain respects, influenced by painters of monumental artworks. The discovery of no fewer than eight similar objects in tombs of high-ranking personages of ancient Scythia (Ukraine) makes it seem likely that these objects were made in the Greek city of Pantikapaion on the Black Sea. This means that Philip II had other goldsmiths working for him, besides fellow Macedonians.*

No art more effectively portrays Macedonia through the centuries than that of its goldsmiths. Since protohistoric times there were abundant supplies of precious metals in Macedonia, which had direct control over the gold and silver mines of the southern Balkans, from Epirus to Thrace, and privileged access to deposits in the Carpathians. This abundance is attested by documented commercial and cultural links with settlements in Mycenaean southern Greece, from Thessaly to Argolis, and would also seem to be proven

by the long-practiced custom (until the sixth century B.C., at least) of applying gold funeral masks to the faces of dead persons of high social rank.

Like all Macedonian art, the creation of jewelry and artifacts had close ties with the great Greek cultural *koine*—universal Hellenism—from as early as the Geometric period. The splendid jewels found in the Archaic and Classical necropolises of Hagia Paraskevi and Sindos testify to an extremely high artistic level, derived in part from countless stimuli that came from all over Greece and from the East (Macedonia acted as a kind of northern bridge to the Orient). In terms of stylistic sequence, too, its goldsmiths were in step with those of southern Greece, rapidly adding innovative techniques and decorative effects to their "tools" as craftsmen. Macedonian goldsmiths took delight in creating light refraction effects on the surfaces of jewelry, obtained by vigorous

107

108 *The profile of Olympias, first wife of Philip II and mother of Alexander the Great, is reproduced with the noble expressive qualities favored in the early Hellenistic period. This gold medallion is now displayed in Thessaloniki (Archaeological Museum). The grave goods from the tomb at Vergina are also preserved in this museum.*

faceting, granulation, and openwork, or strips with appliqué floral decorations.

On the basis of the evidence available to us, the apex of Macedonian goldwork was reached with the grave goods of Philip II, whose tomb was discovered—miraculously intact—in the autumn of 1977 by Manolis Andronikos at Vergina, close to the ancient Macedonian capital, Aigai.

The tomb belongs to a type of monumental funerary architecture of which no fewer than seventy examples have been found in the Edessa-

covered by a single barrel vault (an important structural innovation that Macedonian architects were the first to introduce in the fourth century B.C.), were the cremated remains of a man and a woman, contained in splendid gold caskets (*làrnakes*).

The tomb contained one of the richest hoards of precious objects ever found: a quiver (*gorytos*) in gilded silver; a gold crown formed of oak leaves; a diadem in gold-plated solid silver; plaques, a pectoral, gold studs bearing the Macedonian "starlike" sun; another crown and diadem; five miniaturized

109 *This gold crown of myrtle leaves, decorated with no fewer than 112 flowers cut from laminae of different thicknesses, is a masterpiece created by Macedonian goldsmiths of the mid-fourth century B.C. It was found in the antechamber of the tomb of Philip II, where Cleopatra, his last wife, was buried.*

Thessaloniki-Katerini triangle: it is a large example of a double burial chamber, with the second chamber accessed from the first. The walls were built of large blocks of *pòros* and carefully whitewashed. The monumental façade created the illusion of a "blind" portico, and the entrance through studded doors was framed by graceful Doric columns. Above them was a colored epistyle and a frieze depicting a hunting scene with men on foot and on horseback (one deliberately personalized) and wild animals in a wintry forest: a work of art of an exceptional level, and totally innovative in its subject matter. Inside the chambers,

ivory heads from statuettes depicting personages from the royal family (including the sovereign), believed with good reason to be connected with portraits of the Argeads created by the sculptor Leochares for the Philippeion in Olympia; a votive offering made by Philip II himself; remains of a fabric and leather breastplate, trimmed with gold bands and plaques; an ornamental shield that, with its variety of scenes and subjects and the richness of the materials employed, is as fine as the one described in the *Iliad* as belonging to Achilles; and an amazing quantity of objects in silver and bronze. All these items are datable between 350 and 330 B.C., which led Andronikos to suppose the tomb to be that of Philip II and his second wife, Cleopatra (his assumption was later confirmed by reconstructive paleo-physiognomic and paleopathological analyses conducted by a team of British scientists).

Wrapped in a regal purple and blue garment embroidered with gold, of which delicate fragments are still preserved, the mortal remains of Philip II, picked from the ashes of the funeral pyre, were placed in a splendid casket (*larnax*) of gold lamina (41 x 34 x 21 centimeters). When creating this stunning object,

Macedonia's talented goldsmiths gave full rein to their imagination, combining elegant and refined decorations with the sumptuousness of the material and its important symbolic function.

Stunningly embossed on the lid is the symbol of the Macedonian Kingdom, a star with sixteen rays; adorning the side panels are rows of rosettes created from gold beads and pale blue *pâte de verre*, framed by graceful plant friezes with lotus buds, acanthus volutes, and palmettes, created in relief and with granulation. There are smaller rosettes on the supports, which are shaped like lion's paws.

With its variety of decorative motifs, the *larnax* exudes a sense of inebriation at the dazzling brilliance of the gold, as though its creator intended its uniqueness to equate the unique and perfect dignity of the monarch.

The decorations on the quiver depict the sack of Troy (*Ilioupersis*), the epic theme par excellence. They therefore allude to Philip's feats, and perhaps also to the anti-Persian leanings of his politics: always, in the collective imagination and historical conscience of the Greek people, Troy metaphorically represented the hostile Orient.

Splendid examples of the art of Macedonian goldsmiths have not only been found in the tomb at Vergina; some outstanding pieces are datable to the age of Alexander the Great. Among them, besides the famous krater of gilded bronze discovered at Dervèni, are numerous testimonies to the inventiveness and creativity of Macedonian artists, as well as to the affluence and ostentation of the incredibly rich aristocracies who were the new lords of Greece and the world.

111

SCYTHIAN GOLD FROM THE STEPPES

112 top *This golden torque, a collar worn by the Nordic peoples, is decorated at the ends with two Scythians on horseback. It was found in a tomb at Kul Oba. It dates to the early fourth century* B.C. *and is housed in the Hermitage Museum in St. Petersburg.*

112 center *This vase in electrum, a precious alloy of gold and silver, is from Kul Oba as well. Its embossed decoration consists of two registers separated by a "guilloche," and describes four different scenes with warriors.*

The Scythians were one of many nomadic peoples who occupied the forests and steppes of Eastern Europe and the Caucasus between the eighth century B.C. and the third century A.D.

Archaeological excavations in the northern Caucasus and the region between the lower course of the Dneiper and the Volga rivers have provided new information about these people, whose origins and territory, known as Scythia, are still obscure. Archaeology's most important contribution was identifying the time frame and historic course of development for the nomadic peoples who in pre-Scythian times occupied the regions north of the Black Sea (northern Pricernomor'je), and clarifying the tribes' relationships with sedentary peoples.

Until the eighth century B.C., the region was occupied by nomadic groups that most sources refer to generically as the Cimmerians. Throughout this

112–113 This scabbard, found in the Chertomlyk barrow, shows a battle scene between barbarians and Greeks. The use of space and the fine execution date it to the late fifth or early fourth century B.C.

113 This refined gold comb found in Solokha shows a battle scene on a frieze of five crouching lions. This is a notable example of Greek-Scythian art from the fourth century B.C.

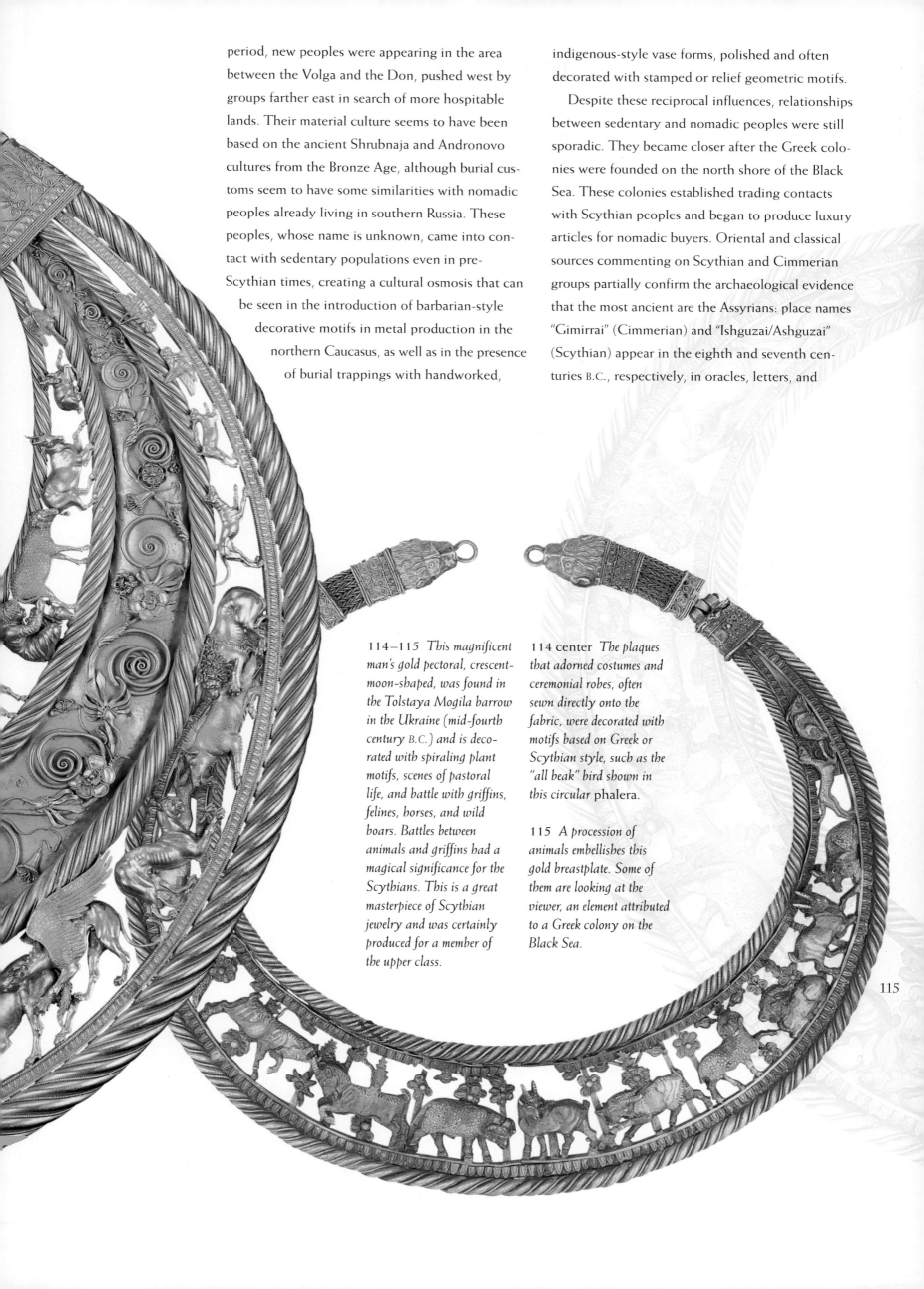

period, new peoples were appearing in the area between the Volga and the Don, pushed west by groups farther east in search of more hospitable lands. Their material culture seems to have been based on the ancient Shrubnaja and Andronovo cultures from the Bronze Age, although burial customs seem to have some similarities with nomadic peoples already living in southern Russia. These peoples, whose name is unknown, came into contact with sedentary populations even in pre-Scythian times, creating a cultural osmosis that can be seen in the introduction of barbarian-style decorative motifs in metal production in the northern Caucasus, as well as in the presence of burial trappings with handworked,

indigenous-style vase forms, polished and often decorated with stamped or relief geometric motifs.

Despite these reciprocal influences, relationships between sedentary and nomadic peoples were still sporadic. They became closer after the Greek colonies were founded on the north shore of the Black Sea. These colonies established trading contacts with Scythian peoples and began to produce luxury articles for nomadic buyers. Oriental and classical sources commenting on Scythian and Cimmerian groups partially confirm the archaeological evidence that the most ancient are the Assyrians: place names "Gimirrai" (Cimmerian) and "Ishguzai/Ashguzai" (Scythian) appear in the eighth and seventh centuries B.C., respectively, in oracles, letters, and

114–115 *This magnificent man's gold pectoral, crescent-moon-shaped, was found in the Tolstaya Mogila barrow in the Ukraine (mid-fourth century B.C.) and is decorated with spiraling plant motifs, scenes of pastoral life, and battle with griffins, felines, horses, and wild boars. Battles between animals and griffins had a magical significance for the Scythians. This is a great masterpiece of Scythian jewelry and was certainly produced for a member of the upper class.*

114 center *The plaques that adorned costumes and ceremonial robes, often sewn directly onto the fabric, were decorated with motifs based on Greek or Scythian style, such as the "all beak" bird shown in this circular phalera.*

115 *A procession of animals embellishes this gold breastplate. Some of them are looking at the viewer, an element attributed to a Greek colony on the Black Sea.*

chronicles. Citations from Achemenid Persian sources are scantier and refer only to the Scythians, indicated in the inscriptions by the generic term "Saka." Nevertheless, Achemenid sources do distinguish various groups: the Saka Haumavarga (haoma eaters), against whom Cyrus the Great had fought and who were already annexed to the empire; the Saka Tigrakauda (with pointed heads); and the Skudra, perhaps from the similarity to Scuthai cited by Herodotus. He provides information on Scythian customs and burial practices gathered during a voyage to the Olbia Empire on the Black Sea and recounted in his fourth book of *Histories*.

The material culture of the Scythians is known solely from discoveries in the necropolises found from 1763 on in the northern Caucasus, Kuban, and the region between the Dnieper and the Volga rivers. The oldest necropolises consisted of circular

116 top *This decorative belt plaque in gold, silver, and colored glass from the eighth century B.C. is attributed to the culture of the Cimmerians. This ancient population inhabited Ukraine prior to the arrival of the Scythians.*

116 bottom *This gold lamina, probably designed to be sewn to a princely feminine headdress, shows a wedding of two local deities. Detailed information on Scythian religious customs is provided by the Histories of Herodotus.*

117 *The pair of jewels shown here belonged to a woman's headdress. They are embossed plaques with a decoration of a battle between a hero and a griffin. They are also enriched with a cascade of trapezoidal and droplet pendants.*

barrows (kurgans), bounded by circles of stones. Inside, ditches dug into the ground constituted the burial chambers, which were connected by corridors with secret recesses. In the fifth century B.C., kurgan structure was distinguished by a dromos that led to a semicylindrical or rectangular well with walls that opened out into burial chambers; in the fourth century B.C., they were often covered with sheets of stone and wooden beams or false vaults. While the kurgans were systematically

117

118 *Small plaques depicting animals (boars, lions, stags, horses) and humans (Bes, Gorgons, or busts of Greek deities) were especially common in nomadic art, and were utilized as decorative elements for horse accoutrements or as religious offerings.*

plundered even in ancient times, the trappings found in the secret chambers that escaped looting show a complex rituality in which the horse, a vitally important animal for the nomads, played a leading role. It was buried in full harness, often saddled as well, in a corner of the main funeral chamber or in a secondary chamber, accompanied by one or more grooms.

The trappings found in sixth century B.C. barrows in the Kuban region and Kelermes reveal not only weapons and horse accoutrements but also splendid gold articles that testify to cultural contacts with the Greek world and the Near East, with

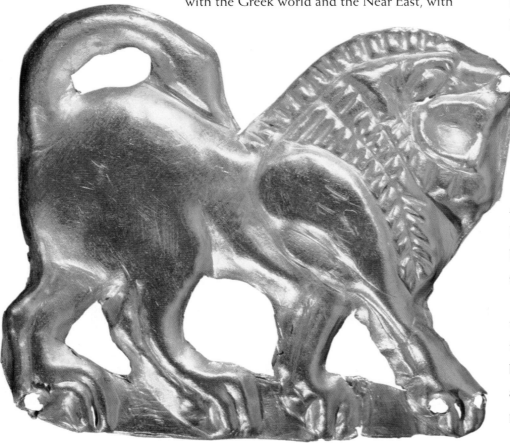

changes in numerous elements to reflect local tastes. Zoomorphic details prevail, taking apart and recomposing animal figures, creating fantastic beings and the "all beak" bird used as an ornamental complement for quivers and dagger sheaths. The classical subjects become cruder in style than the original, as can be seen in the Kelermes mirror.

The birth of the Greek colonies on the northern shores of the Black Sea in the fifth century B.C. marked the beginning of new trading relationships between the settled nomads who controlled the trading centers and nomadic groups. The trappings found in Elizavetinskaya, in the "Seven Brothers" barrows, and at Solokha and Chertomlyk, include imported or original Greek items made in the Black Sea colonies. The pectorals, vases, drinking amphorae, and scabbards show Greek-style decorations inspired by the art of the engraver Dexamenos, or cartoons evoking battles between heroes of classical mythology. There are numerous images of Gorgons, Athena, Heracles, and other deities on small circular plaques that adorned both clothing and horse bridles, while highly stylized animals created scenes that were purely decorative.

In the fourth century B.C., the Scythians began to settle (a process that was completed only in the next century) and to create distinct classes based on wealth. Tombs with simple structures and few trappings begin to appear alongside princely necropolises.

119

119 *This beautiful helmet in chiseled and embossed gold, of Greek-Scythian make, depicts a battle scene among nomads in a background of steppe* *vegetation. The warriors wear the typical nomadic costumes with jacket, trousers, and boots, on which appear to be sewn the decorative plaquettes.*

120 top left *Rectangular plaques depicting a griffin in the center were used to decorate weapons. Griffins were mythical creatures symbolizing the dark forces.*

120–121 top *The gold-plated silver mirror, found in the Kelermes barrow, shows in its figurative part, the back, eight sections depicting scenes in Middle Eastern, Egyptian, and Iranian styles.*

Richer finds with sculpted and painted wooden sarcophagi are testimony to a more developed style than that in use in the fifth century B.C. The schematic design is more decorative, and Greek and Scythian elements merge into a somewhat sober taste, as can be seen in items found in the Kul Oba and Bolshaya Bliznitsa barrows. In the latter, built for the same family, Greek influence prevails not only in the precious items but also in the status of one of the female members, probably a priestess of Demeter, as testified by the presence of a rich *calathos*, a pointed headdress used by clergy in charge of fertility rites.

Starting in the third century B.C., the center of the late Scythian realm moved to the Crimea, while a larger part of the regions of Southern Russia fell under the control of the Sarmatians, a population that spoke the Iranian tongue and

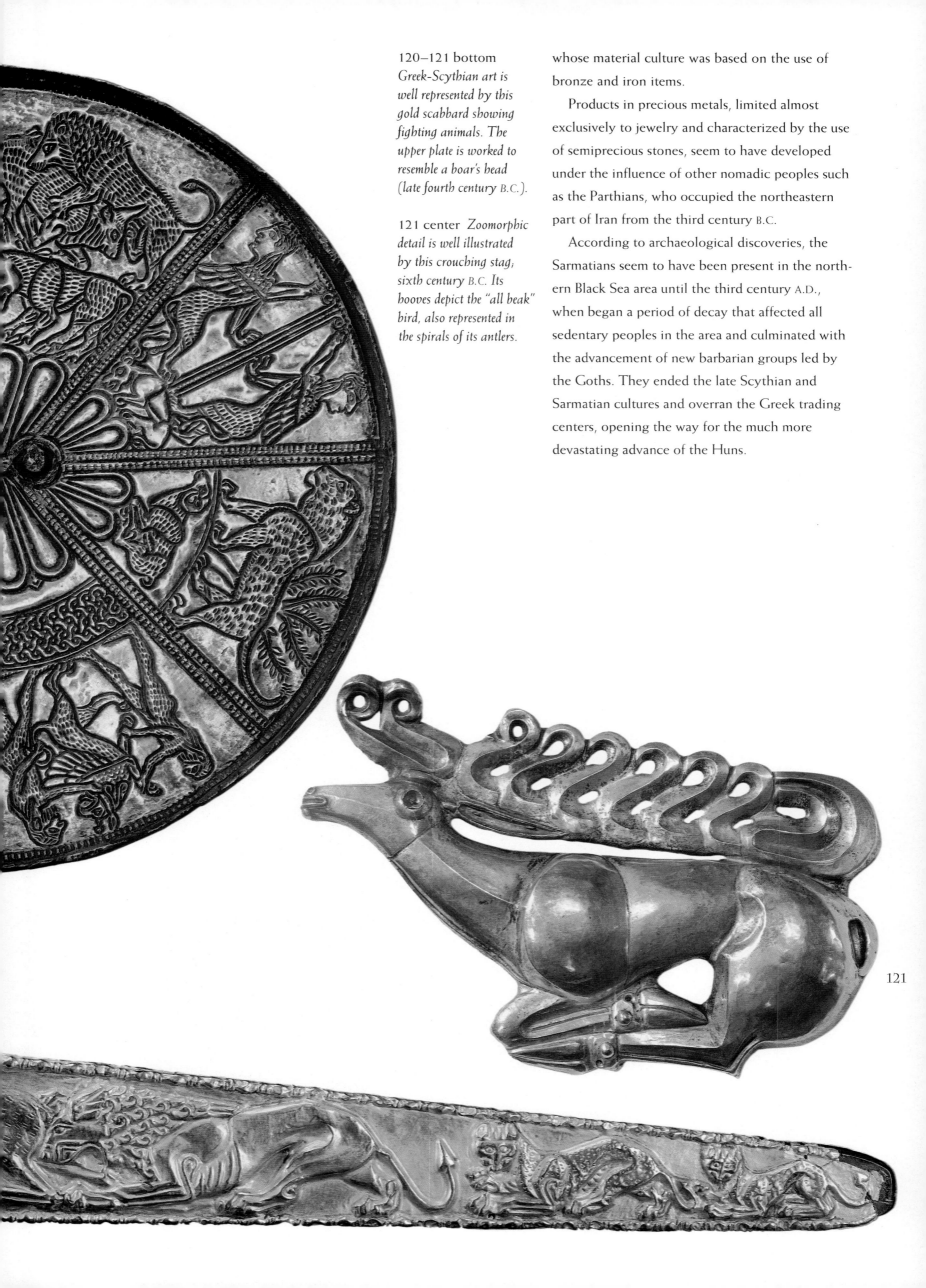

120–121 bottom
Greek-Scythian art is well represented by this gold scabbard showing fighting animals. The upper plate is worked to resemble a boar's head (late fourth century B.C.).

121 center *Zoomorphic detail is well illustrated by this crouching stag, sixth century B.C. Its hooves depict the "all beak" bird, also represented in the spirals of its antlers.*

whose material culture was based on the use of bronze and iron items.

Products in precious metals, limited almost exclusively to jewelry and characterized by the use of semiprecious stones, seem to have developed under the influence of other nomadic peoples such as the Parthians, who occupied the northeastern part of Iran from the third century B.C.

According to archaeological discoveries, the Sarmatians seem to have been present in the northern Black Sea area until the third century A.D., when began a period of decay that affected all sedentary peoples in the area and culminated with the advancement of new barbarian groups led by the Goths. They ended the late Scythian and Sarmatian cultures and overran the Greek trading centers, opening the way for the much more devastating advance of the Huns.

JEWELS FOR THE ETRUSCAN & ARISTOCRACY

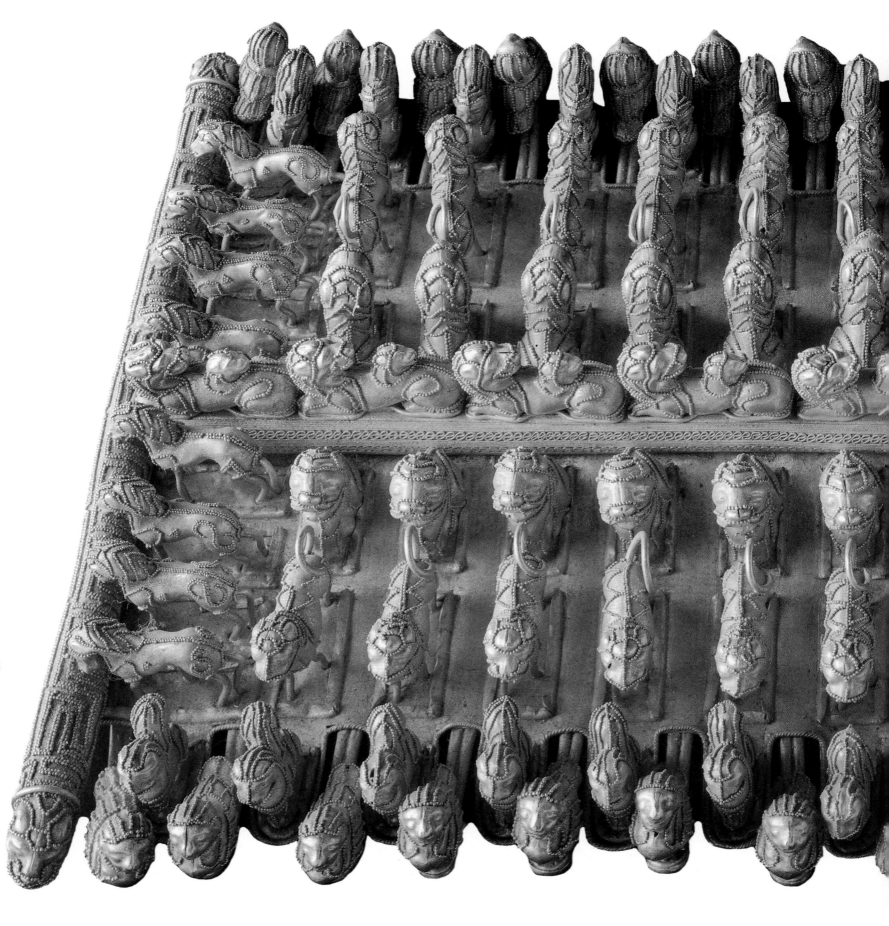

122–123 bottom *Part of the sumptuous grave goods found in the princely Bernardini tomb in Palestrina, dating from the first half of the seventh century* B.C. *The gold plate, with 131 small* figures of animals, both real and fantastic, is decorated using granulation and filigree techniques. The rich aristocrat who owned it used silver pins to attach it at chest height. It is about 17 centimeters long, with the rest of the recovered grave goods, it can be seen at the Villa Giulia Museum in Rome.

123

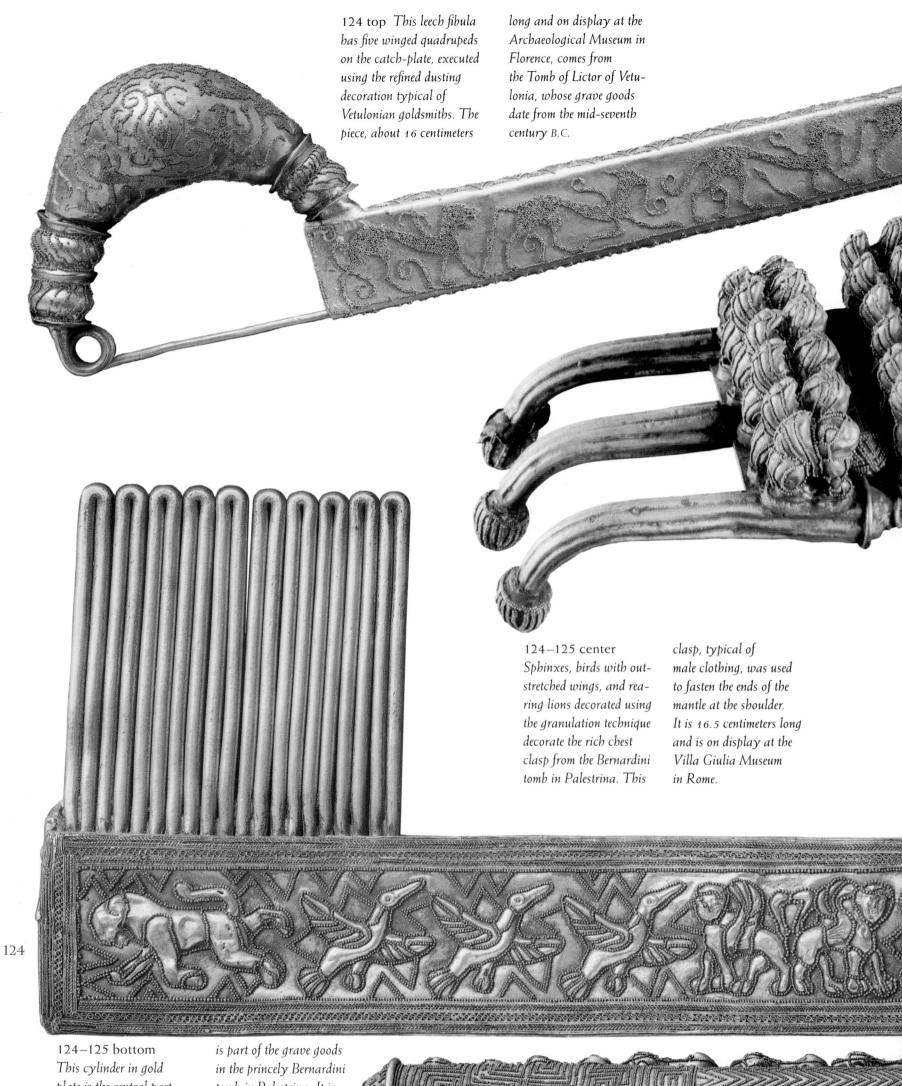

124

124 top *This leech fibula has five winged quadrupeds on the catch-plate, executed using the refined dusting decoration typical of Vetulonian goldsmiths. The piece, about 16 centimeters long and on display at the Archaeological Museum in Florence, comes from the Tomb of Lictor of Vetulonia, whose grave goods date from the mid-seventh century B.C.*

124–125 center *Sphinxes, birds with outstretched wings, and rearing lions decorated using the granulation technique decorate the rich chest clasp from the Bernardini tomb in Palestrina. This clasp, typical of male clothing, was used to fasten the ends of the mantle at the shoulder. It is 16.5 centimeters long and is on display at the Villa Giulia Museum in Rome.*

124–125 bottom *This cylinder in gold plate is the central part of a chest clasp. It is decorated with geometric shapes and figures, using the granulation technique. It, too, is part of the grave goods in the princely Bernardini tomb in Palestrina. It is about 20 centimeters long and is on display at the Villa Giulia Museum in Rome.*

"They entered death splendidly clothed," said the English writer D.H. Lawrence when he visited a burial mound in the Cerveteri necropolis. He imagined its wealthy owners lying on stone beds, adorned with stupendous jewels, surrounded by precious knives, bronze utensils, weapons, and "all that stupendous baggage." It was difficult for this British novelist, who had been wandering the Roman countryside on sunny April afternoons in search of "Etruscan places," to leave the singular fascination of those places. Much less could he resist the magical charm of these "fragile joys of pale gold" in the Regolini-Galassi tomb that he had often admired at the Vatican Museums.

Lawrence's seductive pages, like much literature from this century and previous ones, contributed to the aura of mystery that still today—as we stand before the extraordinary beauty of Etruscan jewelry, the elegance of its decoration, the virtuosity of the refined techniques—invites us to imagine this people, with its vague outlines, surrounded by luxury and splendor and devoted to the pleasures of life. We still love to recall their (false) mysteries, their

124–125 top *This bar chest buckle, another male ornament, consists of curved tubes ending in small spheres decorated with granulation. On the bars are figures of seated sphinxes, executed with the punch technique and decorated with granulation. The jewel, from the Barberini tomb, can be dated to the second half of the seventh century B.C. and is 9.5 centimeters long. It is on display at the Villa Giulia Museum.*

125 bottom right *This magnificent pin found in Vetulonia in the Tomb of Lictor is, like the other jewelry in the grave goods, decorated using the granulation technique. The spherical head and a portion of the pin show refined bands of zoomorphic ornamentation. It is about 20 centimeters long, while the diameter of the head is 2.2 centimeters. The grave goods, from the mid-seventh century B.C., are on display at the Archaeological Museum in Florence.*

125

126 left *The objects on these two pages come from the first half of the seventh century* B.C. *and are part of the grave goods of a high-ranking woman who was buried with other individuals in the Regolini-Galassi tomb in Cerveteri. This tomb, the most sumptuous Orientalizing one ever found, is on display at the Vatican Museums. This gilt silver cup, about 11 centimeters in diameter, has an embossed burin decoration that is quite elaborate both inside and out. A lion-hunting scene with wagons, horsemen, and soldiers covers the object's entire surface.*

126–127 *This surprisingly large, disk-shaped fibula does not appear functional, but rather made solely for ostentation. It has a sumptuous, detailed decoration, with relief figures on the arch, two zigzag-decorated crosspieces, with figures of animals and floral decorations on the large oval disk. All details are done in granulation technique. The fibula is more than 30 centimeters long.*

127 right *This splendid bracelet in gold plate has a series of panels, each one showing three female figures and embossed geometric motifs, enriched with granulation decorations. This object, which was one of an identical pair, is 25 centimeters long.*

obscure origins, incomprehensible language, their silent disappearance.

In reality, nothing could be further from the truth. Despite their extraordinary beauty, these objects are not "timeless" items with no place in historical, social, or economic reality. Rather, due to the total absence of Etruscan literary sources, they have become, along with all other surviving archaeological testimony, a tool for knowledge; we use them to reconstruct the history of the people who made them over a period of eight centuries, from the ninth to the second centuries B.C., when the Etruscan civilization flourished.

Jewelry in precious metals, particularly gold with its clear intrinsic value, was reserved for those of high rank: thus, through its history we can trace the history of the dominant class, with individuals so powerful that they created art to satisfy their needs for luxury in life and proudly recall their caste in death.

Between the tenth and ninth centuries B.C., at the beginning of the Iron Age, various local cultures sprang up all over Italy. One of these was the Villanovan culture, which settled a large area that would later be dominated by the Etruscans. Villanova burials, which always involved cremation, have revealed some gold personal ornamentation, a clear indication that this metal was worked and used very early on.

In cemeteries at the end of the ninth century, and even more so in the eighth century, where funeral rituals had changed from cremation to burial, clear

128 top *This circular gold band, an armlet or an earring, may come from Vulci. It is 4 centimeters in diameter, with embossed and relief decoration with little figures of sphinxes, alternating with female heads. Dating from the second half of the seventh century B.C., it is on display in the British Museum.*

128–129 top and center *This pair of band armillae is decorated with horizontal bands of Phoenician palmettes, small crouching lions, goats, and female heads in an arrangement peculiar to Vetulonia goldsmiths. The objects, about 17 centimeters long, were part of the goods in a cache found in the circular tomb known as the Circle of Silver Lions tomb, from the second half of the seventh century B.C., and are on display at the Archaeological Museum in Florence.*

128 bottom These two braid fasteners consist of four joined threads that end in serpent heads decorated with granulation work. Small studs are soldered onto them and are also adorned with granulation work. The jewels, found in Cerveteri, are 1 centimeter long and are at the Villa Giulia Museum in Rome.

129 right These two small plaques with the figure of a winged woman, embossed and granulated, were used as ornaments for clothing or belts. They were part of the grave goods of an aristocratic woman found at Cerveteri, dating from the late seventh century B.C. They are 3.5 centimeters high and are on display at the Villa Giulia Museum in Rome.

differences emerge indicating the rise of aristocratic classes. In addition to gold objects worked in a variety of ways, these tombs also contain other objects, such as scarabs and faience pendants, that are of Oriental and Egyptian make. These extremely important items are signs of the presence of Phoenician traders and Greek navigators in this area of the Mediterranean, people who plied these waters to trade goods, supply themselves with metals, and seek out landings where they could build new trading centers. This is what the Greeks of Euboea did when they built a settlement on the island of Ischia; archaeological evidence shows that the settlement included peoples of different origins engaged in a variety of activities. Among these, as the sources state, there must have been goldsmiths who brought techniques, styles, decorations, and figures with them from their homelands and introduced them to Tyrhennian Italy.

The second half of the eighth century provides further affirmation of the aristocracy and the birth of the Tyrhennian thalassocracy, Etruscan

130 left This blue-glass bracelet from a Vulci tomb ends in two leonine protomes, enriched with filigree palmettes. It is about 9 centimeters in diameter and dates from the late seventh century B.C.

It is now at the Villa Giulia Museum in Rome. In the center of the bracelet is an elaborate fibula with an elongated, arched catch-plate showing a winged lion; at the end of the clamp is a figure of a sphinx. The object, dating from the second half of the sixth century B.C., is in the Archaeological Museum in Naples.

130–131 This necklace, found somewhere in the Tuscan Maremma, is a particularly indicative example of late archaic production. It uses filigree and granulation techniques, as well as stamped and cast figures with semiprecious stones that provide extraordinary color effects. Dating from the first half of the fifth century B.C., it is 27.6 centimeters in length and can be seen at the British Museum.

130

130 bottom right and 131 bottom left This pair of pendants with embossed and chiseled leonine protomes is of unknown origin.

They are 2 centimeters high and possibly date from the late sixth century B.C.; they are conserved at the Berlin Antikenmuseum.

131 top These three rings, probably women's jewels, have settings with individual figures or figures on different registers, in general real or fantastic animals, decorated using engraving, intaglio, or embossing techniques and enriched with granulation or filigree decorations. Dating from the mid-sixth century B.C., the two on the sides, from the British Museum, may come from Vulci, while the middle one, at the Villa Giulia Museum, may come from Cerveteri.

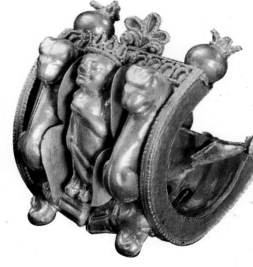

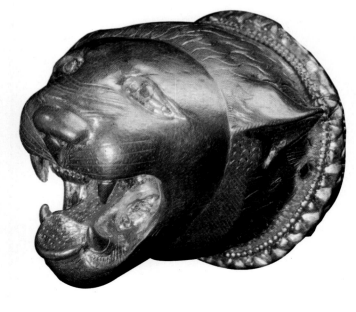

131 bottom right Jewel-box shaped earrings are authentically Etruscan. This pair of earrings, whose origins are unknown, is a good example of the style. They are on display at the Antikenmuseum in Berlin. Decorations come in various forms; in this case, they feature a "Mistress of Animals" between two crouching lions. Dating from the second half of the sixth century B.C., they are 1.2 centimeters in diameter.

132 top *This magnificent example of a disk or stud earring is part of the British Museum collections. It is of Greek-Oriental origin and is about 4 centimeters in diameter. Made of gold plate, it is worked in filigree and granulation with a geometric and plant-shaped decoration with concentric motifs. It is from the sixth century* B.C.

132 bottom *The semicircular gold plate stud used to decorate clothing has an embossed figure of a satyr within. The background is decorated with dusting and granulation techniques. Along the base, in a semicircular setting, is a chalcedony stone. The jewel was found in a tomb in Vignanello in the province of Viterbo, and is 3.5 centimeters wide. It is now on display at the Villa Giulia Museum in Rome. It probably dates from the early fifth century* B.C.

132

132–133 *This rich necklace from Palestrina is formed of nineteen cylindrical beads interspersed with six palmette pendants. All the cylinders are embossed and decorated with granulation work. The central pendant depicts a head of Achelous, whose features are highlighted in granulation and filigree work. This piece, about 37 centimeters long, can be dated to the early fifth century* B.C. *and is in the Antikenmuseum in Berlin.*

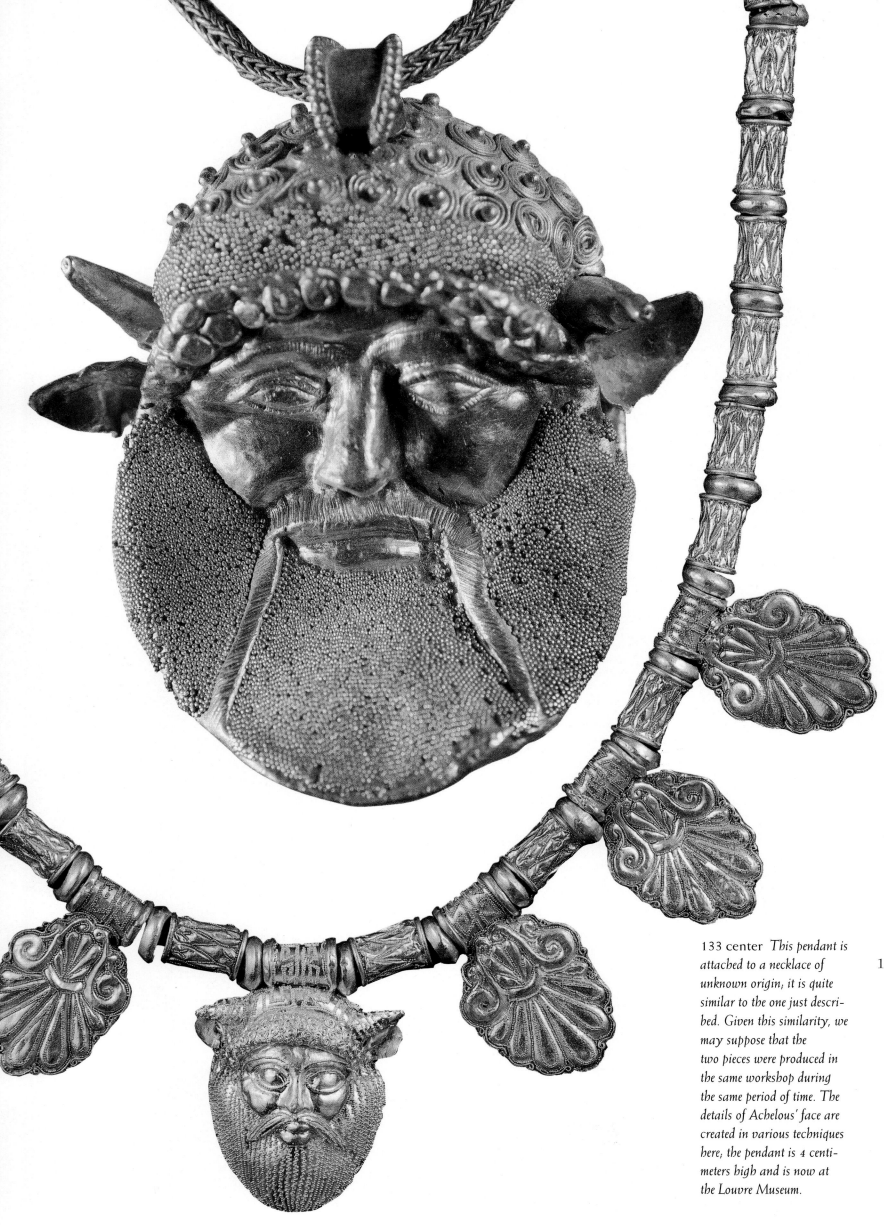

133 center *This pendant is attached to a necklace of unknown origin; it is quite similar to the one just described. Given this similarity, we may suppose that the two pieces were produced in the same workshop during the same period of time. The details of Achelous' face are created in various techniques here; the pendant is 4 centimeters high and is now at the Louvre Museum.*

134 top left *This pair of earrings is from the fifth century* B.C., *found in the necropolis of Spina. Each consists of a curved tube in smooth gold plate, ending in a portrait of the young Achelous. The earrings, 2.5 centimeters in diameter, are at the Archaeological Museum in Ferrara, along with other burial objects.*

domination of the seas, which resulted in an impressive increase in their wealth, and the consequent widespread use of gold.

During the seventh century, the aristocratic classes consolidated their political and economic power through various sources of income; at the same time, through contact with the Greek world, they welcomed and acquired new customs, such as banquets and the practice of oiling the body, as well as new instruments of cultural development, including writing, olive and grape cultivation, and construction crafts. This is clearly shown in archaeological finds, in particular the remains of luxurious palaces built in various areas of Etruria. But once

134 center
Found in a tomb in the Spina necropolis, this original double-plated clasp consists of five rows of small orbs; they are placed vertically and mounted on a palmette pendant. About 3 centimeters high, it can be dated to the early fourth century B.C. *and is on display at the Archaeological Museum in Ferrara.*

134 top right *This type of earring with a disk and pyramid-shaped pendant was quite common between the third and second centuries* B.C., *as can be seen not only in finds of this type of jewelry in tombs but also in portraits of women on alabaster and terra-cotta urns. This example, about 4 centimeters high, was found in a chamber tomb in the Volterra necropolis and is on display at the Guarnacci Museum in Volterra.*

again, Etruscan princes loved to exhibit their wealth in their tombs. More and more objects were added as grave goods and their tombs became increasingly magnificent, with chambers joined under a great burial mound to indicate that they were members of a highly important aristocracy.

Extraordinary noble tombs date to this period, with exceptional grave goods that must have represented the deceased's role in life and reaffirmed the values of his social status, including all the objects related to the new customs. In the Bernardini tomb, a man's grave from the second quarter of the seventh century found in Palestrina, we see objects related to the warrior class, like special parade weapons. In two women's tombs—one in Palestrina, the Barberini tomb from the second quarter of the seventh century, and one at Cerveteri, the Regolini-Galassi tomb from the mid-seventh century—the role of an adult woman is emphasized as an accumulator of

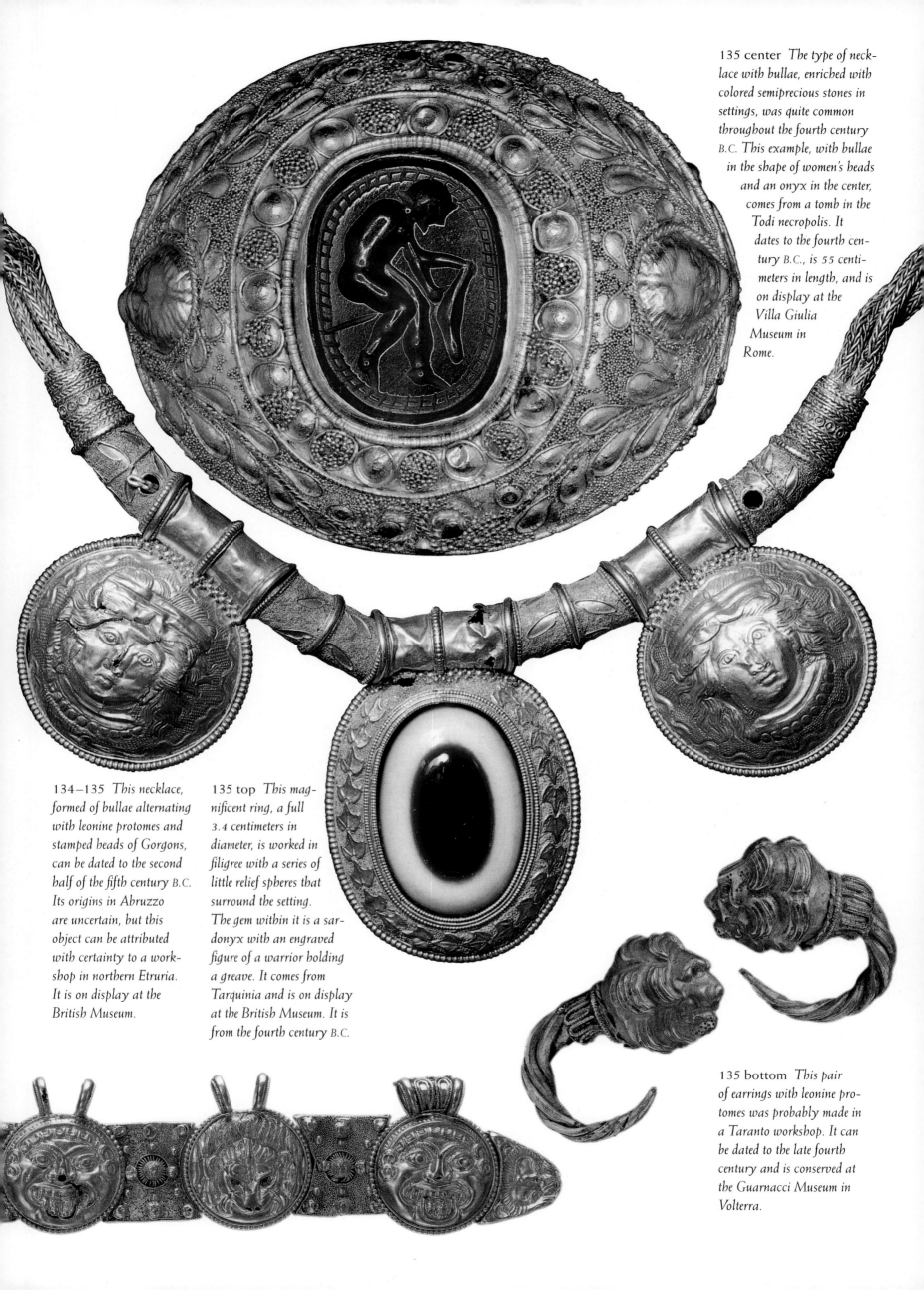

135 center *The type of necklace with bullae, enriched with colored semiprecious stones in settings, was quite common throughout the fourth century B.C. This example, with bullae in the shape of women's heads and an onyx in the center, comes from a tomb in the Todi necropolis. It dates to the fourth century B.C., is 55 centimeters in length, and is on display at the Villa Giulia Museum in Rome.*

134–135 *This necklace, formed of bullae alternating with leonine protomes and stamped heads of Gorgons, can be dated to the second half of the fifth century B.C. Its origins in Abruzzo are uncertain, but this object can be attributed with certainty to a workshop in northern Etruria. It is on display at the British Museum.*

135 top *This magnificent ring, a full 3.4 centimeters in diameter, is worked in filigree with a series of little relief spheres that surround the setting. The gem within it is a sardonyx with an engraved figure of a warrior holding a greave. It comes from Tarquinia and is on display at the British Museum. It is from the fourth century B.C.*

135 bottom *This pair of earrings with leonine protomes was probably made in a Taranto workshop. It can be dated to the late fourth century and is conserved at the Guarnacci Museum in Volterra.*

family goods, such as precious dishware, ivory, and bronze furnishings. Among all these grave goods, both male and female, there are also objects related to banquets, with dishes for eating and drinking wine, and vessels for perfumed body oils.

The most extraordinary aspect is certainly the personal ornamentation, undeniably sumptuous, including coiled arched fibulas and gold and silver buckles for male ornamentation; earrings, pectorals, bracelets, and numerous fibulae for women's attire. These objects were both imported and made locally for wealthy customers, already laden with ornaments in precious metals, for whom foreign artisans made objects to meet local needs. In crafting them, they used not only techniques and decorations already common in Tyrhennian Italy but also new technologies like filigree and granulation, with Oriental motifs used to create a figurative culture that is known as Orientalizing, due to the origin of these artisans.

The workshops, located in a maritime Etrurian town, most probably Caere, settled in Vetulonia in the late seventh century, as shown by splendid aristocratic tombs like the Tomb of Lictor and the Circle of Silver Lions Tomb. Their precious jewelry uses a peculiar "dusting" decoration obtained with gold dust and tiny grains welded to the surface.

In the first half of the sixth century, social and political changes led to the urbanization of southern Etruria's major towns, where the dominant classes invested their wealth in commercial enterprises, as shown by the vast range of Etruscan wares. In the second half of the sixth century, this acceleration and expansion of trade was accompanied by the

136

136–137 top *This crown consists of two bands of gold plate, covered with a series of oak leaves attached by gold thread, converging toward the center. Part of a woman's grave goods found in Vulci, the piece, now at the Vatican Museums, can be dated to the mid-fourth century B.C.*

136 center *These tubular earrings were found in a tomb in the Volterra necropolis and can be dated with certainty to the final decades of the fourth century B.C. They are 4.5 centimeters in diameter and are now at the Guarnacci Museum in Volterra.*

136–137 bottom *This necklace made of eleven stamped pendants, an average of 3 centimeters high, alternates trapezoidal and oval shapes, with figures of sphinxes and women's heads. From the same tomb that gave us the oak leaf crown, it is in the Vatican Museums*

137 bottom This cluster-style earring, of clearly Etruscan make, has a semicircular upper portion decorated with little spheres, a central badge with figures, and a cluster of five globes. It is on display at the Archaeological Museum in Florence.

137 top right The same tomb that gave us the necklace with bullae has revealed these earrings with a pendant in the shape of a woman's head, a more local version of Greek or Magna Graecian production. Little chains, rosettes, female protomes, filigree work, and embossing are utilized to enrich this jewelry from a tomb discovered in the Todi necropolis and dated to the late fourth century B.C. They are 10.7 centimeters high and are on display at the Villa Giulia Museum in Rome.

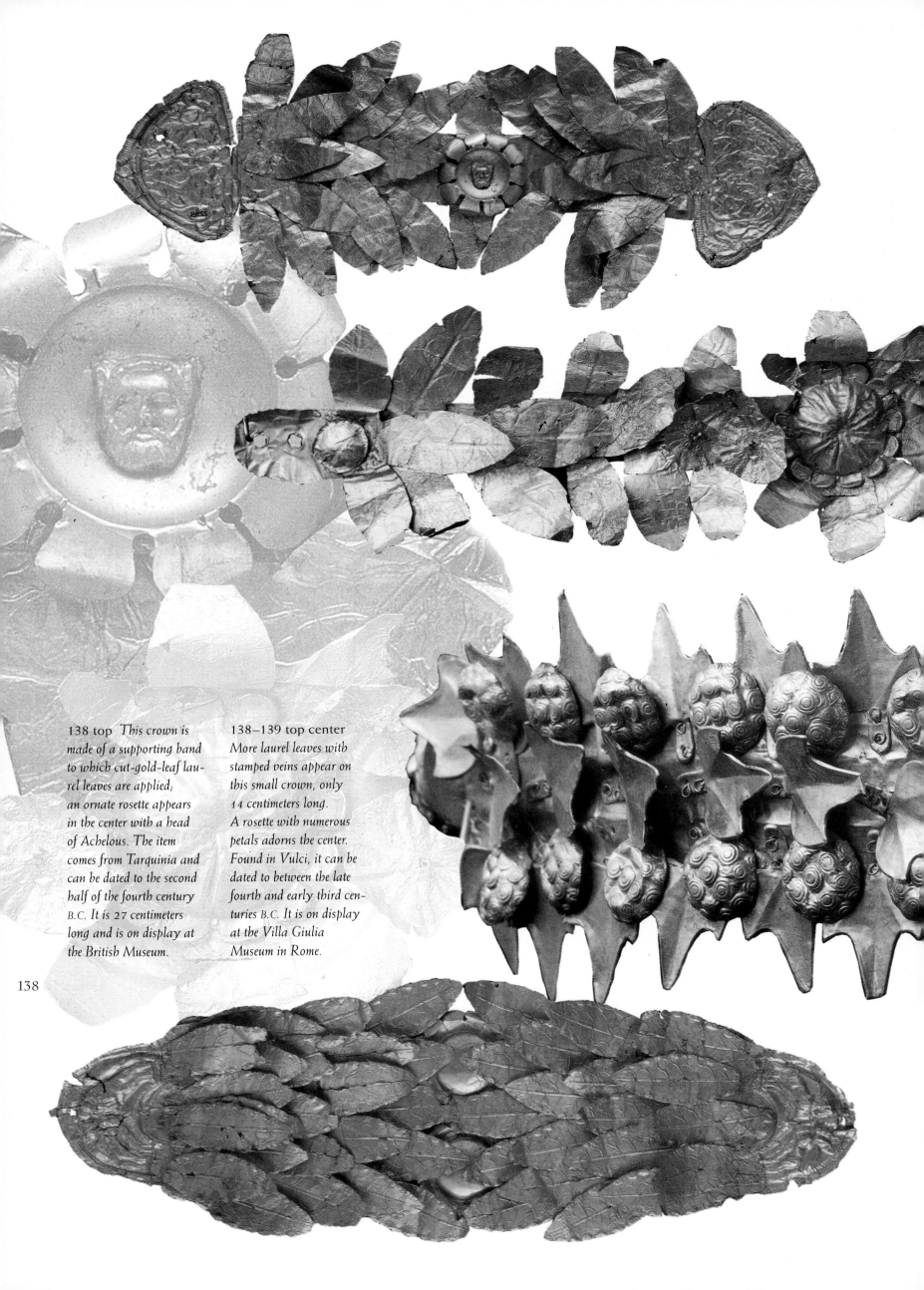

138 top *This crown is made of a supporting band to which cut-gold-leaf laurel leaves are applied; an ornate rosette appears in the center with a head of Achelous. The item comes from Tarquinia and can be dated to the second half of the fourth century* B.C. *It is 27 centimeters long and is on display at the British Museum.*

138–139 top center *More laurel leaves with stamped veins appear on this small crown, only 14 centimeters long. A rosette with numerous petals adorns the center. Found in Vulci, it can be dated to between the late fourth and early third centuries* B.C. *It is on display at the Villa Giulia Museum in Rome.*

138

arrival of the Greeks from Asiatic Ionia. They brought the fabulous riches of the Orient, Lydia, and the legendary treasures of Croesus to the West, as well as items crafted in Greece, of course. As occurred two centuries earlier with the arrival of the Greeks from Euboea, the Etruscan aristocracy was eager to accept the new lifestyle based on the Ionian aristocratic model. The paintings in the tomb of Tarquinia show the new customs adopted, portraying jewel-bedecked aristocrats at a banquet as they participate in dances, games, and shows of every kind.

The jewelry surviving from the second half of the sixth century lacks significant burial context, and it is thus more difficult to draw any useful information from it. For the most part, it is women's gold jewelry with ornaments of distinctly Etruscan creation, such as jewel-box shaped earrings, accompanied by exotic objects like Phoenician-type rings used as seals, and Greek-Oriental type earrings with disk-shaped studs, as well as fibulae with relief figurines, pendants, and necklaces. This jewelry is copiously decorated with granulation and filigree techniques, with the addition of semiprecious stones and glass that create colorful effects. The goldsmiths were probably located in Vulci and Cerveteri, but also in inland Etrurian towns such as Chiusi and Orvieto.

Beginning in the mid-fifth century B.C., archaeological remains become much scantier. The cities of southern Etruria suffered from the fierce naval battles in Cuma between the Syracuse Greeks and the Etruscans. On the other hand, towns in northern Etruria became increasingly important during this period, as shown by the rich grave goods in the necropolises of Spina, a flourishing trading center on the Adriatic coast.

Important political factors that characterized the

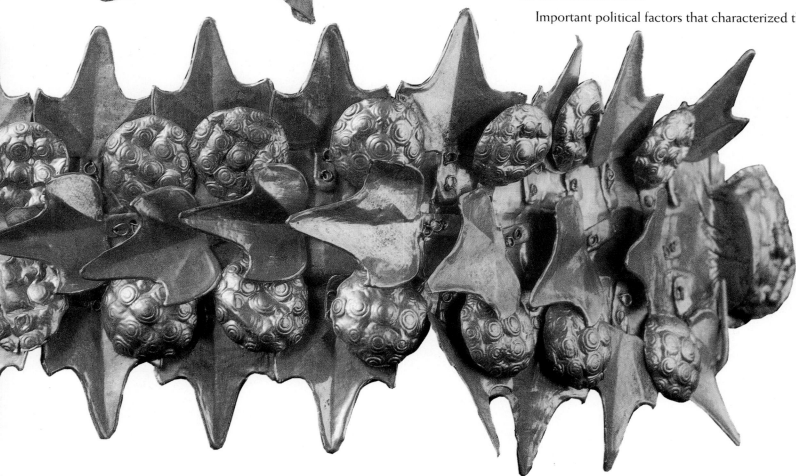

138–139 bottom center *Found with other objects in the tomb of a high-ranking woman, this crown shows that its owner was a member of the cult of Dionysus-Bacchus. Indeed, the crown does not have the usual lau-* *rel leaves but rather a triple row of ivy leaves alternating with berries. The unique grave goods date to the first half of the fourth century B.C. and are on display at the British Museum.*

138 bottom *This crown from Chiusi dates to between the late fourth and early third centuries B.C. It consists of laurel leaves in cut-gold-plate, attached to a* *wide sheet with two quadrigas with galloping horses impressed at the ends. This funeral ornament is 30 centimeters long and can be seen at the British Museum.*

fourth century, including Rome's grip from the south and Gallic incursions to the north, began a lengthy transformation of Etruria that gradually destroyed its economic and social structure. Nevertheless, there was evidence of economic revitalization and renewed artisan activity. Here, the new aristocracy built large hypogea with large inner chambers, numerous beds and burial niches, and large decorated walls. The grave goods feature gold, and jewelry is completely local in style, with elaborate clustered earrings, more simple cylinder-shaped ones, and pendant necklaces. There are also numerous vessels for perfumed substances, decorated both in relief and stamped, and crowns of gold plate leaves that adorned both men and women in this aristocratic class.

There was a clear change in trend in the late fourth century, when the Macedonian army intervened to support Tarentum and put Etruria in contact with the

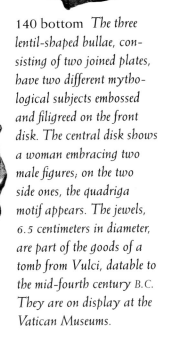

Greek-Macedonian world through Magna Graecia. From this time on, Etruscan production would reflect a single cultural climate common to the whole Hellenistic world.

Based on the model of Macedonian aristocracy, gold seems to have been concentrated in tombs once again. Grave goods contain jewelry that used abandoned techniques like filigree and granulation, fusing local tradition with Greek and Magna Graecian customs. This is reflected, for example, in earrings with multiform or pyramid-shaped pendants, the use of which lasted through the entire second century B.C.

The dominant oligarchs of a number of cities in Etruria offered their support to the emerging power of Rome, ensuring their survival until they were absorbed into the Roman political class between the third and second centuries B.C.

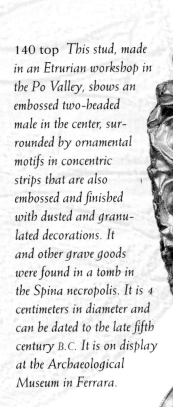

140 top *This stud, made in an Etrurian workshop in the Po Valley, shows an embossed two-headed male in the center, surrounded by ornamental motifs in concentric strips that are also embossed and finished with dusted and granulated decorations. It and other grave goods were found in a tomb in the Spina necropolis. It is 4 centimeters in diameter and can be dated to the late fifth century B.C. It is on display at the Archaeological Museum in Ferrara.*

140 bottom *The three lentil-shaped bullae, consisting of two joined plates, have two different mythological subjects embossed and filigreed on the front disk. The central disk shows a woman embracing two male figures; on the two side ones, the quadriga motif appears. The jewels, 6.5 centimeters in diameter, are part of the goods of a tomb from Vulci, datable to the mid-fourth century B.C. They are on display at the Vatican Museums.*

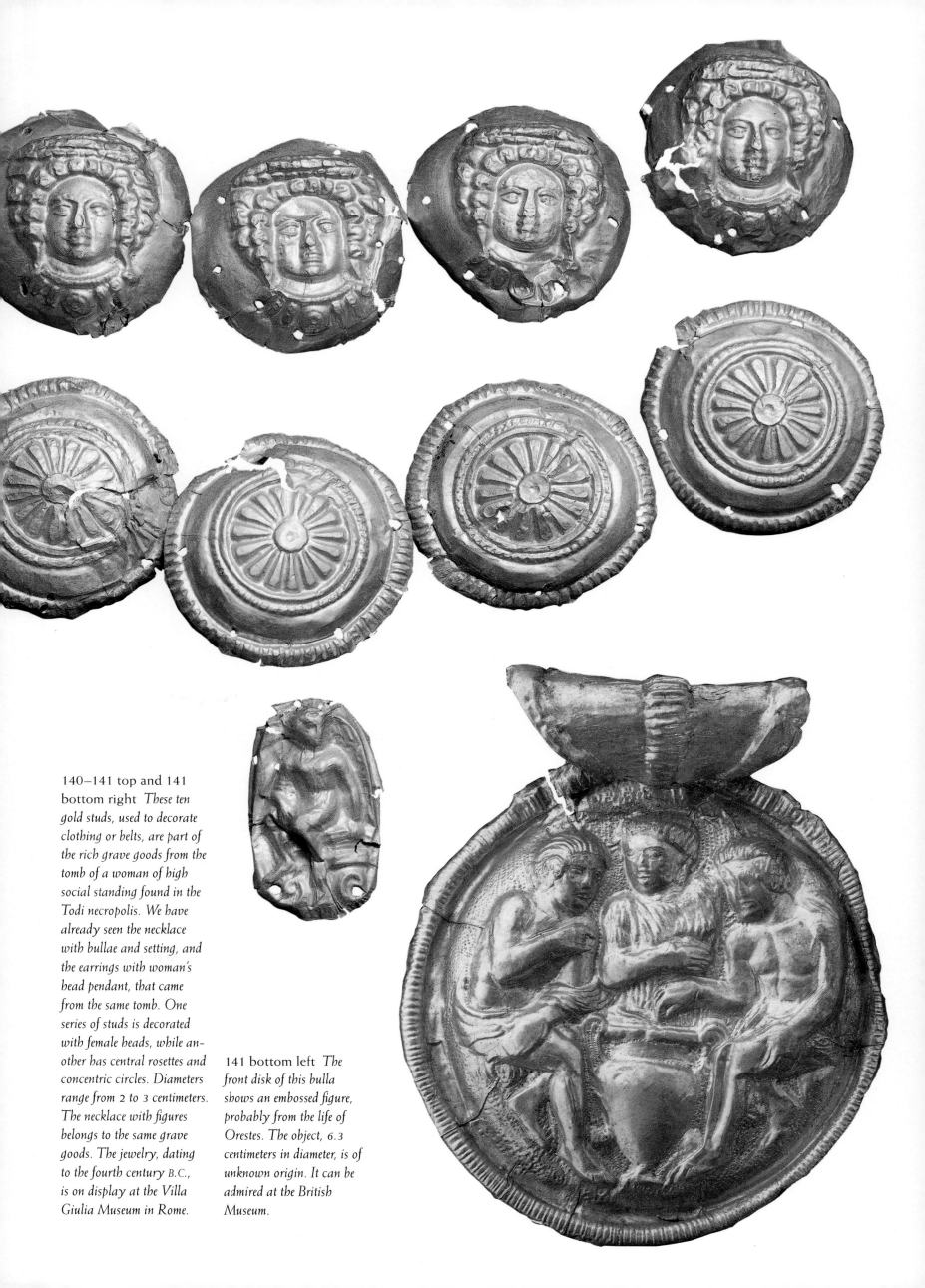

140–141 top and 141 bottom right *These ten gold studs, used to decorate clothing or belts, are part of the rich grave goods from the tomb of a woman of high social standing found in the Todi necropolis. We have already seen the necklace with bullae and setting, and the earrings with woman's head pendant, that came from the same tomb. One series of studs is decorated with female heads, while another has central rosettes and concentric circles. Diameters range from 2 to 3 centimeters. The necklace with figures belongs to the same grave goods. The jewelry, dating to the fourth century B.C., is on display at the Villa Giulia Museum in Rome.*

141 bottom left *The front disk of this bulla shows an embossed figure, probably from the life of Orestes. The object, 6.3 centimeters in diameter, is of unknown origin. It can be admired at the British Museum.*

ROMAN JEWELRY

The encounter of rude Roman soldiers with the populations of monumental, opulent Greek cities—first in southern Italy, then in the Hellenistic realms on the shores of the eastern Mediterranean—was an extraordinary event that signaled the beginning of significant, irreversible changes in Roman society.

On the one hand, the assimilation of a literary, philosophical, and artistic culture that was refined and far-flung ensued. On the other hand, the encounter represented an invasion of uses and customs that would deeply undermine the *mores maiorum*. For this reason, new trends were opposed and reviled by moderates such as Cato the Censor. One of these "fashions" that so worried the dying patrician class was the public display of jewels. Suffice it to consider that, as early as 214 B.C., when Rome was master of all Italy and was engaged in its final battle with Carthage for domination of the Mediterranean, the *Lex Oppia* was promulgated,

prohibiting women from wearing more than half an ounce (about 13 grams) of jewels.

The historian Livy firmly states that ". . . the ostentation of luxury originated in Rome after the army returned from Asia . . . ," i.e., after the wars that resulted in the conquest of Asia Minor and Greece. Roman soldiers brought back great quantities of jewels; they paraded this war booty in a brazen manner to show that they had fought in the wars of conquest and out of simple vanity, and the *Lex Oppia* was soon ignored and then forgotten.

Large numbers of master goldsmiths, chiselers, silversmiths, and engravers arrived along with the jewels. These artisans were disparagingly referred

142 left center and 143 center Beloved by the Romans, cameos first became popular as pendants; subsequently, and ever more frequently, they were used to decorate rings. Particularly refined examples depicted mythological figures draped in filmy veils or imperial portraits and allowed the owners to personalize their jewels. Agate, onyx, carnelian, and sardonyx were the materials of choice.

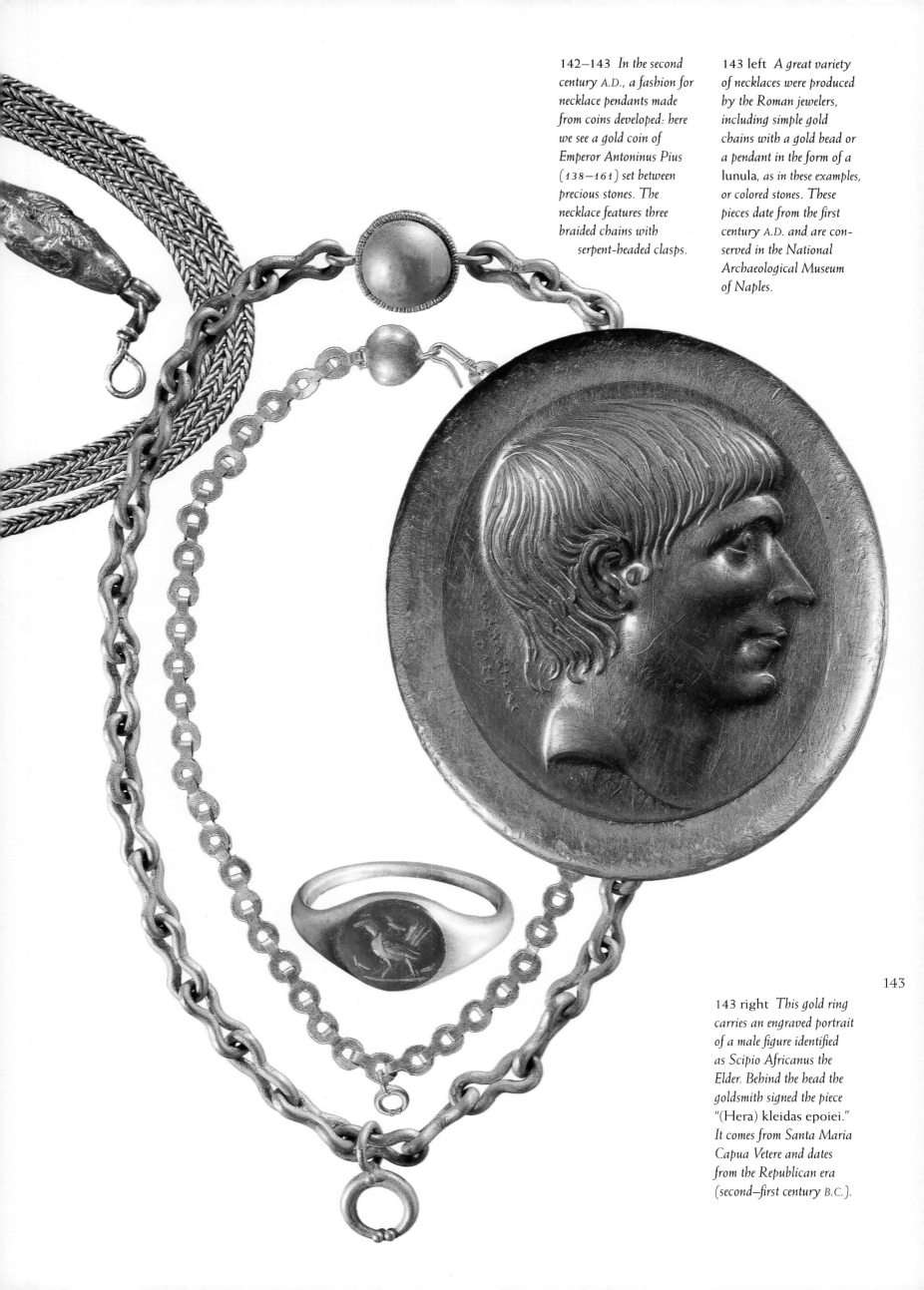

142–143 In the second century A.D., a fashion for necklace pendants made from coins developed: here we see a gold coin of Emperor Antoninus Pius (138–161) set between precious stones. The necklace features three braided chains with serpent-headed clasps.

143 left A great variety of necklaces were produced by the Roman jewelers, including simple gold chains with a gold bead or a pendant in the form of a lunula, as in these examples, or colored stones. These pieces date from the first century A.D. and are conserved in the National Archaeological Museum of Naples.

143

143 right This gold ring carries an engraved portrait of a male figure identified as Scipio Africanus the Elder. Behind the head the goldsmith signed the piece "(Hera)kleidas epoiei." It comes from Santa Maria Capua Vetere and dates from the Republican era (second–first century B.C.).

144 top *Two pairs of earrings from Oplontis, found in the villa attributed to Lucius Crassus Tertium destroyed in the eruption of 79 A.D. Pearls and gold composed in opulent bunches, or pearls paired and rattling with every movement of the face, are original forms of decoration for Roman women's favorite jewels.*

144 bottom *This diadem is unique in the context of Roman goldsmithery. An undulating band enclosed within a knurled frame features three oval settings, inset with large pearls, each decorated on its free side with lanceolate palmettes.*

to as *graeculi*. Their presence naturally encouraged the birth of numerous craft workshops, quickly spreading throughout Italy. The craftsmen were able to meet the needs of a new public that did not always fully appreciate the products of their home-lands. Indeed, while Greek jewelry was character-ized by naturalistic forms and refined decorative motifs from the Greek world, the Romans preferred rounded, smooth lines that brought out the color of the gold, studded with precious stones, especially red (carnelian) and green (emeralds).

Even today, it is debatable whether the roman-ization of the Mediterranean somehow spread and imposed this different taste in the type of jewels, or if Hellenistic goldsmiths continued their tradition,

which later appeared in Byzantine forms. In the workshops that held the *aurifices*, we thus find *aura-tores*, or gilders; *caelatores*, or silversmiths; *bractearii*, who created extremely fine gold leaf; *anularii*, who made rings; and *margariotarii*, who worked with pearls. The gold to be worked came primarily from Spain and Egypt, the precious stones were imported from Oriental countries, and pearls—enjoying great success in the first century A.D.—came from the Red Sea or the Indian Ocean. It is nevertheless extremely difficult to trace a history of tastes in, and forms of, Roman jewelry; the precious nature of the basic material encouraged remelting for different uses. Moreover, it was not common to adorn the dead with jewels.

145 *An interest in polychrome decoration applied to jewelry emerged in the Vesuvian area: these two examples of necklaces in gold chain with emeralds and oval stones, or in gold with* *pearls and semiprecious stones, provide eloquent testimony to the fashion. In contrast with Oriental and Greek jewels, the stones are simply threaded onto a gold wire rather than being inset.*

The only archaeological site that reveals anything significant about the use and type of jewels is the area surrounding Vesuvius, sealed under a blanket of pumice and ash by the eruption of 79 A.D. Patrician residences and important cities such as Herculaneum, Pompeii, Stabiae, and Oplontis were covered in a matter of hours, thus preserving an intact reality with no outside intervention. But analysis of remains in these cities provides only a partial picture of Roman jewels. In fact, while these towns were important, they should be considered provincial. Furthermore, they testify to a way of life in cities undergoing great social, political, and economic upheaval following the numerous earthquakes starting in 62 A.D. Thus, the jewelry found here belongs to a society that was desperately and stubbornly trying to regain its footing. The use and ostentation of jewels should be seen from this socioeconomic perspective, which does not represent the whole Roman world. It is nevertheless an important point of reference that cannot be ignored, due both to the quantities of jewels that Vesuvian towns have revealed and to the pictorial and mosaic decorations that permit us to see how they were used.

Written classical sources are also important, even though they are often ironic and mocking, and give us a broader time frame. Therefore, it is possible to trace a picture of the types of jewels most common in the Roman world during the first century. Rings, or *anuli*, worn on the fingers of the left hand were certainly the most abundant items.

146 top left *These gold earrings are composed of a pair of hemispheres linked by a double-knurled thread terminating in a rosette below. Probably incomplete, the jewels were made from pieces of a bracelet with hemispherical decoration.*

146 bottom left *The apotropaic serpent motif was among the most common in the jewelry of antiquity, both Roman and Oriental. This large ring from Pompeii has carefully engraved scales and other details. Unfortunately, the glass paste traditionally inserted in the eye sockets is missing.*

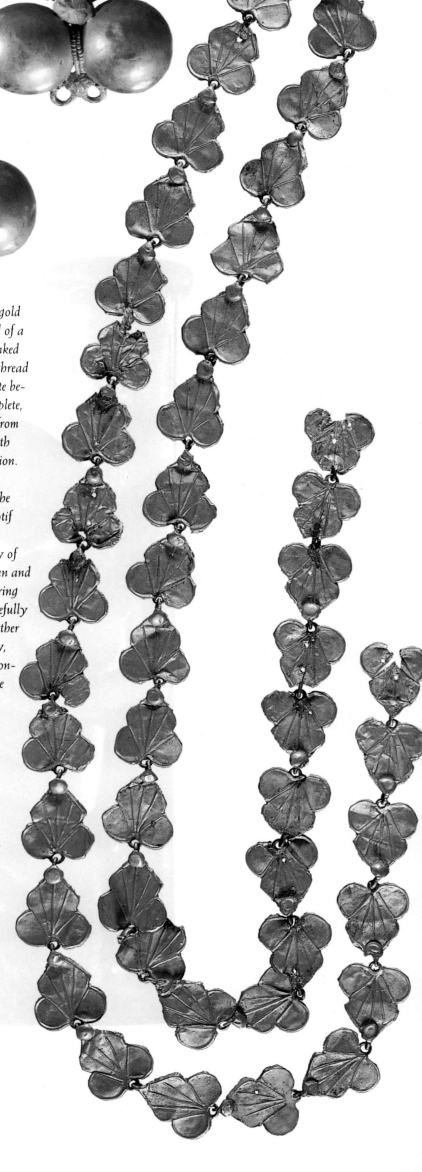

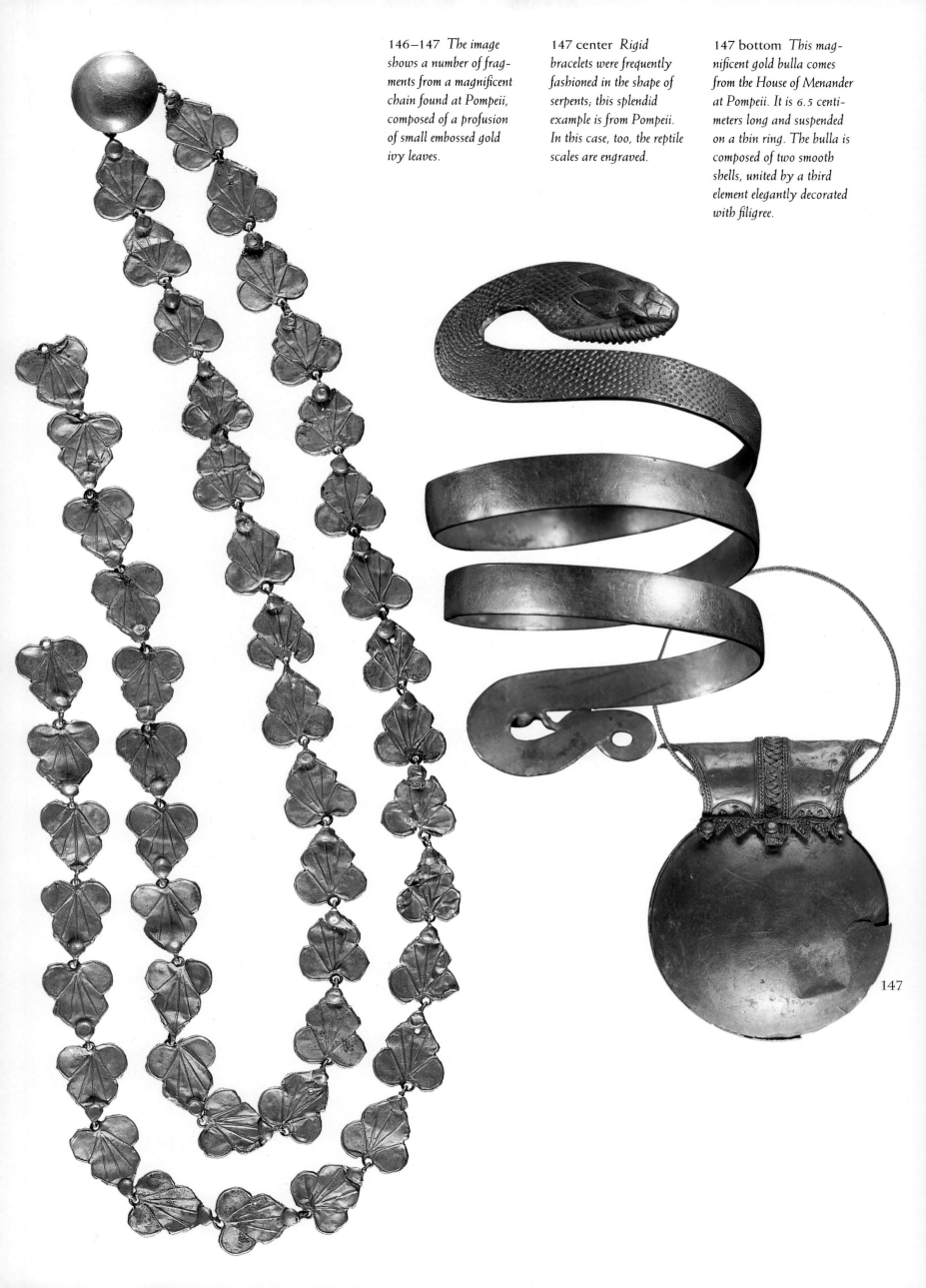

146–147 The image shows a number of fragments from a magnificent chain found at Pompeii, composed of a profusion of small embossed gold ivy leaves.

147 center Rigid bracelets were frequently fashioned in the shape of serpents; this splendid example is from Pompeii. In this case, too, the reptile scales are engraved.

147 bottom This magnificent gold bulla comes from the House of Menander at Pompeii. It is 6.5 centimeters long and suspended on a thin ring. The bulla is composed of two smooth shells, united by a third element elegantly decorated with filigree.

As examples from Pompeii demonstrate, the smooth faces of signet rings were the most popular form with the ancient Romans. The rings lent themselves particularly well to complex intaglio work with precious stones that played on effects of chiaroscuro. The plain gold ring with the oval collet is engraved with an upright male figure holding a spear and a patera. The engraved carnelian of the second depicts a charioteer watering his horses, while the third is embellished with a male portrait in profile.

Throughout the first century, the signet ring indicated the importance of its wearer; whether signet ring or not, if it was made of gold it could belong only to those of the senatorial class. Freedmen wore silver rings, and slaves iron ones. The use of gold rings gradually increased so that by 23 A.D. it was necessary to promulgate a law permitting its use only by those born free by at least two generations. This law was ignored later on, and many authors state that the fashion for ostentation led to wearing a number of rings on the same finger, which conservatives regarded with ill-disguised scorn. The most common and simple gold rings have a thin bar set with a precious stone like an emerald or carnelian but could include cameos or colored glass, mostly square or oval, which brought out the colors and simplicity of the geometric forms popular in Italy. Often the stone was engraved with various motifs.

Another popular item of jewelry was the bracelet, or *armilla*, often worn on both wrists, sometimes in pairs. When worn on the ankle, it was known as

148 top right This gold plaque is decorated with a carnelian depicting Hygeia sitting on a column and leaning in the act of bringing the head of a snake toward a cornucopia. The piece, 1.1 centimeters in diameter, is from the Citarista house at Pompeii.

148 bottom These gold bracelets are made of rows of hollow spheres soldered together. Along with the serpentine version, they represent the most common type of bracelet found at Pompeii.

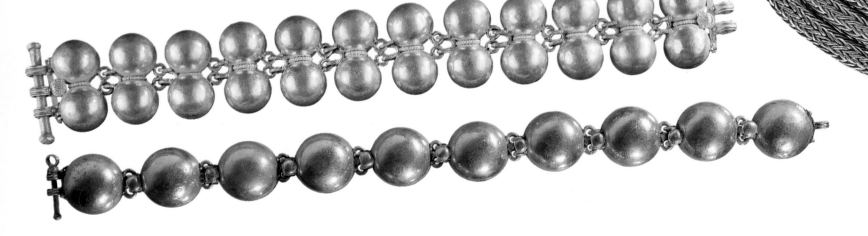

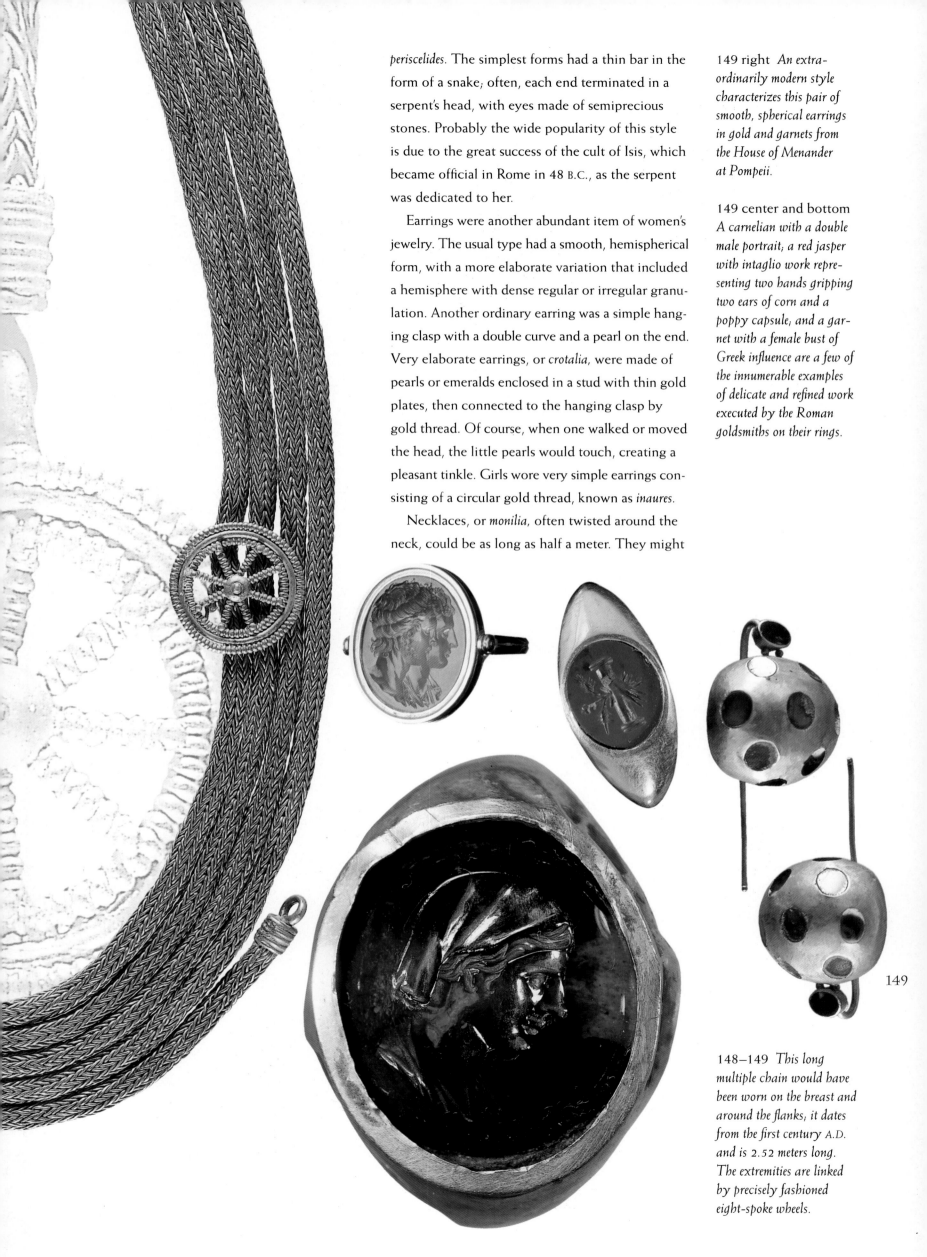

periscelides. The simplest forms had a thin bar in the form of a snake; often, each end terminated in a serpent's head, with eyes made of semiprecious stones. Probably the wide popularity of this style is due to the great success of the cult of Isis, which became official in Rome in 48 B.C., as the serpent was dedicated to her.

Earrings were another abundant item of women's jewelry. The usual type had a smooth, hemispherical form, with a more elaborate variation that included a hemisphere with dense regular or irregular granulation. Another ordinary earring was a simple hanging clasp with a double curve and a pearl on the end. Very elaborate earrings, or *crotalia*, were made of pearls or emeralds enclosed in a stud with thin gold plates, then connected to the hanging clasp by gold thread. Of course, when one walked or moved the head, the little pearls would touch, creating a pleasant tinkle. Girls wore very simple earrings consisting of a circular gold thread, known as *inaures*.

Necklaces, or *monilia*, often twisted around the neck, could be as long as half a meter. They might

149 right *An extra-ordinarily modern style characterizes this pair of smooth, spherical earrings in gold and garnets from the House of Menander at Pompeii.*

149 center and bottom *A carnelian with a double male portrait; a red jasper with intaglio work representing two hands gripping two ears of corn and a poppy capsule; and a garnet with a female bust of Greek influence are a few of the innumerable examples of delicate and refined work executed by the Roman goldsmiths on their rings.*

149

148–149 *This long multiple chain would have been worn on the breast and around the flanks; it dates from the first century A.D. and is 2.52 meters long. The extremities are linked by precisely fashioned eight-spoke wheels.*

be little circular rings inserted into each other to form a chain, or complex constructions in the form of elliptical rings, bent into an arc and pulled together in the center to be attached to each other. They may also be formed in mesh form with eight folds or braided. Often necklaces had a hemispherical pendant known as a *lunula*. The less common chain was a sort of long necklace worn across the shoulder that descended, crossing over on the hips and chest, fastened by studs.

Gold thread was often inserted in the hair, using an *acus crinalis*; in other cases, true gold hairnets, *reticulae aureae*, held the hair. Actual ribbons woven with fine gold threads, or *vittae*, have also been found. Their use is unclear, but

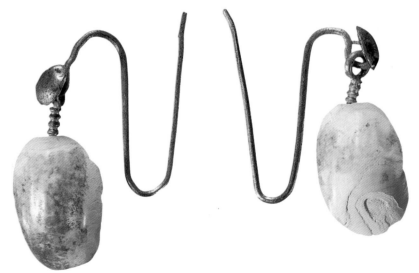

they probably held the hair and were fastened with stickpins.

Brooches, fibulae, and frontlets were also found in the remains buried by Vesuvius, but these carried on the Greek tradition and were the prerogative of matrons of high social rank.

150 top and bottom
Two pairs of earrings from Oplontis date from the first century A.D. *Small collets contain fragments of quartz in the first pair, while the pendants of the second pair are made with two big, long pearls.*

150–151 *This long necklace, measuring 139.6 centimeters, is crafted from two pairs of thin chains with links cut from sheet gold, then folded.*

151 right *This necklace is composed of natural emerald prisms of various sizes, alternating with ovals in sheet metal. It is 28 centimeters long.*

151 center *A simple knurled wire of solid gold with a pearl at the center or a spiraled serpent are used to create bracelets of great sophistication.*

The knurling technique was widely used in ancient Rome: a knurling tool impressed the metal. These jewels were also found at Oplontis.

151

ARBARIC SPLENDORS

152 top *These Bronze Age diadems feature simple, elegant lines. Both terminate with the spiral motif, probably a symbol for the sun. The larger one was found near Örebro, whereas the one with four spirals at both ends is from Nosaby parish, Scania.*

152 center and 153 center *A succession of embossed concentric circles, horizontal lines, and rows of triangles decorate these votive vessels made nearly 3,000 years ago. They weigh only about 70 grams each. Vessels like these are known from Ireland, France, and Germany, as well as from Denmark and Sweden.*

152 bottom *Both the bracelet and the biconical beads from the third century testify to the excellent craftsmanship of the goldsmiths of the Baltic island of Gotland.*

153 bottom *The seven armrings in the shape of coiled snakes were found close together in the sacrificial bog on the Baltic island of Öland. Golden armrings and neckrings with snake-head terminations were symbols of the highest military and political rank during the third century A.D. in Scandinavia.*

The first gold arrived in Scandinavia some 1700 years B.C. at the onset of the Bronze Age and must have been of great rarity. Bronze resembles gold when polished and was important for large ceremonial objects like *lurs* (horns), shields, axes, and jewelry. With the passing of the centuries, gold became more abundant and, particularly between 900 and 600 B.C., golden jewelry, mostly armrings, found its way to the north from southeast Europe. Other objects, such as beautiful vessels, were made. To obtain these bowls, skilled artisans annealed and hammered the soft gold to thin foils. The repoussé ornamentation was produced by pressing the gold foil over a ball of pitch and using various hammers and punches. The vessels were most likely used for pouring libations or for ritual drinking.

The two unique golden diadems with spiral terminations also belong to the Swedish Bronze Age. The diadem with four terminal spirals at both ends turned up in Nosaby parish in Scania, deposited below the surface on a stone slab together with three large axes of bronze. The numerous sites with rock carvings from the Bronze Age in Sweden show scenes of men carrying large, probably ceremonial axes, and we may speculate whether the treasure from Nosaby was not a sacrifice to a male deity whose main attribute was a large bronze axe. The wider diadem, with only one set of spirals, was found somewhere near the town of Örebro, but no other information about this find is available.

The Bronze Age societies of Southern Scandinavia were chiefdoms with well-developed systems for circulation and redistribution of goods. Graves and settlements testify to stratified societies made up of numerous tribes. Goods produced by one tribe were delivered by their chief to a central chieftain, who had the goods redistributed among the tribes according to their needs. The central chieftains were in contact over long distances, and they developed transactions with special, precious, and exotic goods often made of gold and amber. Both men and women of this upper societal strata were buried in monumental burial mounds or cairns.

With the coming of iron technology, gold disappeared from Scandinavia for centuries. Following the Gallic wars, the Roman emperors pressed

153

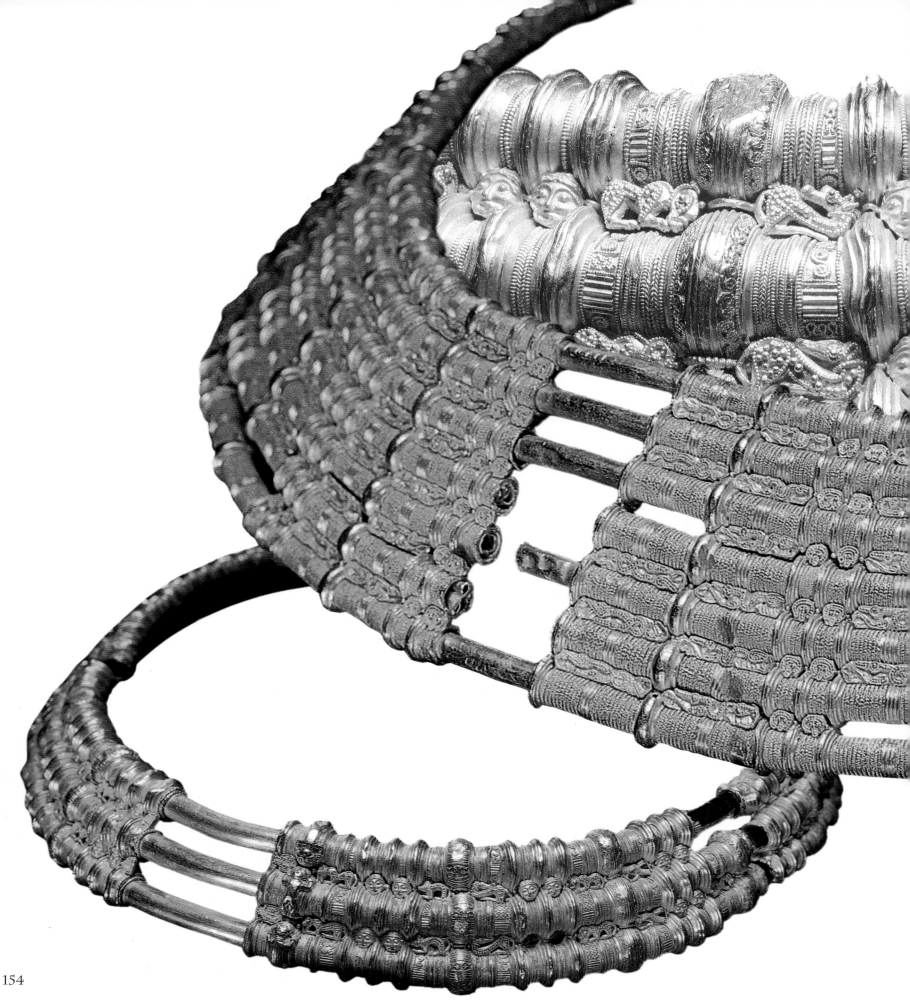

northward, but after the catastrophic defeat of Varus in 9 A.D., they gave up this strategy and fortified the southern embankment of the rivers Rhine and Danube from the North Sea to the Black Sea. In nearly four centuries the military upkeep of the Limes drained Roman society of vital resources, but it also functioned as a magnet. It attracted all kinds of people from the Roman inland who saw the opportunity to do business with the men of the legions and with benevolent Germanic chieftains. Many Roman civilians no doubt felt safer in the neighborhood of the fortifications

than in the countryside where sudden assaults from gangs of Germanic robbers were common. Gold was sought after, and judging by the amount of this precious metal found in graves and deposits in Scandinavia from the third through the sixth centuries, great quantities must have been in circulation.

In the Roman society gold was minted and stamped with the emperor's sacred portrait. Golden solidi brought to Scandinavia were either melted down or kept as coins. When the Roman Empire weakened, the emperors were forced to pay barbarian

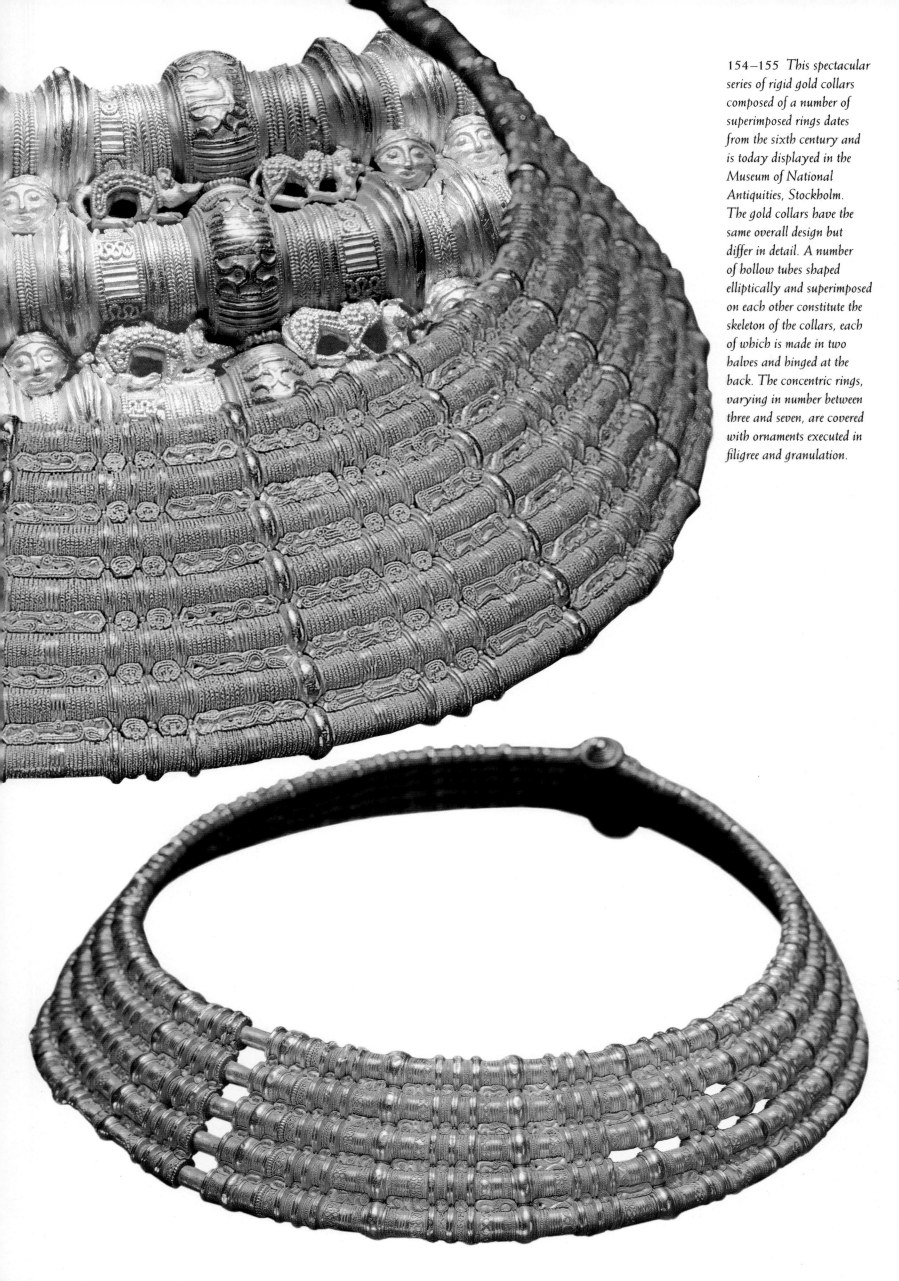

154–155 *This spectacular series of rigid gold collars composed of a number of superimposed rings dates from the sixth century and is today displayed in the Museum of National Antiquities, Stockholm. The gold collars have the same overall design but differ in detail. A number of hollow tubes shaped elliptically and superimposed on each other constitute the skeleton of the collars, each of which is made in two halves and hinged at the back. The concentric rings, varying in number between three and seven, are covered with ornaments executed in filigree and granulation.*

155

156 center *A strap mounting of gilded silver is from Blekinge, Sweden. It depicts Odin the shaman god in trance, with one helping spirit in the form of a hook-beaked bird on each side.*

156 bottom *The gold ring with a mounted carnelian, the two plain rings, and the vase-shaped pendant are part of a richly furnished warlord's grave from* Fullerö in Old Uppsala, Sweden. *This kind of funerary cache could have been the result of plunder, or gifts to a barbarian chieftain for service in the Roman army.*

warlords large sums of solidi to avert attacks on Rome and Constantinople. The amount of gold reaching Scandinavia increased manifold.

During this rather long period, the Germanic societies of Europe underwent important structural changes whereby war became a more honorable profession. Hundreds of young men from different Germanic tribes became Roman soldiers and their leaders became professional officers who won new land for their peoples and returned from war with a rich booty. A Germanic warrior ideology grew, with myths and epic poetry glorifying the courageous and valiant young warriors. Cult and rituals of the gods Odin, Thor, and Tyr became more prominent than those of the fertility and regeneration deities. Gold, soft and malleable and nearly unaffected by air and water, acids and salts, was the metal of the gods. According to Germanic myth, Odin promised every warrior that the golden treasure he had deposited under ground would accompany him to Valhalla.

156–157 *Golden scabbard mountings like this piece are always parts of sacrificial hoards. From Tureholm, Sweden, this belongs to the largest gold hoard from the Migration period in Scandinavia.*

157 bottom *This Germanic gold bracteate, copying a Roman imperial coin portrait, dates to the fourth century* A.D. *These circular pendants were stamped with a motif on one side only. Both men and women used to wear gold bracteates, which functioned as amulets or gifts.*

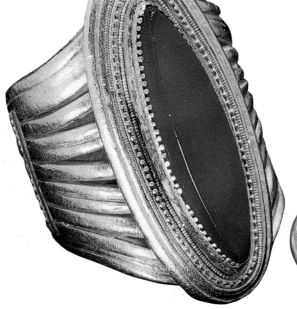

Among the Scandinavian countries, Sweden stands out as the golden land during the third through the sixth centuries A.D. Gold does occur in graves but has mostly been found deposited in bogs and marshland. One such treasure came to light in the seventeenth century in a bog near Hede in Västmanland (page 152 bottom). It consists of a golden armlet from the third century with embossed triangles and three biconical golden beads decorated with filigree and granulation.

In the middle of the Baltic island of Öland lies a sacred bog site, called Skedemosse, where archaeological investigations were conducted between 1959 and 1964. Weapons and the bones of sacrificed animals, such as horses, were the most dominant finds, but the most spectacular were seven golden snake rings coiled up close together in one spot.

The abundance of gold in Scandinavia in the fourth to sixth centuries led to the establishment of workshops where skilled goldsmiths created the most magnificent golden jewelry for powerful families, such as the three gold collars

157

158–159 These three splendid examples of gold bracteates could have been used as amulets or as valuable gifts in sociopolitical transactions between Scandinavian chieftains of the fourth to sixth centuries. Decorating the pendant from Gerete farm, Gotland (page 159), is a man's head above a quadruped. This iconography is related to the Germanic myth of Odin the healer. The amulet from Söderby, Uppland (page 158 bottom), shows Odin the shaman in ecstatic movement with his legs thrown behind him. The pendant (top left) is a much later piece from the Viking Age, from Gotland.

159

found in Sweden. The gold collars must in the Migration period have been connected with certain rituals and were possibly worn by priests or wooden images of gods.

The leading Germanic families in south Scandinavia did not copy directly from Roman art, instead choosing certain motifs adaptable to their own religiopolitical ideology. Among these we find birds of prey with hooked beaks, quadrupeds such as stags and horses, human figures (mostly male), mixed creatures with a human body and head of a bird, or an animal body with a human head plus masks with human and zoomorphic features.

Moreover, the importance of the cult of Odin among the leading north Germanic families is clearly demonstrated by the gold bracteates: circular pendants of thin gold foil, stamped with a motif on one side only and furnished with a frame of gold and

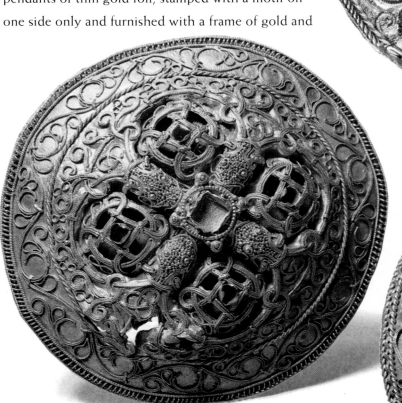

a loop for suspension. More than 900 gold bracteates have been found to date, occurring both as gravefinds and as hoards or sacrificial finds. The gold bracteates are a good example of a Roman type of object taken over and transformed by the Germanic goldsmiths. Four main groups of motifs are present on the gold bracteates: a man's head in profile, a man's head above a quadruped, figural scenes with at least one human figure, and a stylized, ribbonlike animal figure. The iconography of the gold bracteates has been studied for a generation by the German scholar Dr. Karl Hauck. He interprets the majority of them as Odin amulets, emphasizing the different aspects of the god. With the deep sociopolitical changes both on the Continent and in the north Germanic societies

160 top *This brooch in filigree gold from the early eleventh century is completely covered with decorative concentric volute motifs and embellished with four green stones. Brooches such as this were used to fasten the cape in front.*

160 bottom *Intricate gold decoration characterizes these two round fibulae from Jutland, dating from around the year 1000.*

during the sixth century, the flow of gold dwindled and gold bracteates were produced only in Gotland.

During the centuries following the Great Migrations, gold was obviously scarcer than before and the goldsmiths became masters of gilding. The Viking attack on the monastery of the holy St.Cuthbert, Lindisfarne, in the eighth century, was followed by the pillage of churches and monasteries where large treasures in gold and silver were kept.

When the Christianization of Scandinavia was fulfilled during the first half of the eleventh century, people no longer were buried in lavishly furnished graves or hoarded their treasures in bogs or under rocks. Several types of jewelry worn by Viking women went out of use; only the large disk brooch

continued to be made. With these splendid pieces of Scandinavian goldsmiths' art, the Viking Age came to an end. Churches and monasteries were built where pagan gods once were worshipped, and gold, the metal of the Germanic gods, was locked in treasuries to be shown only on special religious feasts, as symbols of the glory of the Christian God.

161 top *The band-shaped golden armring is from Råbylille, Seeland. The twisted golden neckring and armrings and the trefoil brooch all belong to the largest gold board from the Viking Age in Scandinavia, found in Hon, Buskerud, Norway. The spur, the circular belt loop, and the belt mount are a small gold board from Værnö Monastery, Vestfold, Norway.*

161 bottom *This drum brooch in gilded bronze with ornaments in gold, silver, and niello is of a type used only by the women of Gotland during the Viking Age to fasten the cape in front. Few drum brooches are of such exquisite craftsmanship as this example.*

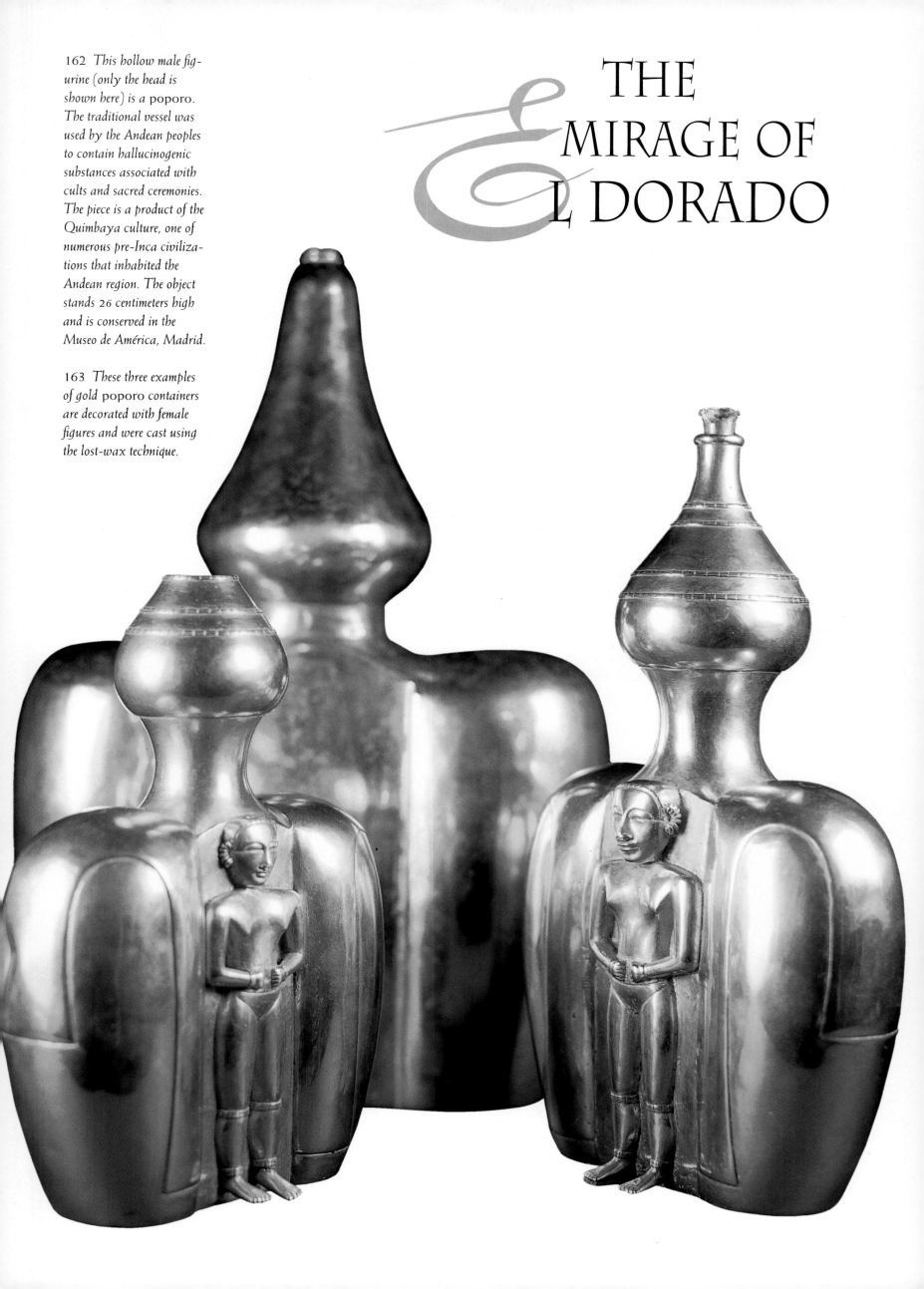

162 *This hollow male figurine (only the head is shown here) is a* poporo. *The traditional vessel was used by the Andean peoples to contain hallucinogenic substances associated with cults and sacred ceremonies. The piece is a product of the Quimbaya culture, one of numerous pre-Inca civilizations that inhabited the Andean region. The object stands 26 centimeters high and is conserved in the Museo de América, Madrid.*

163 *These three examples of gold* poporo *containers are decorated with female figures and were cast using the lost-wax technique.*

Gold, gold, and more gold. The Spanish conquistadores went looking for gold and found it. Columbus himself reported its presence again and again in his diaries. The gold mines of the Antilles multiplied but were soon exhausted.

After the conquest of Mexico and Peru, respectively domains of the Aztec and Inca, Hernán Cortés and Francisco Pizarro were able to find more mines and also to gain possession of huge quantities of gold and silver objects of all kinds; they had these works melted into ingots and sent to Europe. Today

164

we may be astonished and dismayed at their behavior, but it must be regarded as practically emblematic of the tragedy of the Conquista. The history of pre-Columbian goldworking and jewelry-making needs to be analyzed, not only in its own ambit but also in terms of repercussions and interaction with the victorious and destructive Spaniards.

So what did gold represent for the conquistadores? Of course, pure metal; but the destruction of refined works of art should not be interpreted

anachronistically and simply as evidence of ignorant disdain for a civilization. Gold, certainly: "To what do you not push the hearts of mortals, oh despicable hunger for gold?" (*Aeneid* III, 56–57). This was the gold that, once in Europe, was to produce one of the biggest and most widespread inflationary revolutions in history; followed by silver, which replaced it from about 1550 onward; and then the stones. This was gold seen by rapacious eyes and reduced to its natural state of precious metal, discarding all the symbolic and cultural values of the objects it had been used to make.

As Todorov tells us in his book on the subject, now considered a classic, the conquistadores were not men of uniform culture, but neither can they be lumped together as illiterate, uncouth soldiers. They were not unaware of the greatness of the civilizations they had conquered. They observed them with admiration and passed on faithful descriptions of them to the rest of the world. So why the destruction and violence? It is on the hard-to-find answer to this question that the whole interpretation of a complex phenomenon like the Conquista hinges. What was meant, for example, by the destruction of the statues in precious metals, of plants and animals, that decorated the garden of the Sun at Cuzco, by the Temple of the Sun? An expression of intolerance, a burst of uncontrolled, frenzied pillage? Was it pure plunder, or simply a grossly exaggerated evaluation of the material versus the object, the kind of evaluation that has always led people to melt down objects made of precious metals to make more modern ones, or to remount old stones to reflect new fashions?

And what, after all, was the significance of precious objects among the many pre-Columbian civilizations? It may be risky to generalize about the intricate fabric of civilizations that existed for millennia, right up until the sixteenth century. However, even for the pre-Columbian peoples, gold was first and foremost a sign of power and wealth: it was the favorite choice for the grave goods of leaders

165 This ceremonial vase in the form of a seated female figure also belongs to the rich Quimbaya treasure discovered in two Colombian tombs and composed of a series of gold poporo containers and other objects cast with the lost-wax technique. All of these pieces are distinguished by the excellent definition of the forms, especially the nude male and female figures generally portrayed in seated positions. The vase is 29.7 centimeters tall and weighs 1,150 grams. The treasure was discovered in 1891 and presented to the queen of Spain. It is today conserved in the Museo de América, Madrid.

165

167 right *This female statuette in gold is another relic of the La Tolita civilization. A correct interpretation of these technically sophisticated manufactures in precious metals is made all the more difficult by the problem of establishing precise dates, given the lack of scientific archaeological excavations. It is an accepted fact, however, that most of these relics predate the Christian era. This small idol stands 15 centimeters high and is conserved in the Bruning Museum, at Lambayeque.*

and warriors; it marked the distance between rulers and ruled; in objects for everyday use, it served to indicate differences in social status.

None of this alters the fact that gold could also be attributed enormous symbolic value, evident from the presence of countless ritual objects. Among the Aztecs, for example, it was connected with the season of the rains, which made the land fertile; and Xipe Totec, god of the rains, was also the protector of goldsmiths. Among the Incas, it was customary to place silver and gold, as well as coca leaves, in the mouths of the dead: these metals were evident symbols of the two contrasting universal principles (sun/moon, light/darkness). And what about Muiscas? A periodic rite was carried out by *caciques* (native leaders), or by princes about to ascend to the throne. With their bodies covered in gold dust, they plunged into the waters of sacred lakes and offered precious stones to the gods. This was the origin of the legend of El Dorado, the gilded man (dorado) lending his name to the fabulous country of gold: many expeditions searched for this place in vain, especially in the Orinoco lowlands, until the eighteenth century.

When examining the world of pre-Columbian goldworking and jewelry-making, we must take this complex cultural background into account; in addition, the finds on which we can base our arguments are indeed few. Most of the Ameri-

166 *This mask with a conspicuous* nariguera *(an ornament worn in the nose) is a relic of the La Tolita civilization, which flourished in the Esmeraldas region of Ecuador between 600 B.C. and 400 A.D.*

167 left *This medallion features skillfully alternating gold and platinum embossed and spiral decoration.*

168 *The ritual investiture of the sovereign of the Muisca tribe took place on Lake Guatavita in Colombia. The ceremony is symbolically represented in this exceptional gold miniature (20.5 centimeters long) conserved in the Bogotá Gold Museum. A number of persons are depicted on the raft, including one whose size identifies him as a cacique, or chief, and eleven other male figures. The Muisca civilization flourished between 700 and 1500 A.D.*

168–169 *This large semicircular gold earring with gold links was produced by the Sinú civilization, which flourished between 450 and 1500 A.D.*

168

can gold objects, now displayed in the world's museums—particularly in the Museo del Oro in Bogotá, the museum of the same name in Lima, and the Bruning Museum in Lambayeque, in Peru—are the outcome of archaeological finds made long after the discovery of these civilizations, some as late as our own century.

What's more, the two great "states" annihilated by the conquistadores in the sixteenth century— those of the Aztec and Inca—had, themselves, subjugated various peoples and civilizations, in territories and for periods it is not easy to reconstruct with precision. Nor should we forget, where gold objects and jewelry are concerned, the trade between different regions, the mobility of craftsmen, and the survival of techniques and styles passed down from one civilization to the next. Thus the Maya, whose territory offered no sizable gold mines, imported both metal and artifacts; the Aztec, warriors by vocation, used plundered jewelry

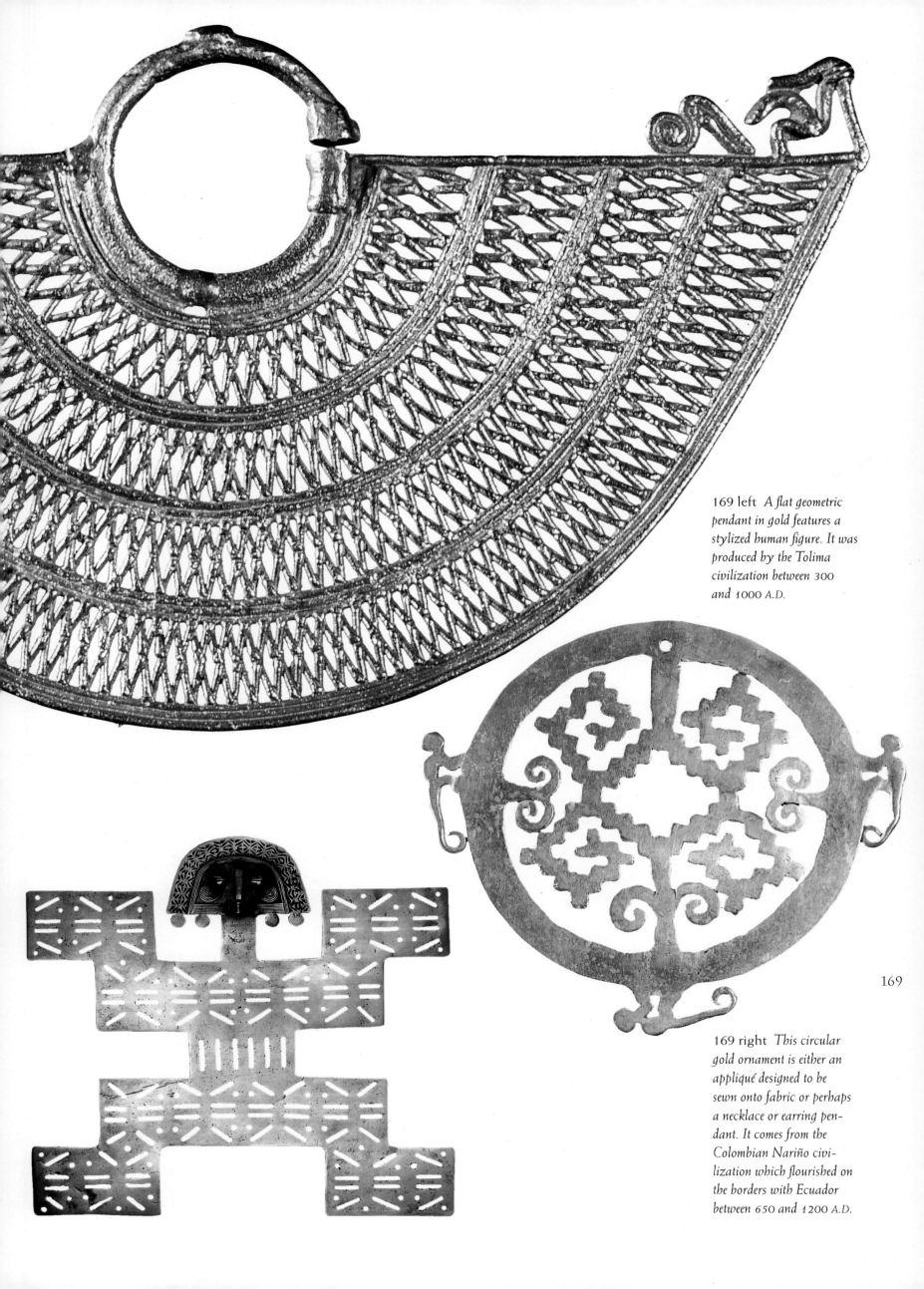

169 left A flat geometric pendant in gold features a stylized human figure. It was produced by the Tolima civilization between 300 and 1000 A.D.

169

169 right This circular gold ornament is either an appliqué designed to be sewn onto fabric or perhaps a necklace or earring pendant. It comes from the Colombian Nariño civilization which flourished on the borders with Ecuador between 650 and 1200 A.D.

170 and 171 bottom left *Large pins were very common ritual jewels produced by the Andean civilizations. Used to fasten clothing during ceremonies, they were, more importantly, employed to extract lime from the poporo containers to chew with coca leaves. The heads of the pins may be flat, domed, fitted with rattles,* *zoomorphic, or, as in these examples from the Colima civilization, anthropomorphic. These pieces are today conserved in the Bogotá Gold Museum. Hallucinogenic substances were and are widely used in the Andean region for the energy they provide. Together with gold, hallucinogens were symbolically associated with the power of the sovereign.*

170

171 top *This votive object (probably a pendant cast in an alloy of gold and copper) comes from the archaeological area of Tairona, in the north of Colombia on the Caribbean* *coast, and has a history dating to 500 A.D. The mythological figure is depicted wearing rich jewels and an elaborate headdress. It is holding a scepter in each hand.*

171

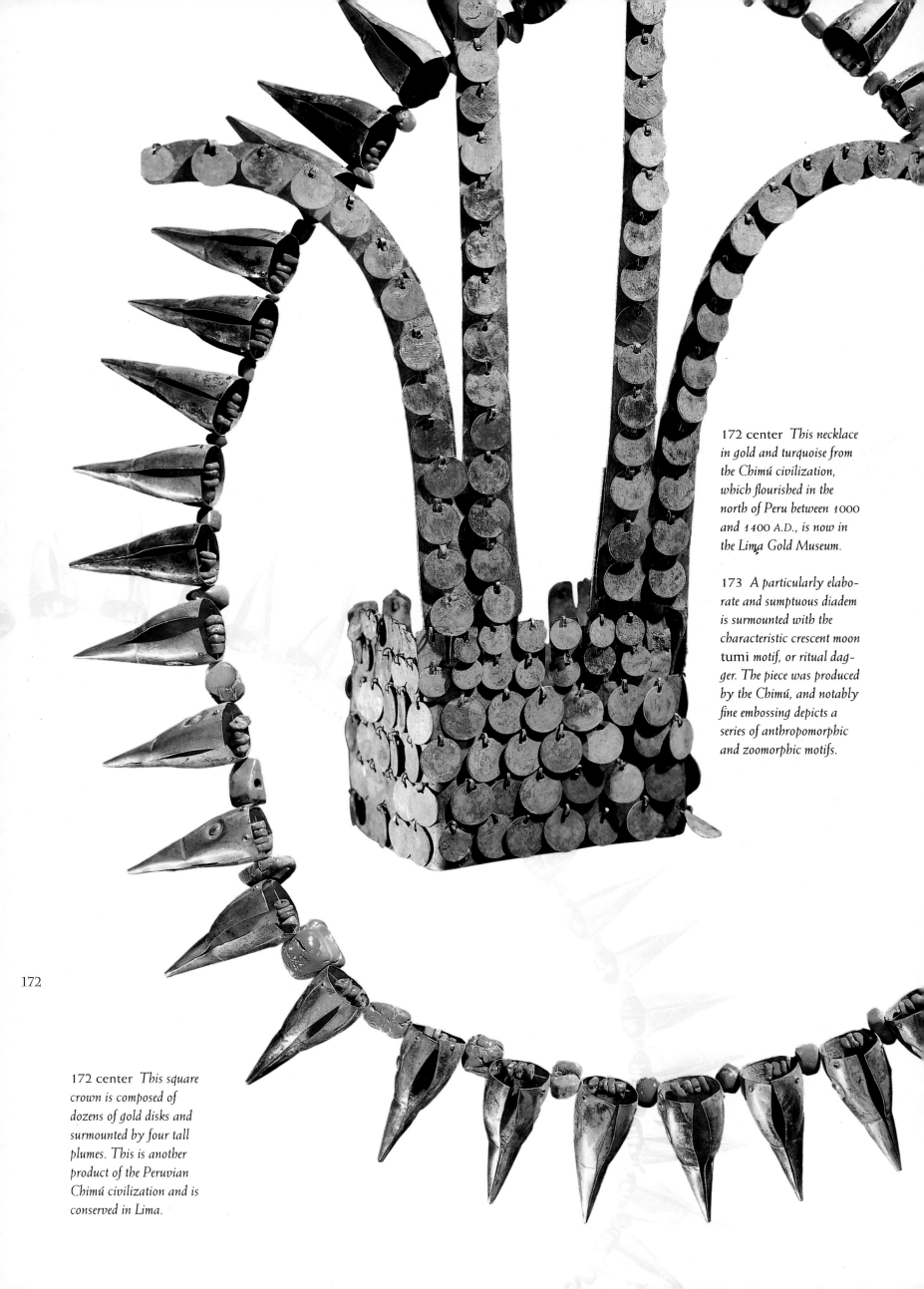

172

172 center *This necklace in gold and turquoise from the Chimú civilization, which flourished in the north of Peru between 1000 and 1400 A.D., is now in the Lima Gold Museum.*

173 *A particularly elaborate and sumptuous diadem is surmounted with the characteristic crescent moon tumi motif, or ritual dagger. The piece was produced by the Chimú, and notably fine embossing depicts a series of anthropomorphic and zoomorphic motifs.*

172 center *This square crown is composed of dozens of gold disks and surmounted by four tall plumes. This is another product of the Peruvian Chimú civilization and is conserved in Lima.*

174

174 bottom *This gold ceremonial vase embellished with turquoise is again a Chimú product and depicts a typical aristocratic figure with a severe and rigid expression.*

174–175 top *This gold funerary mask conserved in Lima was produced by a craftsman from the Andean Lambayeque civilization, documented between 700 and 1100 A.D. The elongated form of the eyes is typical of the anthropomorphic motifs used by this civilization.*

174–175 bottom
This magnificent rigid gold pectoral is also a Chimú product. The embossed motif of the crowned head of the sovereign is a design that frequently recurs.

175 right *This sacrificial knife or axe, known as a tumi, is one of the most significant relics of the Chimú. The gold and silver handle depicts the divinity with outspread arms holding two disks of uncertain symbolism, and wearing a crescent moon crown in filigree with inset turquoise. The piece, from the eighth century, is conserved in the Lima Gold Museum.*

176

176 The relics presented here are again products of the Chimú-Lambayeque people, who gave life to a vast kingdom extending for 700 kilometers along the northern coast of Peru. The gold ritual vase features an embossed male head mythicized with the "winged" eyes found on numerous other objects in metal and pottery.

177 top left This small bird-shaped vessel was used as a container in sacred ceremonies and is made of gold with turquoise eyes.

177 top and right This jar with a chamfered body is another ceremonial vessel, decorated with stylized anthropomorphic and zoomorphic figures. It stands 25 centimeters tall and is conserved in the Lima Gold Museum.

177 bottom The crested feline with a long tongue and curled tail is, together with the bird of prey, the jaguar, and the feline-fanged god, one of the recurrent motifs of the Andean mythical bestiary. This jewel is part of a ceremonial parure in gold and is 29 centimeters tall. It is today conserved in the Bruning Musuem, Lambayeque, and dates from 1200 to 1470 A.D.

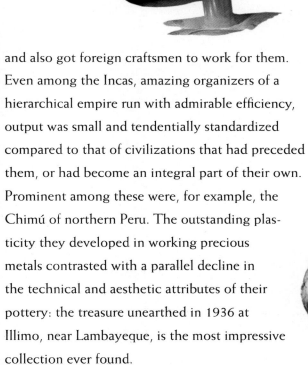

and also got foreign craftsmen to work for them. Even among the Incas, amazing organizers of a hierarchical empire run with admirable efficiency, output was small and tendentially standardized compared to that of civilizations that had preceded them, or had become an integral part of their own. Prominent among these were, for example, the Chimú of northern Peru. The outstanding plasticity they developed in working precious metals contrasted with a parallel decline in the technical and aesthetic attributes of their pottery: the treasure unearthed in 1936 at Illimo, near Lambayeque, is the most impressive collection ever found.

Other examples are offered by the Moche (Mochica) or by the Nazca civilization, further south, which produced fascinating objects distinguished by a profusion of zoomorphic decorations, and by use of the gold-leaf technique: typical of these objects are flat, stylized pendants, sometimes reminiscent of the mysterious animal-like figures

178–179 top *The Sun Cloak is a fabulous gold jewel that adorned the sovereign on the occasion of ceremonial rituals. It is part of a series of jewels, all in precious metals, produced by the Moche civilization that flourished in Peru between 200 B.C. and 600 A.D.*

178 bottom *A great number of different precious objects were produced by the Moche, including this diadem. It bears one of the most typical ornamental motifs used by coastal peoples on vases and sculpture, sacred and secular buildings, religious objects, and fabrics.*

that the Nazca traced in their desert. The Inca never conquered the territory of present-day Colombia which, on account of its rugged and inaccessible terrain, was not the cultural link that might have been expected between South America and Mesoamerica. Preeminent in this region was the Muisca (or Chibcha) culture on the meseta of Bogotá, or the splendid Quimbaya civilization, in the middle and upper valley of the river Cauca. Stunning surviving objects created by both these peoples possibly represent the aesthetic zenith of pre-Columbian goldwork.

Expertise was developed in all techniques; frequent use was made of the lost-wax process; the art of gilding copper and silver was known to them. Materials worked in addition to gold were platinum, silver, and *tumbaga* (copper and gold alloy). Polychromy was not infrequent, using stones (turquoise, emerald, lapis lazuli), corals, shells, and vegetable dyes fixed to the metal with complicated chemical processes. Prevailing among stylistic trends were a taste for eye-catching ornamentation (in particular with beautifully executed repoussé) and accentuated use of geometric

178–179 bottom
Geometric motifs and
anthropomorphic figures
alternate in the decoration
of this Moche gold scepter.
It is conserved, along with
most of the other relics of
this civilization, in the
Lima Gold Museum.

179 One of the strangest objects produced by most of the Andean peoples was the instrument for depilation: this example in gold and turquoise is composed of a blade in the form of a two-headed snake with a human figure at the center. It was used as a pendant and, judging by the numerous examples found, it was a common object.

shapes (often with infinite repetition of the same element: metal strip, leaf, simple decorative motifs).

What remained of pre-Columbian tradition in the splendid colonial goldwork that flourished in both civil and religious life? In many of its manifestations, Latin American civilization was, and still is, a hybrid, a lively synthesis of various cultures. It is, therefore, hardly surprising that precious metalwork in Spanish America in the sixteenth and seventeenth centuries, encouraged by intensive

silver mining, was informed by the techniques of both victor and vanquished. On one hand, the ornate taste of Spanish goldwork was exported to America, and European techniques generally asserted their superiority. On the other hand, in areas such as cutting and mounting precious stones and polishing metals, the craftsmen of Indio origin, with their more accomplished working methods, had the upper hand. Colonial goldwork acquired its own distinctive physiognomy, even recognized back in Spain, to which large numbers of objects were exported. Its distinguishing traits were over-emphatic baroque ornamentation verging on the scholastic and provincial, combined with the zoomorphic and floral designs much favored in indigenous art, and certain tendentiously un-European proportions (particularly evident in objects created for clients of a lower social rank, living in outlying places).

180 top left A rigid gold bracelet with relief decoration produced by the Nazca, also known as the Paraca, who lived in the central Andes between 400 B.C. and 550 A.D.

180 top right This ceremonial vase in gold, a relic of the Nazca civilization, is characterized by a body made of concentric degrading volumes.

180 bottom Reproduced here in beaten and soldered gold and silver, llamas were held to be sacred animals by the Inca and were the property of the emperor. They were frequently used during ceremonies to evoke fertility. Small examples of this kind of statuette have, in fact, been found buried in fields to encourage abundant harvests.

180

181 left *This female idol in gold is a typical example of an Inca votive statuette found in the rare tombs and sanctuaries that survived the fury of the Spanish conquistadores. This object is exhibited in the Archaeological Museum at Cuzco.*

181 right *This small male statue, again in gold, belongs to the same culture and is today conserved in the Lima Gold Museum. The Inca expansion began around the middle of the fifteenth century before the civilization was wiped out by the Spanish conquistador Francisco Pizarro in 1532.*

THE TREASURE OF SIPÁN

182 and 183 The striking grimace of this feline divinity in gilded copper with red shell, turquoise, and colored stones characterizes one of the most potent and enig-matic pieces among those found in the tomb of the Old Lord of Sipán. The full-length view shows the two-headed serpent decorating the forehead, the crown covering the head, the human limbs which terminate in accu-rately embossed feline paws and claws. The closeup of the face highlights the con-cave pupils and the presence of double ears: according to shamanic and esoteric beliefs, the right eye symbol-izes extrasensory perception and the double ears mark a heightened power of hearing.

184 and 185 *Among the objects displaying the highest levels of craftsmanship found in the tomb of the Old Lord of Sipán is this gold ritual scepter-knife decorated with relief scenes. It depicts a richly dressed warrior chieftain falling with notable violence upon a seated prisoner pleading at his feet. The silver handle of the royal scepter carries exquisite relief decoration depicting a military costume complete with a crescent-moon-shaped helmet, throat and neck guards, breastplate, and shield.*

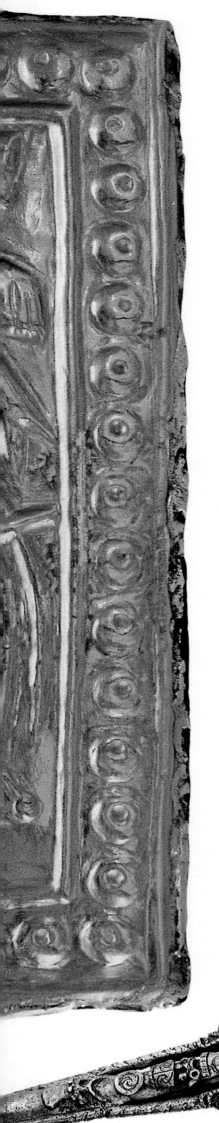

A priceless contribution to our gradually increasing knowledge of the pre-Columbian civilizations is made by archaeological excavations. In Peru, in particular, several schemes conducted in the 1970s and 1980s produced interesting results. It was during one of these systematic excavation programs that the tombs of Sipán, not far from Lambayeque in northern Peru, came to light. This amazing discovery, in 1987, came about due to the efforts of Peruvian archaeologist Walter Alva, director of the Bruning Museum, where most of the pieces unearthed are now housed.

Never before had such an important archaeological discovery been made in Peru. Among three still-intact tombs found on the site was the burial place of a Moche notable. In it was a rich collection of grave goods, including various priceless pieces made of gold, silver, and gilded copper. In terms of importance, the find can justifiably be compared with Howard Carter's discovery of the tomb of Tutankhamen in 1922.

In Peru, as in Egypt, archaeological treasures had for centuries offered easy prey for predators with varying levels of interest in antiquity. After the conquistadores came despicable grave robbers, called *huaqueros* (from *huaca*, an Indio tomb, among the Moche a small pyramid made of unfired earth

bricks). After being informed by the police about the presence on the black market of exceptionally valuable pieces (including a mask with eyes of lapis lazuli), Alva decided to press on with his search, digging deeper and deeper until the discovery of the tomb of the Lord of Sipán, as it was later called. It was assumed the tomb's occupant, a man about age 35, had been a prominent political figure in the city. Later (the discovery was announced in 1990), Alva's team unearthed another tomb, that of the "Old Lord of Sipán." Its occupant was presumed to be a less important notable: nevertheless, the grave goods buried with him consisted of about 150 pieces of gold, silver, and copper.

The importance of the discovery goes far beyond the history of goldworking and jewelry making. Excavation continues and other discoveries are expected. The three tombs so far unearthed (including a third one known as "the Tomb of the Priest") provide an insight into the lifestyle of the Moche (or Mochica) people, a primarily agricultural civilization that developed along the northern shores of Peru between 100 and 700 A.D. This civilization was known to us mainly through its pottery: scenes painted on vases or realistically portrayed by statuettes (some of distinctly erotic content) provided a picture of the Moche and the way they lived.

186–187 Perhaps the most precious object from the funerary cache found in the tomb of the Old Lord of Sipán is this extremely rich earring pendant in gold and turquoise. The jewel is a circular ornament with a diameter of 92 millimeters, framed by a ring of gold spheres. A representation of an elaborately adorned warrior chieftain is at the center, displaying all the attributes of power on his face and in his hands. This is a true three-dimensional micro-sculpture rendered with remarkable realism.

187 Another pair of circular ornaments sur-rounded the skull of the lord. Simpler but still displaying fine crafts-manship, a mosaic of gold and turquoise depicts a water bird that is now extinct but often seen in the local iconography.

188

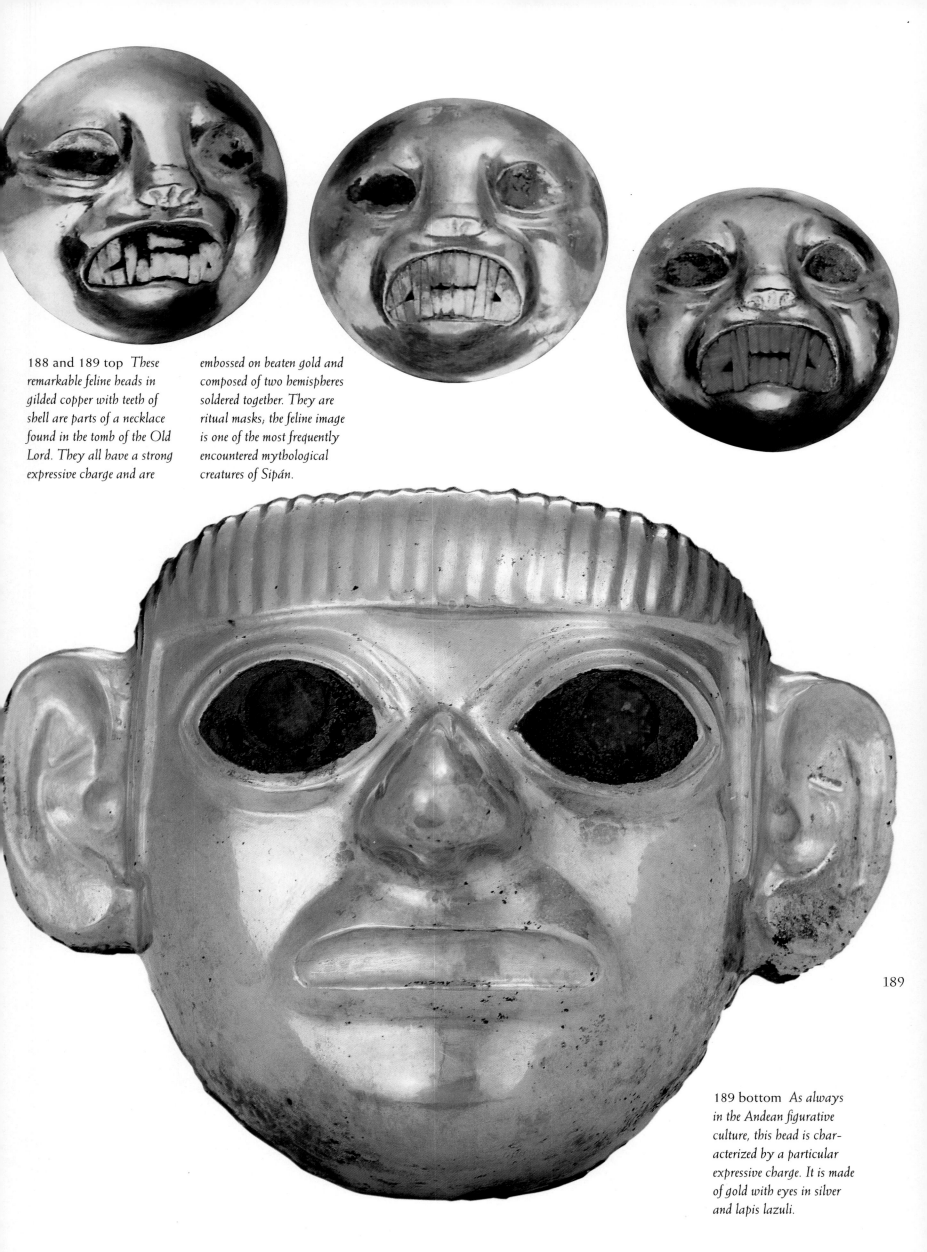

188 and 189 top *These remarkable feline heads in gilded copper with teeth of shell are parts of a necklace found in the tomb of the Old Lord. They all have a strong expressive charge and are* embossed on beaten gold and composed of two hemispheres soldered together. They are ritual masks; the feline image is one of the most frequently encountered mythological creatures of Sipán.

189 bottom *As always in the Andean figurative culture, this head is characterized by a particular expressive charge. It is made of gold with eyes in silver and lapis lazuli.*

190 This statue of a warrior in gilded copper, standing 27.4 centimeters high, depicts the upright figure of a guardian with a crescent-shaped headdress. The figure is holding a kind of mace in his hands that lends him a rather martial air. This figure was part of a richly ornate standard that, together with other emblems, harnesses, and offerings, composed the cache of the tomb of the Old Lord of Sipán.

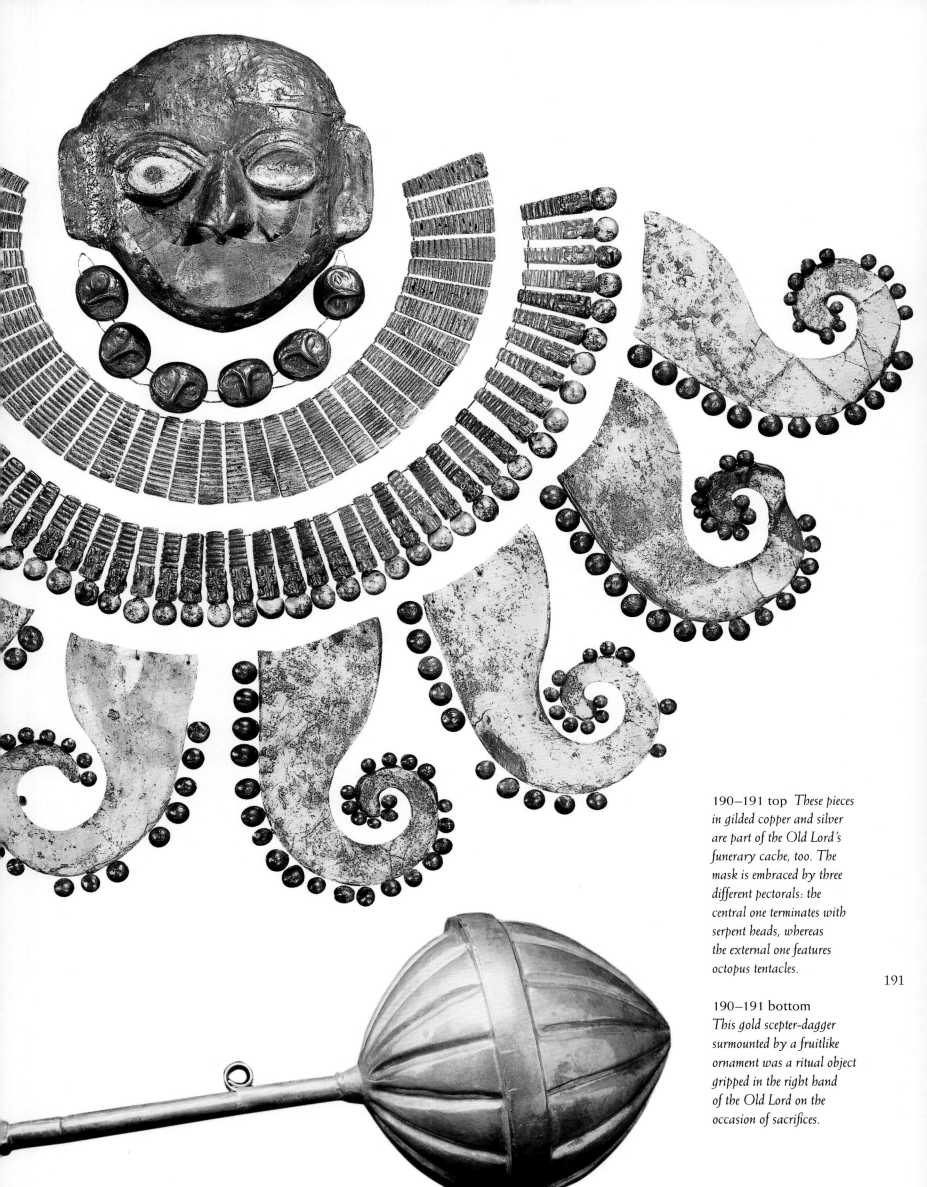

190–191 top *These pieces in gilded copper and silver are part of the Old Lord's funerary cache, too. The mask is embraced by three different pectorals: the central one terminates with serpent heads, whereas the external one features octopus tentacles.*

190–191 bottom *This gold scepter-dagger surmounted by a fruitlike ornament was a ritual object gripped in the right hand of the Old Lord on the occasion of sacrifices.*

The tombs now offer—or confirm—various elements of the culture's social life. Beside the wooden chest containing the remains of the Old Lord of Sipán are the skeletons of three women, possibly his concubines, and those of four men, who were meant to follow the lord in death. The left feet of a woman and a man are missing, both feet of two other men (possibly the guardians) are missing too, as symbolically preventing their fleeing. There are also the bones of a child aged about 10, a dog, and two llamas. Having no written sources to consult, we can but make guesses about the identity of this "lord" and his position in life. It has been suggested, on the basis of similarities between the grave goods and objects present on decorated ceramics, that the two dead men were warrior-priests responsible for the sacrifice of enemies. However, items discovered to date have proved beyond all doubt that the Moche firmly believed in life after death: in the tomb of the Old Lord of Sipán there are also containers with remains of food, clearly intended to provide sustenance for the deceased.

From an aesthetic standpoint the jewels of Sipán have two main features: experimentation with polychromy and repetition of the same decorative motif. On occasions these two forms of expression are found in the same piece, for instance the "groundnut" necklace (groundnuts were one of the crops grown by the Moche, and accounted for a significant portion of their diet), half gold, half silver. An idol instead displays the eye-catching effects produced by shells and stones on its face;

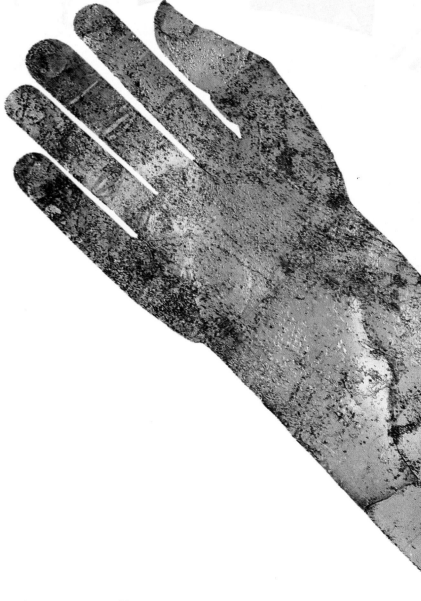

192

193 top *The technical virtuosity of the goldsmiths of Sipán can be admired in this remarkable* nariguera, *or nose ornament, in gold, silver, and turquoise. It depicts a warrior chieftain with a fighting stick and shield. Minuscule earrings and a* nariguera *in gold are part of his sumptuous costume which culminates in a crown in the form of an owl with huge outspread wings made of sheets of gold that vibrate in imitation of the bird's plumage. It has been suggested that this opulent effigy is a portrait of the Old Lord of Sipán.*

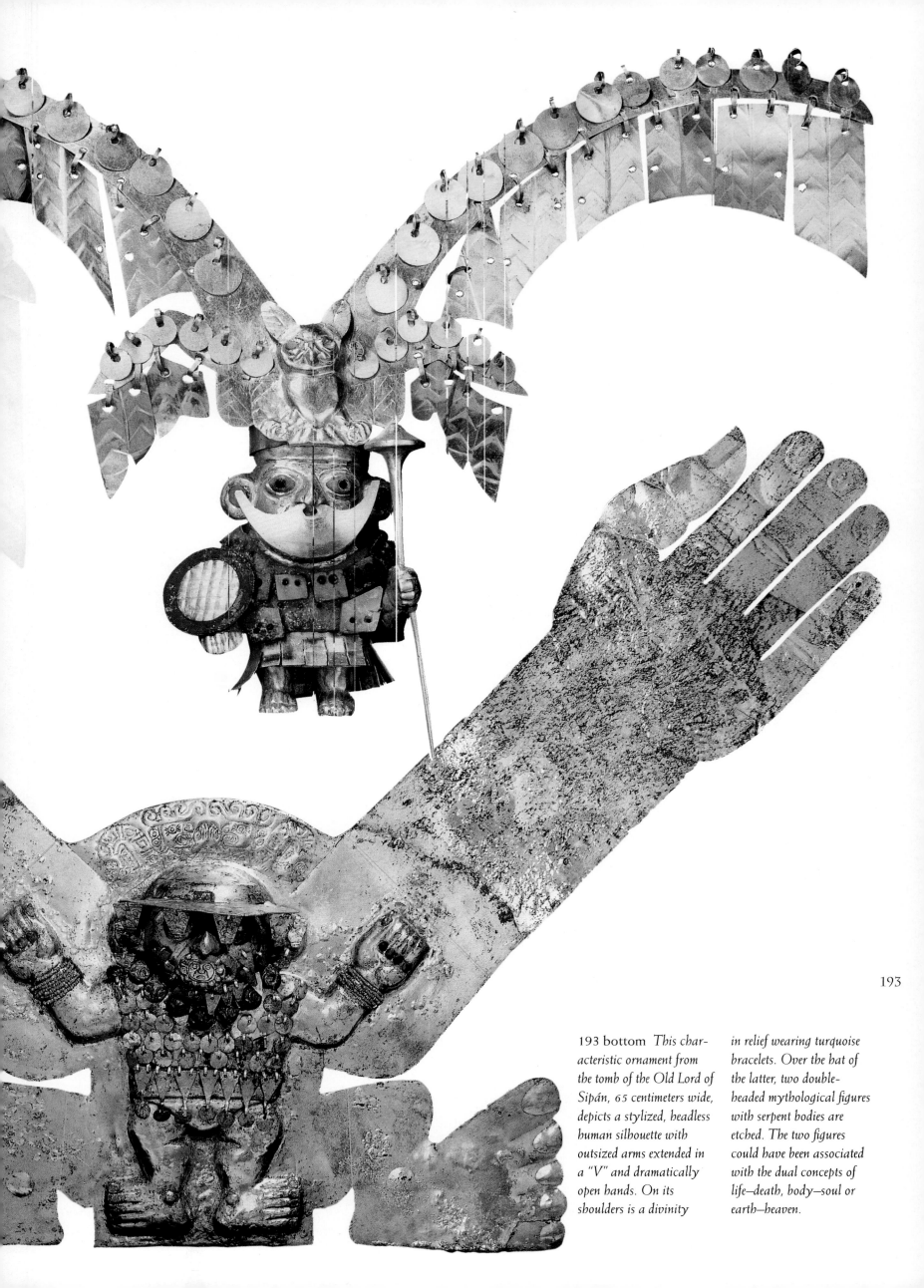

193 bottom This characteristic ornament from the tomb of the Old Lord of Sipán, 65 centimeters wide, depicts a stylized, headless human silhouette with outsized arms extended in a "V" and dramatically open hands. On its shoulders is a divinity in relief wearing turquoise bracelets. Over the hat of the latter, two double-headed mythological figures with serpent bodies are etched. The two figures could have been associated with the dual concepts of life–death, body–soul or earth–heaven.

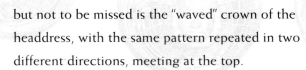

but not to be missed is the "waved" crown of the headdress, with the same pattern repeated in two different directions, meeting at the top.

Polychromy is produced by using both different metals and precious stones and shells, sometimes imported by the Moche from far-off regions. In some cases—for instance, with the idol already mentioned—the objective was to combine different colors, albeit symmetrically arranged; in others, striking bichromic effects were favored (gold and turquoise, for example). Further evidence of the attention paid by the Moche to color comes from the frequent and expertly executed gilding of silver and copper: they used electrolytic and chemical processes, and fixed the results with heat.

Their practice of repeating the same decorative motif is seen, for example, on the spheres of circular ornaments, or in the repetition of large trinkets

195 *This circular standard in gold representing the "ulluchus" fruit divinity is framed by reliefs depicting the same mythical fruit. Today extinct, this fruit is often encountered in* the figurative art of the Moche people. Its anticoagulant properties meant that it was used in sacrificial rituals in which the blood of prisoners was customarily drunk.

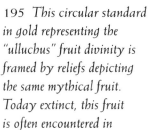

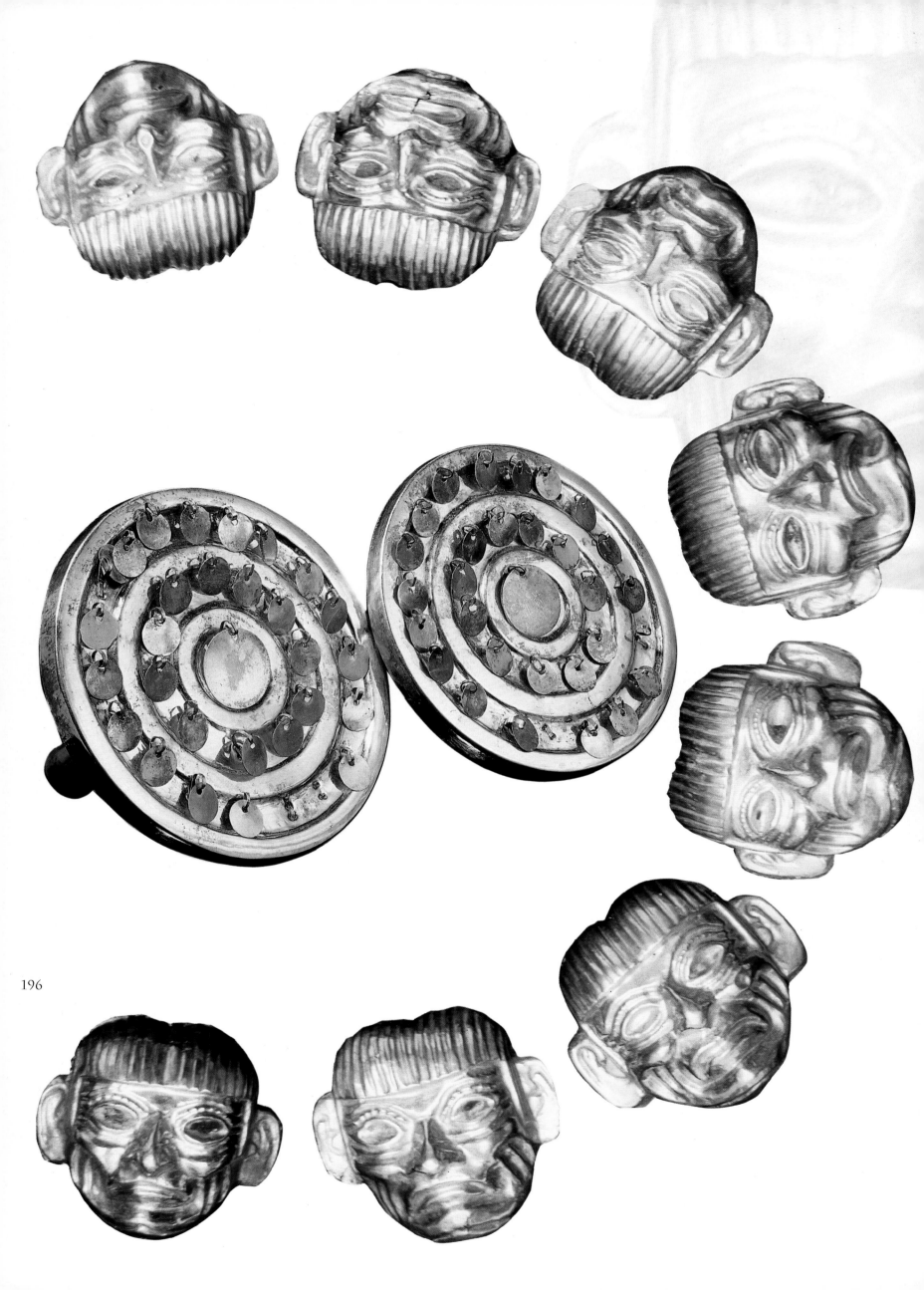

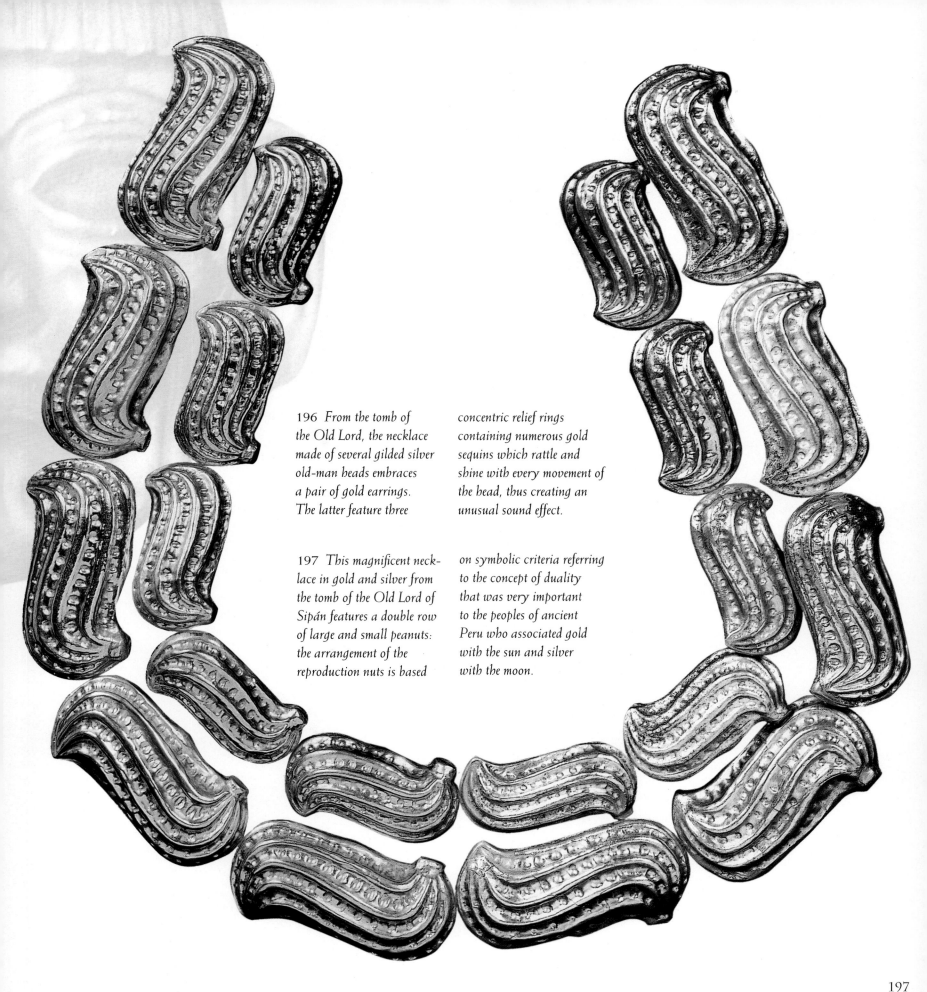

196 From the tomb of
the Old Lord, the necklace
made of several gilded silver
old-man heads embraces
a pair of gold earrings.
The latter feature three
concentric relief rings
containing numerous gold
sequins which rattle and
shine with every movement of
the head, thus creating an
unusual sound effect.

197 This magnificent necklace in gold and silver from
the tomb of the Old Lord of
Sipán features a double row
of large and small peanuts:
the arrangement of the
reproduction nuts is based
on symbolic criteria referring
to the concept of duality
that was very important
to the peoples of ancient
Peru who associated gold
with the sun and silver
with the moon.

in necklaces, or of patterns, such as crests of waves
again, on a breastplate.

A strong sense of self-awareness is evident in
the Moche practice of modeling jewelry and
adornments on themselves. In a large pendant
depicting a warrior, we see objects (the scepter
and necklace in particular) found in the tombs,
and the same goes for tiny statuettes of warriors,
especially a *nariguera*, wearing a nose decoration.

It is possible that these images are connected
with some particular belief, or are instead to be
interpreted as portraits of the deceased; it is
nevertheless certain that we cannot classify as
primitive an art form capable of reproducing the
culture in scale, with precision, by associating
the real (the dead man in his tomb) and the
imaginary (the idea and reproduction of the
universals of the lord and the warrior).

THE TREASURE DESIRED BY THEODELINDA

Among cathedral treasures, that of the Basilica of St. John the Baptist at Monza is distinguished by the remoteness of its origins, the magnificence of its gold and silver, the continuity of its presence on the same site, and for its close ties with the history of the kingdom of Italy because of the Iron Crown. The history of the treasure is a history of gestures of devotion, of obedience to vows, and of demonstrations of pride that have contributed to the formation of a collection of sophisticated beauty.

Such was the importance attached by the city and its church to the treasure that it is depicted at the entrance to the basilica, sculptured in 1320 with archaistic taste but notarial precision in the lunette of the main door. Those who commissioned the lunette had Theodelinda, the queen of the Lombards and the founder of the basilica, portrayed in the act of consigning the Iron Crown and a cross to St. John the Baptist. The chalices, the Cross of the Kingdom, and

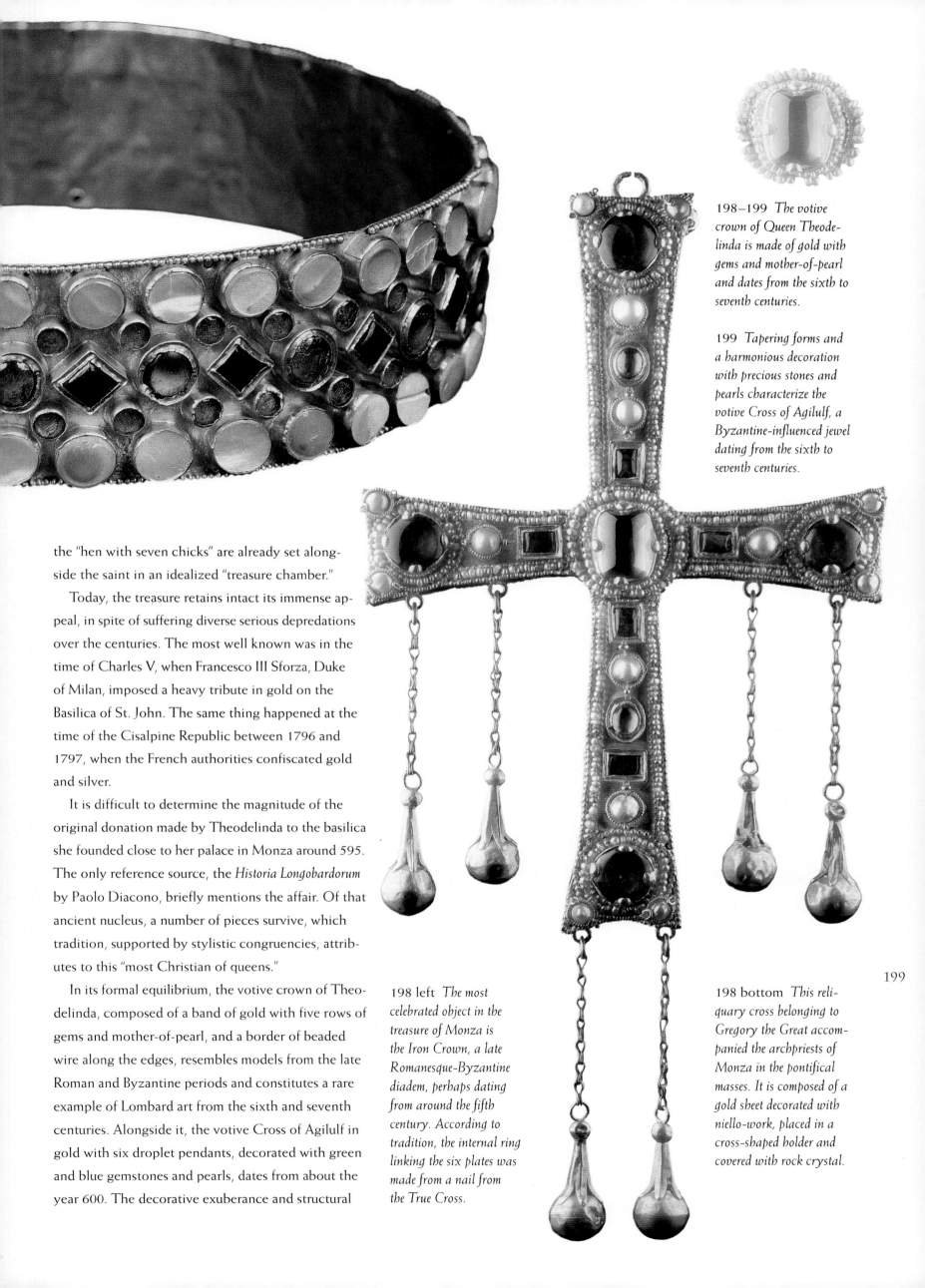

198–199 *The votive crown of Queen Theodelinda is made of gold with gems and mother-of-pearl and dates from the sixth to seventh centuries.*

199 *Tapering forms and a harmonious decoration with precious stones and pearls characterize the votive Cross of Agilulf, a Byzantine-influenced jewel dating from the sixth to seventh centuries.*

the "hen with seven chicks" are already set alongside the saint in an idealized "treasure chamber."

Today, the treasure retains intact its immense appeal, in spite of suffering diverse serious depredations over the centuries. The most well known was in the time of Charles V, when Francesco III Sforza, Duke of Milan, imposed a heavy tribute in gold on the Basilica of St. John. The same thing happened at the time of the Cisalpine Republic between 1796 and 1797, when the French authorities confiscated gold and silver.

It is difficult to determine the magnitude of the original donation made by Theodelinda to the basilica she founded close to her palace in Monza around 595. The only reference source, the *Historia Longobardorum* by Paolo Diacono, briefly mentions the affair. Of that ancient nucleus, a number of pieces survive, which tradition, supported by stylistic congruencies, attributes to this "most Christian of queens."

In its formal equilibrium, the votive crown of Theodelinda, composed of a band of gold with five rows of gems and mother-of-pearl, and a border of beaded wire along the edges, resembles models from the late Roman and Byzantine periods and constitutes a rare example of Lombard art from the sixth and seventh centuries. Alongside it, the votive Cross of Agilulf in gold with six droplet pendants, decorated with green and blue gemstones and pearls, dates from about the year 600. The decorative exuberance and structural

198 left *The most celebrated object in the treasure of Monza is the Iron Crown, a late Romanesque-Byzantine diadem, perhaps dating from around the fifth century. According to tradition, the internal ring linking the six plates was made from a nail from the True Cross.*

198 bottom *This reliquary cross belonging to Gregory the Great accompanied the archpriests of Monza in the pontifical masses. It is composed of a gold sheet decorated with niello-work, placed in a cross-shaped holder and covered with rock crystal.*

200 *The gold reliquary of St. John the Baptist (ninth century) takes the form of a purse studded with gemstones and pearls, at the center of which is set a large garnet in an exposed mount. The free spaces are covered with a dense pattern of filigree and the embossed reverse side depicts a crucifixion. Among the countless gems, two are inscribed with Kufic characters, one of which exalts Allah.*

harmony of the piece reveal a Byzantine taste that by no means excludes the possibility that it was made in a goldsmith's workshop in northern Italy.

A cup that was once thought to be of sapphire due to the intense blue of the blown and cut glass is also associated with the queen. Tradition has it that she drank from this cup with her fiancé, the future King Agilulf, during their first meeting at Lomello, thus sealing their engagement. The piece is a rare and precious example of Roman glassworking of the Augustan Age, while the Renaissance stem in lost-wax technique and chased gold is the fruit of a restoration undertaken late in the fifteenth century.

A different symbolic value is attributed to the "hen with seven chicks," one of the most unusual and enigmatic pieces in the treasure of the Duomo of Monza. The life-size hen is made of embossed, chased, and gilded silver with a sophisticated technique that succeeds in realistically reproducing the plumage and anatomical details of the bird. The chicks are, on the other hand, distinguished by accentuated stylization. One interpretation of the group suggests that it represents the queen surrounded by the Lombard dukes. A more pertinent, if less appealing, version identifies the composition as a symbol of the Church gathering the faithful around itself.

and is a sacred symbol of the kingdom of Italy. It is a diadem dating from late antiquity, probably made around the fifth century, possibly at Constantinople. Composed of six curved rectangular plates, the crown is 15 centimeters in diameter and 5.3 centimeters high. Originally, there were eight plates linked by hinges. Each plate features decoration composed of three aligned gems and a central cabochon set amid four embossed gold rosettes arranged in a cross. Green, blue, and white enamels trace ramifications, spreading out symmetrically from the central gem. A circlet of white metal set inside the crown prevents the plates from moving; legend has it that this is a relic of one of the nails used in the Crucifixion of Christ and forged into a diadem for Constantine by his mother Helen.

In 603, having received news of the baptism of Adaloald, heir to the Lombard throne, Pope Gregory the Great sent a number of precious gifts to his mother, Theodelinda. These included a reliquary of the True Cross composed of a thick, carved piece of rock crystal; it is adorned with a crucifixion scene in niello-work on sheet gold, with a cruciform case in gold. The panel closing the rear of the reliquary is decorated with plant motif friezes on a pointillé background. This small reliquary was used with great solemnity by the archpriests of the Duomo of Monza as a pectoral cross; in January 1963, Pope Paul VI decided to carry it with him on his journey to Palestine.

Another object traditionally recognized as being a gift from Pope Gregory the Great to Theodelinda is a sumptuous bookbinding in sheet gold with gems and cameos dating from the Roman era. The arrangement of the decoration on both plates is symmetrical, the classical composition being characterized by an extreme severity combined with echoes of Byzantine forms and motifs typical of barbarian art. The gold fillet running across both sides carries a dedication from the queen and was inserted when the piece was donated to the Basilica of St. John.

The beauty and prestige of the Iron Crown are impossible to resist. The jewel is the pride of Monza

201

201 *The Cross of the Kingdom is made of gold with the front face richly embellished by gemstones and pearls. An oval amethyst hangs from the lower arm, a Roman gem from the third century A.D. with the figure of Artemis engraved on it.*

Whatever the origins of the relic, the history of
the crown is to be seen in relation to that of Monza
as the "capital of the kingdom" and the setting for
the coronation ceremonies of the kings of Italy.
The tradition of coronations at Monza dates at least
as far back as 1026, when the archbishop of Milan,
Aribert, crowned the emperor Conrad II. During the
age of the Lombard city-states it was Frederick
Barbarossa who received the sacred diadem, succeeded by Charles IV of Luxembourg in 1355,
Frederick III of Hapsburg in 1453, Charles V in
1530, Napoleon Bonaparte in 1805, and Ferdinand
of Austria in 1838.

Three centuries after the donation by Theodelinda, Berengar I, crowned king of
Italy around 888,

expanded the treasury with a conspicuous donation
of furnishings and other sumptuous objects. Among
these was the Cross of the Kingdom, a large reliquary of the True Cross; it has arms of equal length
on which gems and pearls are set according to a precise chromatic rhythm on three levels raised by low
arches. At the intersection of the arms, a stone rose
with a magnificent sapphire in the center takes pride
of place. The cross is to be seen in close relation
with the "baglike" reliquary of St. John, glowing with
stones, pearls, and filigree-work that betray the barbarian taste for excess. The careful arrangement of
the gems that radiate outward from a central garnet

creates an eight-pointed star effect on the front of
the piece. On the rear is a solemn, punched
crucifixion that can be traced back to late
Carolingian models.

While the age of the Viscontis has
left the Duomo with examples of
supreme Gothic goldsmithing, the
successive eras were no less generous in terms of
donations to the treasure. One of the last was
made by one of the archpriests of the Duomo,
Pietro Crugnola who, in 1808, bequeathed a
chalice, a magnificent example of the art of the
Hungarian goldsmiths.

204–205 One of the most famous objects from the treasury of Monza is the splendid gospel cover presented by Pope Gregory the Great to Queen Theodelinda in 603. The cover is composed of a sheet of gold with gems, engraved cameos, and pearls. The decoration combines Classical, Byzantine, and barbarian motifs.

202 This "hen with seven chicks" is made of beaten and gilded silver on a wooden frame; the hen's eyes are garnets and the left eye (reproduced below) is engraved with the figure of a warrior. The chicks' eyes are blue glass. Tradition has it that this ensemble, found in the sarcophagus of Theodelinda, represents the queen and the seven counties of her realm. (See accompanying text for other explanatory legends.) According to a Lombard custom, the dead were buried with a chicken at their feet, symbol of the birth of a new life.

203 These two chalices are representative of the rich cache of liturgical objects conserved in the treasury of Monza: at left, a chalice in silver, filigree, emeralds, and pearls from the Hungarian sanctuary of Szèkelymàrk dates from 1510. On the right, the "sapphire cup," a Roman glass vessel colored with cobalt, is from the first century, with a gold stem from the fifteenth century.

VENICE AND BYZANTIUM IN SAINT MARK'S TREASURE

206 *This icon, perhaps a rich Bible cover, comes from Constantinople and dates from the late tenth century. It features a bust of the Archangel Michael with sharply defined facial features, surrounded by effigies of saints within*

gold medallions. The piece is in gilded silver with inserts in cloisonné enamel, precious stones, pearls, and vitreous paste.

207 *This icon represents a full-length figure of St. Michael in a solemn*

pose; the symbolic setting evokes a paradisaical garden. This splendid jewel, like most of those documented here, arrived in Venice as the spoils of the Fourth Crusade conducted at Constantinople in 1204.

The treasure of St. Mark's is composed of a collection of 283 pieces in silver, gold, semiprecious stones, glass, and other precious materials. It is conserved in three chambers (the Ante-Treasury, the Sanctuary, and the Treasury) within the powerful northwestern tower of the Parteciaco doges' Castellum Ducale (ninth century). The nucleus of the oldest pieces was put together at the time of the sack of Constantinople (1204–1261), the conquest of Tyre, and, subsequently, the abandonment of Candia (Crete): on this occasion numerous priceless objects flowed into Venice. Later, the gifts of popes and princes, purchases, and bequests were added. Entrusted to the care of the procurators of St. Mark's, the Treasury was opened only five times a year on ceremonial occasions.

The fall of the Venetian Republic in 1797 was a veritable coup de grâce for the Marciano Treasury; on the orders of the new French government, the precious manufactures were transported to the Zecca (the mint) and dismantled: the precious metal was valued at 29,223 ducats, and the pearls and precious stones at around 30,000 ducats. When the Austrian government was installed at Venice, it had all the jewels restored to the Basilica. In 1806 the Municipality of Venice passed back into the hands of the French until 1814 and the fall of Napoleon. When it once again fell under Austrian domination, a sale of pearls and precious stones was arranged to raise funds for urgent repairs to the Basilica.

With the treasure having been returned to its original and restored chambers, the *Pala d'Oro*, or gold altarpiece, was itself restored with the replacement of a number of missing precious stones between 1836 and 1842. In 1901 the halls of the Museo Marciano were opened, annexed to the Treasury for the exhibition of paintings, antique

mosaics, sacred furnishings, tapestries, carpets and, from 1983, the famous bronze horses. At the Cloisters in New York, we can admire an unimaginable concentration of the sacred arts of the Western medieval period; likewise, the Treasury of St. Mark's boasts the richest collection of the work of goldsmiths, silversmiths, and gem cutters. All the most refined work produced for the churches and palaces of Byzantium, as well as the cream of the Western medieval and Renaissance work of Europe, is conserved in the Treasury. The Marciano Treasury contains the icon of the Madonna of Nicopeia, the work of a Byzantine painter from the tenth century inspired by the enthroned Madonna in mosaic above the south door of Hagia Sophia in Constantinople. Due to its remarkable beauty, the icon was believed to be *achiopìta*; that is to say, not created by human hands but rather by the Apostle Luke through divine inspiration.

However, the most precious, most sophisticated and most important jewel, the fruit of the metaphysical genius of Byzantium and the cult of light as an anagogical element and prerequisite of the Western Gothic style, is the *Pala d'Oro* placed above the slab of the high altar that covers the sarcophagus containing the relics of St. Mark. The doge Ordelaffo Falier commissioned the *Pala* in 1105: three registers illustrate the announcement of the coming of Christ by the Prophets; the revelation of Christ's presence on Earth, expressed by the Pantocrator dominating the center of the *Pala*; the four Evangelists and the twelve Apostles; and the Parousia symbolized by the throne ready (Etimasia) for the second coming of Christ, worshipped by the cherubim, angels, and archangels. In 1105 these cloisonné enamels, all clearly Byzantine, were mounted in a more sober frame. In 1209, when the Venetians imported seven large cloisonné and found

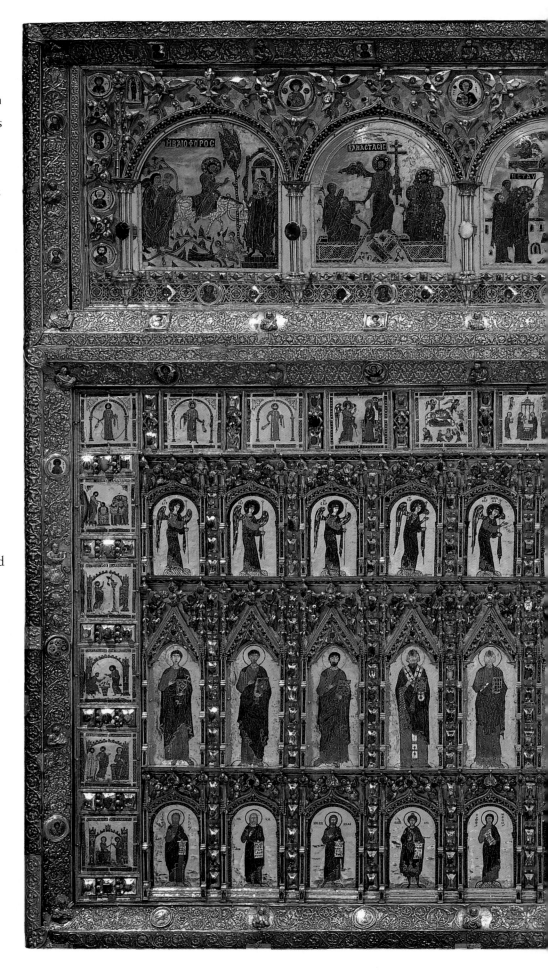

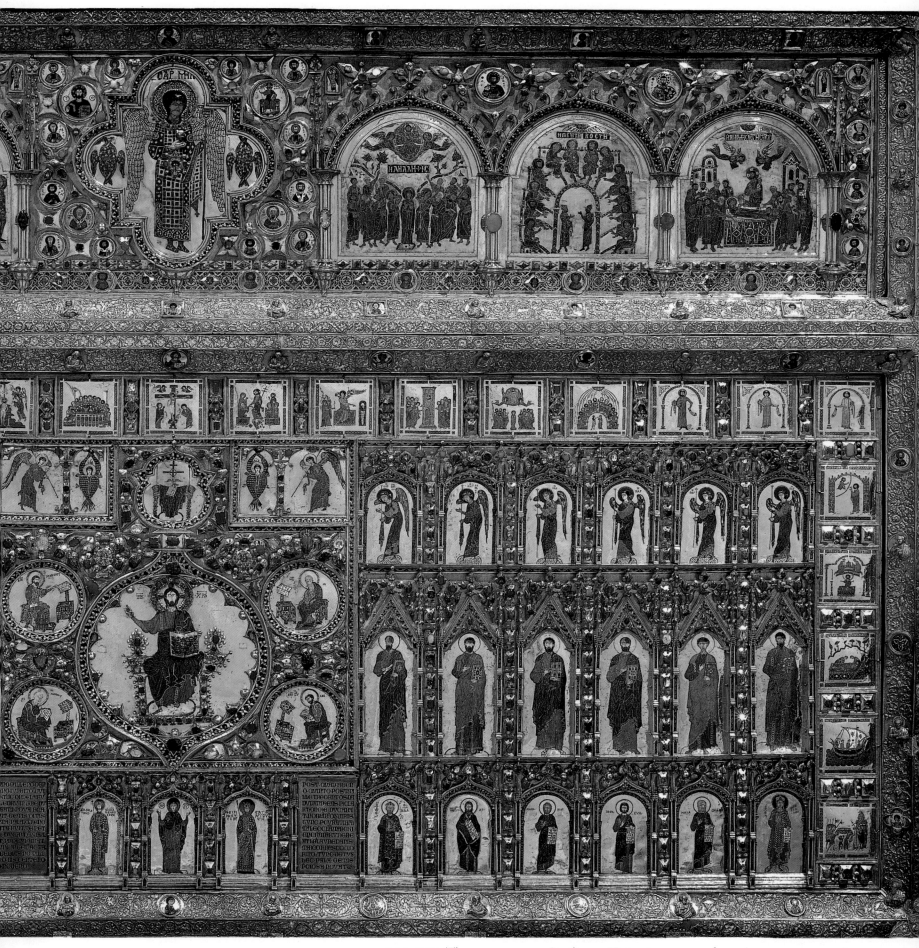

208–209 *The exceptional light emanated by the Pala d'Oro, today located above the main altar in St. Mark's* *Basilica at Venice, is explained by the presence of some of the most precious Byzantine enamels. The Gothic* *frame (1.40 x 3.48 meters) was added between 1343 and 1345 at the behest of Andrea Dandolo, doge of Venice.*

210 *Details of the Pala d'Oro emphasize its transparency, the splendor of the gemstones, the extremely fine tracery, a golden spider's web that sheds a warm sparkling light on the colored enamels. In the upper section of the Pala, a four-lobed medallion frames the Archangel Michael.*

répoussé panels from the church of St. Michael in the Monastery of Christ the Pantocrator at Constantinople (the Venetians' podesta between 1204 and 1261), a large upper frieze was added and further enamels were contextualized within it. Between 1343 and 1345 Andrea Dandolo, later to become doge, had a new Gothic-style gilded silver frame, rich in pearls and gems, made by the goldsmith Giovanni Paolo Bonesegna. His genius was responsible for the creation of the highest and most unimaginable harmony between the chromatic and linear abstraction of the Byzantine enamels and the Gothic architecture of the new frame, based on the concept of ana-

gogical light that leads to God. The enamels with their metaphysical light take their place in Gothic architecture with the same absolute sense of fitness as stained-glass windows in the great cathedrals. With this architectural frame, Andrea Dandolo intended to present an image of Venice as the Celestial Jerusalem, and for this reason he replaced the face of the Byzantine emperor Alexius I Comnenus with a likeness of the doge of Venice, Ordelaffo Falier.

Filippo Calendario was apparently inspired by this structure in the creation of the Palazzo Ducale, with the central balcony for the doge's ceremonial appearances corresponding to the position of the Almighty

211 *At the center of the Pala, a large panel frames an image of a solemn, enthroned Christ the Almighty. As is well known, the gemstones and the enamels date from various eras between the end of the tenth and fourth centuries and are the result of the particularly fruitful encounter between the Byzantine and Venetian gold-working traditions.*

210

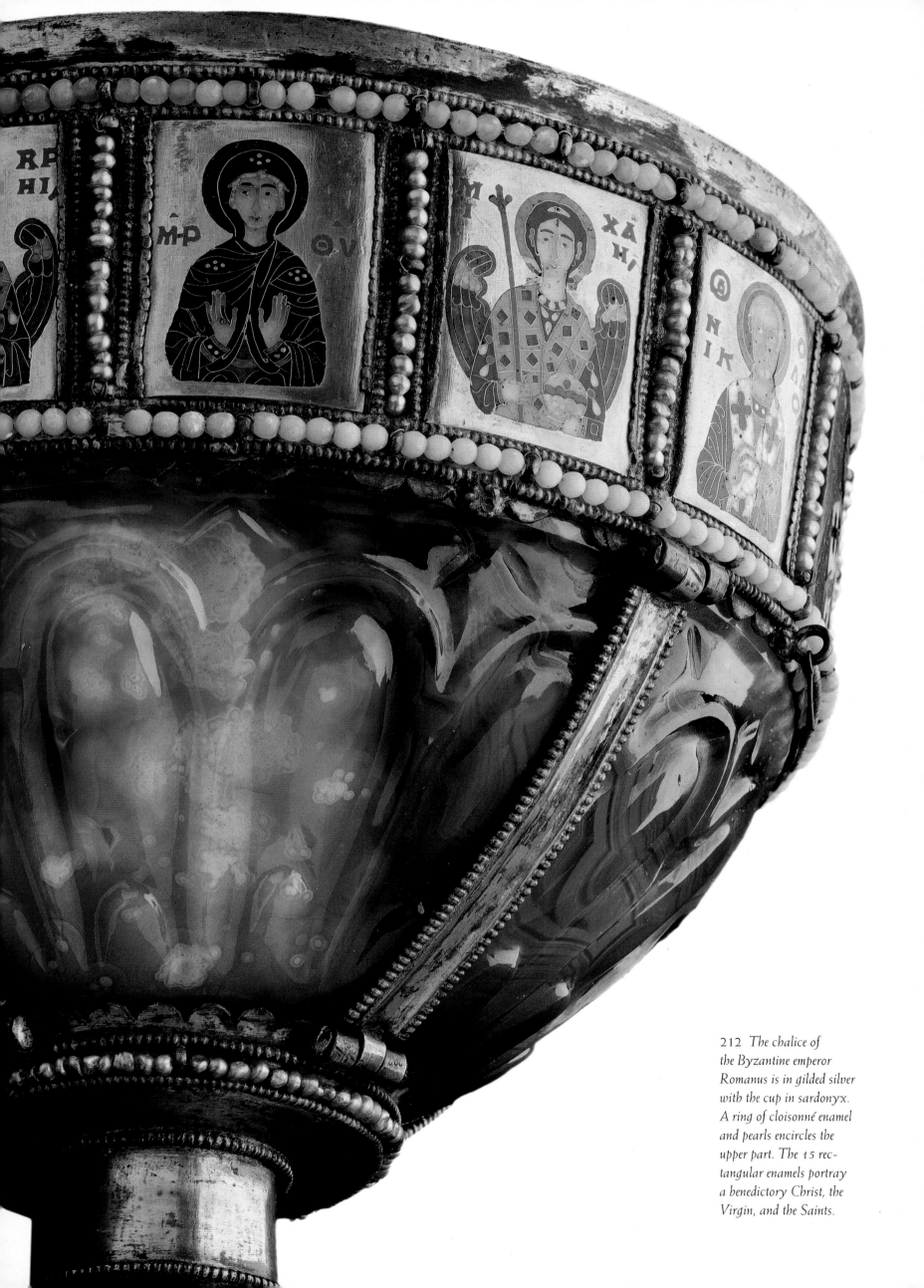

212 The chalice of
the Byzantine emperor
Romanus is in gilded silver
with the cup in sardonyx.
A ring of cloisonné enamel
and pearls encircles the
upper part. The 15 rec-
tangular enamels portray
a benedictory Christ, the
Virgin, and the Saints.

213 top *The hexagonal Byzantine vase in rock crystal and silver dates from the tenth to eleventh centuries and stands almost 20 centimeters high, with a maximum diameter of 10 centimeters. The mount in gilded silver is embellished with insets of colored glass.*

213 bottom *Considered to be one of the finest sardonyx chalices in the Treasury of St. Mark's, the cup—including the handles—is in fact composed of a notably large single piece of stone. A virtuoso piece of carving, created by a workshop active in the early period of the Roman Empire. A series of enamels dating from the tenth century, with paired effigies of Christ and the Virgin and Archangels and Saints, decorates the upper rim and the base of this exceptional piece.*

at the center of the *Pala*, and stacked loggias where dignitaries stood corresponding to the positions of the Prophets, Apostles, Archangels and Angel. The Palazzo Ducale was in fact the symbol of Venice the Celestial City, the chosen city of God.

As well as the most precious relics, almost all imported from Constantinople, chalices, patens, lamps, and other objects in glass and rock crystal, reliquaries, enameled icons, jewel cases, amphorae, monstrances, gold roses, and all the highest expressions of the work of the goldsmiths and artists of ancient Venice, Byzantium, and medieval Europe, constitute a dazzling spectacle of light and color in the principal chamber of the Treasury. Among these masterpieces is the icon featuring an embossed bust of St. Michael in gilded silver, cloisonné enamel, and inset gemstones, a work datable to the turn of the eleventh century; another icon depicting the standing Archangel Michael in the costume of a warrior dates from the threshold of the twelfth century. The same soft modeling of the face in the icon described above reappears in this St. Michael, but the entire surface is covered with enamel, as is his armor, his halo, and the background. The works are two matchless examples of the highest metaphysical abstraction attained by the Byzantine artists and patrons.

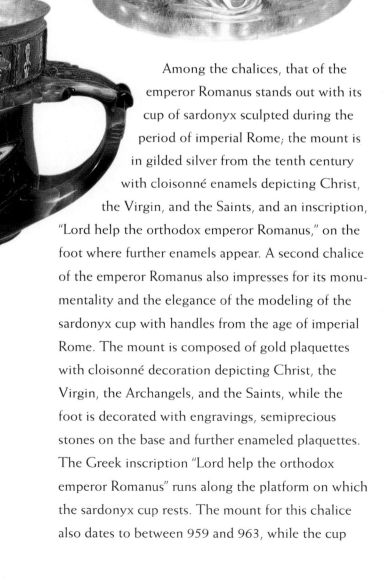

Among the chalices, that of the emperor Romanus stands out with its cup of sardonyx sculpted during the period of imperial Rome; the mount is in gilded silver from the tenth century with cloisonné enamels depicting Christ, the Virgin, and the Saints, and an inscription, "Lord help the orthodox emperor Romanus," on the foot where further enamels appear. A second chalice of the emperor Romanus also impresses for its monumentality and the elegance of the modeling of the sardonyx cup with handles from the age of imperial Rome. The mount is composed of gold plaquettes with cloisonné decoration depicting Christ, the Virgin, the Archangels, and the Saints, while the foot is decorated with engravings, semiprecious stones on the base and further enameled plaquettes. The Greek inscription "Lord help the orthodox emperor Romanus" runs along the platform on which the sardonyx cup rests. The mount for this chalice also dates to between 959 and 963, while the cup

213

214 *This paten in alabaster, silver, and pearls was part of the altar service of the Hagia Sophia in Constantinople. The style is that of the so-called Macedon Renaissance, dating from the tenth to eleventh centuries and inspired by Roman forms. At the center is an enameled bust of Christ surrounded by an inscription in Greek with the words pronounced by the priest during the Holy Communion service.*

itself is from the first century. The chalice of rock crystal and gilded silver inlaid with glass paste of reds and blues, thus mounted in the eleventh century, has a foot that originally belonged to a vase, evidently damaged, made in Iran or Iraq in the ninth century. It was reused in Byzantium as a cup with a mount of gilded silver inlaid with six rectangular plaques of smooth rock crystal. The effect is one of fabulous light and color, a prerequisite of Byzantine aesthetics.

Among the various objects in the Treasury, another that immediately catches the eye is the tenth-century paten in alabaster because of the sophistication of the shaping of the disk, the preciousness of the

gilded silver border with cabochon gems, and the abstract figure of Christ in the central cloisonné medallion surrounded by the Greek inscription "Take, eat, this is my body." The gilded silver shrine covered with five domes arranged in a cross shape and four lateral towers dates from the late twelfth century. The piece was created at Byzantium as an *artoforion*, or tabernacle (a container for the Eucharist), and transformed into a container for the reliquary of the Precious Blood of Beirut following its arrival in Venice in the thirteenth century. Two virtues, prudence and courage, are symbolized on the miniature doors, while the vices are embossed along the base of the temple which, in its upper parts and on the domes, is pierced by clathrate arches symbolizing the borders of Eden, and by trees of life. Given the sacred iconography incorporated in it, this tabernacle was undoubtedly made with a purely religious function in mind. Below the base and on the lower listel bounding the central dome (which can be opened to insert the vial of Precious Blood) appears a monogram with an entwined Latin V and M read as "Votum Marco" (dedicated to Mark), incised after the piece had reached the Basilica.

Numerous other objects in the Treasury of St. Mark's document the convergence in Venice of the most precious and sophisticated products of Byzantium and the Roman and, later, Gothic West, and testify to the perfection of the Venetian ateliers celebrated throughout Europe.

215 *This curious reliquary of the Sacred Blood reproduces in miniature the form of a cathedral in gilded silver. The lower part of this little church carries a series of profane figures, including lions, griffins, mermaids, and centaurs. It dates from the end of the twelfth century and was made in a workshop in the south of Italy. It is 36 centimeters high and 30 centimeters wide.*

A SACRED CROWN FOR THE *H*UNGARIAN ROYAL FAMILY

All the prerequisites for the birth and constitution of the Hungarian state symbolically converge in the Holy Crown of St. Stephen. The Hungarian territory was conquered in the first century B.C. by the Romans and subsequently dominated from the fourth century A.D. by various peoples, including the Avars who were themselves conquered late in the eighth century by Charlemagne. In 896, the Magyars established an embryonic state under Prince Arpád.

Duke Stephen completed the work of his father, Géza I, by organizing the state and converting the people to Christianity. He was also the first figure to bear the title of king, an honor conferred upon him by Pope Sylvester II, together with the powers of legate to the Holy See for the ecclesiastical organization of the kingdom.

216 *Two views, one from the top and one from the inside, of the venerated Holy Crown of St. Stephen allow us to admire the unusual enamel decoration, the signs of assembly, and the repairs carried out on the jewel. The crown is composed of* *two parts: the lower section, known as the "Greek crown," and the upper "Latin crown," dating from circa 1000 A.D. The top image depicts one of the magnificent ancient gems, in this case a sapphire, decorating the crown.*

217 *The crown in all its glory displays the delicate setting of the gems and the enamels representing Christ Almighty, St. George, and the archangels Michael and Gabriel. After myriad adventures, trials, and migrations, the diadem, which dates back from the tenth to eleventh centuries, can today be admired in the National Museum at Budapest.*

Two originally separate elements are combined in the Holy Crown: the lower part, the "Greek crown," of Byzantine origin, was donated to Hungary by the Emperor of Byzantium Michael VII Dukas; the upper "Latin crown" was sent by Pope Sylvester II for the coronation of Stephen in the year 1000. The depiction on the diadem of Géza I (who died in 997) alongside Dukas and his son Constantine clearly excludes the possibility that it was a gift from the second to the first, but Géza I perhaps symbolizes the Hungarian state—at that time faithful to Byzantium—and was thus rewarded with a crown. This hypothesis is supported by the inscription *despotes pistós* (faithful) to the side of the portrait of Géza. The warrior saints Demetrius and George are placed to either side in defense of the sovereigns.

The iconography in the composition of cloisonné plaques inserted in the Greek crown is therefore clear: the emperor is the reflection of the power of Christ Pantocrator in Celestial Jerusalem (symbolized within its boundary walls by the clathrate panels on the sides) that could be wholly realized on Earth if the sovereign were assisted by faithful governors, such as his son Constantine and the king of Hungary.

The Latin crown is composed of two arching supports set crosswise, with eight cloisonné enamel plaques. The central plaque, at the summit, represents the enthroned Christ while the other seven depict the Apostles. Leaving aside the iconographical lacunae of the missing five apostles (probably attributable to

the reworking of the precious diadem), the figures allude to the revelation and the diffusion of the Word of Christ. The evangelical work of St. Stephen of Hungary, who led his people to Christianity, is thus referred to by association. The plaques are Byzantine and the Latin inscriptions have the same characters as the inscriptions on the gold altarpiece of Venice and are therefore also Byzantine.

The fusion of the two crowns has accentuated the significance of the consecration of the Hungarian sovereign with a power that was not simply a reflection of that of the Almighty but was above all the result of the proselytizing work of St. Stephen, inspired by the Holy Spirit. With their luminosity and chromatic splendor, gold, enamels, gems, and pearls confer upon the sovereign a fabulous image bathed in the symbolic light of the Holy Spirit who appointed him leader of his people.

218 top and center
This gold coin-seal from the reign of Sigismund (fourteenth to fifteenth centuries) depicts the royal coat of arms and the sovereign's name (top) and his illustrious predecessor Ladislas I, crowned as king in 1077.

218 bottom *The coronation orb in gilded silver dates from the reign of Charles I, in the first half of the fourteenth century. Together with St. Stephen's Crown, the orb is one of the oldest and most venerated Hungarian relics.*

219 *The scepter in gold and rock crystal features delicate filigree work decorating the head. The carved crystal is an Egyptian piece from the tenth century, while the goldwork dates from the first half of the eleventh century.*

219

A GOLDEN EAGLE
FOR EMPRESS
GISELA

220

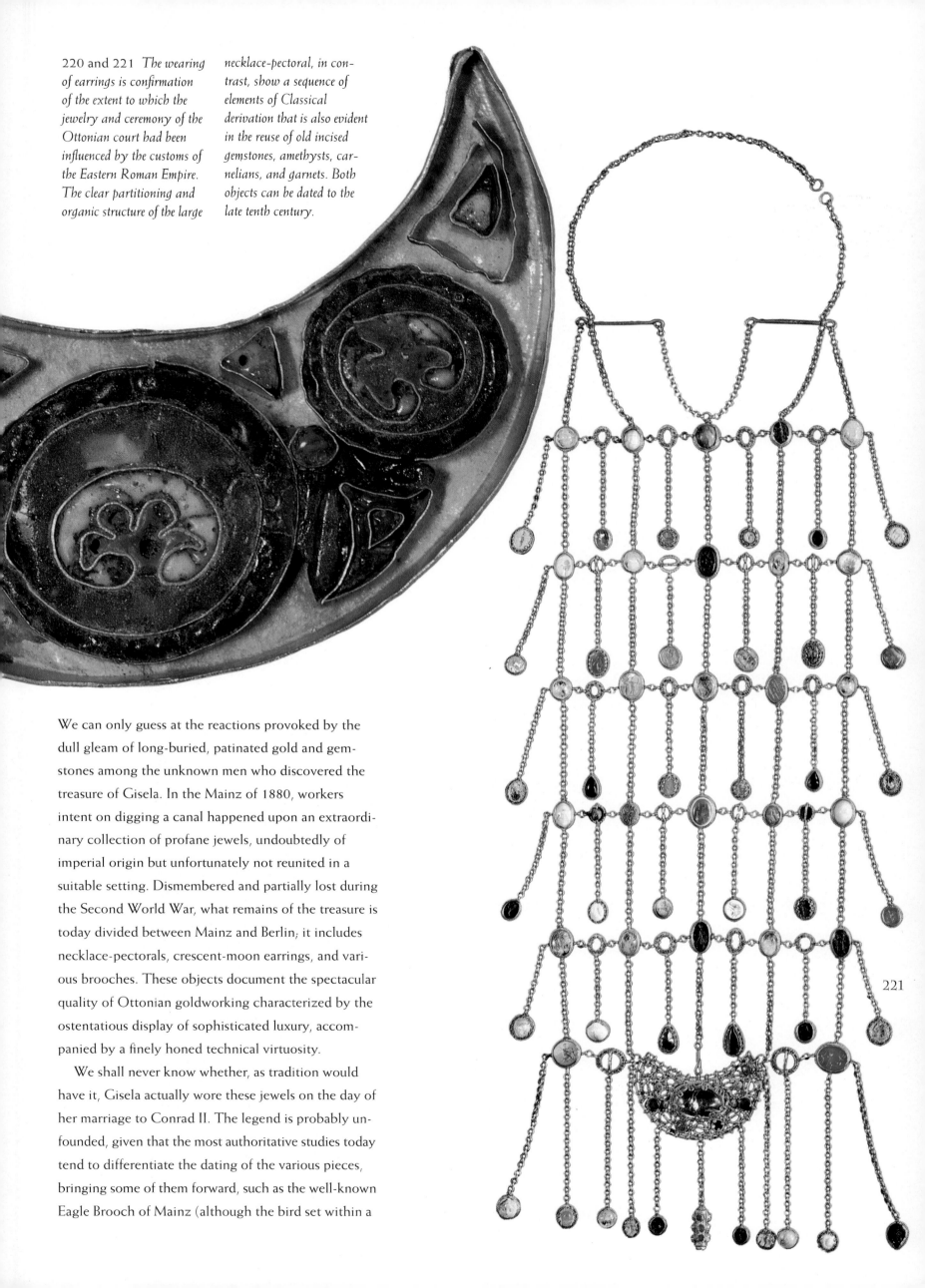

220 and 221 The wearing of earrings is confirmation of the extent to which the jewelry and ceremony of the Ottonian court had been influenced by the customs of the Eastern Roman Empire. The clear partitioning and organic structure of the large necklace-pectoral, in contrast, show a sequence of elements of Classical derivation that is also evident in the reuse of old incised gemstones, amethysts, carnelians, and garnets. Both objects can be dated to the late tenth century.

We can only guess at the reactions provoked by the dull gleam of long-buried, patinated gold and gemstones among the unknown men who discovered the treasure of Gisela. In the Mainz of 1880, workers intent on digging a canal happened upon an extraordinary collection of profane jewels, undoubtedly of imperial origin but unfortunately not reunited in a suitable setting. Dismembered and partially lost during the Second World War, what remains of the treasure is today divided between Mainz and Berlin; it includes necklace-pectorals, crescent-moon earrings, and various brooches. These objects document the spectacular quality of Ottonian goldworking characterized by the ostentatious display of sophisticated luxury, accompanied by a finely honed technical virtuosity.

We shall never know whether, as tradition would have it, Gisela actually wore these jewels on the day of her marriage to Conrad II. The legend is probably unfounded, given that the most authoritative studies today tend to differentiate the dating of the various pieces, bringing some of them forward, such as the well-known Eagle Brooch of Mainz (although the bird set within a

221

perforated circle of gold and enamels might just as easily represent a peacock, given its sumptuous blue-green livery), while postdating others.

An extreme opulence characterizes the German works from the hundred-year period running from the middle of the ninth to the middle of the tenth centuries. Flourishing under the auspices of, and always associated with, commissions from the imperial court, goldworking reflected the medieval passion for gold, the material most appropriate to the emperor, the true intermediary between God and man. There were active goldsmiths' workshops throughout the empire; the artists working in them combined the heritage of the Carolingian style with accents of barbaric splendor evident in the predilection for polychromatic stones and filigree-work. Together they accommodated the demands of Classical decorative themes and the Byzantine style introduced to the German court by Princess Theophano, who married Otto II in 973. Cameos and incised gems were incorporated,

clear evidence of the search for an aristocratic and bravely achieved opulence. This informed imitation of Byzantine models characterizes many of the jewels in the Mainz Treasury. The collection is representative of the jewelry of the high medieval period with all of the salient characteristics being present: the love of heavy forms with an emphasis on three-dimensionality, complex surface treatments obtained through a lavish use of gold and filigree, and cloisonné enamels and cabochon gemstones with high or hooked settings.

It is a pleasure, therefore, to evoke the *Giselaschmuck*, starting with the precious *Evangelario* of Henry III (Madrid, El Escorial), written and illuminated between 1043 and 1046. The emperor requested portraits of his parents, Conrad II and Gisela, kneeling in adoration of Christ, alongside those of himself and his wife. Gisela, who died in 1043, perhaps did actually wear one of the most spectacular pieces in the treasury, a kind of pectoral composed of thin gold chains

222

222 *Blue and green cloisonné enamel, gold and gems confer the evocative appeal of an heraldic symbol upon the Eagle Brooch; an appeal finely translated into the unwavering purity of the metal and precious stones with sophisticated technical mastery.*

223 *A profusion of gold, precious stones, glass paste, and rock crystal characterizes this late-tenth-century brooch of eye-catching and clearly barbarian splendor. The unusual conical form resembles the boss of a dress shield.*

intersecting at right angles with the intersections featuring pearls, precious stones, and incised gems. The piece was perhaps once attached to a fabric base, according to a court fashion of distinctly Byzantine origins.

A dense decorative richness distinguishes the brooches, the most common form of jewelry in the early medieval period. Reproduced here is an example (conserved in Berlin, as are the other pieces illustrated) that would originally have carried a central sapphire, the best-loved stone of medieval man, subsequently replaced with glass paste. The jewel, embellished with pearls, enamels, and filigree-work, is characterized by a kind of conical structure, emphasized by the protuberance of eight cabochons set around the edge and fixed with claws that allow the light to penetrate the depths of the gems and generate a precious effect of transparency. In accordance with the tastes of the period, pearls were used to frame the stones, or set between them to exalt the contrast between their iridescent whiteness and the depth of the colors.

A second fine brooch, the smaller of the two eagle pieces, is a work of consummate skill, distinguished by a border of undulating precious metal circumscribing the bird rendered in cloisonné enamel, the preferred technique in Western Europe until the dawn of the Gothic Age and probably adopted in the tenth century.

A last group of jewels from the treasury once again introduces the tradition clearly inspired by Byzantium and the countries of the Mediterranean basin: five crescent-moon earrings decorated with precious stones, filigree-work, and enamels. Here, too, we can recognize a still barbarian and less sophisticated idiom, wherein the surfaces of the jewels were loaded with precious decoration, a *horror vacui* pervading each piece. However, they retain a more vigorous strength with respect to their Byzantine prototypes. From those models the Ottonian craftsmen, perhaps in some cases Gisela's own jewelers, drew inspiration for the creation of extraordinary masterpieces, dazzling jewels rich in flashing color and sumptuous light, worthy of the sacred majesty of the empress.

OVIEDO: MEDIEVAL SACRED GOLD

224 and 225 The Agate Coffer is so-called because of the rich decoration in the stones covering all sides, together with delicate goldwork. The object is actually a reliquary casket and was made in 910. It measures 42.4 by 27.1 centimeters at the base and stands 16.5 centimeters high. The upper part of the cover is made of a plaque of gold set over the casket and decorated with extremely delicate enamels and colored stones including garnets, topazes, and pearls. It is thought that it was originally a precious belt clasp or a pectoral of Franco-Carolingian manufacture, dating from the year 800.

224

The precious old jewels exhibited in museums and collections across the globe can be moved, if necessary, from place to place: not so the splendid treasures housed in the Cathedral of Oviedo, capital of Asturias in northern Spain. While capital of a Christian kingdom in the Middle Ages, the city was never conquered by the Moors and figured large in the Reconquista. Still preserved in the Cámara Santa of its Cathedral are the relics brought from Toledo—so the legend goes—occupied by the Moors. They were transported in the Arca Santa, a cedarwood chest still to be seen today, silverplated in the eleventh century and embossed with episodes from the Gospels. As well as the relics, there are splendid jewels donated by Asturian kings to

the cathedral they had founded. The most precious pieces were stolen in 1977. Eventually recovered, but by then dismembered, their meticulous restoration was completed in 1986.

Prominent among them is the Cross of Victory: it was raised high by Pelayo, founder of the Asturian monarchy, at the decisive battle of Covadonga (718?) fought against the infidels, and donated in 908 (the date is engraved on the back) by Alfonso III the Great. Other stunning pieces include the Agate Coffer, donated by Fruela II in 910, when he was still a prince, and the angels' cross.

The arts blossomed in the "Golden Age" of the kingdom of Asturias. The pre-Romanesque churches that still dot the region were generously endowed

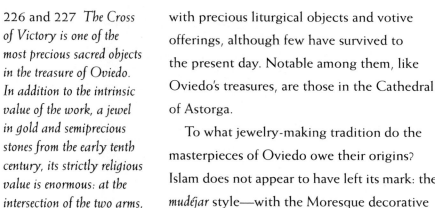

227

226 and 227 *The Cross of Victory is one of the most precious sacred objects in the treasure of Oviedo. In addition to the intrinsic value of the work, a jewel in gold and semiprecious stones from the early tenth century, its strictly religious value is enormous: at the intersection of the two arms, the face of the cross contains a miniature reliquary. The cross stands 92 centimeters high and is 72 wide. With its intricate decoration in magnificent polychrome enamels, with zoomorphic and floral motifs, it has been compared with other celebrated works of the Carolingian school, particularly the reliquary altar by Volvinio in the Basilica of Sant'Ambrogio in Milan, and the Iron Crown of Monza.*

with precious liturgical objects and votive offerings, although few have survived to the present day. Notable among them, like Oviedo's treasures, are those in the Cathedral of Astorga.

To what jewelry-making tradition do the masterpieces of Oviedo owe their origins? Islam does not appear to have left its mark: the *mudéjar* style—with the Moresque decorative elements typically found in the art of Christian Spain—later influenced jewelry too (and still survives in the finest Spanish craftsmanship) but was absent in the tenth century. Nor was there any evidence of the jewelry-making techniques of the Visigoths, the invaders whose Roman-barbarian reign in Spain was swept away in 711 by the invading Moors. Visigoth jewelry reached exceptional heights, on a par with that of other barbarian reigns, and toward the end of their rule bore a definite Byzantine stamp. The votive crowns displayed in the Museo Arqueológico in Madrid are particularly fine examples.

An affinity in terms of techniques (granulated filigree, mounting), as well as taste, is instead seen with celebrated pieces in northern Italy and, above all, Carolingian France. We therefore have to look beyond the Pyrenees and assume that there were foreign goldsmiths working in the region (perhaps, moving to the realm of legend,

the "angels" who supposedly created one of Oviedo's two most famous crosses). The fact that these pieces were made somewhere in Asturias is nonetheless beyond question.

Medieval jewels need to be examined unhurriedly: each tiny detail must be savored without forgetting the one before and without losing the capacity to be no less amazed by the one that follows. Stand too distant from the Cross of Victory and its enameled zoomorphic and floral motifs would pass unnoticed; too close and it would be impossible to appreciate its overall structure, symbolically organized around the central circle and hinged essentially on the polychromy of the symmetrically arranged stones (in some cases, as was common in the Middle Ages, mere colored glass). And each of the stones sparkles with its own colors and light (in part due to the relatively backward cutting techniques): here art does not engulf nature but embraces it, as underlined by the prominent claws of the collet.

On the Agate Coffer, too, the unevenness of the sheets of onyx and the important decorative function of their markings help produce the same effect. They also offer a striking contrast—hardly harmonious, but nonetheless pleasing—with the top of the lid, formed of a Carolingian ornamental plaque.

GEMS AND HARDSTONE VASES OF THE MEDICEAN TREASURY

228 top left *This delicate droplet pendant is a piece of amber featuring a Crucifixion scene set within a chased gold and enameled frame. Along with many other examples of ancient stones mounted as jewels, this piece forms part of one of the most evocative assortments of art and wonders in the history of collecting. The Medici collections, known as the treasury of the Medici, reflect the exquisitely Renaissance taste for precious objects in which art and nature blend in masterpieces of sublime beauty and originality.*

It is thought that Cosimo de' Medici, "Pater Patriae" (1389–1464), must have started the collection in the palace in Via Larga (now Via Cavour), built for him by Michelozzo di Bartolommeo. The hardstone cups and vases, identified by inventories kept by his successors—in particular Piero (1416–1469)—were soon joined by gems. These included intaglio pieces, like the carnelian that belonged to Giovanni di Piero, mentioned by Lorenzo Ghiberti (1378–1455) in his *Commentarii*, as well as cameos.

Some Medicean gems were exceptionally famous, including one depicting Apollo and Marsyas mentioned by Ghiberti, well known even in the fifteenth century on account of numerous copies that Lorenzo de' Medici (1449–1492) had cast in bronze for the use of scholars and artists. Many of the gems collected in the fifteenth century are conserved in the Museo Archeologico Nazionale in Naples because, when the Medici were driven out of Florence, most of these treasures remained in the hands of their trusted supporters.

In various ways the gems were eventually returned to Duke Alessandro de' Medici (1511–1537) and Margaret of Austria (1522–1586), his wife and illegitimate daughter of Emperor Charles V. Upon Alessandro's death, she married again; her second husband was Ottavio Farnese (1524–1586), founder of the dynasty that ruled the duchy of Parma. The Bourbons eventually succeeded to Parma and transferred the family collections to Naples.

Among the gems conserved in the Museo degli Argenti and in the Museo Archeologico in Florence, where antiquarians tried to classify the antique pieces, there is not a single one of the glyptic works once

228 top right
On the oval chalcedony pendant, is an intaglio depiction of Athena making a sacrifice before a burning altar. The fine fragmentary intaglio work is integrated in gold, according to tradition by Benvenuto Cellini, a good example of the Renaissance humanist spirit that measured itself against antiquity.

228–229 *The magnificent Crown of the Madonna della Fontenuova at Monsummano in Pistoia province dates from the early seventeenth century. The work, commissioned by Ferdinando I de' Medici as a votive offering, is made in gold with magnificent precious stones and opaque and translucent enamels. Created by a master goldsmith-jeweler of international culture and fine taste, it comes from the grand-ducal workshops.*

owned by the Medici who lived in Michelozzo's palace. But the extent of their passion for collecting rare objects fashioned from precious materials transpires from numerous letters left. These testify to countless negotiations and transactions that served to obtain objects of this type, as well as what they believed to be medals but were actually large bronze coins, documentary evidence of the appearance of great emperors and rulers of the past. Gems and coins were presented together until very recent times, when different criteria (only apparently more rational) were applied to the arrangement of collections.

With the return to Florence of the second duke, Cosimo de' Medici (1519–1574), who was grand duke from 1569 onward, the ruler worked to restore his state's collecting tradition. He bought ancient statuary and procured stone of the finest quality. Before long porphyry and serpentine, chalcedony from Volterra, and alabaster from the Orient started to arrive in Florence. He also ordered the sardonyx used in 1562 by Milanese sculptor Giovanni Antonio de' Rossi, working to a drawing by Giorgio Vasari, to create the portrait of the various members of the family, placing Cosimo face-to-face with his wife, Eleonora of Toledo, daughter of the Viceroy of Naples. Still visible in Palazzo Pitti, this gem is possibly the most remarkable produced in modern times.

But Cosimo was not content to simply collect refined objects; he made it his major concern to get artists of great talent in the decorative arts to move to Florence. Cellini (1500–1571) thus returned to his service, leaving the court of the king of France. It may not be possible to prove that it was actually Cellini who restored, in gold, two ancient gems depicting, respectively, Athena and a chariot (Museo Archeologico, Florence); however, there is no doubt that this exquisitely executed work demonstrates the amazing skills of the master craftsmen in the service of the Medici. It is also evidence of the loving care taken to save

228 center *This oval cameo features the fall of a charioteer, inspired by that of Phaeton. The figures are depicted with a notable degree of plasticity. This piece has belonged to the grand-ducal collection since the sixteenth century.*

even fragments of the great art of the past. No less importance was attributed to precious marble remains: Cellini's Ganymede (Museo Nazionale del Bargello, Florence), is a masterpiece created by restoring an antique torso, almost for fun or—more likely—to compete with the ancients. Thanks to Pliny's *Natural History*, which dealt at length with the arts, stones, and carved gems, and to increasingly frequent finds of intaglio pieces and cameos, the upper classes eventually learned to appreciate the finer aesthetic qualities of artifacts of this kind.

Demand was so great that the same model was sometimes used several times in different colored stones. Displayed in the Museo degli Argenti, for instance, are a cup in lapis lazuli from the court of the Valois and an identical one—again in the form of a marine monster grasping a shell—that Cosimo I had carved by Gasparo Miseroni from green heliotrope.

In Florence there was a precedent that undoubtedly encouraged the court searching for sophisticated ideas for artifacts created from stone. It was the treasure of San Lorenzo, comprising numerous reliquaries put on public view on important feast days in the so-called Tribuna delle Reliquie, built to a project by Michelangelo Buonarroti. These reliquaries

230 top *This bas-relief lunette in beaten gold with a jasper ground depicts the Belvedere fortress in the presence of Grand Duke Ferdinando I. The work was carried out to the designs of the architect Buontalenti in the late sixteenth century. The lunette measures 6.5 x 15.7 centimeters and was part of the extremely rich decoration of a cabinet in the form of a miniature temple commissioned from the same artist for the Tribuna. The work was dismantled in* the eighteenth century and some of the countless semi-precious stones and objects composing the decoration are today conserved in the Museo degli Argenti, Florence.

230 bottom *An attractive view of Piazza della Signoria with the equestrian monument to Cosimo I in the foreground. Precisely aligned in the background are the Neptune Fountain by Ammannati; Donatello's Marzocco; Michelangelo's* David; Bandinelli's Hercules and Cacus; Cellini's Perseus; and Giambologna's Rape of the Sabine, all in relief or chased in gold or painted on the back of rock crystal. This is a veritable hymn to the splendid Tuscan sculptural tradition depicted in miniature in an exceptional jewel that once decorated the niche of Ferdinando I's Studiolo Grande. The piece measures 18 x 25.5 centimeters.

were in fact "recycled" hardstone vases that the Medicean popes had reacquired after the dismantling of the treasure of Lorenzo il Magnifico. With an ad hoc papal bull in 1532, Clement VII had assigned a large number of these vessels to the basilica; their continued presence there is documented right up until the time when the dukes of Lorraine became rulers of the grand-duchy. Then, with the pretext that the rock-crystal vases allowed the contents to be seen—whereas the hardstone ones were an impediment to the devout veneration of the faithful—the house of Hapsburg Lorraine managed to get its hands on these precious objects, replacing them with admittedly splendid pieces of sacred silverware. Eventually exhibited in the Galleria degli Uffizi, they served to offer a comparison with what the Medicis had amassed, from the sixteenth century onward.

Francesco I (1541–1587) was an even more determined collector and patron than his father. He had

hardstone vessels fashioned in Florence which certainly included the pieces in lapis lazuli still in the city today, among them the celebrated flask designed by Bernardo Buontalenti and mounted by the Flemish goldsmith Jacques Bylivert, dated 1583. The most similar piece known is the ewer Gian Stefano Caroni carved, again from lapis lazuli, and Bylivert completed with an enameled gold setting; this has been conserved in Vienna ever since it was presented by Ferdinando II (1610–1670) to the emperor who was his namesake. Bylivert also created the splendid Medici crown, now known only from pictures and drawings. Comparable in splendor is the crown of the Virgin of Fontenuova at Monsummano, near Pistoia. A votive offering of Ferdinando I de' Medici (1549–1608), delivered to the church only in 1609 by Cosimo II (1590–1620), it is assumed to be the work of Leonard Zarles, a goldsmith from Antwerp long courted by

231 *The ex-voto of Cosimo II combines the technique of inlay with semiprecious stones with that of sculptural mosaic in a magnificent portrait of the kneeling grand duke, clothed in regal robes studded with emeralds and diamonds. The background shows an attractive view of Florence. The panel measures 54.5 x 64.5 centimeters and probably dates from 1624. Originally set in a gold piece for the altar of San Carlo Borromeo, Milan, today it is in the Museo degli Argenti.*

231

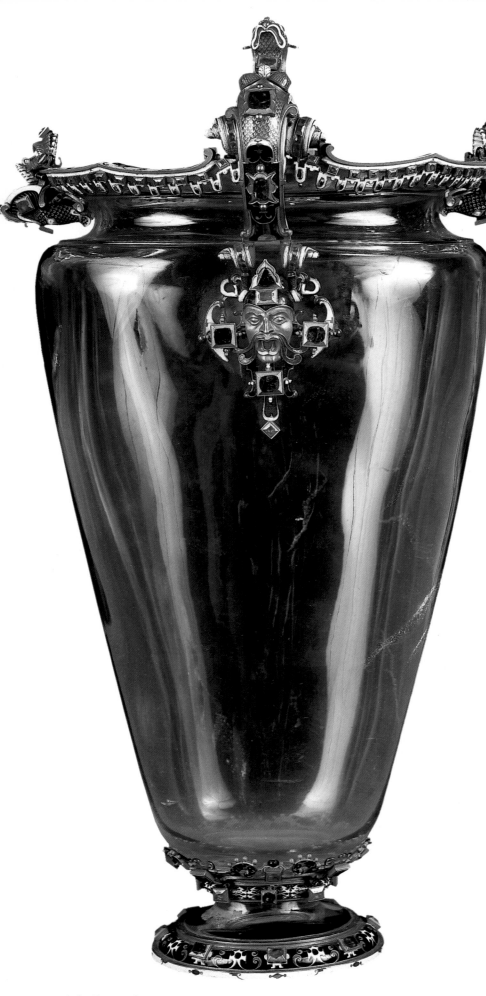

pompilius. Nearby were tortoiseshell bowls, amber vases, Oriental and European daggers with handles made of jade or studded with gems, their blades damascened in gold and their sheaths in red or black velvet mounted in gold and silver, with enamel and niello work.

A large cabinet stood in the center of the room, as it had since this octagonal building was first erected (its form was reminiscent of martiria and baptistries, with cosmic references in the design of the floor plan). This piece of furniture and its companion—a no-less-monumental wall cabinet made for Ferdinando I— were richly ornamented, with hardstone columns, with miniatures, and gold reliefs; some remains of these creations are still preserved in the Museo degli Argenti.

Preeminent among the artisans of the period were Bernardino Gaffuri and Jacques Bylivert, with their plaque depicting Piazza della Signoria: a unique example of how glyptic ornamentation can produce an illusionistic impression in defining architectural and geometric spaces, aided by finely executed details emerging in low relief, such as the statues in front of Palazzo Vecchio. Its almost metaphysical effect testifies to the rational spirit underlying the creations of Florentine workshops in those years.

232 left *Executed in 1618 during Cosimo II's rule, this large vase in rock crystal with emeralds and rubies was mounted in gold and enamel by the French goldsmith Odoardo Vallet. It is 32 centimeters high and represents one of the most sophisticated examples of this type of object for personal use.*

Ferdinando I in the hope of getting him to settle permanently in Florence. This object, made during the period when Zarles was staying in Florence, conveys a good idea of the artifacts that comprised the Medicean treasure.

Contained in wall cabinets in the Tribuna degli Uffizi, built to a design by Buontalenti, were vases, saltcellars, cups, and various other sumptuous objects, often made from unusual and exotic materials, such as shells from Oriental seas, predominantly *nautilus*

In five of the rooms where the art gallery of the Uffizi is situated today was the armory. This too was generously endowed with rare and remarkable objects: Japanese armor and arms, some of which were laquered; plumed hats worn by Turkish janissaries; Mesoamerican cloaks of feathers that had arrived from those far-distant regions before the end of the sixeenth century.

With their collections, this group of rooms combined museological and celebratory functions. From a certain perspective there was an evident affinity with medieval treasures: at the Topkapi Palace in Istanbul and even in the White Tower in London, the juxtaposition of arms and gems was normal practice. After all, it made good sense to use space in the armory for this purpose, in case it was necessary to defend the possessions of the crown; as a result these two categories of objects were kept relatively close to one another. Moreover, the arms themselves were richly bejeweled or decorated as virile symbols of power, and they were in fact often masterpieces of the goldsmith's art.

We know enough about the structure of the Medici collections to be able to affirm that the pieces kept in the Uffizi were considered the treasure of the dynasty. This explains why the dowries of princesses who married members of the Medici family came to be found in this impressive place. In the last room before the short arm of the gallery overlooking the river, Christine of Lorraine, wife of Ferdinando I, placed the hardstone vases with mountings in gold, silver, precious stones, and pearls that she had inherited from Catherine de'Medici, wife of Henri II of Valois.

The room became known as the "Gabinetto di Madama" and it made a pair with the Tribuna, where other vases—the ones Ferdinando I had made to celebrate the marriage—had meanwhile been installed. The finest of this collection was a boat-shaped vase in rock crystal: a marine centaur with an arched back decorated the lid, while at the stern was a castle in the form of a cylindrical tower, presumably designed to allow spices to be mixed with the wine contained in the vessel. In actual fact, the majority of these objects made from hardstone were intended to have a practical function. There were ornamental water jugs, sugar shakers, flasks, ice holders, washbasins, ewers, spice pots, fruitstands, sauceboats, and saltcellars, often in sets or at least in

232 right *The gilded silver and enamel mount of this magnificent jasper vase dates from 1485 and is the work of Giusto da Firenze. It belonged to the private collection of Lorenzo the Magnificent.*

233 *This large flask in lapis lazuli was made by Bernardo Buontalenti, in collaboration with Jacques Bylivert, the most famous court goldsmith of the era and a native of Delft in Holland, who was responsible for the mount in gold. Measuring 40.5 centimeters high, this is one of the collection's most celebrated pieces and dates from 1583.*

233

235 top *A table fountain in the form of a galley was a sophisticated piece for the wedding table of Christine of Lorraine and the Grand Duke Ferdinando I. As ingenious as it was sophisticated, the bowl carries engraved scenes of the life of Moses, while the cover takes the form of a sea monster. The turret at one end could be filled with water or spiced wine, which would then flow from three cannons into the bowl below. The piece was crafted at Milan in the workshop of the Saracchi brothers in 1589.*

234 This magnificent flask, 30 centimeters high, was made by joining two Oriental nautilus shells to form a jug in gilded silver. It is a typical Mannerist object, perhaps executed at Antwerp or Nuremberg in the mid-sixteenth century, and bears witness to the fashion for unusual manufactures of exotic and bizarre appearance.

pairs. Two saltcellars that arrived in Florence in the way described above were created by François Crevecueur, court goldsmith of Henri II, using Canton shells engraved and set in silver mounts. Extremely ornate objects of this type, even for everyday use, were not uncommon at the Medici court. A fine example is offered by a pitcher that once belonged to Francesco I: the goldsmith who created it—possibly Flemish, but more probably close to Wenzel Jamnitzer, who worked in Nuremberg—based his design on two smoothed nautilus shells, set face-to-face and joined with the heads

of a horse, a dragon, humans, and any other weird and wonderful figures that northern European Mannerist tradition could offer.

More treasures were added to the collection under Cosimo II: he died before he was able to adorn the altar of San Carlo Borromeo with the antependium intended as a votive offering in appreciation for his recovery. This outstanding piece was made between 1617 and 1624 by Michele Castrucci, Gualtiero Cecchi, goldsmith Cosimo Merlini, and jeweler Jonas Falck to a design by Giulio Parigi. Again commissioned from Cosimo, Odoardo Vallet, between 1618 and 1619, fashioned a beautiful rock-crystal vase, its surface left without engravings, probably to show off the almost optical quality of the material. It can still be seen in the Museo degli Argenti, regrettably with a handle missing (due to one of the far-from-rare thefts perpetrated during the Lorraine era by less-than-honest custodians).

Ferdinando II must have had a definite preference for hardstone and exotic objects, rather than ornate gold and silver in creations of this type. During his years as ruler of the state, additions to the treasures were more often gifts than commissions. But the finest commissioned works in hardstones, both carved and plain, were produced under Cosimo III (1642–1723), although he certainly appreciated glyptic ornamentation, too. Antique gems were a particular passion of Cardinal Leopoldo de' Medici (1617–1675), an avid collector of paintings, sculptures, and ivory; his nephew, on the other hand, purchased a large number of contemporary works.

It must certainly have been difficult to resist the splendors created by Francesco Gaetano Ghinghi; two effigies of the grand duke, credibly attributed to this master craftsman, are conserved in the Palazzo Pitti collection. Giuseppe Antonio Torricelli is traditionally believed to have fashioned the splendid cameo depicting Cosimo III and Tuscany in front of the Temple of Peace, carved from chalcedony following a medal design by Massimiliano Soldani Benzi. There were a great many master engravers working at the court, a fact that makes it difficult

235 bottom *This saltcellar, made of mother-of-pearl and cast, chased, and gilded silver, stands 16 centimeters high. The shell, engraved with colorful Chinese scenes from Canton, was mounted by the Parisian goldsmith François Crevecueur, who was active in the second half of the sixteenth century. The piece was probably part of the dowry of Christine of Lorraine.*

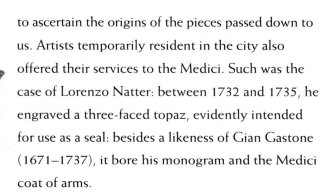

to ascertain the origins of the pieces passed down to us. Artists temporarily resident in the city also offered their services to the Medici. Such was the case of Lorenzo Natter: between 1732 and 1735, he engraved a three-faced topaz, evidently intended for use as a seal: besides a likeness of Gian Gastone (1671–1737), it bore his monogram and the Medici coat of arms.

With the extinction of the male line of the dynasty, the collections were at last sorted out and classified according to the desire of Annamaria Luisa de' Medici (1672–1741). The state of the collections was documented by an antiquarian, Anton Francesco Gori: the first two volumes of his monumental work *Museum Florentinum*, dealing with the gems, were published in 1731–1732. Due to a senseless mania for reclassification, between the Enlightenment and the present day the collections have been scattered among numerous sites: the most sizable collection of surviving pieces is now in the Museo degli Argenti, in Palazzo Pitti, having been transferred there, somewhat piecemeal, between 1925 and 1931.

235

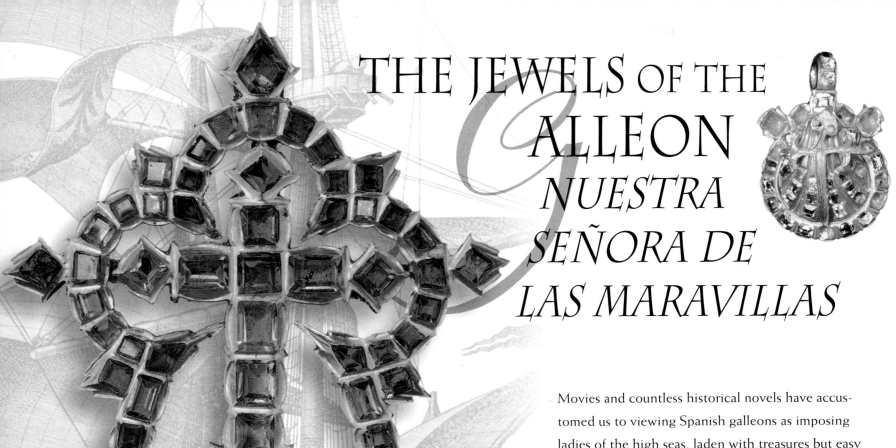

THE JEWELS OF THE GALLEON NUESTRA SEÑORA DE LAS MARAVILLAS

Movies and countless historical novels have accustomed us to viewing Spanish galleons as imposing ladies of the high seas, laden with treasures but easy prey for the French, British, and Dutch pirates and at the mercy of the waves. This image, while essentially accurate, is nonetheless rather simplistic; it fails to highlight significant aspects of the economic and commercial organization that characterized marine traffic following the discovery of the American continent.

First, the Atlantic routes of the sixteenth and seventeenth centuries were traced according to the spheres of influence of the powers involved—to the north the British, in the center and south, the Spanish and Portuguese. The ports of departure and arrival and the eventual supply stations were thus determined. Neither should it be forgotten that the routes involved in transportation and commerce in gold, silver, and other precious metals were by no means restricted to those between Europe and America. From the Mexican port of Acapulco on the Pacific coast, in fact, Spanish ships sailed to Manila, the capital of the Philippines, from whence they joined the trade with Japan, India, and China. Not infrequently, Portuguese merchants took part in this trade alongside the Spaniards, especially during the sixty years when the kings of Spain were also the kings of Portugal (1580–1640). The traffic was, moreover, institutionalized with the *Galeón de Manila*, also known as the *Nao de Cina*, making an annual voyage between the Mexican coast and the Philippines and back, exporting textiles, arms, silver, and munitions and importing spices, tea, silk, and

236 left This magnificent cross pectoral in gold and emeralds with a lobed outline dates from the middle of the seventeenth century and is 10 centimeters long. No less than 66 Colombian emeralds decorate this fabulous jewel, which is also richly decorated on the reverse side. There are, in fact, engraved four-leafed clovers and crosses, with traces of the original black enamel or niello-work. Together with rings in emeralds and gold, and the other treasures illustrated here, it is part of the cargo of the Spanish galleon that sank in the middle of the seventeenth century off the Bahamas and was fortuitously salvaged only a dozen or so years ago.

236

236 top right Among the other treasure objects of unusual form that were found was this small shell-like reliquary of the Order of Santiago, used as a pendant.

other precious fabrics, as well as *objets d'art* such as porcelain, lacquerware, furniture, inlays, and painted screens (the sought-after *biombos*).

The Orient was also accessed directly from Europe: by way of the Ottoman Empire, the famous *reales de a ocho* (Spanish silver coins struck in various mints throughout the empire) found their way to India and China.

The enormous quantities of precious metals (silver in particular) that the Spanish brought to market made the development of long-distance international trade a viable proposition. However, exploiting the wealth of the Americas involved complex logistics and galleons played a vital role. Developed from the galley, galleons could have a displacement of up to

maritime expertise with finely honed military skills. For reasons of safety, an ordinance issued in 1543 imposed a minimum displacement of 100 metric tons for the ships that were to cross the Atlantic and decreed the crossing was to be completed in fleets of at least ten ships. In order to reduce the prohibitive costs of armed escorts, costs that weighed particularly heavily upon merchants and the crown, in 1564 the departure of two fleets annually was prescribed, one bound for the Antilles and the other for South America. The first set sail in April and the second in August; in March of the following year all the ships, having wintered in America, reunited at Havana for the return voyage to Spain. During that voyage, the value—if not the volume—of the cargo

237 top *This large circular Spanish colonial brooch in gold features no less than 81 square or rectangular Colombian emeralds and has a diameter of 6 centimeters.*

1,000 metric tons and represented a synthesis of the requirements of naval and merchant vessels. Equipped with three or four masts, two of which were rigged with square sails, the others with lateens, galleons were longer and higher than earlier ships. They had extremely large holds and a very respectable defensive armament that, not infrequently, included fifty bronze cannons, the weapon that permitted European colonial and commercial expansion starting in the sixteenth century.

The commanders of these vessels were particularly able and the crews were required to combine

237 bottom *This beautiful ring, datable to circa 1650, is mounted with a central amethyst and a ring of square topazes. For the attire worn on the most important social occasions, colored stones were harmonious elements both in the form of jewelry and applied on clothes.*

transported was composed mainly of treasure: gold and silver in ingots or coins (struck in the American mints) and precious objects, especially jewels.

All passengers (functionaries, military figures, ladies, and priests) attempted to exploit their return voyage to Europe by carrying as much in the way of precious goods as they could. Often with the connivance of officials, they omitted registering them or paying the duties owed, the famous *avería* that, calculated as a percentage of the value of the goods, was levied to offset expenses sustained by the treasury for the protection of the fleet.

The voyage did not always go smoothly. By about 1600, the risk of attack by corsairs or pirates was notably reduced, but the potential for natural disaster was still high. The reports of shipwreck survivors constitutes a classic genre of Spanish and Portuguese

literature and the *História trágico-marítima* is a collection of all the known accounts compiled in the eighteenth century. The great Iberian Baroque theater frequently drew inspiration from the tragedies that occurred at sea.

Professional groups of treasure hunters today devote themselves to the recovery of wrecks and all they contain and are obliged to tackle extremely complex technical and legal problems. Among these groups is the team led by Captain Herbert Humphreys Jr. that, in 1986, recovered the treasure of the galleon *Nuestra Señora de las Maravillas*, which sank off the coast of the Bahamas on January 5, 1656, following a collision with another galleon from the fleet of fourteen ships with which it sailed.

The dramatic event aroused considerable attention and we have been left with a vivid account by one of

239 left *The marks impressed on the surface of these four gold rods indicate their weight, the metal purity (checked by a royal officer), and the identity of the person who melted them.*

239 right *This unusual earring, perhaps a pendant of a particularly elaborate form, is 8 centimeters long overall.*

the survivors, Diego Portichuelo de Rivadeneyra, a priest with an important ecclesiastical position at Lima. Almost all the passengers died in the wreck, and the treasures carried by the vessel were lost beneath the waves. We are able to reconstruct the route followed and the cargo carried by the *Maravillas* due to the documents conserved in the all-important *Archivio de Indias* at Seville. Commanded by Matías de Orellana, *Nuestra Señora de las Maravillas* was the *almiranta* (flagship) of the fleet. The *Nuestra Señora de la limpia Concepción*, commanded by the Marqués de Montalegre, was the captain. The fleet left Spain for the Canaries, where victuals were loaded and new passengers were taken aboard, then sailed to Colombia where the ships were loaded with gold, emeralds, and silver. On March 25, 1655, the *Nuestra Señora de las Maravillas* reached Porto Bello, an almost obligatory port of call in the region of the Isthmus, where a solid gold Madonna more than a meter and a half high, and a panel studded with precious stones weighing 170 kilograms were loaded; the galleon then rejoined the other members of the fleet and departed for Havana on July 3, 1655, before being obliged to double back following the sighting of threatening English vessels. The Cuban port was regained on October 10 and, following important repairs to the ships, the *Maravillas* included, the fleet set sail once again on January 1, 1656.

Following the sinking the wreck did not lie in peace for long: the Spanish governor of Cartagena ordered salvage operations to begin; they enjoyed considerable success and further attempts were made up until 1678.

In 1972 Robert Marx identified the wreck and it was finally explored by Humphreys in the 1980s with the help of the *Beacon*, his boat equipped for the salvaging of submerged treasures. Among the objects recovered, splendid pieces of colonial jewelry were brought to the surface that were remarkable for the profusion of precious stones and the sophistication of their manufacture, which revealed Asian influences. Chinese artists were, in fact, active both at Manila and in Mexico. The arrival in Europe of similar jewels naturally transcended the mechanics of economic law and reflected a conscious aesthetic choice as colonial jewelry was long revered in the Spanish homeland.

The appeal of these jewels is enhanced by their romantic history and the centuries spent in the depths of the ocean until tenacity and courage brought them to light once again.

Humphreys has declared, "Recovering submerged treasure is at times boring, monotonous, expensive and dangerous. But it is also one of the most exciting adventures still open to man. Diving and picking up a weapon, a coin, a jewel or a tool [that] belonged to an unknown person who died many years ago is something that few can experience. I have seen the stuff of dreams."

ST. PETER'S BASILICA: A TREASURY OF FAITH AND ART

240 left *Among the liturgical objects used during church services, along with the chalice there is always a paten, a shallow metal plate with a broad rim that may be decorated to a greater or lesser extent. This example in gold features delicate engraving at the center.*

240 right *This cross in gold and rock crystal is known as the Palace Cross and is one of the oldest conserved in the treasury of St. Peter's. It is the work of a goldsmith active in the fifteenth century and conserves a wooden fragment of the True Cross at the center.*

The objects used by the sovereign pontiffs during religious ceremonies and the votive offerings donated by monarchs and believers as signs of their devotion to the shrine of St. Peter constitute one of Christianity's oldest treasures. Ever since St. Peter's Basilica was founded by the Roman Emperor Constantine in 324, the Vatican Treasury has reflected the alternating fortunes of the papal seat itself: enriched by an uninterrupted series of generous donations, it was gravely impoverished by the sackings of the Visigoths, the Ostrogoths, and the Saracens, and by the substantial depredations of Napoleonic occupation. This collection, subjected to frequent historic vicissitudes, has nonetheless conserved, over a period of no less than sixteen centuries, a series of precious liturgical objects and masterpieces of the goldsmiths' art that have miraculously survived numerous disasters.

Exhibited in the prestigious chambers of the Sacristy of the Incumbents, chalices, ciboria, bishops' miters, extraordinary monstrances, altar cards, ampul-

lae, and decorative vases are tangible evidence of faith *and* a tribute to the heights achieved by European goldsmithing.

A more complete artistic-historical analysis of this rich collection is possible due to the wealth of information contained in the *Liber Pontificalis,* a form of inventory that is all the more precious because it records details of objects that are lost forever. The register, in fact, lists with absolute precision the papal riches in their entirety. Each object is recorded with a description of its form and materials, its weight, and the identity of the donor. This source thus allows us to appreciate the extent to which the tastes of the artists and goldsmiths were influenced by new fashions, how the Gothic forms of religious furnishings were, compared with profane objects, slow to adopt the new and flamboyant fifteenth-century models, or how, toward the end of the sixteenth century, candelabra, crosiers, and altar crosses began to reflect the ostentatious splendor typical of the baroque style.

While the present collection is largely composed of eighteenth century and modern objects, it boasts a number of exhibits of exceptional interest. These include the *Crux Vaticana* or *Vatican Cross*, the oldest piece in the collection. Of Paleo-

241 The Vatican Cross covered with gilded and beaten silver is considered to be the oldest piece in the treasury. It has miraculously survived all the numerous, dramatic upheavals which have afflicted Rome. The cross was a gift from Emperor Justinian II, who ruled the Byzantine Empire during the sixth century A.D. and who, when gravely ill, decided to send the cross as an offering in thanks for his recovery. His wife, Sophia, gave up many of her personal jewels to render the cross particularly attractive: it is studded with colored stones including emeralds, jasper, agate, mother-of-pearl, alabaster, aquamarines, and glass paste.

christian origin, it conserves fragments of the True Cross in a capsella. Donated to St. Peter's Basilica in the second half of the sixth century by the Eastern Roman Emperor Justinian II, the cross is embellished with the personal jewels of his wife Sophia and the solemn inscription: "Wood with which Christ defeated the enemy of humankind. Justinian sends aid to the city of Rome and his bride an ornament of honor."

Fashioned in gilded sheet silver on a copper frame, along its borders the piece features a series of rectangular and round settings that contain glass paste, alabaster, agate, hyacinth, and jasper. The reverse side, chased with refined decorative sensitivity, is adorned with five relief medallions; the two on the vertical arm portray Christ with the Bible and Christ benedictory, while the pair on the horizontal arm feature effigies of the emperor and the empress paying devout tribute to the Lamb of God embossed on the central medallion.

Originally, the reliquary was surrounded by a series of sixteen large Oriental pearls, but these were removed in 1798 by the commissars of the Roman Republic. Conserved at Maastricht during the French revolution, the *Crux Vaticana* was brought back to Rome in 1837. Similar good fortune preserved the rock crystal cross that, as tradition would have it, was donated to the basilica by Constantine on his return from the Orient as a manifestation of his approval of the Christian doctrine.

The relic, encased in a pectoral cross from the tenth century decorated with polychrome enamels and pearls, occupies a gold reliquary datable to around the year 1000. The reliquary doors feature finely embossed figures of the Madonna and seven saints, while the internal plaque carries an effigy of Constantine the Great. This object, a work of exquisite Byzantine craftsmanship, stands on a tall eighteenth-century pedestal commissioned from the Roman goldsmith Borgognoni by Pope Gregory XVI.

242 left *This Gothic chalice in gilded silver and translucent enamels dates from the fourteenth century. The almost conical cup is supported by enameled leaves and the node features three series of small medallions with effigies of saints. The chalice was added to the treasury of St. Peter's Basilica in 1601 and came from the ancient Benedictine abbey of San Martino al Cimino (Viterbo).*

The conservation and veneration of relics was a custom deriving from the eastern church that, from the fourth century, permitted the translation of saints. The bodily remains and the objects belonging to the martyrs were presented to the faithful, being first exhibited in the cities of the Middle East and then in the largest urban centers in the West. The spread of this practice throughout Europe led to a progressive development in the production of urns, cases, chests, and ampullae that during the High Middle Ages were enriched with symbolic meaning; in this period reliquaries were produced with architectural forms such as aedicules, towers, and temples, or they were of the

242 right *The Reliquary of the True Cross is made of silver; it takes the form of a rectangular tabernacle, set within two Corinthian pillars and a classical tympanum with two attractive statuettes of angels alongside. The work is from the Roman school of the sixteenth century and contains fragments of the wooden cross used in the Crucifixion.*

"speaking," anthropomorphic type, the shapes of which alluded to their contents, be they an arm, a finger, or a leg. Among the most interesting examples in the Vatican collection are the reliquaries of St. Sebastian and the True Cross, both embellished with pilasters with Corinthian capitals and classical tympana. The first, produced in the fifteenth century, takes the form of a sarcophagus set on leaflike feet with a tiled roof and walls lighted by the transparency of eight windows. *The Reliquary of the True Cross* is a small sixteenth-century tabernacle in gilded silver, supported on a sumptuous base composed of stylized floral motifs, a cherub's head, and a pair of praying angels turned toward the fragment of wood.

The splendor of the museum is enriched by the *Dalmatic of Charlemagne,* donated to Rome by the patriarch of Constantinople, Isidore of Kiev, in 1439. This sacred imperial robe, circa eleventh century, is a true masterpiece of the art of embroidery. A fine weave of thin gold and silver threads traces a composition of scenes deriving from the Byzantine iconography on a background of light blue silk scattered with Greek

crosses. Tradition has it that the robe was worn by Charlemagne at his coronation on Christmas night in the year 800, in the presence of Leo III.

Thanks to the continual commissions received from the Church, a phenomenon particularly intense in the seventeenth century, goldsmithing in the Italian peninsula retained a degree of vitality that was lost elsewhere. The demand for new furniture and furnishings led to a refinement in the working of precious metals, niello-work decoration, and techniques employing colored enamels. The museum cases contain pieces that testify to the exceptional skills of the chasers and gem setters, such as the *Ring of the Fisherman,* which belonged to Sixtus IV, who occupied the papal throne between 1471 and 1484. In gilded bronze with a sparkling rock crystal, this is a rare example of a piscatory ring, so-called in reference to the background of the apostle St. Peter. A personal symbol of papal authority, piscatory rings have been used since the thirteenth century with a specific function as seals; they always

243 bottom left The Reliquary of St. Sebastian, another fifteenth-century piece, in silver, partially gilded and decorated with enamels. It contains the relics of the saint. The casket, in the form of a miniature rectangular building, is equipped with a number of windows to allow the head of the martyr to be seen.

243 top right The ring of Pope Sixtus IV, from the late fifteenth century, is made of gilded bronze and set with a rock crystal. On the sides can be seen the emblems of the apostles, while the curved surface features angels with St. Peter's keys.

symbolizing the Holy Spirit, a pectoral cross studded with rubies, and a gilded silver papal tiara.

Among the numerous *ex votos* and objects of exquisite taste with which nobles, pilgrims, and artists of all ages paid tribute to the Prince of the Apostles, of particularly distinguished beauty are the pectoral cross completely covered with pearls, brilliants, and rubies, donated by Emperor Franz Josef to Pius X; and the chalice that the Portuguese monarchs sent to Leo XIII in 1833, the dense decorations and accentuated relief of the figure reflecting the majesty of the Portuguese style.

The extent to which, from the Renaissance onward, the goldsmith's art drew closer to that of the sculptor is demonstrated by the magnificent cross decorated with lapis lazuli and the two gilded bronze altar candelabra by the well-known silversmiths Antonio Gentili of Faenza and Sebastiano

244 top This magnificent jewel is a precious clasp for a cope, the voluminous liturgical cloak worn by the pope. It features large stones with a fine topaz in the center. The ring dates from the eighteenth century.

244 bottom center This gold dove surrounded by precious stones is an eighteenth-century clasp for a cope, normally used for the statue of St. Peter.

carry a depiction of St. Peter. The emblem of the pontiff is engraved on the collet, which is broken upon the Holy Father's death to indicate the end of the papacy.

The bronze statue of the patron saint of the basilica has been paraded during the festival of Sts. Peter and Paul, on June 29 since 1736. The jewels accompanying the statue include an eye-catching ring composed of a garnet surrounded by eleven rock crystal rosettes, a "rational" from the eighteenth century studded with faceted gems and featuring the dove

Torrigiani, and a pair of monumental candlesticks by Antonio Pollaiolo. Complex festoons, plant motifs, columns, emblems, cartouches, variously channeled volutes, small fauns, tritons, sphinxes, and masks completely cover these works, the functional aspect of which appears to be lost in the exuberance of the baroque imagination.

A monstrance in partially gilded silver, clearly influenced by Bernini, combines the exaltation of the consecrated Host with that of the figurative art of the seventeenth century, the representative nature

245 left *The sumptuous Bernini-esque monstrance is thus described due to the reproduction of the celebrated canopy, fruit of the great Baroque artist's imagination in 1633. The work is in gilded silver with precious stones, pearls, enamels, and an infinite variety of statuettes animating the remarkable construction. It was presented to Pope Leo XIII in 1896.*

245 right *This pectoral cross with chain, a gift from Pius X, is embellished with a series of emeralds of notable size, encircled by brilliants.*

of which reinforces perspective and confers movement to the forms. The slim crescent moon placed at the center of the canopy, a copy of the one designed for the basilica by Bernini, is crowned by a magnificent halo with diamonds and by angels celebrating with long trumpets the sacrament of the Eucharist. This tribute to the triumphant figure of Christ is dominated by the intense gold reflections.

Among the contemporary pieces, of particular originality are the chalice and the ciborium in silver and bronze by the sculptor Vittorio di Colbertaldo; the unusual chalice in ivory and gold donated by the African bishops to Pope Paul VI on the occasion of the Jubilee in 1975; and the hammer and the trowel created by the sculptor Tot and presented to Pope Paul VI by the Sampietrini, the craftsmen dedicated to the maintenance of St. Peter's Basilica.

This abundance of magnificent works of art continues to enrich a treasury that is unique in terms of its religious, historical, and human values: a symbol of a faith that transcends space and time.

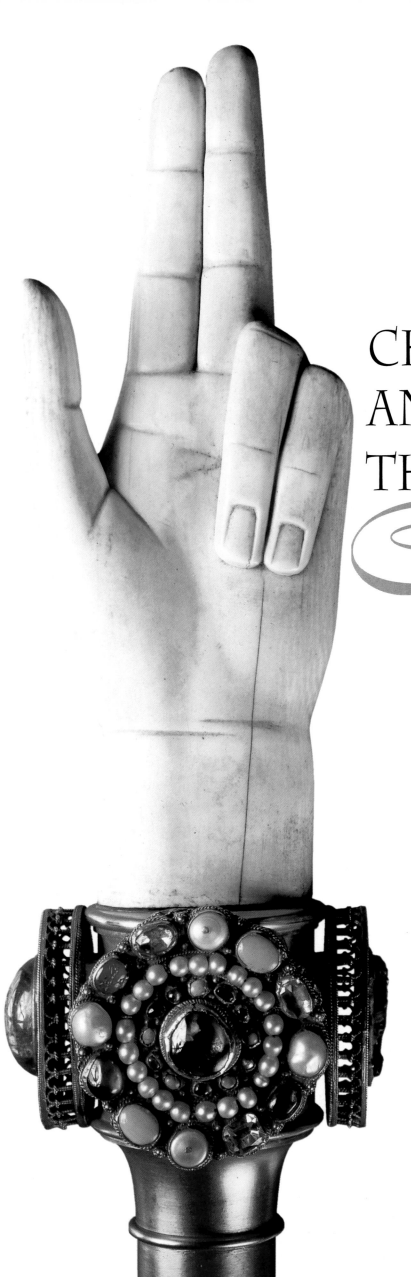

CHARM AND LUXURY IN THE GOLD OF FRANCE

French civilization has given us some of the most brilliant chapters in the history of gold and jewelry. With its elegant, perfected technique, its jeweled objects at times created a fashion eagerly adopted by other civilizations and countries in Western Europe, especially in the nineteenth century, when France had its greatest influence on international politics.

The most successful seasons of these works can be grouped into four periods: the Merovingian and Carolingian Age; the Gothic Age; the period from the beginning of the reign of Louis XIV (1643) to the end of the reign of Louis XVI (1792); and, finally, the great, auspicious nineteenth century that began with the coronation of Napoleon I and ended with the fall of Napoleon III (1870).

Unfortunately, few examples of French jewelry have escaped the vicissitudes of time; due to war or revolutionary fervor, masterpieces of universal value were melted down and destroyed. What now remains is no more than a pale flicker of what was once a radiant universe.

We can begin our brief look at French jewelry in the sixth century, as we consider the burial trappings of Childeric (436–481), king of the Franks, found in 1653 when his tomb in the cathedral of Tournai

246–247 *The Hand of Justice of the Kings of France, one of the so-called Honours of Charlemagne in gilded silver, ivory, filigree, and precious stones, is one of the French regal insignia of greatest symbolic value. It was made on the occasion of the consecration of Charles X. This scepter is embellished with the* Ring of Saint-Denis, *a rare example of a papal ring from the early eleventh century which gives a particularly venerable appearance to the piece. The ring is joined by three old carved stones, an amethyst (center), a cameo on a clear sapphire (bottom) and a rock crystal cameo (top). These jewels are what remain of the lost treasure of the ancient abbey of St. Denis and date from the twelfth century.*

was opened, and now in safekeeping at the Cabinet des Médailles in Paris. A number of gold bees had been applied to his mantle, because in ancient Rome, these insects were one of the attributes of imperial dignity; the barbarian king, who had proclaimed himself Rex Romanorum, wanted to use this symbol as a sign of the Franks' claims to autonomy, based on a supposed continuity of Roman civilization under his rule.

Subsequently, we can consider some works produced several decades later by St. Eloi (588–660), the heavenly patron of goldsmiths, who was a highly skilled goldsmith and official of the mint at the Merovingian court, as well as bishop of Noyon (641). He worked for Clotard II, for whom he made two gold thrones, as well as various religious objects, and for Dagobert, for whom he made a bronze throne that can still be seen at the National Library in Paris.

The profusion of gems increased significantly under Charlemagne (800–814) when he became the first sovereign of the Holy Roman Empire. By becoming "the heir of Caesar" and asserting that Irene had no claim to the Imperial Throne of the Orient, Charlemagne yielded to Byzantine tradition,

247

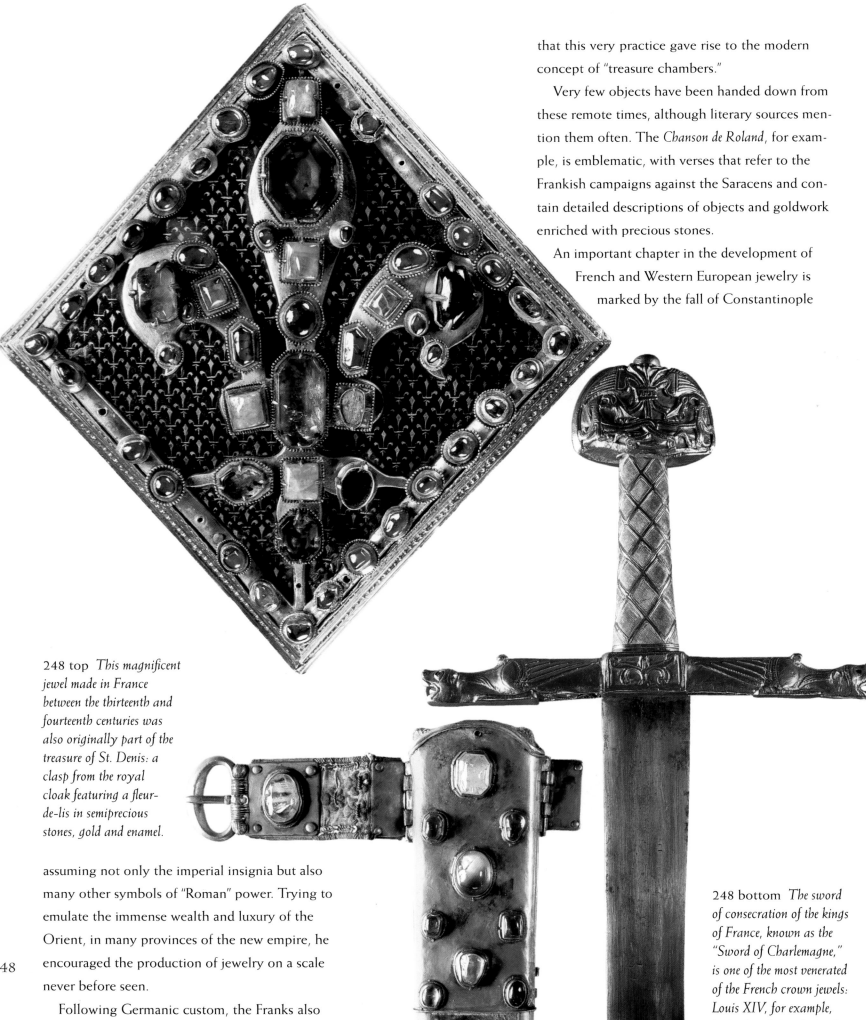

that this very practice gave rise to the modern concept of "treasure chambers."

Very few objects have been handed down from these remote times, although literary sources mention them often. The *Chanson de Roland*, for example, is emblematic, with verses that refer to the Frankish campaigns against the Saracens and contain detailed descriptions of objects and goldwork enriched with precious stones.

An important chapter in the development of French and Western European jewelry is marked by the fall of Constantinople

248 top *This magnificent jewel made in France between the thirteenth and fourteenth centuries was also originally part of the treasure of St. Denis: a clasp from the royal cloak featuring a fleur-de-lis in semiprecious stones, gold and enamel.*

assuming not only the imperial insignia but also many other symbols of "Roman" power. Trying to emulate the immense wealth and luxury of the Orient, in many provinces of the new empire, he encouraged the production of jewelry on a scale never before seen.

Following Germanic custom, the Franks also had the tendency to accumulate great quantities of gold, precious stones, and jewels in a single place, as their possession could guarantee the legitimacy of royal power. Vestiges of this custom were still alive at the time of Ludwig the Pious who, after the death of Charlemagne, wanted to see that "all paternal treasures of gold and silver, precious stones and vessels" were exhibited. It is believed

248 bottom *The sword of consecration of the kings of France, known as the "Sword of Charlemagne," is one of the most venerated of the French crown jewels: Louis XIV, for example, insisted on being depicted with it while wearing the coronation cloak in his official portrait by the court painter Rigaud. The scabbard in gilded silver is embellished with blue and yellow sapphires, four amethysts, a garnet, and a rock crystal.*

into Latin hands in 1204 during the Fourth Crusade. At this time, an enormous quantity of relics and jewels was taken as war booty. The rapacity of the Crusades did not stop even before the tombs of emperors, which were profaned and looted of their contents. When they reached France, these items caused not only admiration from the local craftsmen but also encouraged the production of imitations and commissions of objects that reflected influences mediated by a single new language.

The most important treasures of French gold and jewelry were historically those of the abbey of St. Denis and the dukes of Burgundy, the Crown Jewels , the Jewels of the Holy Chapel, and those of the Order of the Holy Spirit. Obviously, these were not the only collections. Indeed, in all the major cathedrals, in monasteries, abbeys, and in important families, superb collections grew up over time that only in rare cases have survived to this day. One example is the so-called Treasure of the Grand Dauphin, which Louis XIV gave to his nephew, the future Philip V of Spain. It is now at the Prado in Madrid.

When we think of gold and jewelry, we often do not remember the people who made these remarkable works, and yet there are numerous goldsmiths, primarily Parisians or Burgundians, who supplied many European markets from their workshops through a widespread commercial network. Over the centuries, many artists left their mark on French jewelry. In addition to St. Eloi, the patron of European goldsmiths, there were Germain, Odiot, Biennais, Nitot, Foncierg, as well as gem cutters like Coldoré, Rey, Barrier, Guay, Certain, and many other singular figures.

Trade between France and neighboring countries, in particular Italy, Spain, and the Empire, facilitated reciprocal "migrations" of artisans. Great financial means, artistic sensitivity, and patronage by French sovereigns made it possible to bring the best artists of the time to court and to collect many works through the widespread network of ambassadors and correspondents. Some examples are the

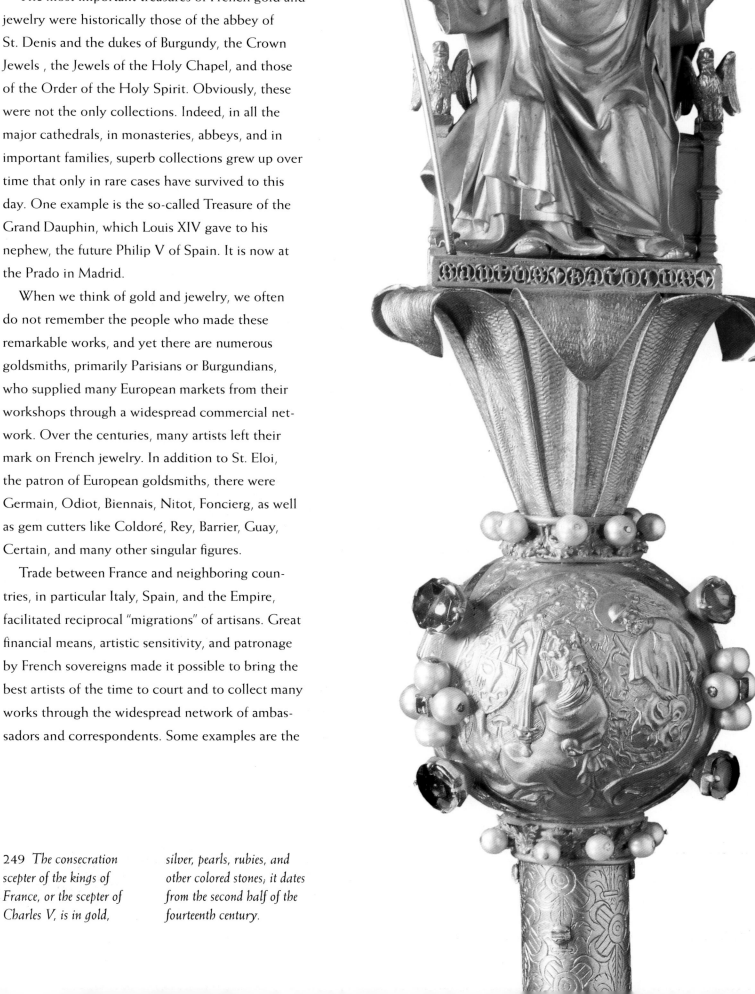

249

249 *The consecration scepter of the kings of France, or the scepter of Charles V, is in gold,* *silver, pearls, rubies, and other colored stones; it dates from the second half of the fourteenth century.*

250 left *One of the most celebrated objects from the royal treasury of the Valois era was this opulent gold reliquary from the fifteenth century. With figures in enameled gold, embellished with pearls, spinels (a variety of ruby), and sapphires, it was offered by Henry III to the Order of the Holy Spirit.*

relationship between François I and Cellini for the famous gold saltcellars (now at the Kunsthistorisches in Vienna), or the king's relationship with Valerio Belli, who created two candlesticks and a crucifix with remarkable rock crystal carvings (now at the Victoria and Albert Museum in London). Sadly, François I never enjoyed the latter, as he was taken prisoner in the battle of Pavia in 1525 and was deprived not only of his liberty but also of the means to pay for luxuries.

We now come to the treasure of St. Denis, the most prestigious abbey in France, named after the sainted bishop of Paris, who lived in the third century. Under royal patronage, this Benedictine abbey became a royal necropolis, as well as a storehouse for regalia, including the insignia of royalty, and caretaker for a number of famous relics. Due to these circumstances, the abbey eventually housed the most prestigious collection of gold art in

France, including a jewel case holding all the jewels connected to official State history. Very little of this treasure remains, as it was plundered and destroyed in 1793 during the Revolution. Nevertheless, a precious volume, *L'Histoire de l'abbaye royale de Saint Denys en France*, edited by Michel Féliben and printed in Paris in 1706, allows us to imagine the treasure with surprising accuracy, as the works are drawn in great detail. Within this collection were several works actually made by St. Eloi, the legendary founder of the abbey's treasure. For example, there was the famous cross that hung from the top of the choir; only a gold fragment of it survives today, at the Cabinet des Médailles in Paris. The complete work is shown in an extremely rare painting (at the National Gallery in London) showing the Mass of St. Gil celebrated before the gold pallium of Charles the Bald.

Dagobert's generosity was responsible for the various objects commissioned to the holy bishop and goldsmith. Among these, the most famous were the Dagobert lance, the Dagobert scepter, and the Dagobert clasp. The opulence of the treasure is mentioned in numerous inventories that were periodically taken. The most interesting of these is the one kept by the abbot. Many of the objects listed no longer exist, like the crowns of the sovereigns

that were stored here after the most valuable precious stones were replaced, as was the custom, to be once again placed among the "crown jewels." Among these, those of Philip II and Henry IV were particularly precious, but the most famous was that known as the Holy Crown, because it had been used by St. Louis. Along with these insignia, the Oratory and the Cross of Philip Augustus were lost, as well as the gem-studded busts of St. Denis and St. Benedict, and many other masterpieces.

Some of the objects lucky enough to escape the revolutionary thirst for destruction were various works commissioned by Abbot Suger. Today, these works and many others from medieval times are in the Apollo Gallery in the Louvre. They include Charlemagne's sword, which he used to invest

252 *Known as Charle-magne's Crown, this work was created by the court goldsmith Biennais for Napoleon's coronation. At the last minute, the emperor changed his mind and decided to use a gold laurel crown, as can be seen in the famous painting by David.*

sovereigns, vessels in semiprecious stones and crystal, the so-called St. Louis clasp, and Charles V's scepter. Of the sovereigns' crowns, the one used by Louis XV, who was crowned in 1722, is the only one of the *ancien régime* that has survived to the present. Various objects of exceptional historic and artistic value are conserved at the National Library of Paris, primarily missal bindings, sacred books, some cut gems, cameos, and surviving precious stones, like those that were once at the top of Charlemagne's Chair,

along with several engraved vessels, such as the sardonyx cup of the Ptolemys.

Almost nothing remains of the treasure of the dukes of Burgundy. When Burgundy, one of the richest states of France, independent until 1477, was annexed to the hereditary domains of the French crown, it owned a legendary amount of goldwork and jewels that it passed on to its last representative, Marie, the wife of the emperor Maximilian. Along with the jewels, the duchess'

dowry included the Order of
the Golden Fleece, created by Philip
the Good in 1429. This decoration
became the most exclusive knightly distinction,
and its insignia were often scattered with large,
high-quality diamonds, emeralds, and rubies, as the
decorations in the best public collections testify.

Unfortunately, the treasure of the Royal House,
known more generally as the Crown Jewels, which
was undoubtedly the most important collection
of precious stones in France, was almost totally
lost due to well-known historical events. Made up
of high-quality, high-carat gems, the collection
grew significantly through the patronage of the
kings, in particular François I, Louis XIV, and
the duke of Orleans, regent for Louis XV. This
superb collection included the gems of Montespan
and those of the Fontagnes, donated by the Sun
King, as well as the famous diamonds of Cardinal
Mazarin. There were also two diamonds that
were said to be the fourth and fifth largest in the
world (as noted in a Venetian chronicle written
around 1740), the Regent Diamond and the
Grand Sancy. A singular aspect of this collection
of stones is the fact that they were used as
needed in official jewels. Then, before storing
the object at St. Denis, they were removed
and put back into the deposit, so they
could be used in new works. One
example is the Regent Diamond,

253

253 *The consecration
swords, created in the
Napoleonic era and
featuring extraordinarily
rich decoration in precious
stones, are today conserved
at Fontainebleau in the
Musée Napoléon.*

254 top *Among the most precious objects from the collection of gems and jewels of the French Crown is this clasp, known as the Eagle of Poland. Made in Germany between the seventeenth and eighteenth centuries, it is formed by a* large central zircon and 150 small square rubies mounted in enameled gold. In 1791 it was a pendant hanging from a thin chain on a Chinese teapot decorated with gold.

254 bottom *This ruby or spinel, known as* Côte de Bretagne, *weighs an exceptional 107.88 carats. It is the oldest stone in the French crown that has survived to this day. The court goldsmith J. Quay set it into a dragon-shaped jewel for Louis XV.*

which was used in Louis XV's crown, Napoleon's sword, Charles X's sword, and the diadem of the Empress Eugénie.

Speaking of diamonds and royal gems, we should note that this collection does not contain the famous Queen's Necklace, a parure made by the jewelers Bohemer and Bassagne in 1781. Made of 593 extremely high-quality diamonds, it was offered to Marie Antoinette when the Dauphin was born. This piece of jewelry proved to be an ill omen for the queen, who unknowingly became

involved in a scandal, which Alexandre Dumas used as inspiration for a novel.

The Crown Jewels included not only gems but also other objects of great value, which grew in number after the Revolution, when the entire treasure of the Order of the Holy Spirit was encompassed. It has survived almost completely intact to this day, and is safeguarded in the Galerie d'Apollon in the Louvre.

Because of their importance and dissemination among most contemporary jewelers, the French objects of the nineteenth century deserve mention, in particular those of Napoleonic origin, almost all of which have survived intact. Among these are Charlemagne's Crown, an idealized historical reconstruction, in which numerous Roman cameos are set; they come from the bust of St. Benedict (once stored at St. Denis and destroyed in 1793). Made in 1804 for Napoleon's coronation, it was instead used for that of Charles X, as the emperor decided to use a gold laurel crown. Two swords studded with diamonds were added and used for the same occasion, along with other jewels, now in the Apollo Gallery of the Louvre. A testimony to the luxury and refinement of jewelry in the new Empire style can be seen in paintings, particularly that by David depicting Napoleon's coronation, where a large number of glittering diadems ripple on the heads of the ladies attending the ceremony.

In later years, the Bourbon star still shone. For Charles X's coronation, Odiot created an imposing pontifical service that the sovereign, exiled in Gorizia, bequeathed upon his death to the cathedral of that secluded city in the Austrian monarchy. As the course of history changed, the Bonapartes returned with Napoleon III; the last of the great French gold art was produced during this period. Extraordinary works were created such

255 *This crown was used for the solemn coronation of Louis XV in 1722 in the cathedral of Reims, where all the kings of France were crowned during the* ancien régime. *The celebrated Regent Diamond and the Grand Sancy were set into it.*

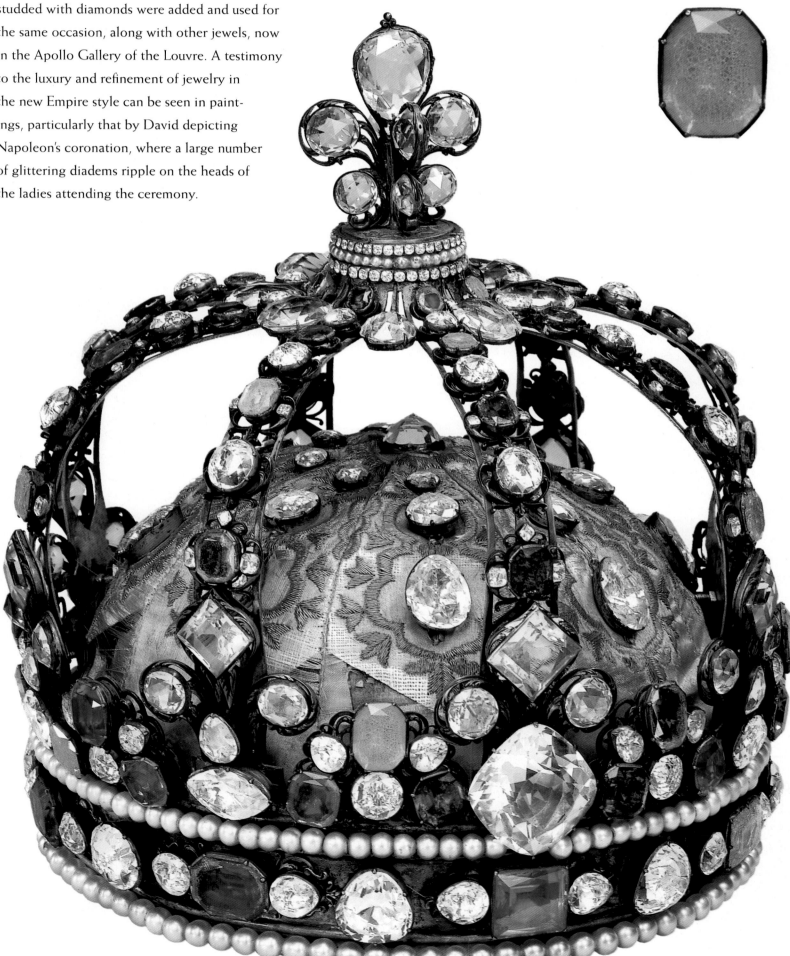

255

256 as those for the Empress Eugénie, even using
stones from the crown, which had in the meantime
become the property of the French government.
Some of these works include the crown, a diadem,
two bracelets, a necklace and pendant studded
with brilliants, pearls, and rubies, and many other
jewels, most of which can still be seen in the
Apollo Gallery collections of the Louvre, which
holds what remains of the most precious goldwork
in French history.

256 This magnificent necklace of rubies and diamonds was part of a parure that also included earrings and a ring. It was sold at a Christie's auction in 1982. In its center there is the diamond brooch of the Empress Eugénie, with its long tapering pendant, designed by the jeweler Alfred Bapst in 1855. In this period, fashion required the setting to disappear almost completely in favor of the stones it contained, displaying the gems to best effect.

257 top This pair of bracelets is studded with rubies and diamonds in oblong shapes and various sizes: it was designed by Evrard Bapst in the nineteenth century for the duchess of Angoulême.

257 center The crown of the Empress Eugénie, in gold, diamonds, and emeralds, was designed by the court jeweler Gabriel Lemonnier for the coronation of 1855.

257 bottom This diadem was part of the parure of pearls belonging to the Empress Eugénie and is today part of the personal collection of the Princess Thurn und Taxis.

257

THE BRITISH CROWN JEWELS

The Crown Jewels kept today in the Tower of London consist largely of the regalia made for the coronation of the sovereigns of England. Britain is the only European country that continues to perform the ancient ritual of coronation, which has symbolized the sovereign authority of the monarch since at least the eighth century.

Until the middle of the seventeenth century, there were two separate collections of regalia, one kept in Westminster Abbey and one in the Tower of London. The former comprised the crown and ornaments made for King Edward the Confessor (1042–1066), which were placed in the Abbey for safe-keeping and came to have the status of holy relics after the Confessor's canonization in 1161. It was these pieces of regalia that became associated specifically with the coronation of the sovereign; King Henry III (1216–1272) was invested with them at his coronation in 1220, and they were used in this way for the following 400 years. In contrast, the regalia kept in the Tower of London was the personal or state regalia of the sovereign, which was used on all manner of ceremonial occasions.

258

The establishment of a republican regime in England in the mid-seventeenth century had disastrous consequences for both the institution and the equipment of monarchy. After the execution of King Charles I (1625–1649), the government resolved to "melt down the Gold and Silver" of the regalia, and to "sell the jewels for the best Advantage of the Commonwealth." Thus the English regalia, accumulated over 600 years, was disbanded and dismantled, being considered the ultimate symbol of the "detestable rule of Kings."

258 left and 259 bottom right *Queen Mary of Modena's State Crown and Diadem (1685) were supplied for King James II's consort to wear at their coronation. The diadem (left) and the crown (right) were temporarily set with precious stones hired for the occasion, but today contain crystals and cultured pearls.*

259 bottom center *The Coronation Rings (1831) were made for King William IV and Queen Adelaide. Traditionally, the coronation ring remained the personal possession of the monarch, but these rings became part of the Crown Jewels in 1901 and have been used at every coronation since. The Sovereign's Ring (left) is set with a sapphire, 16 diamonds, and 5 rubies in the shape of a cross. The Consort's Ring (right) contains 15 rubies and 14 diamonds.*

After the restoration of the monarchy in 1660, King Charles II (1660–1685) appointed Sir Edward Walker to oversee the re-creation of the English regalia. Lists of Charles I's regalia were used to establish what was required, and Walker recommended that two crowns be made for Charles II, "one named St. Edwards Crowne & the other an Imperiall Crowne," perpetuating the ancient distinction between the state regalia and the coronation regalia, though the Confessor's treasures themselves had been lost. The form and function of some pieces of the medieval regalia had been

258 right and 259 top *St. Edward's Crown (1661) is used solely for the coronation of the monarch. Set with 444 semiprecious stones and made of solid gold, it weighs over 2 kilograms. The crown was rarely used during the eighteenth and nineteenth centuries, but resumed its central role in the coronation ceremony in 1911.*

259 bottom left *Queen Victoria's Coronation Ring (1838) is a miniature version of that made for William IV, which was found to be too large for the Queen's small fingers.*

forgotten altogether, and the goldsmiths had more-or-less to re-invent "St. Edward's Staff," the purpose of which had long been something of a mystery.

The only item of the coronation regalia to survive the Interregnum was the twelfth-century silver-gilt anointing spoon, purchased by a member of Charles I's household in 1649, then returned to Charles II on his restoration. For this reason, much of the coronation regalia kept in the Tower of London today dates from 1660–1661, including the solid gold coronation crown, still known as St. Edward's Crown, made by the royal goldsmith Robert Viner, for Charles II. Also made by Viner were the Sovereign's Orb, which symbolizes Christian sovereignty over the earth, and the Sovereign's Sceptre with Cross, which symbolizes the monarch's temporal power under the cross. The Sovereign's Sceptre with Cross was modified in 1910 to receive the largest top-quality cut diamond in the world, known as Cullinan I or The First Star of Africa. St. Edward's Crown, the Sovereign's Orb, and the Sovereign's Sceptre with Cross were all used at the coronation of Queen Elizabeth II in 1953.

In the seventeenth and eighteenth centuries, it was common practice for the stones set in the crown used at the coronation to be hired from jewelers for the occasion and returned afterward, whereas the stones in the state crown tended to be permanently set. Thus, at the coronation of Charles II, St. Edward's crown was set with stones hired for four weeks for four percent of their value. This practice was most pronounced at the beginning of the nineteenth century, when King George IV (1820–1830) borrowed £65,250 worth of diamonds to adorn his new coronation crown. The King's attempt to persuade the government to buy the diamonds outright proved unsuccessful and the stones were returned in 1823. The frame, still empty of jewels, can be seen in the Martin Tower in the Tower of London.

260 top *The Imperial State Crown (1937) was made for George VI, and altered slightly in 1953 for the use of Queen Elizabeth II. It contains some of the most famous jewels in the regalia, including the huge balas known as the Black Prince's Ruby and the second largest top-quality cut diamond in the world, Cullinan II, which is set in the band at the front. The sapphire in the cross that surmounts the crown is said to have belonged to Edward the Confessor.*

260 bottom left *Queen Mary's Crown (1911) is currently set with nearly 2,200 diamonds. The larger stones with which it was originally adorned were removed to be used elsewhere, and have been replaced with rock crystals.*

260 bottom center *The Crown of Queen Elizabeth the Queen Mother (1937) is made of platinum and can be worn without the arches as a circlet. In addition to the 105-carat Koh-i-Nûr, the crown is set with some 2,800 smaller*

diamonds, but remains unusually light, weighing only around 0.5 kilograms.

260 bottom right *The Sovereign's Sceptre with Cross (1661) was made for the coronation of Charles II. It has been used at every subsequent coronation. The scepter was altered in 1910 to receive Cullinan I, the largest top-quality cut diamond in the world, which weighs an extraordinary 530.2 carats.*

261 *The Imperial Crown of India (1911) was made for George V to wear while receiving the homage of the princes of India in Delhi. A new crown was required because it is illegal for the English regalia to leave Britain; it is adorned with emeralds, rubies, sapphires, and approximately 6,200 diamonds.*

As Charles II was still a bachelor at the time of his coronation, the creation of regalia for a queen consort was thought unnecessary, and it was not until the coronation of James II (1685–1688) and his wife, Mary of Modena, that a second set of regalia was provided for the use of the queen. Like the sovereign, the consort was also equipped with two crowns (one of which does not survive), an ivory rod surmounted by a dove, and a scepter topped with a cross. As well as these items, the Jewel House at the Tower of London also contains the diadem made for Mary of Modena to wear on the procession to Westminster Abbey.

New regalia had to be created again, in 1689, when William III (1689–1702) and Mary II (1689–1694) were crowned joint sovereigns of England. The regalia made for Mary of Modena was suitable only for a queen consort, while Mary II was queen in her own right. For this reason, a second orb was made, and a second scepter with dove. These pieces have not been used at a coronation since.

Until the eighteenth century the coronation ceremony was preceded by a great procession from the Tower of London, and until the nineteenth century,

followed by a lavish banquet in Westminster Hall. Many of the pieces now in the Tower are associated with the procession and banquet, rather than with the coronation itself. These items include the ceremonial maces and swords carried in the procession, and the plate used at the banquet. The magnificent altar plate is displayed in Westminster Abbey during the ceremony, beneath the royal gallery and on the altar itself.

While St. Edward's Crown is used for the investiture of the sovereign, the Imperial State Crown is worn by the monarch on departure from Westminster Abbey at the end of the coronation ceremony, and also at the State Opening of Parliament in the autumn of each year. The Imperial State Crown that is used today was made for King George VI (1936–1952) in 1937, but the shape of the crown and the stones which adorn it have remained largely the same since at least the early eighteenth century.

The state crown made for King George I (1714–1727) in 1715 was permanently abandoned in 1838 when "the whole of the diamonds and precious stones" that it had contained were removed and reset into a similar new frame for Queen Victoria (1837–1901). Queen Victoria abandoned the practice of using two different crowns: her new crown of 1838 was used both for the coronation and on occasions of state. However, she found the weight of the great crown uncomfortable, and in 1870 the delicate Small Diamond Crown was made for her to wear instead, while the state crown was carried before her on a cushion. On one occasion in 1845, this had rather unfortunate consequences: the Duke of Argyll, who was bearing the cushion, tripped and fell, dropping the crown on the floor. Queen Victoria described the crumpled crown in her diary as "looking like a pudding that has sat down." The stones were removed from Queen Victoria's crown in 1937, to be set into a new

262 top right *The Ampulla (1661) contains the holy oil with which the sovereign is anointed. The oil is poured from the ampulla, which is shaped like an eagle, through the beak.*

262 bottom left *Queen Mary II's Orb (1689) was made for the coronation of William III and Mary II as joint sovereigns of England. The precious stones with which it was originally set were hired for the occasion; today the orb is decorated with imitation stones and cultured pearls.*

263 top left *The Sovereign's Orb (1661) was made for Charles II and has been used at every coronation since the Restoration. Made of gold, the orb is hollow and is adorned with about 600 precious stones, many in enameled settings. The orb was slightly damaged in 1671 during an attempted theft of the Crown Jewels by Colonel Thomas Blood.*

263 top right *Queen Victoria's Small Diamond Crown (1870), though less than 10 centimeters high, contains some 1,300 diamonds. Queen Victoria was devastated by the death of her husband in 1861, and frequently wore this minute crown on top of her widow's veil.*

263 center *The Jewelled Sword of Offering (1820) was made for the coronation of George IV, and is adorned with emblems representing England, Scotland, and Ireland.*

263 bottom *The Armills of Queen Elizabeth II (1952–1953) were given to the Queen by the governments of seven Commonwealth countries for her coronation in 1953. Known as the Bracelets of Sincerity and Wisdom, the armills were worn about the Sovereign's wrists, and closed with clasps in the form of Tudor roses.*

264 left *Queen Mary II's Sceptre with Dove (1689) features a dove with outstretched wings, indicating that it is the scepter of a sovereign, not a consort. Made of gold and silver it is decorated with jewels and enameling.*

264 top and 265 *The Prince of Wales's Crown (1901) was made for George, the eldest son of Edward VII, to wear at his father's coronation in 1902.*

264 center *The Golden Spurs (1660–1661) symbolize knighthood. They were made for Charles II to replace the pair melted down during the Interregnum. They have remained essentially unaltered since.*

frame for George VI, but both George I's and Queen Victoria's discarded crown frames have now returned to the Tower of London, and can be seen in the Martin Tower.

King Edward VII (1901–1910) suggested that the practice of using St. Edward's Crown for the coronation be reintroduced; although ill health prevented him from wearing the crown himself, it was to be used for this purpose by every subsequent monarch.

The period of British sovereignty in India saw two extraordinary additions to the Crown Jewels. In 1850, after the British annexation of the Punjab, the Maharajah of that territory presented Queen Victoria with the exquisite and mysterious Koh-i-Nûr Diamond. The jewel, recut in 1852, was a personal possession of Queen Victoria, but became part of the Crown Jewels upon her death in 1901. It has since been worn as the centerpiece of the crown of every queen consort, and currently adorns the crown of Queen Elizabeth the Queen Mother. The collection also contains the Imperial Crown of India, which was made for King George V (1910–1936) as Emperor of India in 1911.

The Tower of London has been home to English regalia for some 700 years, and today houses a collection unique in a multitude of ways. When so many collections of regalia have lain unused for so long, the English regalia is perhaps most remarkable for remaining in active use, despite the destruction and dissipation of the seventeenth century, almost a millennium after its first pieces were wrought for the Anglo-Saxon king, Edward the Confessor.

VIENNA'S IMPERIAL TREASURE

The Imperial Treasury of Vienna, or the Treasury of the House of Hapsburg, contains the objects of fantasy of a family that ruled Austria and, at times, large sections of Europe, for over six centuries. Like the originally non-Viennese, internationally oriented family that assembled it, however, the treasury is of truly European scope and is only casually related to the grand city in which it has been located for centuries. Only a few of its objects are actually of Viennese production.

As the wonders of the treasury show, many of the Hapsburg rulers were men of exquisite and refined taste who consistently sought to gratify these tastes on an international, rather than a local, scale. The collection is, therefore, a truly imperial collection, of a family with a consistently imperial outlook and vision. Although we are justified in dating the treasury to the mid-fourteenth century, what the late medieval Hapsburg rulers assembled could not properly be termed a collection. Throughout the fifteenth century, the treasury was viewed as a source of emergency revenue; the rulers frequently pawned items, including the royal crown, when in need of funds. Despite this essentially utilitarian attitude toward the treasure, there was some indication, even at a rather early date, of special attachment to certain items. In 1395 three ancient gemstones and two golden vessels were deemed too valuable to be taken from the land.

Not until the reign of Ferdinand I (1558–1564), with the infusion of humanistic ideas of the Italian Renaissance, did the treasure actually become a collection, assembled for aesthetic considerations as well as monetary worth. At Ferdinand's death in 1564, his sons agreed that certain items were of such significance that they would be declared inalienable heirlooms of the House of Austria. At this point the treasure was clearly transformed into a collection,

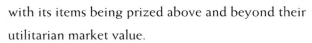

with its items being prized above and beyond their utilitarian market value.

During the late Middle Ages, with individual pieces being pawned—and redeemed generations later, or not at all—the treasury's content and the location of individual pieces was very fluid. Despite the development of a collection under Ferdinand I, the situation did not really stabilize; upon his death, that ruler divided the collection among his sons, with many items being sent to Innsbruck and Graz. These items were in large part bought back to Vienna by Rudolf II and his brother and successor, Mathias. The final stabilization of the collection in Vienna came in the early seventeenth century under Ferdinand II, who declared that the treasury belonged by right of primogeniture "to the House as its inalienable property," which made further division of the collection through inheritance impossible. Since then the collection has been housed in the Schatzkammer of the Royal Palace and in the Kunsthistorisches Museum of Vienna.

266 left *The Imperial Scepter of Austria was made by the court goldsmith Andreas Osenbruck in 1612. A series of spectacular enamels, diamonds, rubies, a sapphire, and a pearl are mounted on a narwhal tusk. Traditionally, this tusk was believed to belong to the legendary unicorn, which was thought to be one of the symbols of Christ. This explains its presence among the insignia of the sovereign. The scepter is 75.5 centimeters long.*

266 right *The Imperial Orb was made at the same time as the scepter, complementary pieces to the crown, during the reign of Emperor Matthias, brother and successor to Rudolf II. The decorative design of the gold sphere in fact echoes the decoration of the crown with its enamels, diamonds, rubies, pearls, and single sapphire. It stands 27.4 centimeters high and was made in the workshops of the imperial court at Prague early in the seventeenth century. Since 1804, the orb has been a part of the Imperial Austrian Crown Jewels.*

267 *The crown of Emperor Rudolf II became the Imperial Austrian Crown in 1804 but dates from 1602. It was probably the work of the court goldsmith Jan Vermeyen, who was active at Prague in the company of a great number of artists, magicians, astrologers, and philosophers with whom the eccentric sovereign loved to surround himself. The form of the jewel reflects the taste of the late medieval period; it is embellished with relief decoration depicting the salient moments of the sovereign's coronation as the Holy Roman Emperor, King of Bohemia and King of Hungary.*

The Hapsburg treasury is traditionally divided into three parts: objects acquired by the Hapsburgs in their official role as rulers of the House of Austria; objects obtained as rulers of the Holy Roman Empire; and the so-called Burgundian inheritance, or objects obtained through the marriage of Maximilian I of Austria to Maria of Burgundy in 1477.

Among those treasures belonging to the House of Austria, perhaps the most beautiful and at the same time most enigmatic are those created for Emperor Rudolf II, who ruled from 1576 to 1612. Rudolf decided to move the entire Imperial

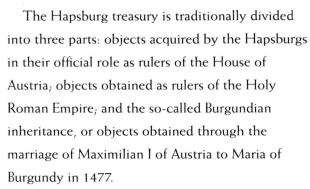

268 left The Imperial Sword, also known as the Sword of St. Maurice, is a German piece from the first half of the eleventh century. It is 110 centimeters long; the scabbard in olive wood is covered with beaten gold and enamels. It was carried in front of the sovereign during ceremonies and solemn processions.

Court from Vienna to Prague in 1583. Why this young emperor, who had been given the strictest Catholic education under his Spanish uncle Philip II, chose Prague, which was still a largely Protestant city, and why he seemed both tolerant and largely indifferent to the religious conflicts which, in a few decades, would create the bloodiest conflict in pre-industrial European history, is still not fully understood. What is incontestable is that in Prague Rudolf created one of the most brilliant artistic and intellectual centers of late Renaissance Europe. Brilliant, without a doubt, but also one given to emphasize the melancholic, irrational side of Renaissance thought. Rudolf brought to Prague many of the finest artists, artisans, and scientists

268 right The Imperial Cross is decorated with precious stones and niello-work on the sides and back; it dates from 1024. It was the primitive receptacle containing the relics belonging to the empire, including the Holy Nail and a fragment of the True Cross. The cross stands 77 centimeters high and was commissioned by the emperor Henry II but completed during the reign of Conrad II, his successor.

269 *The medieval Imperial Crown is a jewel dating back to 962 and was made for the Holy Roman Emperor Otto the Great. It was crafted in a workshop in the west of Germany. The eight gold plaques, enamels, and stones have different sizes, proportional to their significance. The four principal elements at the front are decorated with precious stones, while the others depict sacred scenes in cloisonné enamel. The choice and arrangement of the precious stones, and the octagonal form of the crown, have particular symbolic meanings. The figure 8 is in fact a symbol of perfection, frequently found in works associated with the Holy Roman Empire.*

of late-sixteenth-century Europe, but he also filled his court with astrologers, alchemists, and magicians. The crises in confidence of the late humanistic Renaissance in man's ability to understand the universe produced the tragedies of Shakespeare in England and the humanistic skepticism of Montaigne in France. In the Catholic Hapsburg court in Prague, it produced a retreat from reality into the brilliant but extreme Mannerism of the painters Hans von Aachen and Bartholomeus Spranger, as well as an

obsession with magic and a decades-long search for the fabled Philosopher's Stone, which would turn base metal into gold.

It is in this context that we must consider the beautiful objects from Rudolf's court presented in this volume, particularly his imperial crown. It is harmonious and beautiful in itself, but these aesthetic considerations bring us to only a partial understanding of the crown's significance. There is symbolism in the three parts of the crown: the circlet, or base, with its fleur de lis mounts, symbolizing kingship; the miter, which recalls the shape of a bishop's hat, or that of a biblical Jewish priest, symbolizing the emperor's status as Pontifex by divine right; and the imperial high arch, from the brow to the neck. These symbolic levels, however, still do not fully explain the profound significance that this object had for Rudolf and his court. For the sage steeped in Renaissance magic, precious stones were more than beautiful, valuable objects that dazzled and conferred wealth and prestige. For the Renaissance magus precious stones had far more import than they had even for the medieval allegorist, although a complex allegorical level is also clearly present in the stones of Rudolf's crown. For such a magus, precious stones, along with certain plants and images, constituted talismans that could actually bring down the power of the stars and planets for their owner. That Rudolf believed

270–271 *This oval basin with relief decoration illustrates the myth of Europa. An exquisitely crafted piece, it is attributed to the artist Christoph Lencker, a member of the well-known family of goldsmiths from Augsburg. It dates from the last decades of the sixteenth century and bears eloquent testimony to the fashion and taste of the era.*

this is indicated in the writings of his physician, Anslemus Boetius de Boot, who, in *Gemmarium et lapidarium historia*, printed in 1609, explains: "The Emperor loves precious stones . . . in order to behold . . . the greatness and ineffable power of God, who in such minute bodies seems to have united the beauty of the whole world and enclosed the powers of all other things." In short, the stones are talismans, and the crown is a magic object that channels the power of the heavens to its owner. This is hardly the place to hazard a full interpretation of the talismanic program of Rudolf's crown. We can, however, mention

the dominant use of pearls, which were thought to have been formed by oysters that rose to the surface and drank heavenly dust and the beams of the sun, moon, and stars. Hence they were the talismanic stone par excellence.

Another notable feature is the iconographically heterodox placement of the magnificent sapphire above the cross on top of the crown. This placement becomes more understandable when we consider that the sapphire is the stone of the sun, the source of all light and good in neo-Platonic cosmology, a force likened to the Godhead itself.

271 top left *This brooch is a Dutch jewel from the middle of the fifteenth century that was part of the Burgundy treasure. It came into the hands of the Hapsburgs following the politically inspired marriages recorded in the accompanying text. Made of partially enameled gold, with decorations of pearls and precious stones, the graceful jewel depicts a betrothed couple in a garden setting and has a diameter of 5 centimeters.*

271 right *This ewer and basin were made by Christoff Jamnitzer. Its bas-reliefs portray an allegory of the Victory and Defeat of Love, expressing the self-conscious tastes of late-sixteenth-century Mannerism.*

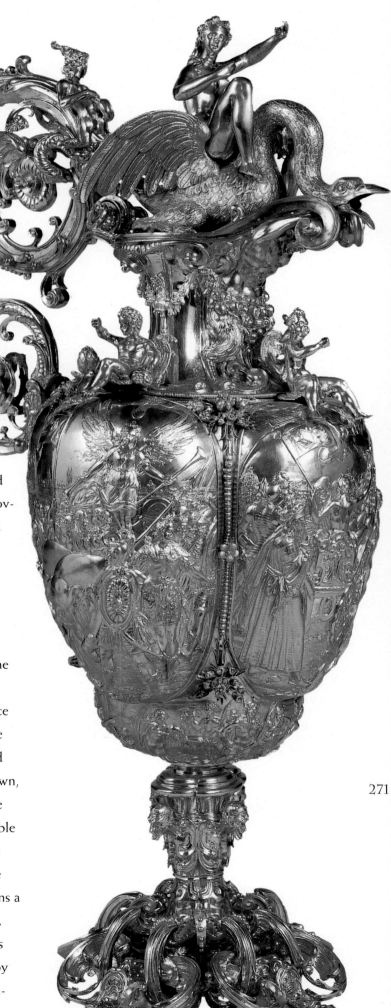

It is also worth noting that the crown, completed in 1602, must have been commissioned about 1600, a year during which Rudolf fell ill, both physically and mentally. Quite contrary to his nature, Rudolf frequently became violent and even attempted suicide. He also developed an aggressive hatred of the Church, and feared he was going to be killed by a priest. He recovered physically, but historians doubt his full mental recovery. It would not be surprising if during this period the emperor's abiding interest in magic and neo-Platonic cosmology intensified, leading to what is perhaps a dominance of magical over Catholic significance in his crown.

Another aspect of the art of Rudolf's court can be seen in the magnificent ewer made for him by the Augsburg goldsmith Christoff Jamnitzer, whom he brought to Prague. The ewer is the companion piece to a basin, also in the Vienna treasury; together, the pieces contain bas reliefs depicting the triumph and defeat of Amor. Again, as in the case of Rudolf's crown, full appreciation of the object goes way beyond the piece's visual, aesthetic effect. While it is also possible that the images depicted have talismanic value, it is their extremely complicated allegorical significance that interests us here. The bowl of the basin contains a straightforward, typical Renaissance *Trionfo d'Amore,* but around the rim of the basin are depicted various scenes from classical mythology: Love conquered by Chastity; Chastity conquered by Death; Death conquered by Fame; and Fame conquered by Eternity.

272 left *Ferdinand of Tyrol was also the owner of this unusual chalice made from an ostrich's egg and surmounted with coral decoration. This is an example of the so-called pokal, characteristic German mugs from the sixteenth century.*

Their meaning is hardly apparent to the casual viewer and is revealed only to those who understood the moral values the Renaissance scholars put upon the events of classical mythology.

When we go to the ewer, the allegory becomes even more complicated, since the scenes of the defeat of Love are here transposed, with the same meaning, to scenes from the legend of the poet Petrarch and his Lady Laura. Needless to say, a great deal is made of Laura, who can be made to represent not only Love and Chastity but also, through her name, Fame. Quite clearly, communication of the allegory's content is quite secondary to the intellectual challenge of deciphering it. Knowledge is no longer an instrument for understanding the universe but rather an end in itself, a sophisticated game for the initiated. The ewer and its

272 right *This nautilus cup mounted in gilded silver is also a German work from the late sixteenth century. Attributed to the goldsmith Kornblum Marx, it documents the typical Mannerist fashion for highly wrought and bizarre objects, manag-* *ing to combine the most exotic and wild forms of nature with the virtuosity of art.*

273 top *These rock crystal herons were among the exquisite objects belonging to Ferdinand of Tyrol. They* *were made in Italy in the late sixteenth century in the workshop of the Saracchi brothers. Like other objects in the collections of the Austrian crown, they are today exhibited in the Kunsthistorisches Museum, Vienna.*

can understand some of the immense scope and range of the Hapsburg treasury. As the family that assembled it well understood, the jewels of the treasury represent far more than their monetary and aesthetic worth. In contemplating them, we come into immediate contact with over six hundred years of European history.

accompanying basin incarnate, therefore, the essence of late-sixteenth-century Mannerism.

The rulers of the House of Austria were also, for long periods of time, emperors of the Holy Roman Empire. Many of the insignia of that ill-named empire became part of the Hapsburg treasury, the most artistically and historically significant of which is the Imperial Crown. This treasure, begun in western Germany during the second half of the tenth century and finished during the first quarter of the eleventh, is a masterpiece of Ottonian art. The period of the Ottos saw the first major wave of influence of Byzantine art and ideas north of the Alps. The crown, from its use of cloisonné enamel techniques, to the symbolic vocabulary of its choice of precious stones, to the style of the biblical figures representing kingship on its enameled plaques, is a piece of strong Byzantine inspiration. It uses motifs that were specifically associated with the Byzantine emperor, such as the form of the crown itself and the color scheme of green, blue, and white stones, a color combination that could be used only by the Byzantine emperor, for the side plates of the crown. The fashioners of the crown quite clearly wanted to add the legitimacy of the Byzantine emperor to the references of biblical king and priesthood represented on the enameled plaques, strengthening even further its wearer's claim to absolute sovereignty. In the priceless treasures illustrated on these pages, one

273

273 bottom *This particularly elaborate jasper jug was part of the personal collection of Rudolf II, grandson of Ferdinand of Tyrol. The piece is from the goldsmiths Ottavio Miseroni and Paulus van Vianen; it dates from the first decade of the seventeenth century.*

CROWNS AND JEWELS OF BAVARIA

With more than 1,250 art works, the Treasure Chamber of the Munich Residence is one of the most significant of its kind in Europe. It dates to Duke Albrecht V of the House of Wittelsbach, which ruled Bavaria from 1180 until 1918.

In 1565, Duke Albrecht V and his consort, Anna, declared their personal collection of precious artifacts a family treasure. They decreed that the nineteen pieces of selected jewels and artistic goldwork, to which ten other pieces were added in the years leading to 1579, could not be sold. This treasure was to be conserved forever in the ducal palace at Munich, the Wittelsbach capital, passing to the firstborn male heir.

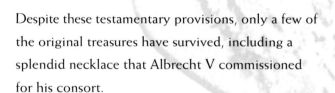

Despite these testamentary provisions, only a few of the original treasures have survived, including a splendid necklace that Albrecht V commissioned for his consort.

Successive generations of rulers enriched the Wittelsbach jewel collection. In addition to various interpretations of the Bavarian royal coat of arms and other heraldic symbols, it now includes priceless jewels and medals, as well as lavishly decorated daily objects such as precious vases in rock crystal inlaid with colored carvings. Masterpieces from the collection also include goblets in ivory and rhinoceros horn, as well as religious works from the treasures of churches and monasteries. The collection also features goldwork from the early Middle Ages up to Classicism, bearing witness to exotic artistic craftsmanship. The masterpieces of the Munich Treasure Chamber indisputably highlight the Wittelsbachs' passion for collection and patronage of the arts, since they cover over a thousand years of artistic craftsmanship.

274–275 The crown of the king of Bavaria was designed in 1806–1807 by the goldsmith Jean-Baptiste De Lasne, who drew inspiration from the jewels of the court of Napoleon. The crown is studded with precious stones, emeralds, and sapphires of notable dimensions. Like the other regal insignia, the crown was not worn by the sovereign. It was exhibited on a cushion at his feet during official ceremonies in the throne room of his official residence.

275 The design of the queen's crown, with alternating pearls and diamonds, was the work of the jeweler Guillaume Biennais; it was later modified by Gottfried Merk at the court of King Ludwig II in 1867.

276 left *Gold, sapphires, emeralds, rubies, and diamonds decorate the imperial orb, one of the classic symbols of sovereignty. Frederick V, the Elector of the Palatinate, commissioned it for his coronation as King of Bohemia at Prague, November 4, 1619.*

276 right and 276–277 top *The Bavarian imperial orb and the enameled sword with a hilt studded with gems are dated to 1806; along with the crown, they form part of the insignia of the kingdom of Bavaria, designed by the Parisian goldsmiths Biennais and De Lasne.*

277 One of the oldest crowns of the treasury of Munich is said to have belonged to "an English Queen." It dates from the 1370s or 1380s. Also known as the "Palatinate crown," it was part of the dowry of Princess Blanche on her marriage to the Elector Palatinate Ludwig III in 1402.

Duke Maximilian I of Bavaria, a passionate art collector, enriched his grandfather's collection by a total of forty-eight masterpieces. The most significant contribution was made in 1617 with the statuette of St. George on horseback. Because of its high artistry and expressive force, it has now become the symbol of the Munich Treasure Chamber. The work was commissioned to commemorate a gift of a relic of St. George, made by the Archbishop of Cologne to his brother, Duke Wilhelm V of Bavaria, in 1586. The statuette was completed

about 1597 from a drawing by Friedrich Sustris, by master goldsmiths from Munich and Augsburg. The Bavarian coat of arms was added onto the plinth that holds the relic of St. George, patron of the court of Munich, between 1638 and 1641. On special feast days, the sculpture was placed on the altar of the royal chapel. The holy knight appears on horseback just after having killed the dragon. The visor of his helmet can be opened and hides the boxwood sculpted face of Duke Wilhelm V, who is thereby depicted as the holy knight. During

the Counter-Reformation, the relic became the monument of the Catholic princely house.

Similar political significance is attached to the imperial orb of Bohemia and the Palatinate. During the Thirty Years' War, Duke Maximilian I of Bavaria fought alongside the emperor and the Catholic League. In 1620, at the battle of White Mountain near Prague, he defeated the Elector Frederick V of the Palatinate, who sided with the Evangelicals and Lutherans and who was crowned King of Bohemia on November 4, 1619. It was for this occasion that Frederick had commissioned the royal orb in Augsburg. Following Maximilian's victory over Frederick, the right of the Elector passed from the Palatinate to Bavaria in 1623. Later, Frederick's royal orb also fell into the hands of the Wittelsbachs of Bavaria.

In 1806, the Emperor Napoleon raised Bavaria to the status of kingdom. King Maximilian I Joseph commissioned the Parisian goldsmiths Jean-Baptiste De Lasne and Martin Guillaume Biennais, who was considered the greatest goldsmith of his time, to craft the royal symbols of his new kingdom. Design was entrusted to no less a master than the architect Charles Percier. The royal crown by De Lasne was based on the design of the crown of Louis XV of France, with a gold frame richly encrusted with gems and pearls. The blue Wittelsbach Diamond that adorns the royal orb of the crown came to the Wittelsbachs of Bavaria through Spain and Austria, as part of dowries. The stone later ended up on the international diamond market and is now replaced by a copy on the crown.

The smaller crown for the queen, richly encrusted with pearls, was crafted by Biennais in 1806–1807. Queen Theresa of Bavaria used to wear it together with a diamond diadem. In 1867, King Louis II of Bavaria had the crown modified by his court jeweler, Gottfried Merck, who en-

278

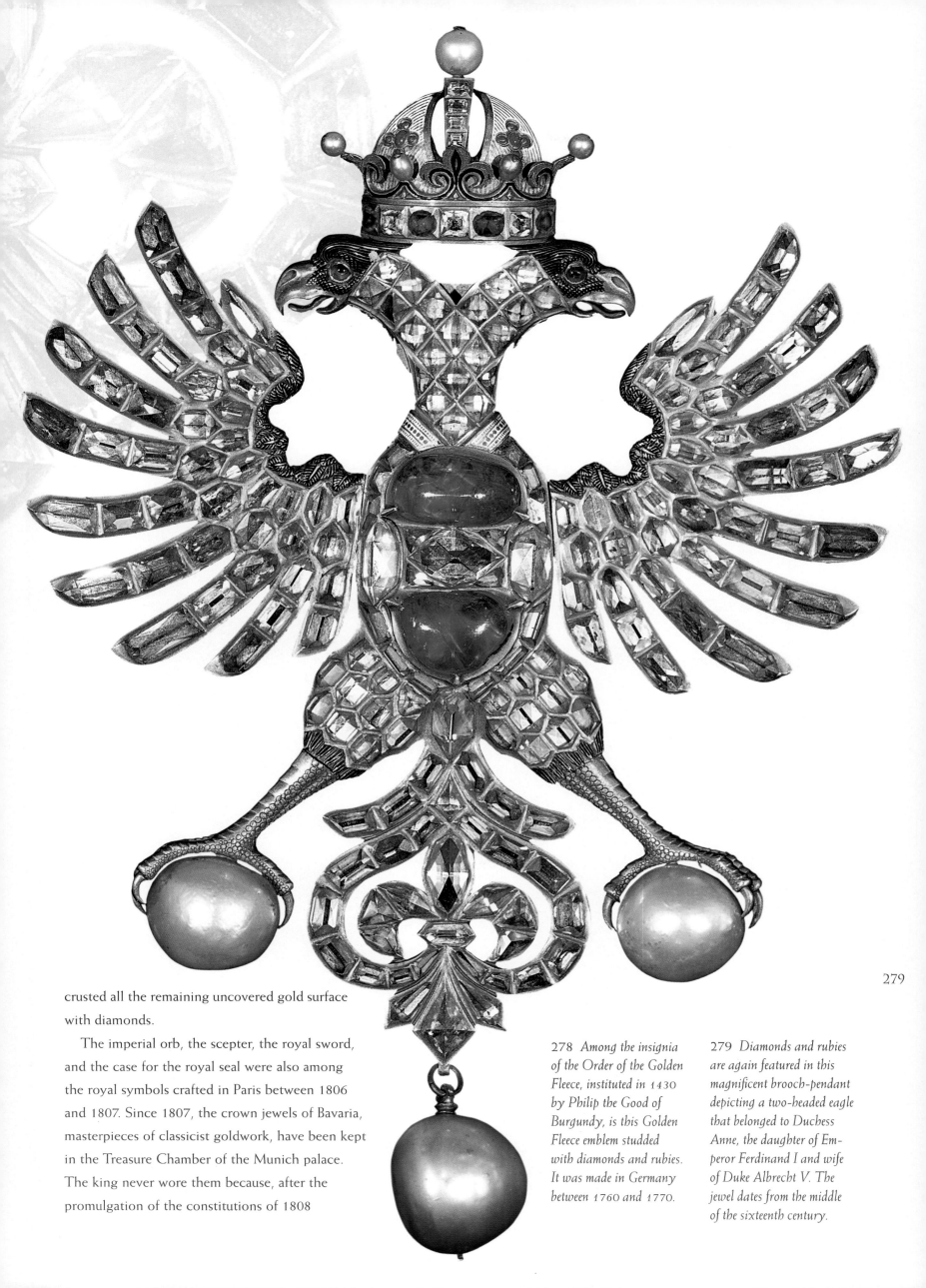

crusted all the remaining uncovered gold surface with diamonds.

The imperial orb, the scepter, the royal sword, and the case for the royal seal were also among the royal symbols crafted in Paris between 1806 and 1807. Since 1807, the crown jewels of Bavaria, masterpieces of classicist goldwork, have been kept in the Treasure Chamber of the Munich palace. The king never wore them because, after the promulgation of the constitutions of 1808

278 Among the insignia of the Order of the Golden Fleece, instituted in 1430 by Philip the Good of Burgundy, is this Golden Fleece emblem studded with diamonds and rubies. It was made in Germany between 1760 and 1770.

279 Diamonds and rubies are again featured in this magnificent brooch-pendant depicting a two-headed eagle that belonged to Duchess Anne, the daughter of Emperor Ferdinand I and wife of Duke Albrecht V. The jewel dates from the middle of the sixteenth century.

280 top *The "Crown of Henry" dates from 1280 and was made posthumously. It was manufactured either in France or the west of Germany. It features a delicate cameo in onyx, together with a profusion of precious stones and pearls. It belonged to the treasury of the cathedral of Bamberg, where it was used as the decoration for the reliquary bust of Emperor Henry II, canonized in 1146.*

and 1818, no coronation was held in Bavaria. The royal symbols were presented to the king on gold-embroidered red velvet cushions after he swore allegiance to the constitution; they were also presented before the king in the throne room of the palace on festive occasions.

Among the three crowns of the Wittelsbach collection, great significance is attached to the crown of an English queen. The gold filigree crown with lily motifs on the diadem is encrusted with rubies, sapphires, diamonds, pearls, and crafted pieces of enamel. The Gothic crown was crafted in western France between 1370 and 1380 and was first referred to in England in 1399 as an ancient jewel. This English crown, the oldest in existence, was given as a wedding gift to Princess Blanche, one of the daughters of Henry IV of England, when she

married the Elector Ludwig III of the Palatinate. The crown became part of the Wittelsbach collection when the so-called Treasure of the Palatinate fell to Bavaria. In 1779, the treasure chambers of the Wittelsbach princes of the Palatinate, at their residences in Heidelberg, Düsseldorf, and Mannheim, were shifted to Munich since the collateral line of the Palatinate became the main line of succession of Munich that was left without direct heirs.

The Munich Treasure Chamber was further enriched with secularization, that is to say, the closure of monasteries in 1803. Priceless early medieval church treasures were then kept in the Munich Residence and thus escaped being melted down by then Crown Prince Louis, who later became King Louis I. The most important works in this group that are still in the collection today

280

280 bottom *This precious gold belt clasp decorated with diamonds and rubies belonged to a Turkish pasha of the seventeenth century.*

281

281 This ornamental chain in gold, enamels, emeralds, spinel rubies, diamonds, and pearls dates from 1575. It was probably designed by the celebrated German goldsmith Hans Mielich. The chain was worn by the Bavarian kings in the nineteenth century in their role as Grand Masters of the Order during the ceremonies of the Knights of St. George. The Hohenstaufen eagle cameo carved in onyx in its center dates from 1230: the mount and the beautiful frame in gold, silver, and brilliants was the work of a Viennese craftsman and dates from 1720.

include the altar ciborium of King Arnulf of Carinthia, a portable altar crafted in Reims before the year 900; the "staurotheque" of the Emperor Henry II, dating to circa 1000, as well as the cross from more or less the same period that Queen Gisela of Hungary commissioned for the tomb of her mother, who was also her namesake, in Regensburg. The crown of the Empress Kunigund, a diadem in five parts encrusted with gems and pearls and decorated with gold filigree work, dates to about 1010–1020 and comes from the treasure of the Bamberg Cathedral, together with the crown of her husband, Emperor Henry II, although it was not crafted during his lifetime. This "Crown of Henry" was produced around 1280, either in

southern Germany or in France, as an ornamental reliquary for the head of the emperor who was canonized in 1146. The crown, made up of five lily-shaped plates, is embellished by an openwork wreath of gold-plated silver leaves, gems, pearls, and onyx cameos, as well as angel figures on the hinges. Lastly, the collection includes a chalice from the old chapel in Regensburg. This rock crystal chalice features cut-glass palm trees and was made in Egypt around the year 1000; it was transformed into a twin-handled chalice in a gold-plated silver version in the twelfth century.

Throughout the centuries, the Bavarian royal family bequeathed individual jewels or works of art to the collection. Anne of Austria, wife to Albrecht V

of Bavaria and daughter of the Hapsburg Emperor Ferdinand I, left a jewel in the form of a two-headed eagle that was undoubtedly created in Italy in 1550; it features the shield of Austria on its breast and the imperial crown of the Hapsburgs on its head. Empress Amalia, daughter of Emperor Joseph I and wife of the Elector Karl Albert of Bavaria, who, in 1742, became Emperor Charles VII, left a precious box made in Vienna around 1720; it has a cameo depicting the Hohenstaufen imperial eagle at its center. The stonecutting that dates to 1230 is the largest of its kind known.

283 top This medieval object of extraordinary elegance is a two-handled chalice in rock crystal, silver, and precious stones. The crystal dates to the year 1000, while the mount— probably German—is from the twelfth century.

283 bottom Of imperial taste, this finely engraved gold and silver seal box was crafted by the French goldsmith Biennais. It is part of the insignia of the Bavarian crown.

283

In the eighteenth century the male heirs of the House of Wittelsbach bequeathed a series of precious decorations of various royal orders. These include the jewels of the two orders of the House of Wittelsbach, the Order of the Knights of St. George, and the Order of the Knights of St. Hubert, but also priceless pieces of the Order of the Golden Fleece. One such fleece, dating to 1760–1770, is decorated with a large Oriental garnet and an almandine. The Bavarian Elector Maximilian Emanuel seems to have taken a large number of Ottoman artistic objects as spoils of war from the Turks, including a seventeenth-century belt buckle in gold encrusted with diamonds and rubies. Significant pieces of exotic craftsmanship were gifted to the Wittelsbach collection, including sixteenth-century ivory chests from Ceylon and a gold ring with an eagle's head that is one of the rare works from the Monte Albán tombs in Mexico that escaped melting by Spanish conquistadores.

A considerable proportion of the Munich Treasure Chamber is made up of works from goldsmithing centers in southern Germany, Nuremberg and Augsburg. The most significant goldsmith from Nuremberg, Wenzel Jamnitzer, is represented with an entire series of his masterpieces. A working sketch for one of his jewelry boxes dated to 1550–1560, depicting the deeds of Hercules and bequeathed by Duke Wilhelm V of Bavaria, is even preserved in Berlin. The goldsmithing tradition of Augsburg during the seventeenth and eighteenth centuries is represented by precious tablewares, especially tea and dinner services or drinking vessels. The Treasure Chamber also houses a small collection of rare watches; the most noteworthy is a piece richly decorated with enamels, gems, and cut shells from the House of Hapsburg.

Since 1958, the precious pieces of the Wittelsbach collection are exhibited in ten halls of the Royal Palace of Munich, open to the general public.

284 Among the most remarkable and precious baroque objects in the treasury is this table clock. Crafted at Augsburg, of gilded silver, enamels, cameos, and precious stones, it dates to 1680. The two-headed imperial eagle decorates the summit of the clock.

285 This statue of St. George is today a cult object for Bavarians; created in 1597 as a reliquary, probably to the designs of Friedrich Sustris, it is an exercise in extraordinary technical virtuosity. The goldsmith has succeeded in combining gold, silver, enamels, and a blaze of precious and semiprecious stones.

THE KREMLIN'S DIAMONDS

286 The "small" imperial crown in silver completely covered with diamonds of exceptional quality belonged to Empress Elizabeth, wife of Czar Alexander I. Designed by the French court goldsmiths Jacob and Jean Duval in 1801, the jewel is well proportioned and extremely elegant with its repeated cloverleaf motif.

286–287 This image shows the solemn moment when Alexander III placed the small crown on the head of his wife, Maria Fyodorovna, in 1882. The photograph is taken from the official album of the emperor's coronation.

287 *The large crown created by the court jeweler J. Posier in 1762 for the coronation of Catherine II is made of silver, brilliants, pearls, and ruby spinels. It is traditional in form with two open hemispheres; at the center is located a strap with an orb and cross. The brilliants trace a laurel leaf pattern symbolizing power and glory. This jewel is today one of the prized possessions of the State Diamond Fund in the Kremlin.*

The Kremlin, the first walled city in Russia, was built after Khan Toqtamis burned and sacked the city of Moscow in 1386. Ever since, the Kremlin has been Russia's citadel of power, the inaccessible place that controls the city and the whole immense country, stretching from the Baltic to the Pacific Ocean. But the Kremlin is also the heart of Russia's spiritual and cultural life: beginning in the mid-fifteenth century, Italian architects built cathedrals within its protective walls, and the workshops that produced everything necessary for displaying the grandeur of the state were also concentrated here.

The history of the Kremlin's treasure retraces the history of Moscow, the youngest of the great Russian cities, which in less than two centuries became the capital of an immense empire. The first mention of the treasure dates to 1476–78, when, as the chronicler states, "300 carts of pearls, gold, silver and precious stones" reached Moscow from Novgorod, which had just been conquered. A few years later,

288 These three bow brooches have an extremely delicate appearance because of their lacelike structure with brilliants of various sizes. The largest piece weighs 155 grams and the two smaller ones 98 grams. They date from the middle of the eighteenth century and are conserved in the Kremlin as part of the State Diamond Fund.

288–289 This analogous jewel, which dates to 1810, is made of gold, silver, and brilliants. It is embellished with a 13-carat square pinky brilliant and weighs about 200 grams. Its lower circumference is 33 centimeters.

between 1484 and 1485, the building later known as *Kamennyj dvor*, or "the Stone Court," was built; it was destined to become the site of the prince's private treasure and later the state treasury.

The various ateliers appeared in the first half of the sixteenth century; the most important were the *Oružejnaja palata*, or Kremlin Armory; the *Postel'naja*, which made the fabrics used for the sovereign's clothing and court furnishings; and the *Zolotaja* and *Serebrjannaja*, gold and silver workshops, respectively.

The Kremlin Armory, where the Kremlin's treasure is currently displayed, was originally a production and storage site for the weapons of the sovereign and the court. But the best craftsmen gathered around it, called from every corner of Russia, as well as from Germany, Italy, Poland, and Bohemia. It constantly sought new technologies, but within a strict adherence to Russian tradition that bordered on cult worship. At the end of the seventeenth century, the activity of the Kremlin's ateliers slowed abruptly, and in the early eighteenth century, when all master craftsmen were transferred to the new capital, St. Petersburg, activity ceased altogether.

Almost foretelling the modern-day museum, the armory was given the task of safeguarding the

289 *The scepter in gold, silver, enamel, and diamonds is a jewel designed at St. Petersburg in 1770. It includes the celebrated Orlov Diamond, one of the largest and purest gemstones in the Russian collection (189.62 carats). Numerous legends have grown up around this extraordinary gem found in India, where, in the seventeenth century, it adorned an idol of a god at Srirangam. The following century it was stolen from the temple and, in a roundabout fashion, reached the Shah of Persia, Nadir. In the 1770s it was acquired by Count Orlov for 400,000 rubles and presented to Empress Catherine II.*

290 top Four magnificent rubies embellish the insignia of the Order of St. Anne, one of the highest Russian honors conferred for particular services to the state. Made of gold, silver, rubies, and enamel, it dates from the late eighteenth century and weighs 20 grams.

290 bottom This rich semicircular diadem is made of gold, silver, brilliants, and rubies, measures 8.5 x 8.5 centimeters, and also dates from the late eighteenth century.

290–291 *This extremely elegant clasp reveals the French taste of its creator, the court jeweler J. Posier. It was made at St. Petersburg in the middle of the eighteenth century.*

291 bottom left *This pair of earrings with drop pendants is composed of a series of diamonds framing magnificent rubies. It is also a design from the second half of the eighteenth century and measures 6 x 4.5 centimeters.*

291 bottom right *This esclavage bow in gold, silver, brilliants, and spinel rubies is a jewel designed by the court goldsmith L. Pfisterer in 1764. It weighs 153 grams and is 11.3 centimeters wide.*

291

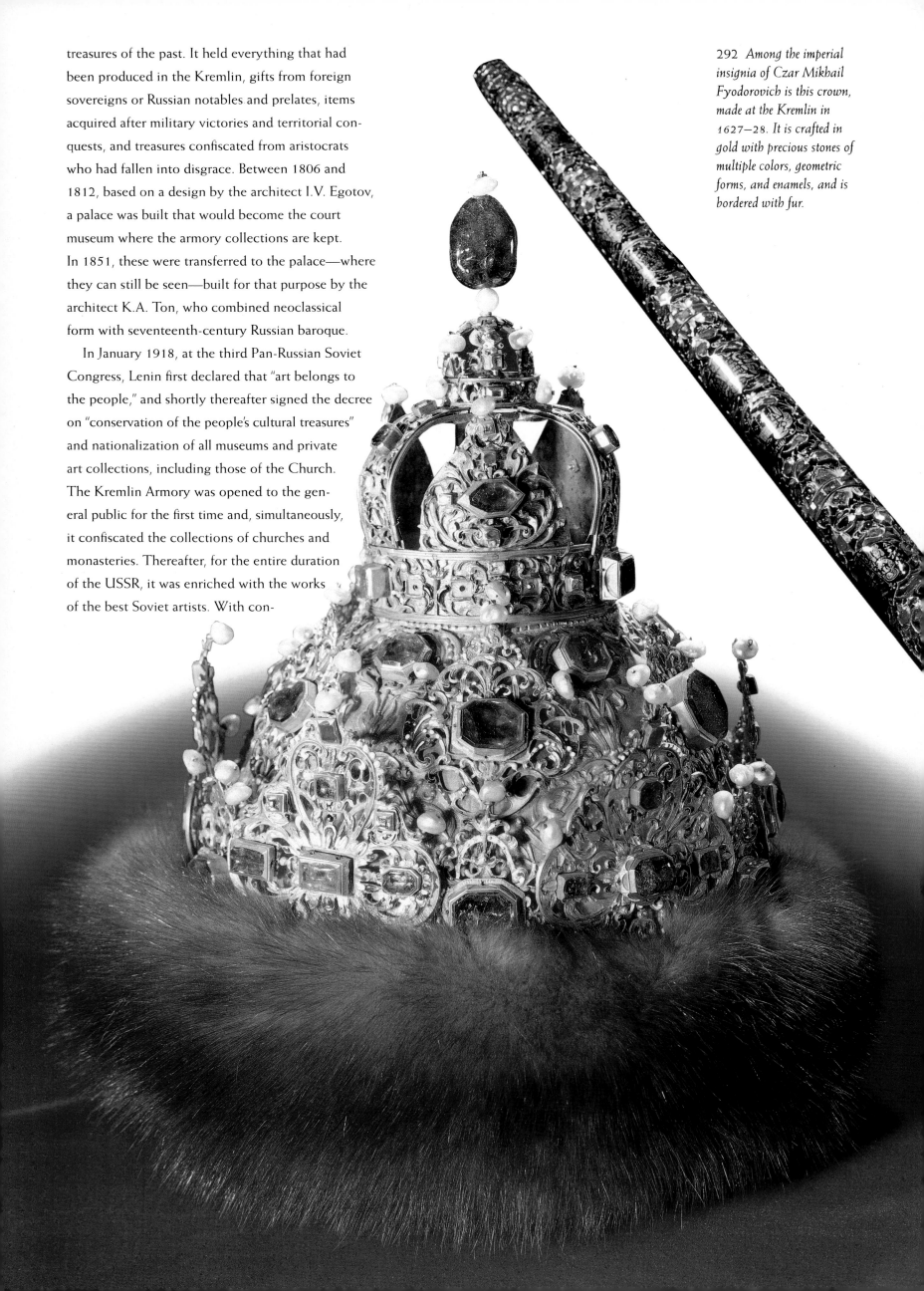

treasures of the past. It held everything that had
been produced in the Kremlin, gifts from foreign
sovereigns or Russian notables and prelates, items
acquired after military victories and territorial conquests, and treasures confiscated from aristocrats
who had fallen into disgrace. Between 1806 and
1812, based on a design by the architect I.V. Egotov,
a palace was built that would become the court
museum where the armory collections are kept.
In 1851, these were transferred to the palace—where
they can still be seen—built for that purpose by the
architect K.A. Ton, who combined neoclassical
form with seventeenth-century Russian baroque.

In January 1918, at the third Pan-Russian Soviet
Congress, Lenin first declared that "art belongs to
the people," and shortly thereafter signed the decree
on "conservation of the people's cultural treasures"
and nationalization of all museums and private
art collections, including those of the Church.
The Kremlin Armory was opened to the general public for the first time and, simultaneously,
it confiscated the collections of churches and
monasteries. Thereafter, for the entire duration
of the USSR, it was enriched with the works
of the best Soviet artists. With con-

292 *Among the imperial
insignia of Czar Mikhail
Fyodorovich is this crown,
made at the Kremlin in
1627–28. It is crafted in
gold with precious stones of
multiple colors, geometric
forms, and enamels, and is
bordered with fur.*

tinued zeal, these metalsmiths and lapidaries followed in the steps of their eighteenth- and nineteenth-century predecessors, drawing inspiration from models of classical purity in the Russian tradition.

The continuity of the tradition is particularly visible in the crowns. Czar Mikhail Fyodorovich's crown is a faithful reproduction of another piece displayed in the armory, the Monomachus Crown, said to have been donated by the Eastern Roman Emperor Constantine Monomachus to the prince of Kiev, Vladimir Vsevolodovich, as a sign of his imperial dignity and that of his descendants. It is a half-circle of gold edged with fur and studded with precious stones. The only difference is that the Romanesque simplicity of the older crown is replaced by the baroque imperial magniloquence of the more recent version. The difference between these crowns and later ones is that the former are not art objects but simply symbols of power, while the second ones are also objects of art.

In the so-called great crown, first used at the coronation of Catherine II in 1762, and in the small one, made in the early nineteenth century to crown the czar's wife, the cap opens into two hemispheres and is surmounted by a small cross, based on the one on the Monomachus Crown. The use of diamonds —the only precious stone not found in the soil of the Russian/Soviet empire, which is incredibly rich in gold and gems of every kind—only underscores the power and grandeur of the person who wears them. It is no coincidence that

293

292–293 and 293
The scepter and the orb of Czar Alexander are of Ottoman origin, made in Istanbul in the seventeenth century. The extraordinary coloring and decoration *that leaves no free space but rather superimposes brightly colored precious stones over enamels, along with the intricate gilded frame, reveal the works' origins.*

294–295 *The beautiful Russian Field Diadem, so-called for its delicate ears of corn traced in diamonds, is made of platinum, gold, and brilliants. This modern piece was designed in 1980. Almost 600 grams in weight, it features a splendid 35.52-carat yellow brilliant at the center.*

some of the motifs of the imperial crown and diadem can also be seen in Soviet-made jewels, which also use a large quantity of diamonds. The scepter and orb (in Russian, *deržava*, which also means "power"), which the Russian czars inherited from the Eastern Roman emperors, are also of ancient origins, according to two complementary legends from the sixteenth century: one says that the princes of Moscow descended from Augustus; the other speaks of Moscow as the "third Rome," stating that after the first two fell because of their sins, the third would live on forever.

In the late-eighteenth-century scepter appears a two-headed eagle, the imperial symbol par excellence, representing Constantinople, the Hapsburgs, and the Mongol khans. The two-headed eagle was the Russian coat of arms from the end of the fifteenth century to the Bolshevik Revolution; in 1991, President Yeltsin used it to replace the hammer and sickle.

The history of art is inseparably bound to that of power in a country like Russia, which has always been messianic and imperial in nature, and even now shows no signs of changing.

295 Both the earring with pendants and the "Anniversary" necklace in platinum, gold, brilliants, and rubies are contemporary pieces made in the 1980s. The droplet motifs alternate with rosettes to form an extremely elegant composition.

296 This diadem, known as the Russian Beauty, is a contemporary piece created by a group of Russian jewelers in 1987. Platinum, brilliants, and 25 pearls are combined in a composition that is notably airy and elegant in spite of weighing almost 400 grams.

297 This extraordinary parure of jewels is dominated by the green of its exceptional emeralds, alternating with the sparkle of the brilliants. The necklace and the rigid bracelet with pendants are contemporary works made in the 1970s by Soviet jewelers.

THE GOLDEN TALE OF THE TOPKAPI

For anyone passionately fond of gold and jewelry, who thrills at the sight of precious stones beautifully set in precious metals—art and nature fused in a single object—few places could hold more appeal than the Topkapi Palace Museum in Istanbul. The world of cinema contributes to the fascination of the visit: who, after all, does not remember the movie *Topkapi*, centered on the theft of the famous dagger?

From around 1470, when the first buildings were constructed by Mehmed the Conqueror, to 1839, the Topkapi was the official residence of the sultan. Today it is one of the world's outstanding museums, with vast collections of documents of unique importance to the history of the Ottoman empire. Between 1453 (siege and conquest of Constantinople) and 1923 (proclamation of the Turkish Republic) the Ottoman sultans—members of the dynasty started by Osman I in the late thirteenth century—were protagonists of an extraordinary period of history. The Turks gained control of much of the Mediterranean and established an empire that eventually had direct political rule over a large part of the Muslim world (as Braudel has pointed out, its rise had amazing symmetries with that of the Spanish empire under Philip II).

These two ceremonial helmets date from the mid-sixteenth century. The frames in iron are completely covered with damasked gold, niello work, and enamels; they are studded with turquoise and rubies as if in imitation of an extraordinary illuminated manuscript. The verses from the Koran praising Allah, along the base of the helmet on the right, are also highly decorative.

299

298 top *This gold dagger studded with diamonds and three enormous emeralds is one of the most famous and highly symbolic objects contained in the Topkapi Treasury. At the top of the handle, a large octagonal hinged and faceted emerald conceals* *a miniature English clock. This is a jewel of exquisite craftsmanship made in the first half of the eighteenth century as a gift for the Shah of Persia Nadir. After his death it returned to the palace of the sultans.*

This important chapter in world history culminated in 1571 with the Battle of Lepanto, a naval defeat for the Turks at the hands of the Christian fleet comprised particularly of Spanish and Venetian ships (the effective outcome of the battle, however, was to institutionalize the coexistence of the two empires in the Mediterranean).

The decline of the Ottoman state became increasingly evident from the seventeenth century onward. The real task of government was left more and more in the hands of court officials. The intrinsic weakness of the Ottoman empire was to have created not a nation but an administration preoccupied with collecting taxes and little concerned with developing a comprehensive plan for different peoples and situations. It was hardly surprising that its subjects became increasingly restless, and foreign interference was a constant threat. In the 1800s, the century of European colonial expansion, the Ottoman empire started to fall apart and efforts directed at its modernization by recent sultans, in particular Mahmud II (1808–1839), proved to little avail. With Mahmud gone, the Topkapi Palace was abandoned as official residence (many regarded it as a cumbersome symbol of a Turkey they were anxious to leave behind).

The sultans had other splendid palaces built; the most prominent was the Dolmabahçe, erected on the Bosphorus between 1843 and 1856. Decorating these more modern, more "European" buildings—amid crystal balustrades and Murano chandeliers—were paintings of Turkish scenes by Italian and French Orientalist artists: a curious sign of the Turkish courtiers' desire to see themselves in the

300 top One of the greatest attractions of the Topkapi is this incredible stone known as the "spoon-merchant's diamond" (Kasikçi), surrounded by 49 smaller diamonds in a double row for a total of 86 carats. As with all legendary stones, there are fantastic stories associated with this diamond, said to have been purchased in 1774 by the Maharajah of Madras before passing to Napoleon's mother and finally being sold in Turkey.

300 right A veritable cascade of diamonds, pearls, and colored precious stones composes a splendid turban jewel dating from the seventeenth century.

301 top The star of the oldest Persian knightly order, that of the Lion and the Sun, features a lion at the center brandishing a scimitar surmounted by the crown worn by the Qajar sovereigns of Iran. Made of gold, diamonds, and enamels, it was presented to the sultan Abdul Hamid II late in the nineteenth century.

301

301 center This jewel of extraordinary elegance is an Islamic piece from the eighteenth century and plays on the alternation of emeralds, pearls and red enamel. In spite of the exceptional dimensions of some of the stones, an effect of airy lightness is obtained.

301 bottom This Turkish watch dates from the middle of the seventeenth century. With its round face encrusted with rubies, emeralds, and turquoise, it is an object of extremely fine craftsmanship, testimony to the remarkable skills of the Ottoman jewelers and goldsmiths of the era.

image that "the others" had of them. Meanwhile, a new emphasis on archaeology developed in Turkey, of German positivist stamp, as these were the years when the Kaiser was attempting to bring the Ottoman empire within his sphere of influence. The Topkapi Palace was thus turned into an outstanding museum of the Ottoman sultanate and civilization. Contained within its walls today are thousands of everyday objects used by hundreds of individuals who at some time lived in the building, and archival documents with which it is possible to reconstruct their lives.

Visitors to the museum's four treasure rooms had better be prepared for the overwhelming effects such profusion can produce (the initial sense of wonder degenerates into nausea as a consequence of such an abundant amount of gems). It is advisable to ignore the exact carats of the stones (their huge size is in any case obvious) or the number of rubies set in a jug flaunted by the

302 bottom The Festival Throne was used by the sultans exclusively on the occasion of the great religious celebrations of the Muslim year. Made of walnut covered with gold, it is studded with 954 peridots of various shapes and sizes. The throne can be dismantled into ten panels and, in the past, it would have featured a canopy now lost. The overall design of this imposing piece dates from the late sixteenth century, while the heavy gold-embroidered upholstery is from the ninteenth century.

302–303 top *This regal Ottoman cradle covered with gilded silver is also decorated with countless diamonds, rubies, and emeralds; it dates from the seventeenth century.*

303 right *The canopied throne of the sultan Ahmed I, who reigned early in the seventeenth century, is studded with mother-of-pearl, rock crystal, ivory, and dazzling precious stones tracing a dense pattern of stylized floral motifs. The throne is topped by a polygonal lantern in gold, rubies, and emeralds, and a pennant in rock crystal. A fabulous jewel with a large emerald and delicate rows of pearls hangs from the canopy, the oldest of those conserved in the Topkapi Treasury.*

guide. What matters is to unravel the collection's historical significance.

It is relevant to remember that many important treasures are in fact exhibited in other sections of the museum among arms, apparel, and horses' harnesses. In addition, the items displayed should not simply be taken at face value for they represent not real life but its expositive projection. It would be silly to suppose that the sultan and members of his household "played ball" with the amazing diamonds and emeralds that fill a whole series of glass cases. Besides being part of the sultan's riches, a guarantee of the economic health of the Sublime Porte, jewels were essentially a symbol, intended to shine primarily on ritual social occasions at court. Viewed from another perspective, they were emblematic of the sultan's isolation from the social life of his dominions, as his role gradually shrank to that of an invisible queen bee.

Western visitors must also be on their guard against anachronistic exoticism. We may consider Turkish civilization to bear the fragrance of the Orient, in far-away scenarios set by *The Thousand and One Nights*. It is true that, for Christian Europe of the sixteenth and seventeenth centuries, the empire did represent a different world, but a very real one with which there was constant confrontation. Very close links existed between these two worlds. The sultan was not a dozy gentleman who wore diadems and drank coffee from diamond-studded cups; he was instead the symbol of an enemy state that, besides being efficient and well structured, was also often more tolerant of ethnic and cultural minorities than the Christian kingdoms. And these

306 *A faceted emerald is set at the center of this binding for the Koran and encrusted with brilliants. The floral motifs set within* *geometric frames reveal the influence of Western European taste and allows this jewel to be dated to the early nineteenth century.*

307 *This bookbinding is exceptionally opulent and belonged to the sultan Murad III, who reigned in the late sixteenth century. The decoration and the juxtapositioning of precious* *stones fills every available space. Medallions encrusted with stones alternate with sinuous decoration and the undulating lines of the inscriptions in a triumph of golden light.*

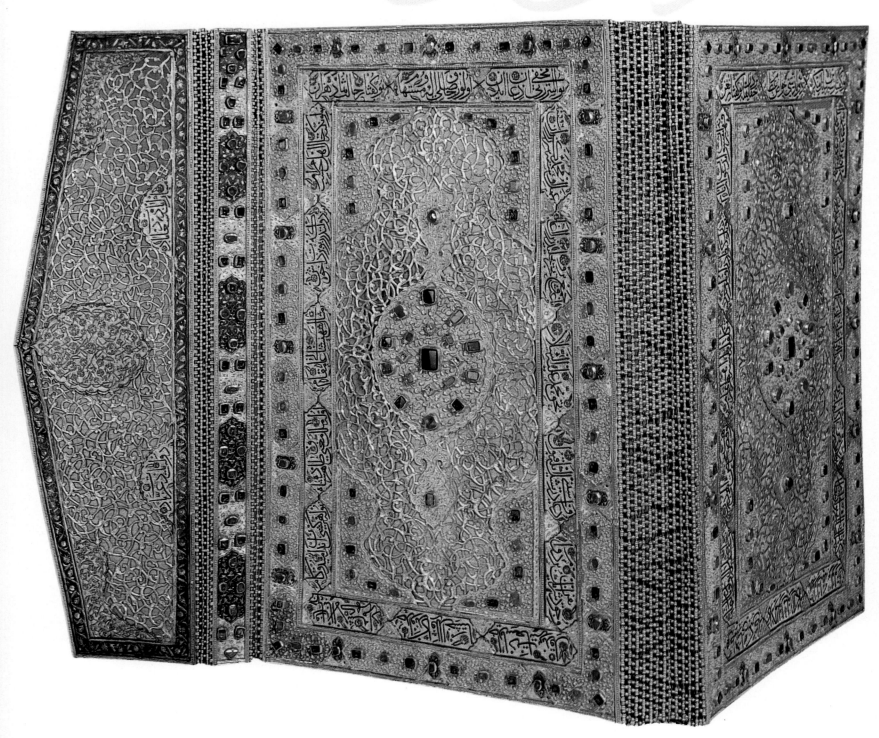

minorities were the bone of contention on which the diplomatic efforts of the great powers were focused.

Each of the precious gems exhibited in the Topkapi Palace has many tales to tell: many have lived more than one life, having passed from one object to another in a slow but interminable process of change. Widely assorted styles and every kind of goldsmithing technique are displayed side by side. The evolution of taste is self-evident: toward the end of the 1700s the conventions of European jewelry making had been fully accepted here too, and European modes and fashions were extended to other

aspects of everyday life in Turkey, including clothing and furnishings.

The stated history of each individual piece is merely indicative: How did it come to be in the palace? Who donated it? Why was it commissioned? It is important to remember that in past centuries jewels much less important than those of the Topkapi collections were ordered directly from the craftsman by the buyer; they were therefore designed to suit the buyer's taste, his economic limitations, and the intended user. The cultural importance of jewelry meant that every instant of daily life and every

307

social ritual of *homo ludens* (to use the term neatly coined by Huizinga), from table to battlefield, were marked by the possible presence of extremely precious objects: swords and glasses, perfume-holders, cases for copies of the Koran. For in the Islamic world, the plastic and figurative arts are essentially applied arts: even when an object's function is clearly secondary to its beauty and preciousness, it must still be visible and recognizable. This explains why—to a far greater degree than in the gold and jewelry-making traditions of other civilizations—there are relatively few purely decorative objects. Many parallels are to be found in beautifully executed everyday objects of infinitely lower value: the forms attributed to a coffee pot, dinner plate, even the case in which the Sacred Writings are kept, are not substantially different from corresponding items made of pewter or leather. The gold or gilded cradle and beds have the same design as furniture used by Anatolian peasants or members of the urban bourgeois.

It is interesting to note how the political and religious history of the Ottoman empire is reflected in these jewels, and not only in connection with specific occasions for which they were made and taken to Istanbul. Persia's influence on gold and

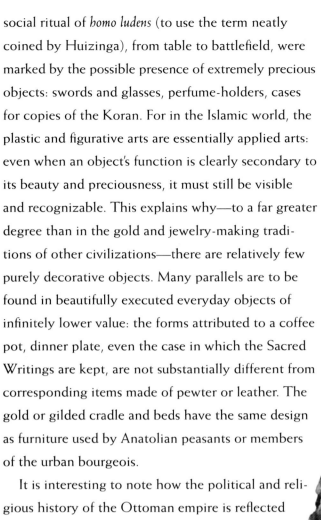

308

308 *Fine examples of ceremonial tableware, these two sumptuous lidded mugs from the sixteenth or seventeenth century feature magnificent rubies and emeralds set in a chased gold tracery.*

308–309 *Rubies, emeralds, and rock crystal medallions cover this box from the late sixteenth century containing a writing set.*

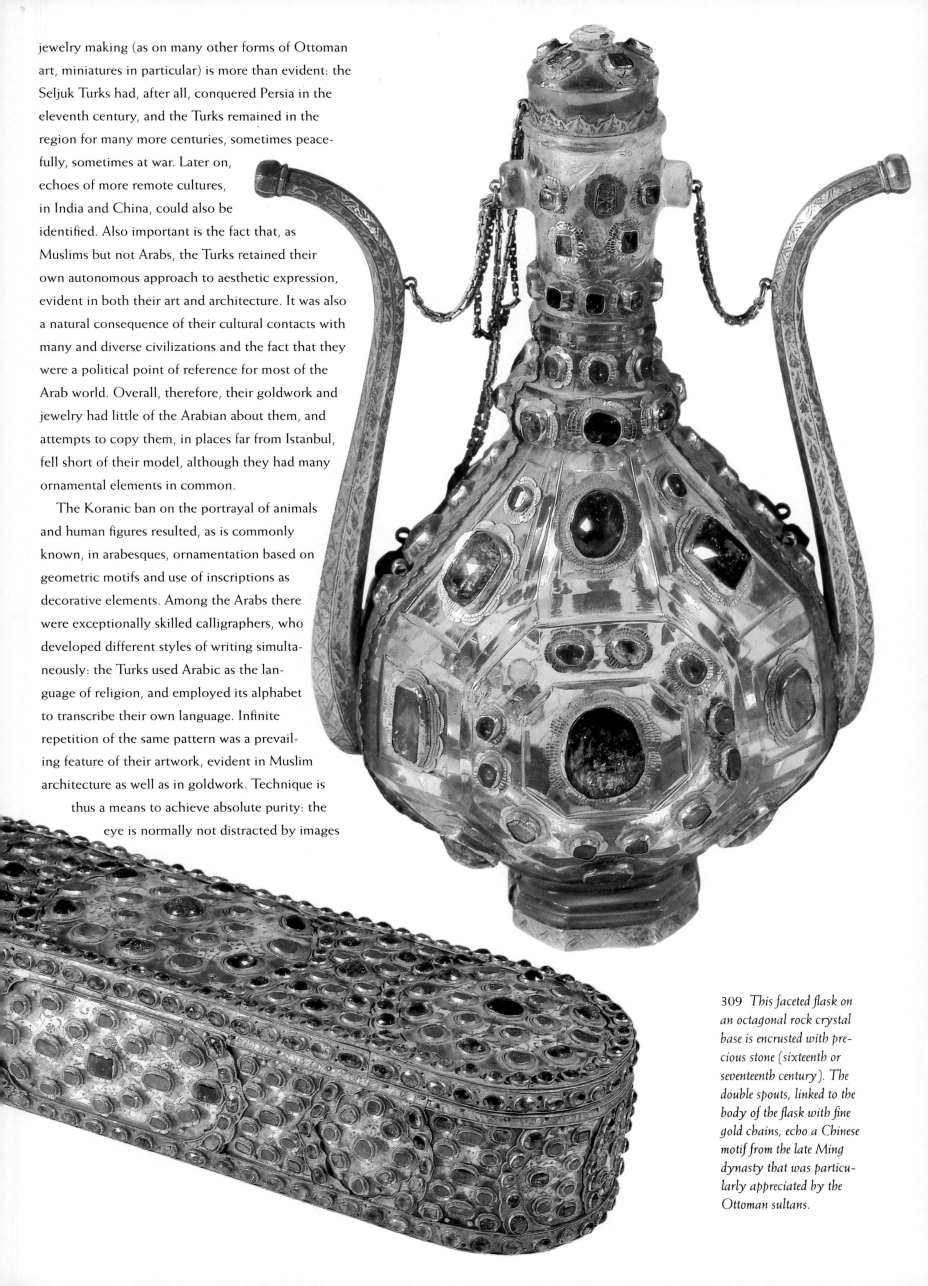

jewelry making (as on many other forms of Ottoman art, miniatures in particular) is more than evident: the Seljuk Turks had, after all, conquered Persia in the eleventh century, and the Turks remained in the region for many more centuries, sometimes peacefully, sometimes at war. Later on, echoes of more remote cultures, in India and China, could also be identified. Also important is the fact that, as Muslims but not Arabs, the Turks retained their own autonomous approach to aesthetic expression, evident in both their art and architecture. It was also a natural consequence of their cultural contacts with many and diverse civilizations and the fact that they were a political point of reference for most of the Arab world. Overall, therefore, their goldwork and jewelry had little of the Arabian about them, and attempts to copy them, in places far from Istanbul, fell short of their model, although they had many ornamental elements in common.

The Koranic ban on the portrayal of animals and human figures resulted, as is commonly known, in arabesques, ornamentation based on geometric motifs and use of inscriptions as decorative elements. Among the Arabs there were exceptionally skilled calligraphers, who developed different styles of writing simultaneously: the Turks used Arabic as the language of religion, and employed its alphabet to transcribe their own language. Infinite repetition of the same pattern was a prevailing feature of their artwork, evident in Muslim architecture as well as in goldwork. Technique is thus a means to achieve absolute purity: the eye is normally not distracted by images

309 This faceted flask on an octagonal rock crystal base is encrusted with precious stone (sixteenth or seventeenth century). The double spouts, linked to the body of the flask with fine gold chains, echo a Chinese motif from the late Ming dynasty that was particularly appreciated by the Ottoman sultans.

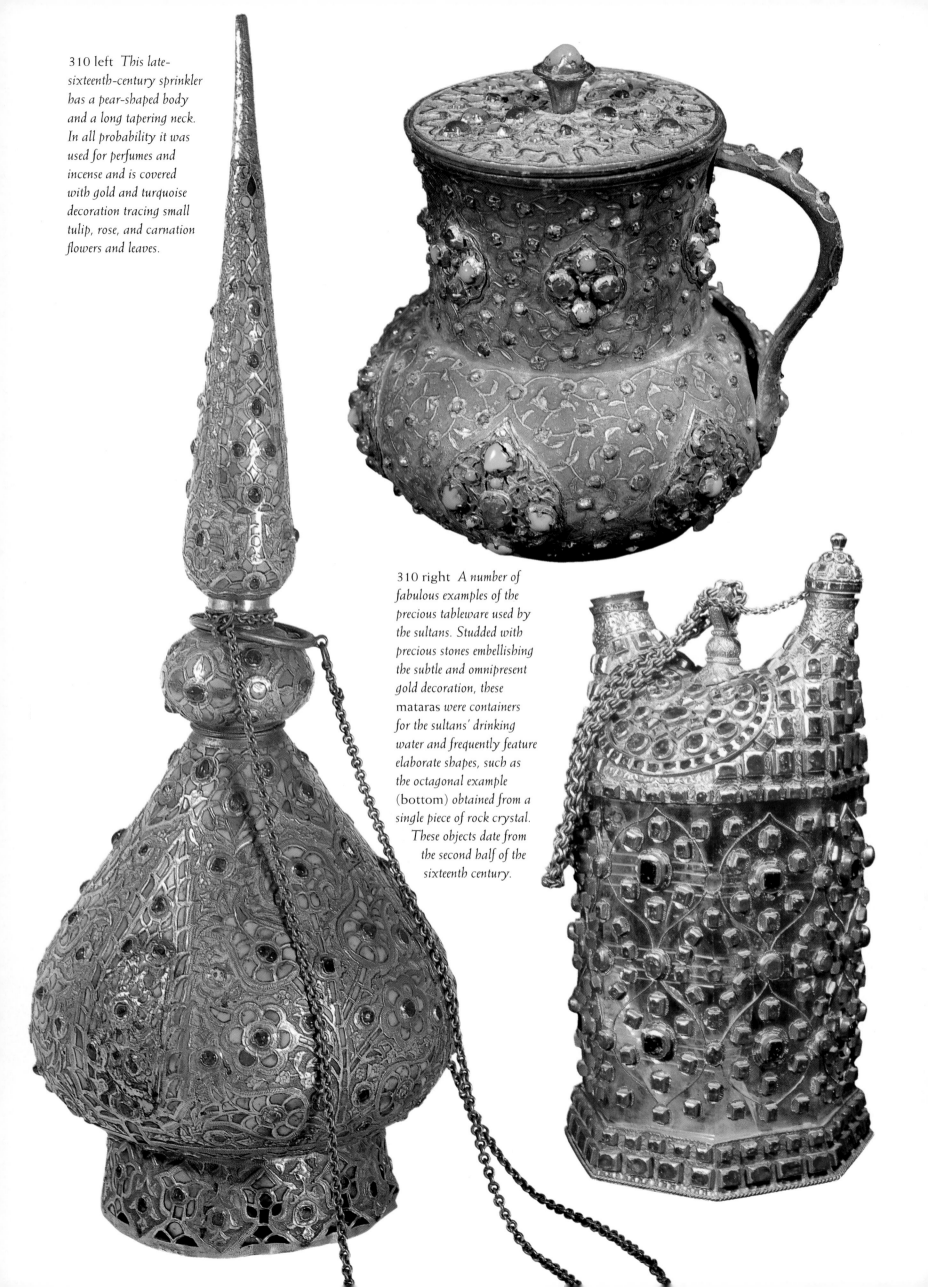

310 left *This late-sixteenth-century sprinkler has a pear-shaped body and a long tapering neck. In all probability it was used for perfumes and incense and is covered with gold and turquoise decoration tracing small tulip, rose, and carnation flowers and leaves.*

310 right *A number of fabulous examples of the precious tableware used by the sultans. Studded with precious stones embellishing the subtle and omnipresent gold decoration, these* mataras *were containers for the sultans' drinking water and frequently feature elaborate shapes, such as the octagonal example (bottom) obtained from a single piece of rock crystal. These objects date from the second half of the sixteenth century.*

311 left *This small jug features oval medallions that closely resemble the designs on Oriental fabrics, framing splendid gemstones, including emeralds, rubies, and sapphires.*

311 right *This unusually simple and plain gold candlestick reveals its Oriental origins through the Arabic writing that decorates the base.*

created by precious stones, nor by figures to which fili-gree gives form in other goldworking traditions. Light—the light of the sun—enhances the abstract beauty of man's artifacts, on which a verse from the Koran can serve as a reminder of both the presence of God, Allah, the absolute Being, and that of man who adores Him with heart and mind. By now the old Islamic ban on using objects made of solid gold and silver had lost currency in the Ottoman capital. It was in any case a thing of the past, having been circumvented in various ways: for instance, by gold-plating or gilding pieces in bronze, copper, or iron; or by getting Christian or Jewish infidels to make pieces of jewelry. The stunning gold and gems of Topkapi therefore remain as a permanent testimonial to the Ottoman civilization's outstanding taste for beauty, as well as to the power and far-reaching influence of its empire.

311

STATUES IN GOLD FROM MYSTERIOUS THAILAND

312 The magnificent 18-centimeter-high representation of Buddha in gilded wood comes from the crypt of the Wat (temple) Ratchaburana at Ayutthaya (late fifteenth century). Buddha is depicted in the bhumisparsamudra pose: seated with his legs crossed, the left hand resting on the ankle of the right leg and the right arm extended toward the ground. This position represents Buddha calling on the Earth to witness in the face of evil. The half-closed eyes and a barely sketched serene smile—clearly influenced by the Khmer style—are characteristic of Buddha's state of meditation. The usnisa, in the form of a flame, typical of the Thai images of Buddha, can be seen on the head of the statue: this represents the moment of complete enlightenment.

313 *These two repoussé gold plaques represent Buddha in two different mudras, or poses: in the bhumisparsamudra, seated on a lotus flower throne, and in the abhayamudra, the gesture of dispelling fear that symbolizes Buddha's first sermon in the Deer Park at Sarnath.*

Intensive cultural exchanges took place between East and West during the first five centuries of the first millennium, a continual movement of goods and ideas that is documented in both archaeological terms and through the works of the Greek, Latin, and Indian historians and geographers. Between the fourth and sixth centuries, the relationship of cultural interaction between India and the regions of Indochina and Indonesia led virtually the entire population of continental and insular Southeast Asia to adopt writing systems from India (Sanskrit and Pali), the Hindu and Buddhist religions, and the Indian concept of regality.

In the Indian texts we find passages in which "a land of riches and abundance beyond the setting sun" is located to the east of the Gulf of Bengal. In the majority of cases, the noun *gold* or the adjective *golden* is used, as in the terms *Suvarnadripa* and *Suvarnabhumi* (which mean,

313

respectively, "Land of Gold" and "Islands of Gold") or *Suvarnakudya* ("Wall" or "Frontier of Gold").

In the contemporary Greek and Latin literature the regions "beyond the rising sun" in which "the soil was gold" had been well known. Here, too, the place-names chosen were associated with the two precious metals: *Chryse, Argyre, Chryse Chora, Chryse Cheronesus,* and *Auren Cheronesus*.

In terms of archaeological prestige, however, it is by no means Thailand that "shines" in terms of the discoveries of gold or other precious metals: a few beads made from fine gold-leaf have been found at levels datable to between the fourth and seventh centuries A.D. at the Tha Kae site, while at Kantarawichai in northeast Thailand, 66 finely worked repoussé silver plaquettes with scenes of Buddhist inspiration have been

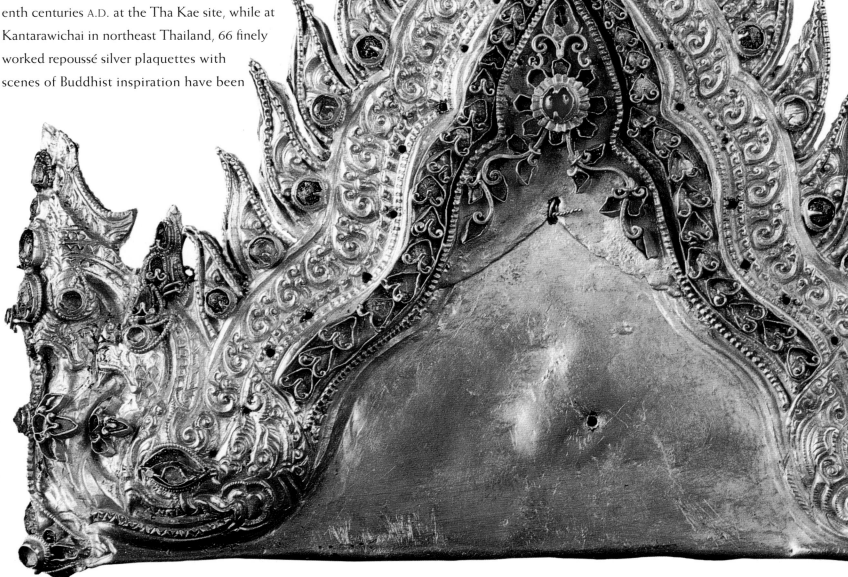

found. A number of small ornaments in gold have, furthermore, been discovered at Oc Eo in Vietnam, also datable to between the fourth and sixth centuries.

The true "Eastern El Dorado," the land described and dreamed of in the ancient Greek, Latin, and Indian literature, is instead to be sought in the archipelagoes between Indonesia and Borneo, where the most sophisticated gold manufactures of Southeast Asia have been found. The principal center of production of these treasures was Java.

Java was, in fact, the source of stunningly beautiful ornaments dating from the prehistoric era (500 B.C.– 500 A.D.): finely cut thin sheets of gold laid over the

eyes, nose, and mouth of the deceased; earrings in the form of open ovals and rings in braided gold wire datable to the late prehistoric period (second through seventh centuries A.D.); marvellous rings with inscribed collets or repoussé gold plaques datable to between the seventh and tenth centuries; and, finally, regal earrings with *makara* masks from the Majapahit period (fourteenth to fifteenth centuries). This is the goldworking tradition that profoundly influenced all the kingdoms of Indochina, including that of the Khmer. For most of us, discussion of the art of the kingdom of the Khmer evokes images of the sumptuous architecture of the tem-

314 *The goldsmiths of Ayutthaya were influenced by the Indonesian and Indian traditions. They achieved high technical sophistication, the metal being worked in the filigree and embossing techniques, with the insertion of precious stones. This piece is a decorative element of the pediment of a miniature shrine (Prang), found in the crypt of the main Prang at Wat Ratchaburana.*

314

ple-palace at Angkor, the statues of Buddha, the long serpentine handrails, and the myriad divinities of an extensive pantheon sculptured in stone.

Of Khmer goldsmithing, little has survived; however, much can be deduced from the opulent jewels adorning the countless divinities sculptured to fill every nook and cranny of the local architecture and the bronze statues, in the casting of which the Khmer were masters.

Between the ninth and twelfth centuries, the Khmer Kingdom absorbed much of present-day Thailand between the Mekong and the valley of the Chao Phraya, with the sole exception of the Chiang Mai region where the Mon kingdom of Haripunjaya flourished.

A new ethnopolitical structure began to emerge

315 This fabulous antefix has a number of stepped levels, decorated with floral garlands in extremely fine open filigree and studded with precious and semiprecious stones. It was part of a miniature building, also found in the crypt of the main Prang of Wat Ratchaburana.

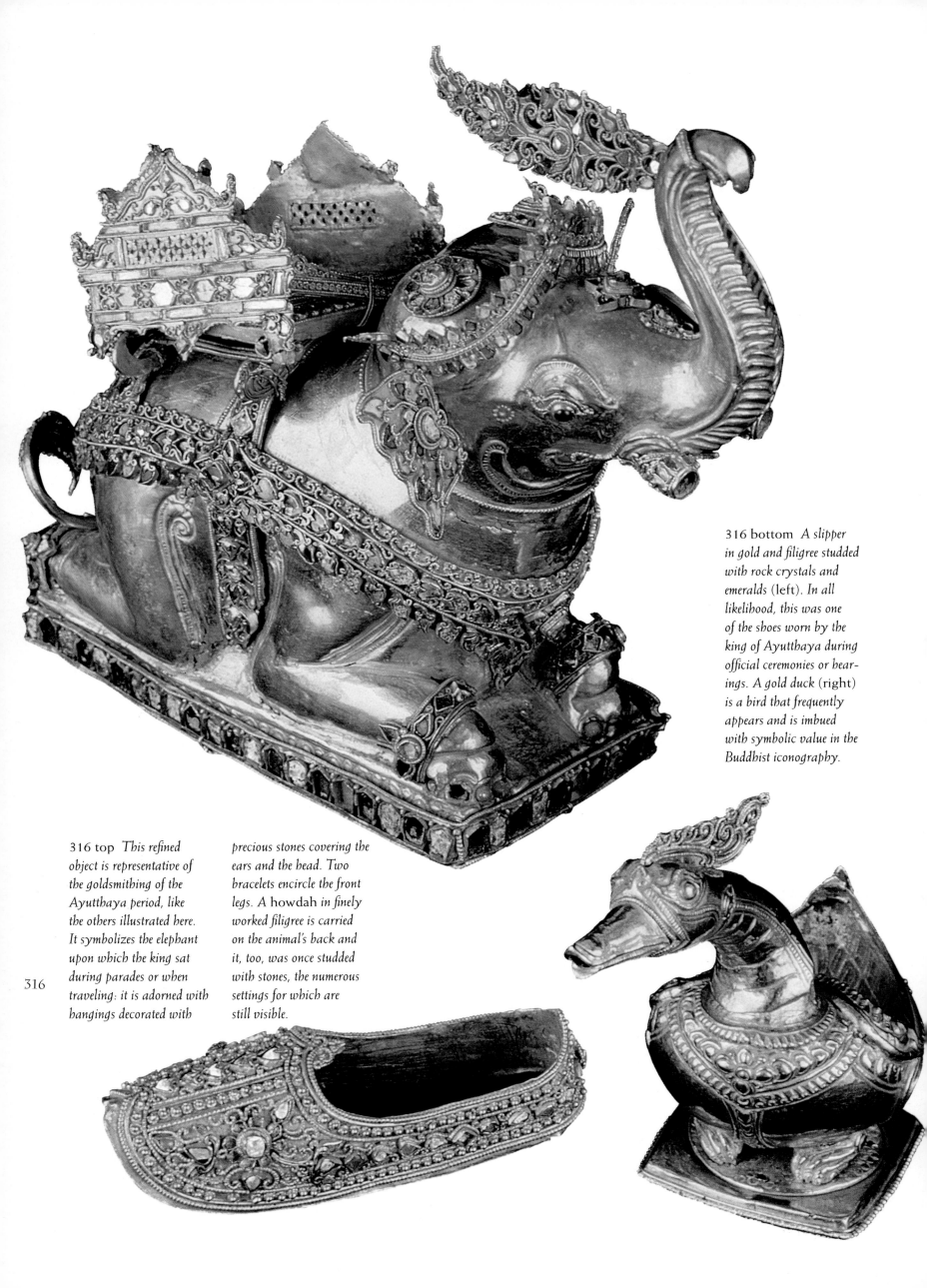

316 bottom A slipper in gold and filigree studded with rock crystals and emeralds (left). In all likelihood, this was one of the shoes worn by the king of Ayutthaya during official ceremonies or hearings. A gold duck (right) is a bird that frequently appears and is imbued with symbolic value in the Buddhist iconography.

316

316 top This refined object is representative of the goldsmithing of the Ayutthaya period, like the others illustrated here. It symbolizes the elephant upon which the king sat during parades or when traveling: it is adorned with hangings decorated with precious stones covering the ears and the head. Two bracelets encircle the front legs. A howdah in finely worked filigree is carried on the animal's back and it, too, was once studded with stones, the numerous settings for which are still visible.

in the Chao Phraya valley during the thirteenth century: the Tai people who, within a few decades, were to conquer the entire region. The decline of Khmer power permitted the Tai elite—warriors and farmers—to establish diverse regional political entities along the entire valley of the Menam Chao Phraya as far as the Khorat plateau. Of these Tai political regions or "principalities," initially the most powerful seemed to be the one with its capital at Sukhothai in the middle of the Chao Phraya valley; it influenced a vast territory roughly corresponding to present-day central Thailand.

Beginning in 1651, however, a new principality imposed itself: the city of Ayutthaya, founded that year in the lower valley of the Chao Phraya. Ayutthaya could be described as a true kingdom and became the principal power in the region, capable of maintaining commercial and political relations with the Chinese empire, the kingdoms and sultanates of Indonesia, India, and Persia, and the kingdoms of Europe and their commercial representatives.

Ayutthaya, with its sacred character as the residence of the king—both the temporal and divine sovereign, in that he was considered to be the reincarnation of Buddha—was enriched with temples and monasteries adorned with splendid glazed ceramics and statues in bronze, wood, or stucco, always covered with gold-leaf or painted in gold. The sovereign and his court made offerings of statues and furnishings in gold and silver, most of which were studded with multicolored precious stones, to the temples containing the golden symbols of the power of the Tai kings.

It was about the middle of the sixteenth century when the power of Ayutthaya began to decline, as it was subjected to the aggression of its most powerful neighbors. When the Burmese laid siege to the city, the jewels were hidden and the gold statues were covered with bitumen to obscure their splendor. This was the case with the monumental gold statue of the gentle

317 *This gold reliquary in the form of a stupa, or chedi, was undoubtedly made for the royal family. The base is in the form of a double lotus flower, finely worked with the repoussé technique. A bell-like dome rests on this base and is studded with precious stones set amid floral filigree elements.*

317

318 *These two objects in fine repoussé gold are ceremonial parasol-fans used by the king or a high-ranking Buddhist priest. The form of the parasol in the background is inspired by the leaf of the pipal tree (or the bodhi tree) beneath which Buddha achieved Enlightenment. The example in the foreground is instead based on the leaf of a palm or banana tree.*

319 top *This ceremonial sword has a handle richly decorated with lozenge, rhomboid, and droplet precious and semiprecious stones, all set as cabochons. It is complete with a scabbard that is itself fully decorated with floral motifs studded with stones. The sword, like the other two objects on this page, was probably part of the king's personal treasure.*

318

Buddha that can today be seen in the Wat Po in Bangkok. Was it also true of the jewels discovered in the Wat Ratchaburana at Ayutthaya? Was this perhaps a last regal gift to the merciful Buddha prior to the final defeat? It was undoubtedly a treasure of great value, including thousands of precious objects: it suffices to say that archaeologists from the Thai Department of Antiquities, who began excavations in the temple in 1957, found in the main *Prang* 2,121 gold objects. Among these were royal regalia, princely ornaments, headdresses, jewels, Buddha images, inscriptions on gold leaf, and some Arab coins. All this, considering that the crypt of the main shrine had just been robbed and a large number of objects had already been stolen: a total weight of 75 kilograms, of which only ten pieces have been recovered.

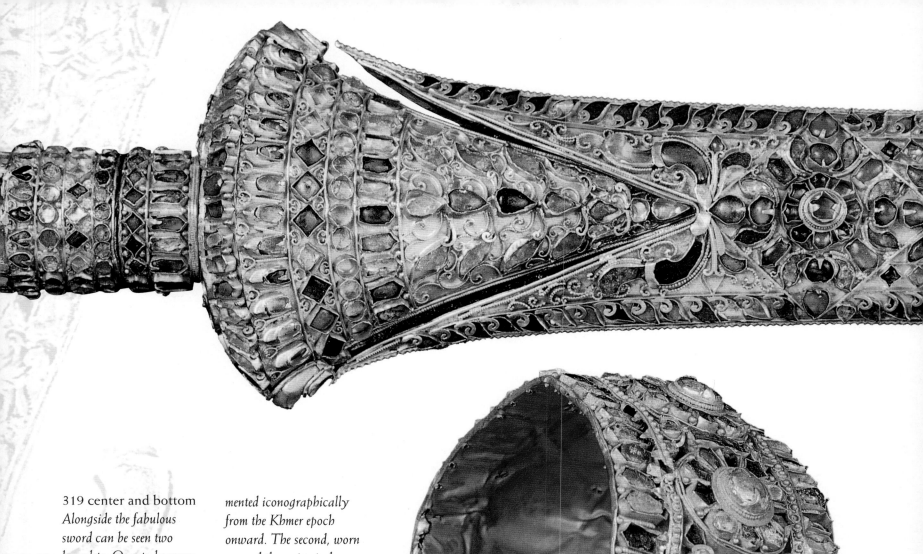

319 center and bottom
*Alongside the fabulous
sword can be seen two
bracelets. One, to be worn
on the forearm, is much
broader and terminates with
two lozenges. This is a
typical ornament, docu-*
*mented iconographically
from the Khmer epoch
onward. The second, worn
around the wrist, is decorated with a central band
filled with a garland of
eight flowers (probably
having a symbolic value).*

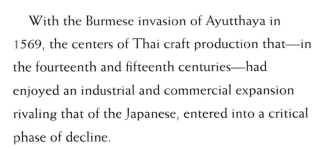

With the Burmese invasion of Ayutthaya in 1569, the centers of Thai craft production that—in the fourteenth and fifteenth centuries—had enjoyed an industrial and commercial expansion rivaling that of the Japanese, entered into a critical phase of decline.

A revival of the arts and crafts occurred with the rise of the Chakri Dynasty and the beginning of the Bangkok period in 1782. The first sovereigns drew on the goldworking models of the Ayutthaya era, further embellishing them with precious stones and colored glass in a triumph of volutes, polychromy, embroidering, and inlays that was to have considerable influence on the goldsmithing of Europe at the threshold of the twentieth century.

319

320 top *This necklace with spinel pendants is decorated on the back with enamel, depicting flowers on settings of gold. It dates from the eighteenth century. It is particularly sumptuous due to the presence of a pendant almost 10 centimeters long and intricately decorated with polychrome enamels.*

320 bottom left *These rigid bracelets studded with gems terminate with two facing tigers' heads, symbols of power. The setting of the stones, embellished with enamels, is a masterpiece of goldworking. All these pieces date from the eighteenth century.*

THE JEWELS OF THE MAHARAJA

321 top *Ten rows of cultivated pearls form an extremely elegant necklace. It features a precious pendant, encrusted with colored stones set in gold.*

321 bottom *These ornaments for the ears are composed of a convex disk encrusted with precious stones forming concentric circles (bottom) and the profile of a peacock within a frame of rubies (top). This type of earring was generally used by the women of the court, as shown in numerous ancient miniatures.*

320 bottom right *Rubies and enamel enrich this kadas —a jewel worn on the forearm—terminating with two dragon heads. The piece, from northern India, is dated late seventeenth century.*

When the gods and demons embarked upon the titanic task of "stirring up" the cosmic ocean, symbol of original chaos, to extract the *amrita*—the nectar of immortality that represented supreme knowledge—from it emerged mythical creatures and numerous fabulous objects. One of them was the *kaustubha*, a splendid jewel that the god Vishnu, lord of providence, chose to adorn his breast.

This was the start of the traditions surrounding famous stones and the fascinating tales about them: for instance, the *mani*, a kind of pearl with magical protective attributes; and the *cintamani*, able to satisfy any desire, enclosed in the golden palace of the *manidvipa*, the "jewel isle" where everything was made of precious materials. And gems were not only concealed beneath the ground: the fantastic *gajamukta*, a sort of pearl, was to be found in the head of elephants, serpents, and legendary aquatic monsters known as *makara*. Jewels could spell danger, too: the tantalizing attribute of the jewel called *syamantaka* (which many men fought bloody battles to possess) was its ability to enhance its owner's characteristics, whether positive or negative.

322 *The beautiful turban ornaments shown here all date from the eighteenth century and represent one of the most evocative examples of the taste and innate elegance of Mogul jewelry, particularly succesful in juxtaposing different forms and colors. Turban jewels were a prerogative of the emperor, his closest relations, and the members of his entourage, including his horse! The center and bottom images reproduce two sides of one jewel.*

322

323 top *This magnificent necklace dates from the late nineteenth century and is composed of a series of lobed plaques. Each is decorated with a facing pair of birds realized in sapphires, brilliants, and rubies on a ground of green enamel. At the center of the necklace is a splendid turban ornament. Both sides show its perfect execution.*

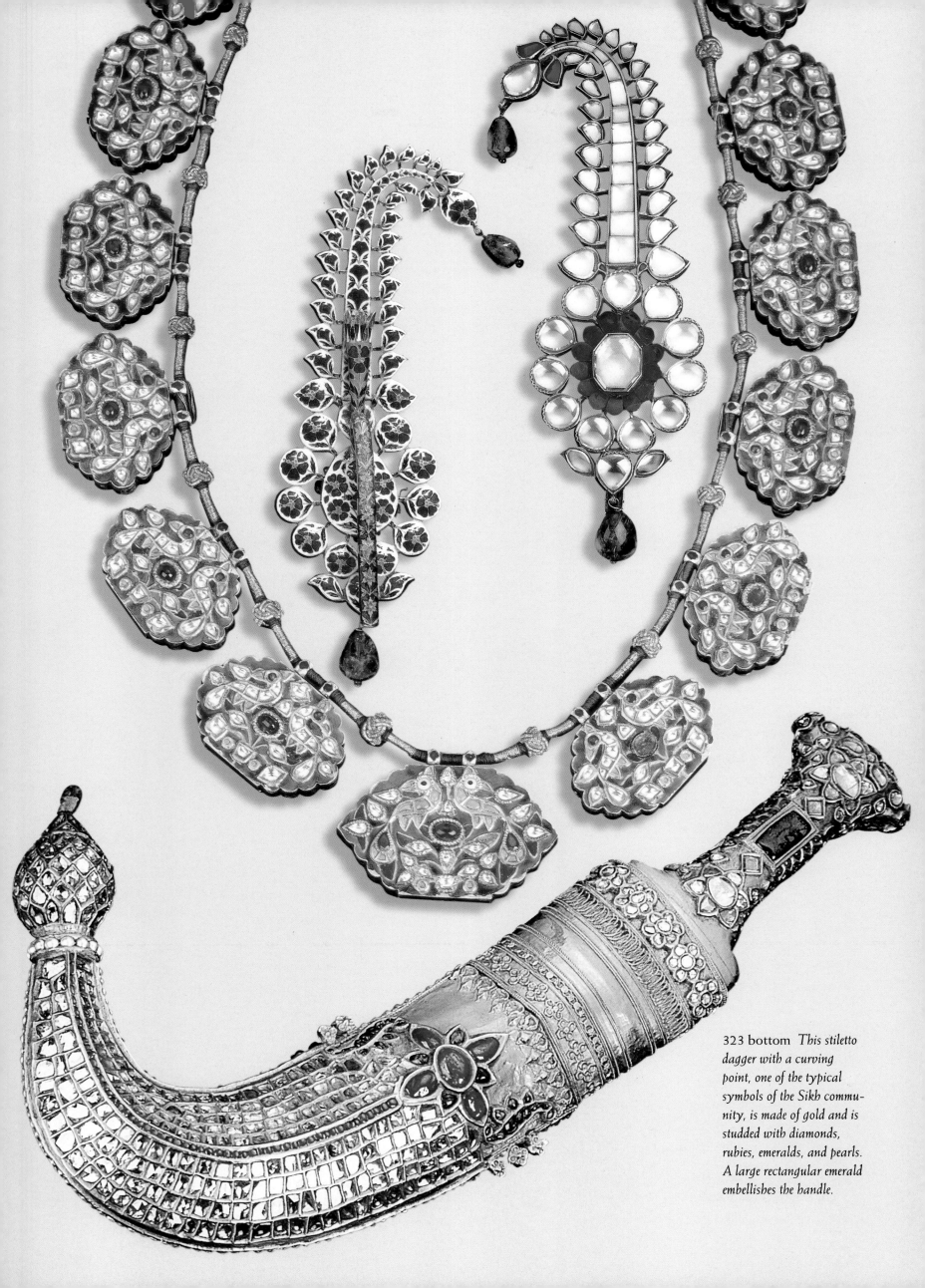

323 bottom *This stiletto dagger with a curving point, one of the typical symbols of the Sikh community, is made of gold and is studded with diamonds, rubies, emeralds, and pearls. A large rectangular emerald embellishes the handle.*

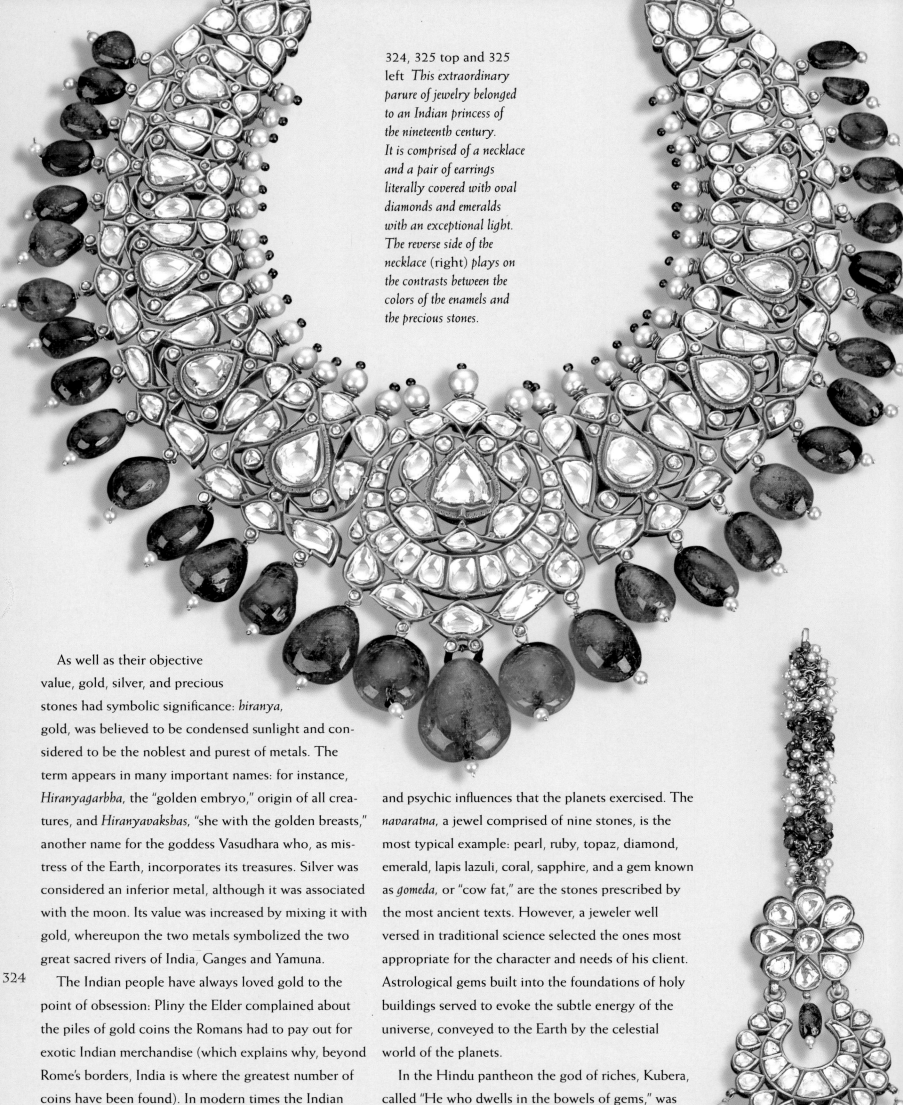

324, 325 top and 325 left *This extraordinary parure of jewelry belonged to an Indian princess of the nineteenth century. It is comprised of a necklace and a pair of earrings literally covered with oval diamonds and emeralds with an exceptional light. The reverse side of the necklace (right) plays on the contrasts between the colors of the enamels and the precious stones.*

As well as their objective value, gold, silver, and precious stones had symbolic significance: *hiranya*, gold, was believed to be condensed sunlight and considered to be the noblest and purest of metals. The term appears in many important names: for instance, *Hiranyagarbha*, the "golden embryo," origin of all creatures, and *Hiranyavakshas*, "she with the golden breasts," another name for the goddess Vasudhara who, as mistress of the Earth, incorporates its treasures. Silver was considered an inferior metal, although it was associated with the moon. Its value was increased by mixing it with gold, whereupon the two metals symbolized the two great sacred rivers of India, Ganges and Yamuna.

324

The Indian people have always loved gold to the point of obsession: Pliny the Elder complained about the piles of gold coins the Romans had to pay out for exotic Indian merchandise (which explains why, beyond Rome's borders, India is where the greatest number of coins have been found). In modern times the Indian government introduced strict limitations on private ownership of gold, which was more than double the Bank of India's gold reserves.

Precious and semiprecious stones were associated with the planets and with a precise group of physical and psychic influences that the planets exercised. The *navaratna*, a jewel comprised of nine stones, is the most typical example: pearl, ruby, topaz, diamond, emerald, lapis lazuli, coral, sapphire, and a gem known as *gomeda*, or "cow fat," are the stones prescribed by the most ancient texts. However, a jeweler well versed in traditional science selected the ones most appropriate for the character and needs of his client. Astrological gems built into the foundations of holy buildings served to evoke the subtle energy of the universe, conveyed to the Earth by the celestial world of the planets.

In the Hindu pantheon the god of riches, Kubera, called "He who dwells in the bowels of gems," was represented by effigies made of gold; he presided over the *yaksha*, pot-bellied spirits of plants believed also to be guardians of the Earth's treasures. The *naga*, mythical snakelike creatures, were also considered custodians of mineral riches and their association

325

325 bottom right *A typical motif of flower alternating with peacock is seen on the back of this drop-shaped pendant encrusted with diamonds on its front side. The exceptional dimensions of the jewel, 13 centimeters high, suggest it was a ceremonial male ornament or even destined for the head of an elephant belonging to a high-ranking family.*

326 top *Here again, alternation of the scintillating white of diamonds and the opaline sheen of pearls dominates this necklace. It is composed of three entwined strings of pearls supporting a magnificent large pendant in the form of a white and yellow flower.*

with jewels was deeply entrenched in the collective imagination, as is borne out by many legends.

Also prominent were esoteric interpretations of gold and gems, referring to a spiritual dimension where virtue and cognitive enlightenment represented true riches.

On a more practical plane, jewelry served as a statement of the position and role of its wearer: adornments varied according to sex, marital status (still today, a single woman does not wear the gems with which a married woman decorates herself), and membership in one of the four traditional Indian castes: the *brahmana*, custodians of spiritual power; *kshatriya*, barons or warriors; *vaishya*, commoners or merchants; and *shudra*, artisans and laborers.

The deities are each assigned their own specific jewels; for instance, the earring of the goddess Parvati,

dropped at Benares, after which one of the most famous *ghat*, or platforms, descending to the Ganges was named: it is called *Manikarnika*, the steps of the "ear gem." Even traditional Indian medicine, *Ayurveda*, includes powdered gold and other precious minerals among its remedies.

It is possible to reconstruct the evolution of Indian jewelry-making—its secrets passed down from father to son in a highly skilled professional caste—from statues and reproductions of necklaces engraved on the pillars and architraves of sacred buildings.

The most famous Indian jewelry of all was created during the Muslim Mogul dynasty, which ruled in India between the sixteenth and eighteenth centuries and had a notable influence on both contemporary and later Hindu princedoms. Descriptions of the

326 center *The Oriental luxury that characterizes the design of splendid jewels literally loaded with precious stones is seen in this necklace, undoubtedly commissioned by a high-ranking figure. Diamonds of various shapes —geometric, oval and droplet—feature in this jewel, made all the more precious by a cascade of pearls ending with tiny, delicate rubies and emeralds.*

326 bottom *This pair of bracelets utilizes tiny geometric rubies to frame a series of splendid diamonds.*

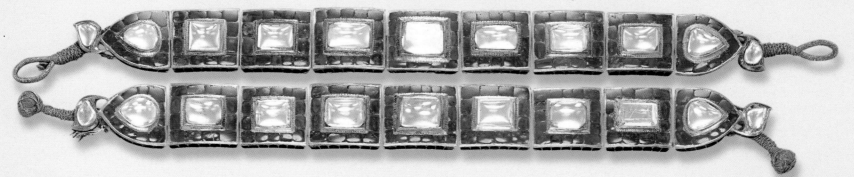

327 left *This necklace is composed of coral beads and terminates with a long gold pendant set with diamonds. The jewels shown here all belong to the Mogul tradition that, from the sixteenth to the middle of the nineteenth century, produced the highest expressions of Indian figurative culture from jewelry to fabric design, from miniatures to decorative objects.*

327 right *Pearls and rubies are, according to Indian traditions, gems worn by sovereigns and their closest courtiers. These stones frequently carry inscriptions with the name of the Mogul emperors. This necklace uses the princely stones to create an original jewel in which bunches of tiny rubies alternate with pearls. A double pendant encrusted with diamonds is the central part of the piece.*

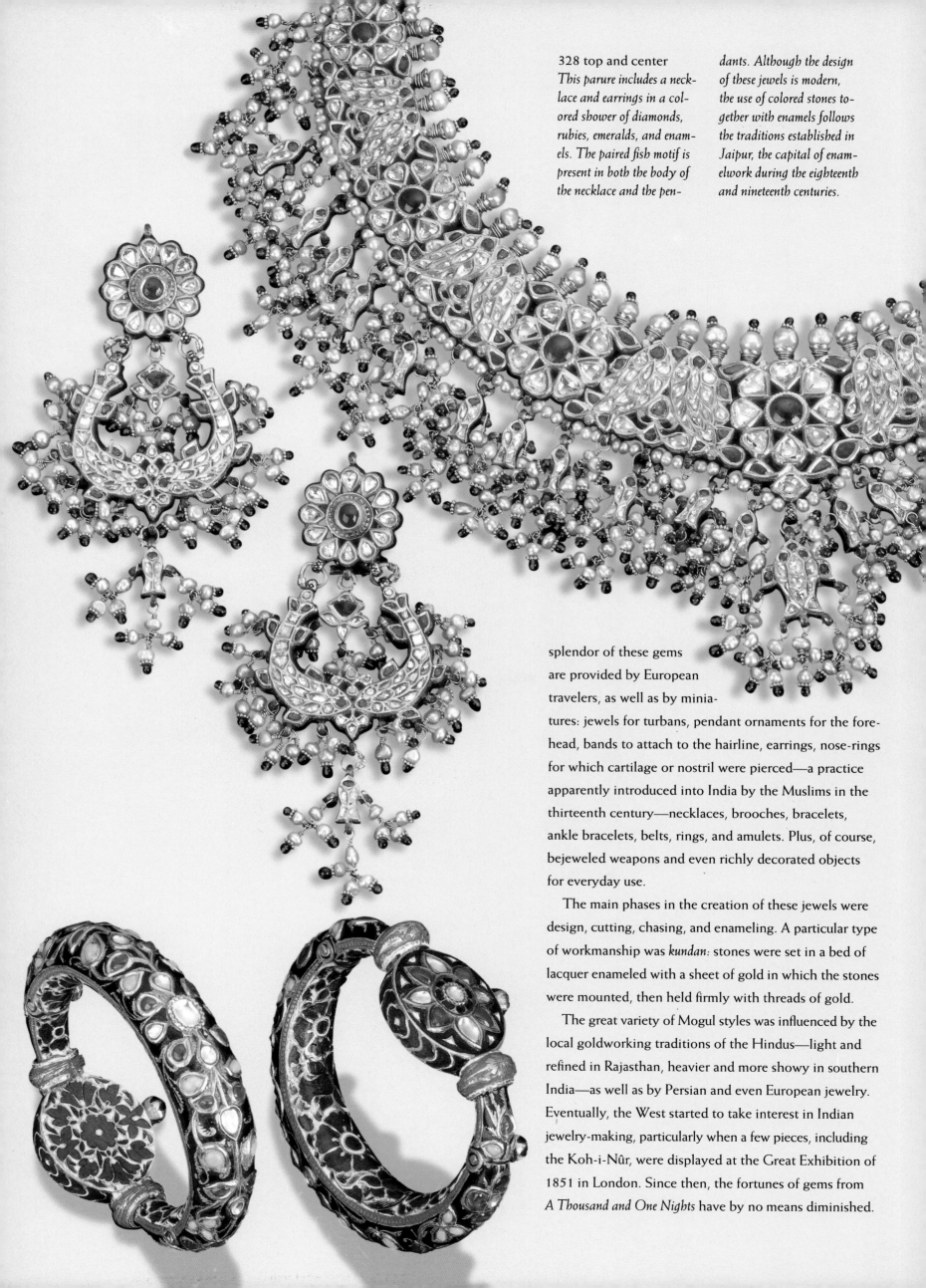

328 top and center
This parure includes a necklace and earrings in a colored shower of diamonds, rubies, emeralds, and enamels. The paired fish motif is present in both the body of the necklace and the pendants. Although the design of these jewels is modern, the use of colored stones together with enamels follows the traditions established in Jaipur, the capital of enamelwork during the eighteenth and nineteenth centuries.

splendor of these gems are provided by European travelers, as well as by miniatures: jewels for turbans, pendant ornaments for the forehead, bands to attach to the hairline, earrings, nose-rings for which cartilage or nostril were pierced—a practice apparently introduced into India by the Muslims in the thirteenth century—necklaces, brooches, bracelets, ankle bracelets, belts, rings, and amulets. Plus, of course, bejeweled weapons and even richly decorated objects for everyday use.

The main phases in the creation of these jewels were design, cutting, chasing, and enameling. A particular type of workmanship was *kundan*: stones were set in a bed of lacquer enameled with a sheet of gold in which the stones were mounted, then held firmly with threads of gold.

The great variety of Mogul styles was influenced by the local goldworking traditions of the Hindus—light and refined in Rajasthan, heavier and more showy in southern India—as well as by Persian and even European jewelry. Eventually, the West started to take interest in Indian jewelry-making, particularly when a few pieces, including the Koh-i-Nûr, were displayed at the Great Exhibition of 1851 in London. Since then, the fortunes of gems from *A Thousand and One Nights* have by no means diminished.

328 bottom *These splendid anklets, sumptuously decorated with a floral enamel motif, even on the inside surface, date from the early nineteenth century. The stones are rubies and turquoises, alternating with diamonds.*

329 top *This rigid bracelet is studded with large diamonds on a background of blue enamel. The internal decoration of this piece is spectacular, with red and green flowers on a gold ground.*

329 center and bottom *This magnificent necklace decorated with flowers of diamonds on a blue enamel ground, with the internal surface enameled in red and green, features a similar type of design. It was one of the most typical motifs used in Jaipur during the nineteenth century.*

CARTIER THE KING OF THE GOLDSMITHS

King of jewelers and jeweler of kings: the name Cartier needs no introduction.

The creator of the dynasty established more than one hundred and fifty years ago was Louis François Cartier. A goldsmith with exceptional flair and entrepreneurial skills, he opened his first workshop in Paris, 29 rue Montorgueil, in 1847. In 1852, he moved close to the Palais Royal and then, in 1859, to the Boulevard des Italiens, where his shop was frequented by the most famous celebrities.

The creations he sold were made mainly by the city's most highly regarded jewelers. Production began in earnest only later, under the supervision of Alfred Cartier, who took over the business from his father in 1894. The rue de la Paix—heart of the French "haute joaillerie" and "haute couture"—welcomed its first Cartier outlet in 1899.

Louis, Alfred's son, married Andrée Worth, daughter of the famous fashion designer, in 1898, a match that produced significant creative and commercial developments, as well as sentimental ties.

The coronation of King Edward VII in London resulted in a great influx of orders for the Cartier business in Paris, placed by members of the English court. And in 1902 the firm's increasing success led it to open a branch in New Burlington Street (moved to New Bond Street in 1909), under the management of Jacques, Louis' younger brother.

In 1908, Pierre, Alfred's second son, took on the management of the New York store that had just been inaugurated on Fifth Avenue.

It was Louis Cartier the designer who coined the new artistic language of the Parisian maison.

Initially he continued to favor gems in the "garland" style popular among his Parisian clientele, and he refused to be influenced by the already immensely successful developments of Art Nouveau. A major change came around 1907, when he started designing jewelry in geometric shapes, a great many years before the style known as Art Deco caught on in a big way at the Exposition Internationale des Arts Décoratifs (1925).

Influenced by the strongly contrasting colors of oriental art, Louis Cartier mixed precious gems and introduced unusual stones such as jade, rock

330 top *A distinctive feature of this ruby ring is its geometric setting, typical of the Art Deco style that came into fashion around 1925.*

330 center *This large, flower-shaped brooch is formed of a cluster of multifaceted diamonds set around a high-carat yellow diamond.*

330 bottom *The geometrically shaped links of this bracelet exemplify the stylistic language of Art Deco; at the center is a splendid oval emerald.*

330–331 *Cartier's confident use of contrasting color is a prominent feature of this lovely necklace of rubies, emeralds, and diamonds; at its center is an original brooch, studded with rubies and diamonds and embellished with pendants. The engraved jade ring below has a distinctive saddle-base setting, much favored by Art Deco with its firm preference for solid shapes and linear design. Beneath it is another ring, this one decorated with a group of semiprecious stones (green chrysoprase /black onyx) and gems (diamonds/rubies).*

crystal, and onyx with materials such as mother-of-pearl and coral. He achieved high levels of refinement in decoration with enameling, an art he mastered by following the example of the great Fabergé firm. After jewels of neo-Egyptian, Persian, Indian, Chinese, and Japanese inspiration came—between the two World Wars—his "tutti frutti" creations: dazzlingly colorful gems set in platinum; compositions with diamonds in simple geometric forms; floral and animal creations.

Many of Cartier's most celebrated pieces—evening bags, cigarette holders, watches, jewels—owe much to the collaboration of Jeanne Toussaint, his companion and associate designer from the 1930s onward. One truly stunning piece was the flamingo created for the Duchess of Windsor, in 1940.

The postwar period saw some of Cartier's most exquisite creations. Possibly the finest of all was

the "Panther" brooch designed, again, for the Duchess of Windsor, in 1949: the animal in diamonds and sapphires is resting on a 152.35 carat cabochon sapphire.

In the 1950s and 1960s the firm's precious output was snapped up by princesses, actresses, and heiresses. Prominent literary figures honored with membership in the Académie Française also received one of Cartier's celebrated tiny swords (Jean Cocteau, Daniel Rops, Maurice Druon, Louis Pauwels).

No roundup of Cartier's triumphs would be complete without mention of his clocks and watches: "Santos," the "Tonneau" watch-cum-bracelet; his first weird and wonderful pendules, table clocks already undeniably Deco in style; the celebrated "Tank," inspired by the tanks used by allied forces in the Great War; plus countless other wonderful and original designs that have continued to make their mark right up to the present day.

332 top *Diamonds and sapphires of various hues are featured in this pair of clip brooches.*

332 center *This elegant short necklace with pendants, decorated with diamonds tracing exquisite bows and love knots, recalls the hedonistic era of the Belle Epoque.*

332 bottom *Shining with diamonds, this Déco-style brooch featuring geometric and rigorous motifs is another product of Cartier's inexhaustible fancy.*

333 This stunning parure plays on the dazzling contrast between diamonds and sapphires, all geometrically cut, some of an impressive size. The pair of bracelets, earrings, ring, and necklace all share the breathtaking but tasteful elegance universally recognized as the trademark of Cartier jewelry. The ring is marked with the designer's name and the parure is dated 1930.

333

INTRODUCTION
Text by Gianni Guadalupi

Gianni Guadalupi has worked for thirty years as a writer, translator, and anthology editor, specializing in nonfictional and fictional travel writing. He is coeditor of *Le Vie del Mondo*, a magazine published by the Italian Touring Club. He edits the *Guide Impossibili* (Impossible Guides), *Antichi Stati* (Ancient States), and *Grand Tour* collections for Franco Maria Ricci. He is also the author of *The Discovery of the Nile* (Stewart, Tabori & Chang, 1997).

Photographic credits: **1** Nicolai Rachmanov/Agence A.N.A.; Kremlin, Moscow; **2–3** Araldo De Luca/Archivio White Star; Cairo Museum; **4–5** State Museum of Figurative Arts/A.C. Pushkin, Moscow; **6–7** Giovanni Dagli Orti; Archaeological Museum Plovdiv, Bulgaria; **8–9** Christie's Images, London; **10–11** Giovanni Dagli Orti; Gold Museum, Lima, Peru; **12–13** Bengt A. Lundberg; Statens Historiska Museum, Stockholm; **14 top** and **14–15 top** Araldo De Luca/Archivio White Star; Cairo Museum; **14–15 bottom** Giovanni Dagli Orti; National Museum of Athens; **15** Araldo De Luca/Archivio White Star; Cairo Museum; **16 top and 16–17** The British Museum, London; **17 top** Emilio F. Simion/Ag. Luisa Ricciarini; Museo Nazionale, Naples; **17 bottom** Fotografica Foglia; Museo Archeologico Nazionale, Naples; **18–19** Archivio Scala; S. Ambrogio, Milan; **20 top and bottom** Archivio Scala; Cathedral of Aachen; **21** Cameraphoto Arte; San Marco, Venice; **22–23, 22 top** Archivio Scala; Museo degli Argenti, Florence; **22 bottom** and **23 top** Kunsthistorisches Museum, Vienna; **23 bottom** Narodni Museum, Prague; **24** Antonio Quattrone; Museo degli Argenti, Florence; **25 top** Kunsthistorisches Museum, Vienna; **25 bottom** Antonio Quattrone; Museo degli Argenti, Florence; **26** The Bridgeman Art Library; Private Collection; **27** Arnaudet/Photo R.M.N.; Louvre Museum, Paris; **28** Chuzeville/Photo R.M.N.; Louvre Museum, Paris; **29 left** Photo R.M.N.; Louvre Museum, Paris; **29 right** Arnaudet/Photo R.M.N.; Louvre Museum, Paris; **30–31** Christie's Images, London; **32–33** Emilio F. Simion/Ag. Luisa Ricciarini Private Collection.

THE PHARAOH'S GOLD
Text by Adela Oppenheim

Adela Oppenheim is a research associate in the Department of Egyptian Art at The Metropolitan Museum of Art, New York. She has participated in ten seasons of excavations at el-Lisht and Dahshur, conducting research on Middle Kingdom royal relief and the jewelry of Queen Weret.

Bibliography

C. Desroches-Noblecourt, *Tutankhamen: Life and Death of a Pharaoh*, London, 1963.
H. Carter, *The Tomb of Tutankhamen*, New York, 1972.
I.E.S. Edwards, *Tutankhamun's Jewelry*, New York, 1976.
I.E.S. Edwards, et. al. *Treasures of Tutankhamun*, exhibition catalogue, The Metropolitan Museum of Art, New York, 1976.
N. Reeves, *The Complete Tutankhamun: The King, the Tomb, the Royal Treasure*, London, 1990.

Photographic credits: **34–55** Araldo De Luca/Archivio White Star; Cairo Museum.

MYCENAE AND THE GOLDEN MASK
Text by Furio Durando

Furio Durando graduated in Classical Literature at the University of Milan, with a postgraduate diploma in archaeology from the University of Bologna. He is an archaeologist and postgraduate teacher who has taken part in a number of excavations, and has published several scientific articles and *Ancient Greece* (Stewart, Tabori & Chang and Thames and Hudson, 1997).

Bibliography

I.A. Sakellarakis, *La Collezione Micenea del Museo Nazionale di Atene*, Athens, 1971.
M. Benzi, "Le oreficerie micenee," in various authors, *L'oro dei Greci*, Novara, 1992.

Photographic credits: **56** Giovanni Dagli Orti; National Archaeological Museum of Athens; **57** AKG Photo; National Archaeological Museum of Athens; **58 top** and **58–59 top** Giovanni Dagli Orti; National Archaeological Museum of Athens; **58–59 bottom** Ag. Luisa Ricciarini; National Archaeological Museum of Athens; **59** Emilio F. Simion/Ag. Luisa Ricciarini; National Archaeological Museum of Athens; **60–61** and **62 top** Giovanni Dagli Orti; National Archaeological Museum of Athens; **62 bottom** Photo Nimatallah/Ag. Luisa Ricciarini; National Archaeological Museum of Athens; **63** and **64–65** Giovanni Dagli Orti; National Archaeological Museum of Athens.

JEWELS FOR THE BEAUTEOUS HELEN
Text by Salvatore Ciro Nappo

Salvatore Ciro Nappo graduated in Classical Literature at the University of Naples with a major in archaeology and attended the Naples Classical Archaeology College. He has taken part in numerous archaeological missions, collaborates with Italian universities and foreign institutes on Pompeiian research, and he has given speeches at various congresses and seminars.

Bibliography

H. Schliemann, *Ilios, the City and Country of the Troians*, London, 1880.
H. Schliemann, *Troy and its Remains*, London, 1875.
L.Vlad Borrelli, *s.v.Troia*, in E.A.A, Rome, 1966.
I. Stone, *The Greek Treasure*, New York, 1975.
Various authors, *Il tesoro di Troia, Gli scavi di Heinrich Schlieman*, Milan, 1996.
G. Cervetti and L.Godart, *L'oro di Troia, La vera storia del tesoro scoperto da Schlieman*, Turin, 1996.
P. Vandenberg, *Alla scoperta del tesoro di Priamo*, Casale Monferrato (AL), 1996.

Photographic credits: **66–67** and **68–69** State Museum of Figurative Arts/A.C. Pushkin, Moscow; **70 left** AKG Photo; **70–77** State Museum of Figurative Arts/A.C. Pushkin, Moscow.

MAGIC IN PHOENICIAN GOLD
Text by Maria Rosaria Visone

Maria Rosaria Visone graduated in Etruscology and Italic Antiquities at the University of Naples. She has taken part in excavations at Pompeii and Cerveteri. One of her most recent research projects is the publication of the miniature decorations of the Archaeological Museum of Santa Maria Capua Vetere.

Bibliography

S. Moscati, *I Fenici*, Catalogue of the Exhibition, Milan, 1988.
G. Pisani, *I gioielli fenici di Tharros nel Museo Nazionale di Cagliari*, Rome, 1974.
G. Pisani, *I gioielli fenici e punici in Italia*, Rome, 1988.
E. Acquaro, *Amuleti egiziani e egitizzanti del Museo Nazionale di Cagliari*, Rome, 1975.

Photographic credits: **78 top** Giovanni Dagli Orti; Museum of Alep, Syria; **78 bottom** Giovanni Dagli Orti; Louvre Museum, Paris; **79** Henri Stierlin; National Museum of Beirut, Lebanon; **80–81 top** and **80 center** Giovanni Dagli Orti; Louvre Museum, Paris; **80 bottom** AKG Photo; Louvre Museum, Paris; **81** AKG Photo; Louvre Museum, Paris; **82** Rcs Rizzoli/Servizio Fototeca; Bard Museum, Tunis; **82–83** Giovanni Dagli Orti; Louvre Museum, Paris; **83 bottom** AKG Photo; Archaeological Museum La Valletta, Malta; **84 top** Rcs Rizzoli/Servizio Fototeca, Museo Archeologico, Cagliari; **84 center** and **84 bottom** Rcs Rizzoli/Servizio Fototeca; Museum of Carthage, Carthage; **85** Giovanni Dagli Orti; Museum of Carthage, Carthage; **85 center** Rcs Rizzoli/Servizio Fototeca; Museum of Carthage, Carthage; **86–87** and **88 top** Rcs Rizzoli/Servizio Fototeca; National Archaeological Museum, Madrid; **88 bottom** and **88–89** Giovanni Dagli Orti; National Archaeological Museum, Madrid; **89 bottom** Rcs Rizzoli/Servizio Fototeca; National Archaeological Museum, Madrid; **90** Rcs Rizzoli/Servizio Fototeca; Museo Archeologico, Cagliari; **90–91 top** Henri Stierlin; Geneva Museum; **90–91 bottom** Giovanni Dagli Orti; Museo Archeologico, Cagliari; **91 right** Henri Stierlin; Geneva Museum.

GOLDEN JEWELS FROM HELLAS
Text by Furio Durando

Bibliography

R.A. Higgins, *Early Greek Jewellery*, in Annual of the British School at Athens LXIV, 1969.
R. Laffineur, *L'Orfèvrerie rhodienne orientalisante*, Paris, 1978.
E.M. De Juliis, *Gli ori di Taranto in età ellenistica*, Milan, 1984.
Various authors, *Traci. Arte e cultura nelle terre di Bulgaria dalle origini alla tarda romanità*, Milan, 1989.
L. Rocchetti, "Il Geometrico e l'Orientalizzante," in various authors, *L'oro dei Greci*, Novara, 1992.
P.G. Guzzo, "L'età arcaica e classica," ibidem.
Id. "Oreficerie dei Greci d'Occidente," in various authors, *I Greci in Occidente*, Milan, 1996.

Photographic credits: **92** Giovanni Dagli Orti; Museum of Delphi, Greece; **93 left** Giovanni Dagli Orti; Louvre Museum, Paris; **93 right** Giovanni Dagli Orti; Museum of Delphi, Greece; **94** Henri Stierlin; Archaeological Museum of Plodiv, Bulgaria; **95** Giovanni Dagli Orti; Archaeological Museum of Plodiv, Bulgaria; **96 bottom** The British Museum, London; **96–97** Giovanni Dagli Orti; Museum of Volos, Greece; **97 top right** Henri Stierlin; Historical Museum of Vraca; **97 bottom** Giovanni Dagli Orti; Museum of Volos, Greece; **98 left** Henri Stierlin; Musée de Tragoviotz; **98 right** Giovanni Dagli Orti; Museum of Volos, Greece; **98–99** Giovanni Dagli Orti; Sovraintendenza Archeologica, Salerno; **99 top left** and **99 top right** The British Museum, London; **99 bottom** Giovanni Dagli Orti; Sovraintendenza Archeologica, Salerno; **100** and **100–101** The British Museum, London; **101 right, 101 right** and **102** Araldo De Luca; Museo Archeologico Nazionale, Taranto; **102–103** and **104 left** The British Museum, London; **104–105** Araldo De Luca; Museo Archeologico Nazionale, Taranto.

THE TREASURE OF PHILIP OF MACEDON
Text by Furio Durando

Bibliography

Various authors, *Arte dei Macedoni dall'età micenea ad Alessandro Magno*, Bologna, 1988.
G. Calcani, "Il Regno di Macedonia," in various authors, *L'oro dei Greci*, Novara, 1992.

Photographic credits: **106–107** Giovanni Dagli Orti; Archaeological Museum of Thessaloniki, Greece; **106 top** The Bridgeman Art Library/Archivio Alinari; Fitzwilliam Museum, University of Cambridge; **108** Giovanni Dagli Orti; Archaeological Museum of Thessaloniki, Greece; **109** Archaeological Museum of Thessaloniki, Greece; **110** Giovanni Dagli Orti; Archaeological Museum of Thessaloniki, Greece; **111 top** The Bridgeman Art Library/Archivio Alinari; Fitzwilliam Museum, University Of Cambridge; **111 bottom** Giovanni Dagli Orti; Archaeological Museum of Thessaloniki, Greece.

SCYTHIAN GOLD FROM THE STEPPES
Text by Paola D'Amore

Paola D'Amore is curator for the Ancient Near and Middle East section of the National Museum of Oriental Art in Rome. She has participated in numerous archaeological expeditions in Syria. She edited the Italian edition of the exibition "Kurgan Treasures of the Northern Caucasus" (Rome 1991) and the scientific edition of the exibition "Oxus" (Rome 1992). She has written numerous articles on Iranian art in the first millennium B.C.

Bibliography

E.H. Minns, *The Art of the Northern Nomads*, Cambridge, 1942.
Herodotus, *The History*, Chicago, 1998.
T. Talbot Rice, *The Scythians*, London, 1957.
K. Jettmar, *Art of the Steppes*, New York, 1964.
M.I. Artamanov, *Treasure from Scythian Tombs*, London, 1969.
T. Sulimirski, *Prehistoric Russia*, London, 1970.
A.M. Khazanov, *Storia sociale degli Sciti*, Moscow, 1970.
A.K. Greyson, *Assyrian and Babylonian Chronicles*, New York, 1975.
P. D'Amore, *Elementi scitici ed assiri nelle guaine iraniche del I millennio a.C.: Vicino Oriente 1*, 1978.
S. Parlato, *La cosiddetta campagna scitica di Dario: Annali dell'Istituto Orientale di Napoli 41*, 1981.
A.M. Khazanov, *The Dawn of Scythian History: Iranica Antiqua 17*, 1982.
P. Briant, *Etat et pasteurs au Moyen Orient ancien*, Paris, 1983.
B. Piotrovsky, *L'art scythe*, Leningrad, 1986.
K. Marcenko and Y. Vinogradov, *The Scythians in the Black Sea region: Antiquity 63*, 1989.
P. D'Amore and G. Lombardo, *Vicino Oriente e Caucaso*, Rome, 1991.
A. Leskov et al, *I tesori dei kurgani del Caucaso settentrionale*, Rome, 1991.
V. Schiltz, *Gli Sciti*, Milan, 1994.

Photographic credits: **112 top** The British Museum, London; State Hermitage Museum, St. Petersburg; **112 center, 112–113** and **113** State Hermitage Museum, St. Petersburg; **114 center** Luciano Pedicini/Archivio dell'Arte; Museum of Oriental Arts, Moscow; **114–115, 115** and **116–117** Ente Fiera di Vicenza, National Historical Museum, Kiev; **118 top** Luciano Pedicini/Archivio dell'Arte; Museum of Oriental Arts, Moscow; **118 bottom** and **119** Ente Fiera di Vicenza; National Historical Museum, Kiev; **120 top** and **120 bottom** Henri Stierlin; Museum of Trogovitz; **120–121 top** and **bottom** Ente Fiera di Vicenza, National Historical Museum, Kiev; **121** Ag. Luisa Ricciarini; State Hermitage Museum, St. Petersburg.

JEWELS FOR THE ETRUSCAN ARISTOCRACY
Text by Antonella Magagnini

Antonella Magagnini graduated in Etruscology and Italic Antiquities at the University of Rome, where she also attended the courses of the National Archaeological School. She currently works in the Capitoline Museums. Since 1995 she has worked in the department of etruscology at the University of Palermo, where she carries out occasional teaching duties. She has published a number of works on archaeology and museum management, has taken part in the scientific organization of exhibitions, and made contributions as speaker to several conventions.

Bibliography

R. Bianchi Bandinelli and A. Giuliano, *Etruschi e Italici prima del dominio di Roma*, Milan, 1973.
M. Cristofani, *L'arte degli Etruschi-Produzione e Consumo*, Turin, 1978.
M. Torelli, *Storia degli Etruschi*, Bari, 1881.
M. Cristofani and M. Martelli, *L'oro degli Etruschi*, Novara, 1992.

Photographic credits: **122–123 top** The British Museum, London; **122–123 bottom** Ag. Luisa Ricciarini; Museo Villa Giulia, Rome; **124–125 top** Ag. Luisa Ricciarini, Museo Archeologico, Florence; **124–125 center top** Photo Nimatallah/Ag. Luisa Ricciarini, Museo Villa Giulia, Rome; **124–125 center bottom** Photo Nimatallah/Ag. Luisa Ricciarini, Museo Villa Giulia, Rome; **124–125 bottom** Photo Nimatallah/Ag. Luisa Ricciarini, Museo Villa Giulia, Rome; **125** Photo Nimatallah/Ag. Luisa Ricciarini, Museo Archeologico, Florence; **126 bottom** Archivio Scala; Museo Etrusco Gregoriano, Vatican; **126–127** Ag. Luisa Ricciarini, Museo Etrusco Gregoriano, Vatican; **127** Archivio Scala; Museo Etrusco Gregoriano, Vatican; **128 top** The British Museum, London; **128–129** Photo Nimatallah/Ag. Luisa Ricciarini; Museo Archeologico, Florence; **128 bottom, 129 right** and **130 left** Photo Nimatallah/Ag. Luisa Ricciarini; Museo Villa Giulia, Rome; **130 left center** Luciano Pedicini/Archivio dell'Arte; Museo Archeologico Nazionale, Naples; **130 bottom right** Jurgen Liepe Bildarchiv Kulturbesitz; Staatliche Museen zu Berlin; **130–131** and **131 top** The British Museum, London; **131 bottom left** and **131 bottom right** Jurgen Liepe Bildarchiv Kulturbesitz; Staatliche Museen Zu Berlin; **132 top** The British Museum, London; **132 bottom** Photo Nimatallah/Ag. Luisa Ricciarini, Museo Villa Giulia, Rome; **132–133** Jurgen Liepe Bildarchiv Kulturbesitz; Staatliche Museen zu Berlin; **133 center** Giovanni Dagli Orti; Louvre Museum, Paris; **134 top**

left Photo Nimatallah/Ag. Luisa Ricciarini; Museo Archeologico, Ferrara; **134 top right** Photo Nimatallah/Ag. Luisa Ricciarini; Museo Guarnacci, Volterra (SI); **134 center** Ag. Luisa Ricciarini; **134–135** and **135 top** The British Museum, London; **135 center** Giovanni Dagli Orti; Museo Villa Giulia, Rome; **135 bottom right** Photo Nimatallah/Ag. Luisa Ricciarini; Museo Guarnacci, Volterra (SI); **136–137 top** Archivio Scala; Museo Etrusco Gregoriano, Vatican; **136 center** Archivio Scala; Museo Ernesto Guarnacci, Volterra (SI); **136–137 bottom** Archivio Scala; Museo Etrusco Gregoriano, Vatican; **137 top right** Giovanni Dagli Orti; Museo Villa Giulia, Rome; **137 bottom** Giovanni Dagli Orti; Museo Archeologico, Florence; **138–139** The British Museum, London; **140 top** Archivio Scala; Museo Archeologico, Ferrara; **140 bottom** Archivio Scala; Museo Etrusco Gregoriano, Vatican; **140–141** and **141 bottom left** Giovanni Dagli Orti; Museo Villa Giulia, Rome; **141 bottom right** The British Museum, London.

ROMAN JEWELRY
Text by Salvatore Ciro Nappo

Bibliography

G. Becatti, *Le orificerie antiche dalle minoiche alle barbariche*, Rome, 1955.
R. Higgins, *Greek and Roman Jewelry*, Los Angeles, 1980.
L.A. Scatozza Horicht, *I monili di Ercolano*, Rome, 1989.
Various authors, *Bellezza e lusso*, exhibition catalogue, Rome, 1992.
L. Pirzio Biroli Stefanelli, *L'oro dei Romani*, Rome, 1992.
A. D'Ambrosio, *Gli ori di Oplontis. Gioielli romani del suburbio pompeiano*, Naples, 1994.
A. D'Ambrosio and E. De Carolis, *I monili dell'area vesuviana*, Rome, 1997.

Photographic credits: 142 left and **142 center** Fotografica Foglia; Museo Archeologico Nazionale, Naples; **142–143** Henri Stierlin; Museum of Sophia; **143 left, 143 center, 143 right, 144–151** Fotografica Foglia; Museo Archeologico Nazionale, Naples.

BARBARIC SPLENDORS
Text by Bente Magnus

Bente Magnus studied at the University of Oslo, the British School of Archaeology at Athens and the University of Bergen, Norway, where she gained her degree. Since 1989 she has been living in Stockholm and is director of her own consulting firm. Among her published works, it is worth mentioning "The Firebed of the Serpent. Myth and Religion in the Migration Period mirrored through some golden Objects," in Leslie Webster and Michelle Brown (eds), *The Transformation of the Roman World A.D. 400–900*, London, 1997.

Bibliography

A. Knape (ed.), *The Magic of Gold in Life and Legend*, Stockholm, 1994.
L. Webster and M. Brown (eds.), *The Transformation of the Roman World A.D. 400–900*, London, 1997.
E. Roesdahl and D. Wilson (eds.) *From Viking to Crusader. Scandinavia and Europe 800–1200*, New York, 1992.

Photographic credits: 152–156 Christer Ahlin Statens Historiska Museum, Stockholm; **156 bottom right** Ulf Bruxe Statens Historiska Museum, Stockholm; **156–157** and **157 bottom** Gunnel Jansson Statens Historiska Museum, Stockholm; **158–159** and **160 top** Christer Ahlin Statens Historiska Museum, Stockholm; **160 bottom** Werner Forman Archive; National Museum, Copenhagen; **161 top left and right** Universites Oldsaksammling, Oslo; **161 bottom** Christer Ahlin Statens Historiska Museum, Stockholm.

THE MIRAGE OF EL DORADO
Text by Giuseppe Mazzocchi

Giuseppe Mazzocchi, lecturer in Spanish culture at the Vercelli-based University of East Piedmont, specializes in Castilian literature from the Middle Ages to baroque, and in cultural contacts between Christendom and Islam in the Spanish area. He has published books and papers about late-medieval Spanish poets (the Comendador Roman, the Comendador Luduena, the Vizconde de Altamira); he has also translated into Italian works by Pablo Picasso, Miguel de Unamuno, Juan de Mena. A bilingual edition of the *Lusíadas* by Camões, with Mazzocchi's translation and annotations, is to be published shortly. In the field of the applied arts he has a particular interest in the history of apparel.

Bibliography

Various authors, *Oreficeria*, in *Enciclopedia Universale dell'arte*, Istituto per la collaborazione culturale X, Venice-Rome, 1963.
E. Gunther, *Americane indigene culture*, in *Enciclopedia Universale dell'arte*, Istituto per la collaborazione culturale I, Venice-Rome, 1958.
V. von Hagen, *L'Eldorado*, Milan, 1993.
T. Todorov, *La conquista dell'America. Il problema dell'altro*, Turin, 1984.

Photographic credits: 162–163 Foto Mayr & Cabal; Museo de America, Madrid; **164** Foto Mayr & Cabal; The British Museum, London; **165** Foto Mayr & Cabal; Museo de America, Madrid; **166** Henri Stierlin; **167 left** Gamma/Foto Olympia; **167 right** Giovanni Dagli Orti; Museo Arqueológico Nacional Bruning de Lambayeque, Lima, Peru; **168 Foto** Mayr & Cabal; Gold Museum, Bogotà, Colombia; **168–169** and **170–171** Henri Stierlin; **172–173** Giovanni Dagli Orti; Museo del Oro Lima, Peru; **174–175 top** Henri Stierlin; Museo del Oro, Lima, Peru; **174 bottom** Henri Stierlin; **174–175 bottom** Gamma/Ag.Olimpia; **175** Mireille Vautier; Museo Arqueológico Nacional Bruning de Lambayeque, Lima, Peru; **176** Gamma/Ag. Olimpia; **177** Giovanni Dagli Orti; Museo Arqueológico Nacional Bruning de Lambayeque, Lima, Peru; **178–179, 180 top** and **180 center** Henri Stierlin; **180 bottom** Mireille Vautier; Museo del Oro, Lima, Peru; **181 left** Henri Stierlin; Archaeological Museum, Cuzco; **181 right** Giovanni Dagli Orti; Museo del Oro, Lima, Peru.

THE TREASURE OF SIPÁN
Text by Giuseppe Mazzocchi

Bibliography

W. Alva, "Discovering the New World's Richest Unlooted Tomb", *National Geographic*, 10/1988.
C.B. Donnan, *Iconography of the Moche. Unraveling the Mystery of the Warrior-Priest*, ibidem.
W. Alva, "New Tomb of Royal Splendor", *National Geographic*, 6/1990.
C.B. Donnan, *Masterworks of Art Reveal a Remarkable Pre-Inca World*, ibidem.

Photographic credits: 182–197 Museo Arqueológico Nacional Bruning de Lambayeque, Lima, Peru.

THE TREASURE DESIRED BY THEODELINDA
Text by Roberto Conti

Roberto Conti has been the Keeper of the Duomo and the curator of the Museum of the Duomo of Monza since 1983. In 1987, he founded the Società di Studi Monzesi of which he is the secretary. He is currently overseeing the extension of the museum which will transform what is now the Museum of the Duomo Treasury into a Museum of Sacred Art.

Bibliography

R. Conti, *Il Tesoro. Guida alla conoscenza del Tesoro del Duomo di Monza*, Monza, 1983.
R. Conti (ed.), *Monza, il Duomo e i suoi tesori*, Milan, 1988.
R. Conti (ed.), *Monza, il Duomo nella storia e nell'arte*, Milan, 1989.
R. Conti and R. Cassanelli (eds.), *Monza, La Cappella di Teodelinda nel Duomo*, Milan, 1991.
R. Conti (ed.), *Monza: il Polittico del Duomo. Un recupero, un restauro*, Milan, 1997.
R. Conti and R. Cassanelli (eds.), *Cinque secoli di pittura a Monza. Opere d'arte restaurate 1980–1995*, Milan, 1997.
R. Conti and R. Cassanelli (eds.), *Il Duomo di Monza. Itinerario barocco*, Milan, 1995.

Photographic credits: 198 Museo del Duomo di Monza e Biblioteca Capitolare Duomo di Monza; **198–199** Giancarlo Costa/Ag. Stradella, Duomo di Monza; **199** and **200–205** Museo del Duomo di Monza e Biblioteca Capitolare Duomo di Monza.

VENICE AND BYZANTIUM IN ST. MARK'S TREASURE
Text by Renato Polacco

Renato Polacco is a professor of the History of Medieval Art at the University of Venice, specializing in high medieval sculpture and Italo-Byzantine mosaics and goldsmithing. He has published about a hundred articles in specialty journals, books, and conference papers as well as entries in the *Encyclopaedia of Medieval Art*. He has also written eleven books, including one dedicated to the Cathedral of Torcello and one to St. Mark's Basilica. He has organized international conferences and is a member of numerous cultural institutions.

Bibliography

H. Hahnloser, *Il Tesoro di San Marco, il Tesoro, il Museo*, Florence, 1971.
Various authors, *Il Tesoro di San Marco*, Milan, 1986.
R. Polacco, *S. Marco—la basilica d'oro*, Milan, 1991.
H. Hahnloser and R. Polacco, *La Pala d'oro, Il Tesoro di San Marco*, Venice, 1994.
R. Polacco (ed.), *Storia dell'Arte Marciana, sculture, tesoro, arazzi*, Venice, 1997.
R. Polacco, *Il cosiddetto "brucia profumi" del Tesoro di San Marco*, in *Ellenismo Italiota*, Athens, 1998 (forthcoming).

Photographic credits: 206–210 Cameraphoto Arte; San Marco, Venice; **211–212** Giovanni Simeone/Sime; San Marco, Venice; **213 top** Cameraphoto Arte; San Marco, Venice; **213 bottom** and **214–215** Archivio Scala; San Marco, Venice.

A SACRED CROWN FOR THE HUNGARIAN ROYAL FAMILY
Text by Renato Polacco

Bibliography

D. Talbot Rice, *Byzantine Art*, London, 1954.
G. Ostrogorsky, *Storia dell'Impero Bizantino*, Turin, 1975.
A. Cutler and J. Nesbitt, *L'Arte Bizantina*, Turin, 1986.
Various authors, *The Glory of Byzanthium*, New York, 1997.

Photographic credits: 216–219 Hungarian Pictures Limited; National Museum, Budapest.

A GOLDEN EAGLE FOR EMPRESS GISELA
Text by Giovanna Baldissin Molli

Giovanna Baldissin Molli teaches History of the Applied Arts at the University of Padua. Her areas of research are concerned especially with the art of the Veneto region over the centuries. She has completed diverse studies of fifteenth-century painting in Verona and, more recently, the work of craftsmen in the field of the applied arts, paying particular attention to goldworking and inlaid wooden manufactures for liturgical use, which she has investigated from the points of view of patronage and the critical historiography of the eighteenth and nineteenth centuries.

Bibliography

O. von Falke, *Der Mainzer Goldschmuck der Kaiserin Gisela*, Berlin, 1913.
M. Schulze Dörrlamm, *Der Schatz der Kaiserin Agnes aus dem mittleren 11. Jahrhundert*, Neue Untersuchung zum sogenannten 'Giselaschmuck,' Siegmaringen, 1991.
R.W. Lightbown, *Medieval European Jewellery*, London, 1992.
P. Lasko, *Ars Sacra 800–1200*, Yale University Press, London, 1994.

Photographic credits: 220–223 Bildarchiv Kulturbesitz; Staatliche Museen zu Berlin.

OVIEDO: MEDIEVAL SACRED GOLD
Text by Giuseppe Mazzocchi

Bibliography

A. Arbeiter and E. F. González, *Asturie*, in *Enciclopedia dell'arte medievale*, Istituto dell'Enciclopedia Italiana, I, Rome, 1991.
A. Bonet Correa, *Imagen del arte pre-románico asturiano*, Barcelona, 1980.
H. Schlunk, *Arte asturiano*, Espasa-Calpe, "Summa artis" II, Madrid, 1947.

Photographic credits: 224–227 Henri Stierlin; Cathedral of Oviedo.

GEMS AND HARDSTONE VASES OF THE MEDICEAN TREASURY
Text by Mario Scalini

Mario Scalini graduated in Florence and specialized in Munich as an Alexander von Humboldt scholar. He has developed his keen interest in metals and sculpture, devoting particular attention to researching artistic techniques and intriguing facets of the Medici collections. He has made contributions to museums both in Italy and abroad, currently as curator of the Armoury of Castel Coira in the Italian Tyrol region, while also working at the Museo degli Argenti, at Palazzo Pitti. His other activities include teaching history of decorative arts at the Opificio delle Pietre Dure and hardstones and antique metalwork restoration workshop at the Università Internazionale dell'Arte, and collaborating with the universities of Siena and Florence. Mario Scalini has published several books including *L'arte italiana del bronzo 1000–1700, toreutica monumentale dall'alto Medioevo al Barocco* (1988), and *L'armeria Trapp di Castel Coira* (1996).

Bibliography

E. Müntz, *Les collections des Médicis au XV siécle*, Paris, 1888.
K. Aschengreen Piacenti, *Il Museo degli Argenti*, Milan, 1967.
D. Heikamp, *Mexico and the Medici*, Florence, 1972.
N. Dacos, A. Grote, M. Giuliano, D. Heikamp, U. Pannuti (eds.), *Il tesoro di Lorenzo il Magnifico*, Florence, 1980.
A. Giusti (ed.), *Splendori di pietre dure*, exhibition catalogue , Florence, 1988.
F. Tuena, A.Massinelli, *Il tesoro dei Medici*, Milan, 1992.
G. Gaeta Bertelà, B. Paolozzi Strozzi, M. Spallanzani (eds.), exhibition catalogue, *Eredità del Magnifico*, Florence, 1992.
K. Aschengreen Piacenti and M. Scalini, (eds.), *Naturalia e arte orafa. Dai tesori medioevali alle raccolte medicee*, in *Di natura e d'invenzione, fantasie orafe dal Rinascimento al Barocco*, catalogue, Arezzo, 1993.
M. Scalini, *Benvenuto Cellini*, Florence, 1995.
S.B. Butters, *The Triumph of Vulcan, Sculptors' Tools Porphyry, and the Prince in the Ducal Florence*, Florence, 1996.
G. Cantelli, *Storia dell'oreficeria e dell'arte tessile in Toscana dal Medioevo all'età moderna*, Florence, 1996.
C. Acidini Luchinat (ed.), *Tesori dalle collezioni medicee*, Florence, 1997.
Magnificenza alla corte dei Medici, exhibition catalogue, Florence, 1997.
C. Acidini Luchinat and M. Scalini (eds.), *Opere d'arte della famiglia Medici*, exhibition catalogue , Cinisello Balsamo, Milan,1997.

Photographic credits: 228 top left Archivio Paolo Tosi; Museo degli Argenti, Florence; **228 top right** Antonio Quattrone; Museo Archeologico, Florence; **228–229** Antonio Quattrone; Chiesa di Santa Maria della Fontenuova; **229 center, 230 top** Massimo Listri; Museo degli Argenti, Florence; **230 bottom** Massimo Listri; Museo degli Argenti, Florence; **231** Giovanni Dagli Orti; Museo degli Argenti, Florence; **232 left** Massimo Listri; Museo degli Argenti, Florence; **232 right** Archivio Scala; Museo degli Argenti, Florence; **233** Massimo Listri; Museo degli Argenti, Florence; **234** Archivio Paolo Tosi; Museo degli Argenti, Florence; **235 top** Antonio Quattrone; Museo degli Argenti, Florence; **235 bottom** Antonio Quattrone; Museo degli Argenti, Florence.

THE JEWELS OF THE GALLEON NUESTRA SEÑORA DE LAS MARAVILLAS
Text by Giuseppe Mazzocchi

Bibliography

C. M. Cipolla, *Vele e cannoni*, Bologna, 1983.
C. M. Cipolla, *Conquistadores, pirati, mercanti: la saga dell'argento spagnuolo*, Bologna, 1996.
G. Lanciani, *Tempeste e naufragi sulla via delle Indie*, Rome, 1991.
O.H.K. Spate, *The Pacific since Magellan: The Spanish Lake*, London, 1978.
J. L. Tippin and H. Humphreys, *In Search of the Golden Madonna*, 1989.

Photographic credits: 236–239 Christie's Images, London.

St. Peter's Basilica: a treasury of faith and art
Text by Msgr. Michele Basso

Msgr. Michele Basso was appointed director of the photographic archive of the Vatican Basilica in 1977. Two years later he graduated in theology at the University of St. Peter's. In 1980 he obtained a diploma in archive management from the Vatican Secret Archive and in 1983 was appointed archive manager of St. Peter's and took up a post in the offices for the excavations of the Vatican Necropolis and the Photographic Archive. In 1985 he graduated in canonical law at the University of Urbania, and in 1994 he became Canon of St. Peter's.

Bibliography

M. Accascina, *L'oreficeria italiana*, Florence, 1934.
M. Msgr. Basso, *La "Crux invicta" in un sarcofago paleocristiano delle Sacre Grotte Vaticane*, Notitiae, 19, 1983.
M. Msgr. Basso, *Guida della Necropoli Vaticana*, Città del Vaticano, 1986.
M. Msgr. Basso, *Storia della costruzione del nuovo San Pietro da Michelangelo a Bernini*, Ennio Francia 1989 da 150 Anni della Messa degli Artisti, 1, 1989.
G. Cascioli, *Il Tesoro di S. Pietro in Vaticano*, "Il Bessarione", 1912.
G. Cascioli, *Guida al Tesoro di S. Pietro*, Rome, 1925.
A. Colasanti, *Il Tesoro di San Pietro*, Rome, 1413.
A. Lipinsky, *Il Tesoro di S. Pietro*, Città del Vaticano, 1950.
E. Müntz and A. L. Fronthingham jr, *Il Tesoro della Basilica di S. Pietro in Vaticano dal XIII al XV secolo*, in "Archivio della Società romana di storia patria", 1883.
P. Toesca, *Il Trecento*, Turin, 1951.
P. Toesca, *Storia dell'arte italiana. Il Medioevo*, Turin, 1927.

Photographic credits: **240** Araldo De Luca; San Pietro, Vatican; **241** Capitolo di San Pietro in Vaticano; San Pietro, Vatican; **242–243** Araldo De Luca; San Pietro, Vatican; **244–245** Capitolo di San Pietro in Vaticano; San Pietro, Vatican.

Charm and luxury in the gold of France
Text by Piero Pazzi

Piero Pazzi is artistic consultant and honorary member of the Venetian Goldsmiths' Society and curator of the Silver Section of the Diocesan Museum of Venice. He has worked with UNESCO and the Cataloguing Center of the Region of Veneto in various cataloguing operations for the antique gold collections in Veneto. In the1994–95 academic year he held the chair in History of Applied Arts and Goldsmith Techniques at the University of Venice. In 1996 he was in charge of the exhibition "The Gold of Venice," organized by the Biblioteca Nazionale Marciana and the Venetian Goldsmiths' Society. He has edited twenty specific publications on Venetian antique gold objects and, on behalf of the Biblioteca Orafa of Sant'Antonio Abate di Venezia, edits the annual editions of *Contributions to the History of Gold, Silver and Jewellery*, coordinating the work of various scholars.

Bibliography

J. Doublet dom, *Histoire de l'Abbaye de S. Denys en France*, Paris, 1625.
G. Millet dom, *Les trésor sacre ou inventaire des saintes reliques et autres précieux joyaux du trésor de l'abbaye royale de Saint Denise en France* (II edition), Paris, 1638.
J.J. Chiflet, *Anastasis Childerici I Francorum Regis sive Theasurus Sepulcralis Tomaci Nervataan essossus, & Commentario Illustratus auctore Ioanne Iacopo Chifletio, Equite, Regio Architrorum Comite, & Archiducali Medico primario*, in Antverpiae (Anversa) ex officina Palatina Balthasaris Moreti MDC LV (1655).
M. Félibien dom, *Histoire de l'abbaye royale de Saint Denys en France*, Paris, 1706.
Various authors, *Tesori Profani d'Europa*, Milan, 1968.
P. Pazzi, *I Diamanti nella Civiltà Veneziana*, Venice, 1986.
P. Pazzi, *I Gioielli nella Civiltà Veneziana*, Treviso, 1995.
P. Pazzi, *Dizionario Aureo: orefici, argentieri, gioiellieri, diamantai, peltrai, orologiai, tornitori d'avorio nei territori della Repubblica Veneta*, Treviso, 1998.
E. Campagnol, *Il Ricamo degli abiti di corte nell'età napoleonica; motivi decorativi e tecnica*, in *Contributi per la Storia dell'Oreficeria, Argenteria e Gioielleria*, Venice, 1996.
A. Nardi, *Lo sviluppo della produzione orafa durante la prima metà del XIX secolo*, in *Contributi per la Storia dell'Oreficeria, Argenteria e Gioielleria*, Venice, 1996.

Photographic credits: **246–255** Photo R.M.N.; Louvre Museum, Paris; **256** Christie's Images, London; **257** Photo R.M.N.; Louvre Museum, Paris; **256–257 bottom** Mercatorfonds Paribas, Private collection.

The British crown jewels
Text by Anna Keay

Anna Keay is Assistant Curator of Historic Royal Palaces, with responsibility for Hampton Court, the Tower of London, Kensington Palace, the Banqueting House, Whitehall and Kew Palace. Educated at Magdalen College, Oxford, she has worked for Historic Royal Palaces since 1994, and was closely involved in assembling the exhibition "Crowns and Diamonds: the Making of the Crown Jewels" which opened at the Tower of London in 1996.

Bibliography

B. Claude (ed.), *The Crown Jewels: The History of the Coronation Regalia in the Jewel House of the Tower of London*, London, 1988.
R. Tessa, *The Coronation Ceremony and the Crown Jewels*, London, 1992.
M. Holmes and Major-General H.D.W. Sitwell, *The English Regalia: Their History, Custody and Display*, London, 1972.
R. Lightbown "The King's Regalia, Insignia and Jewellery" in Arthur MacGregor, (ed.), *The Late King's Goods: Collections, Possessions and Patronage of Charles I in the Light of the Commonwealth Sale Inventories*, London, 1989.
Lord Twining, *European Regalia*, London, 1967.

Photographic credits: **258–265** Crown Copyright Historic Royal Palaces, London.

Vienna's imperial treasure
Text by Bruce Leimsidor

Bruce Leimsidor has advanced degrees from Swarthmore College and Princeton University. He has taught at Indiana University, Occidental College, and Oberlin College in the United States. He currently lives in Vienna and Venice.

Bibliography

R. Bauer, et al., *The Secular and Ecclesiastical Treasuries*, Vienna, 1991.
Peter, Casper, Rudolph II, *Dagli archivi di Radio Praha*, Prague, 1997.
H. Fillitz, *Die österreichische Kaiserkrone*, Vienna, Munich, 1959;
F.A. Yates, *Giordano Bruno and the Hermetic Tradition*, New York, 1969.

Photographic credits: **266–273** Kunsthistorisches Museum; Vienna.

Crowns and jewels of Bavaria
Text by Sabine Heym

Sabine Heym graduated in history of art at the University of Munich. Since 1984, she has worked in the museums department of the Bavarian castles, gardens, and lakes administration, where she is responsible for the scientific and artistic conservation of a number of castles, including the Residence of Munich and the Treasury Chambers. Her main scientific interests are textiles and jewelry, and the baroque and rococo architecture of the early nineteenth century.

Bibliography

H. Brunner, *Schatzkammer der Residenz*, catalogue, 3rd edition, Munich, 1970.
H. Brunner, *Kronen und Herrschaftszeichen in der Schatzkammer der Residenz Munchen*, 2nd edition, Munich/Zürich, 1977.
H. Brunner, *Die Kunstschätze der Münchner Residenz*, Albrecht Miller (ed.), Munich, 1977.
H. Ottomeyer, *Die Krominsignien des Königreiches Bayern*, Munich/Zürich, 1979.
L. Seelig, *Pretiosen in der Münchner Schatzkammer*, in Kunst & Antiquitäten V/1987 und VI/1987.
Schatzkammer der Residenz München, Amtlicher Fürer, Bayerische Verwaltung der staalichen Schlösser, Gärten und Seen, Munich, 1992.
S. Heym, *Silberkammer-Schatzkammer-Reiche Kapelle, Augsburger Goldschmiedekunst in der Münchner Residenz*, in: exhibition catalogue "Silber und Gold I, Augsburger Goldschmiedekunst für die Höfe Europas," Munich, 1994.

Photographic credits: **274–285** Bayerisches Verwaltung Der Staatlichen Schlosser Residenz, Munich.

The Kremlin's diamonds
Text by Gianfranco Giraudo

Gianfranco Giraudo graduated in foreign languages and literature at the University of Venice. From 1972 to 1990 he taught the history of Eastern Europe, and in 1990 he became professor of Slavic philology. He is president of the Italian Association of Ukrainian Studies, member of the International Association of Ukrainian Scholars, the Italian Association of Slavic Scholars, and the editorial board of various publications specializing in Slavic studies. Historian, philologist, and lexicographer, he is the author of four books and several articles on history, philology, Ukrainian studies, and the comparative lexicography of the Eastern Slavic nations.

Bibliography

Oruẽejnaja palata, Moskva, Moskovskij Raboëij, Moscow, 1954.
P. Catalano (ed.), *Roma, Costantinopoli, Mosca*, Naples, 1983.
G. Giraudo, *Alle origini dello Stato russo: da Ivan III a Pietro il Grande*, Venice, 1984.
G. Maniscalco Basile, G. Giraudo, *Lessico politico, giuridico ed ecclesiastico della Russia del XVI secolo*, Rome, 1995.

Photographic credits: 286–297 Nicolai Rachmanov/ Agence A.N.A.; Kremlin, Moscow.

The golden tale of the Topkapi
Text by Giuseppe Mazzocchi

Bibliography

Various authors, *Oreficeria* (see The Mirage of El Dorado).
F. Braudel, *The Mediterranean and the Mediterranean World in the Age of Philip II*, London, 1975.
F. Iz, *Topkapi, il palazzo dei sultani*, Novara, 1981.
G. Mandel, *Mamma li turchi*, Bergamo, 1990.

Photographic credits: **298–299**, **300 top left** and **301 top** Namikawa Foundation/Shimane; Topkapi Museum, Istanbul; **301 center** Ag. Luisa Ricciarini; Topkapi Museum, Istanbul; **301 bottom** Ara Güler; Topkapi Museum, Istanbul; **302–307** and **308–309** Namikawa Foundation/Shimane; Topkapi Museum, Istanbul; **310–311** Ara Güler; Topkapi Museum, Istanbul.

Statues in gold from mysterious Thailand
Text by Fiorella Rispoli

Fiorella Rispoli is vice-director of the Thai-Italian Lopburi Regional Archaeological Project, contributes as archaeologist and ceramics expert to the Thai-U.S. "Thailand Archaeometallurgy Project," and is a researcher at the IsIAO's Asian Center for Archaeological Studies and Research. She currently teaches in the training courses of the Xian Center for the Conservation and Restoration of the Historic and Cultural Heritage, in China.

Bibliography

S. van Beek and L. Invernizzi Tettoni, *An Introduction to the Arts of Thailand*, Hong Kong, 1988.
J. Boisselier, *Le Cambodge. Manuel d'Archeologie d'Extreme-Orient* (Asie du Sud-Est), Paris, 1966.
J. Boisselier, *Trends in Khmer Art*. Natasha Eilenberg (ed.), Studies on Southeast Asia, Ithaca, 1989.
D. Ch'ing, "Malay Silver," *Arts of Asia*, March–April 1986.
D.H. Fickle, *Images of the Buddha in Thailand*, Singapore, 1989.
I.C. Glover, *Trade between India and Southeast Asia: a link in the Development of a World Trading System*, Hull, 1989.
C.F.W. Higham, *The Archaeology of Mainland Southeast Asia. From 10,000 B.C. to the Fall of Angkor*, Cambridge, 1989.
B.C. Law, *The light of the history of the Buddha's religion*, London, 1952.
R.C. Majumdar, *Suvarnadvipa, Ancient Indian Colonies in the Far East*, New Delhi, 1986.
J. Miksic, *Old Javanese Gold*, Singapore, 1989.
P. Wheatley, *Nagara and Commandery. Origins of the Southeast Asian Urban Tradition*, Chicago, 1983.

Photographic credits: **312–320** Photobank; Ayutthaya National Museum.

The jewels of the maharaja
Text by Maria Ausilia Albanese

Maria Ausilia Albanese teaches Indian Studies at the Milan School of Oriental Languages and Cultures, of which she is also the director. She is the director of the Lombardy Section of the Italian Institute for Africa and the East in Milan and has written a number of books and papers.

Bibliography

J. Brijbhushan, *Masterpieces of Indian Jewellery*, Bombay, 1979.
F. Brunel, *Jewellery of India. Five thousand years of tradition*, New Delhi, 1972.
Gioielli dall'India dai Moghul al Novecento, exhibition catalogue, Monza 1996.
M. Latif, *Bijoux Moghols*, Brussels, 1982.
Spink & Son Ltd, *Islamic and Hindu Jewellery*, London, 1988.
S. Stronge, N. Smith, and J.C. Harle, *A Golden Treasury. Jewellery from the Indian Subcontinent*, London, 1988.

Photographic credits: **320–329** Christie's Image, London.

Cartier, the king of the goldsmiths
Text by Alessandra Quattordio

Alessandra Quattordio graduated in humanities at the University of Milan. A journalist by profession, she specializes in art and contributes to magazines in this sector (*Flash Art, Arte, Arte In*). A major project she completed in recent years was the section on the twentieth century in *La Storia dell'Arte*, edited by Rossana Bossaglia (1990, Bramante Editrice). Having written extensively for *Vogue Gioielli* for several years, she has acquired specific expertise on the subject of modern and period jewelry.

Bibliography

Various authors, *I gioielli degli anni '20-40- Cartier e i grandi del Déco*, exhibition catalogue , Venice, 1986.
G. Chazal, *L'art de Cartier*, exhibition catalogue , Paris, 1989–90.
F. Cologni and E. Mocchetti, *L'oggetto Cartier*, Milan, 1992.
F. Cologni and E. Nussbaum, *Cartier—L'arte del platino*, Milan, 1995.
J. Rudoe, *Cartier 1900–1939*, exhibition catalogue, New York, London, 1997.

Photographic credits: Christie's Image, London.